Computer Simulation
of
Dynamic Systems

COMPUTER APPLICATIONS
IN ELECTRICAL ENGINEERING SERIES

Franklin F. Kuo, *Editor*

Computer Simulation

of

Dynamic Systems

RALPH J. KOCHENBURGER

Professor of Electrical Engineering
University of Connecticut

PRENTICE-HALL, INC.

Englewood Cliffs, New Jersey

10 9 8 7 6 5 4 3 2 1

ISBN: 0-13-166074-8
Library of Congress Catalog Card Number: 77-39623

Printed in the United States of America

PRENTICE-HALL INTERNATIONAL, INC., *London*
PRENTICE-HALL OF AUSTRALIA, PTY. LTD., *Sydney*
PRENTICE-HALL OF JAPAN, INC., *Tokyo*
PRENTICE-HALL OF CANADA, LTD., *Toronto*
PRENTICE-HALL OF INDIA PRIVATE LTD., *New Delhi*

Contents

4   Nonlinear Operations with Analog Computers   149

5   Implicit Methods of Function Generation   207

9   Simulation of Random Disturbances and Their Effects   405

Preface

This book is intended to serve the dual function of being: (1) a reference book for engineers engaged in research and development involving simulation in industrial, government, and educational institutions, and (2) a teaching text at the advanced senior or graduate level. Even when used as a teaching text, this book has served to fulfill the first function mentioned above. About half of the students who took the University of Connecticut course associated with this text were full-time engineers enrolled as graduate University Extension students who often applied the material to their current work. Through them and the very useful feedback they provided, this book was made more meaningful and more applicable to real life situations than if it had evolved in a purely academic atmosphere. The author's own industrial consulting experience also contributed in a similar manner.

The material in this book has been used at the University of Connecticut in a six-credit course that extended over a full academic year. Although listed as a course in Electrical Engineering, it has been completed very successfully by students from other engineering disciplines. A student with weak or almost no knowledge of electronic circuits will be hampered only slightly as far as the analog-computer techniques discussed here are concerned; he will have no problem at all with digital techniques. On the other hand, some prior knowledge of system theory is essential; the student should know how to use the Laplace transform in at least simple system problems. Some digital-computer programming ability is necessary, but the programming language to which the engineer or student is accustomed is unimportant as long as the language is scientifically oriented. Algorithms are described by general flow diagrams that do not depend upon a knowledge of any particular programming language syntax.

With the two-semester arrangement in use at the University of Connecticut, it was found possible to reach the end of Chapter 5 during the first semester and to cover the entire book by the end of the second term. A few quizzes were found useful for student evaluation during the first semester, but even then, most of the grading was based on individual student projects. Ideas for such projects sometimes arose from the problems suggested at the ends of the chapters, but they also evolved from other problems the students had encountered in related engineering or academic work.

The author has had the satisfaction of seeing a number of students make very effective use of the material in this book in their subsequent research work. For this reason, it is suggested that the student take a related course very early in his academic program enabling him to employ his knowledge of the subject in his thesis or other research efforts.

All of the computer programs proposed here have been tried and their validity verified, using the facilities of the University of Connecticut's Computer Center.

This work was supported in part by funds granted to the Center under National Science Foundation Grant GJ-9.

The author is deeply indebted to those students who, during the past few years, have taken the course related to this book while it was being taught from the author's notes. They not only uncovered a number of errors, but they also made many valuable suggestions that subsequently have been incorporated in the text. They provided the author with considerable encouragement as well. One of these, Mr. George Starkweather, now with Martin Marietta Corp. of Orlando, Florida, did a very conscientious and thorough job of proofreading the galleys.

The author is especially grateful to Mrs. Carolyn J. Turcio for her very excellent typing of the long and tedious manuscript, her painstaking drawing of the artwork of the original notes, and also for her many useful suggestions for improvement in style.

R. J. KOCHENBURGER

Computer Simulation
of
Dynamic Systems

Fundamental Simulation Techniques: An Example

1

1-1 Introduction

The use of computers for the purpose of simulating systems problems is explained most effectively by proceeding directly to a typical example that illustrates the most commonly encountered techniques. The types of simulation problems to be considered here, for the most part, will be *dynamic* problems, involving systems where the performance variation as a function of *time* is of interest. Such dynamic systems are encountered in many engineering problems, [1, 2][1] in operations-research types of problems, in biological systems, and in such sociodynamic areas as econometrics [3].

The example used here will refer to a very simple problem involving a mechanical-dynamic system consisting of a mass suspended on a spring and subjected to damping action. This particular type of problem frequently appears in more complicated form in the study of mechanical vibration and related problems, such as vehicle suspension. It is chosen because the physics involved in the analysis leading to the development of the simulation procedure (programming) will depend on principles that are generally well understood, in contrast to the more specialized fields to which simulation techniques might also be applied.

To avoid undue complication at this stage, the problem chosen as

---

[1] Numbers in brackets refer to the References at the ends of the chapters.

an example happens to be one in which a "pencil-and-paper" analysis could be applied without undue difficulty. The question could therefore be raised as to why computer simulation is advisable. The answer to this is probably obvious; such simulation procedures would not be necessary or show any advantages in so oversimplified a system. On the other hand, so simple a system would never be encountered exactly in practice, except as a very approximate version of a true physical situation. When the approximations are removed to obtain a more realistic version of the true system, an exact understanding of what the system does will be possible only by computer simulation procedures.

1-2   Description of the Problem Used in This Example

The problem used in this example is illustrated in Figure 1-1.

> M is a mass, constrained to move only vertically, of inertia, $M = 0.5$ kg
>
> k is a spring of spring rate, $k = 20$ kg/cm
>
> B is a viscous type of linear damper of damping constant, $B = 0.05$ kg/(cm/sec)
>
> x is the vertical position of the lower support, measured from some fixed reference and positive when upward, measured in centimeters
>
> y is the vertical position of the center of M, considered as zero when k is at "free length" with $x = 0$ and positive when upward, measured in centimeters

It should be noted that the inertia and mass of the spring and the mass and resilience of the damper are all neglected. This is therefore a *lumped-parameter approximation* of a real situation. The assumption of a linear damper, B, is also an approximation of the true nonlinear state of affairs applying in most practical situations.

The above system is to be simulated so that the motion of the mass may

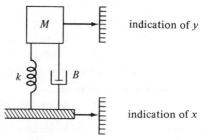

FIGURE 1-1

be expressed in terms of its displacement, y, for various motions of the support [i.e., for various prescribed functions, $x(t)$].

1-3   Block-Diagram Description of the Problem

A more thorough understanding of the system being simulated may be obtained by expressing in the form of a block diagram[2] the various mathematical relations that apply. Such a diagram gives a graphical picture of the flow of "cause and effect." It is useful for a theoretical analysis of systems as well as for the programming of either an analog or a digital simulation procedure.

In the preceding statements, the words "cause and effect" were used with the full realization that in many processes it is difficult to establish which of two related phenomena is the cause and which the effect. In such instances the choice is arbitrary. However, with simulation procedures the fact must be kept in mind that all computation techniques perform integration more readily than differentiation. For this reason it is preferable to establish a cause-and-effect relationship in the block diagram that leads to integral (rather than differential) equation form.

The spring force will be defined as f_k kilograms (positive for compression) and, assuming a linear spring obeying Hooke's law, will be given by

$$f_k = k(x - y) \qquad \text{kg} \tag{1-1}$$

This operation is shown symbolically in the block diagram by a rectangle, as shown in Figure 1-2a.

The dashpot force is defined as f_B kg and (based on the stated assumption of linear damping) is given by the relation

$$f_B = B \frac{d}{dt}(x - y) \qquad \text{kg}$$

The "dot notation" will be employed here; a single dot means the first time derivative, two dots, the second, etc. Then

$$f_B = B(\dot{x} - \dot{y}) \qquad \text{kg} \tag{1-2}$$

This is shown symbolically in Figure 1-2b.

The net force acting on the mass M is the sum of f_k and f_B less the

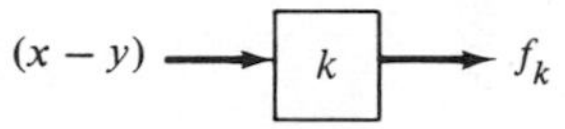

$(x - y) \longrightarrow \boxed{k} \longrightarrow f_k$ $(\dot{x} - \dot{y}) \longrightarrow \boxed{B} \longrightarrow f_B$

FIGURE 1-2a 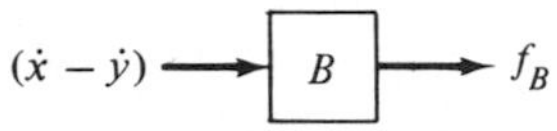   FIGURE 1-2b

[2]A simplified and compact form of block diagram, known as a *signal-flow diagram*, is also used, particularly with complicated configurations.

gravity force of M kg, or

$$f_M = f_k + f_B - M \quad \text{kg} \tag{1-3}$$

This is shown symbolically in Figure 1-2c. (The circular symbol implies algebraic summation. The absence of a minus sign next to an entering arrow indicates that the quantity involved is to be added.)

The acceleration of the mass, expressed in dot notation, will be simply

$$\ddot{y} = \frac{g}{M} f_M \tag{1-4}$$

This is shown symbolically in Figure 1-2d.

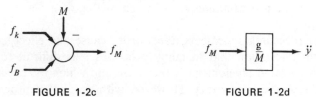

FIGURE 1-2c   FIGURE 1-2d

The velocity of the mass, M, is simply the time integral of the acceleration, or

$$\dot{y} = \int \ddot{y} \, dt$$

This will be written in operational form, where s indicates the operation, d/dt, and hence $1/s$ indicates the operation of time integration, as

$$\dot{y} = \frac{1}{s} \ddot{y} \tag{1-5}$$

shown symbolically in Figure 1-2e. Similarly,

$$y = \frac{1}{s} \dot{y} \tag{1-6}$$

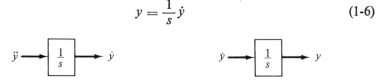

FIGURE 1-2e   FIGURE 1-2f

as shown symbolically in Figure 1-2f. Finally, by algebraic definition,

$$(x - y) = x - y \tag{1-7}$$

$$(\dot{x} - \dot{y}) = \dot{x} - \dot{y} \tag{1-8}$$

as shown by Figures 1-2g and 1-2h.

In summary, all the operations described by relations (1-1) to (1-8) can be expressed in block-diagram form, as shown in Figure 1-3, which is useful for portraying the problem graphically; its configuration is identical

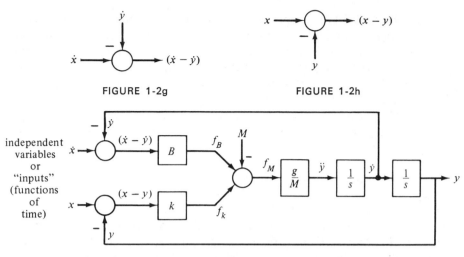

FIGURE 1-2g   FIGURE 1-2h

FIGURE 1-3

to the actual configuration of the connections between elements when an analog computer is employed for simulation. If a digital computer is to be employed for simulation, the direction of cause and effect (indicated by the arrows) is indicative of the sequence in which variables of interest will be computed.

Algebraic simplification of the block diagram is possible. For example, the blocks g/M and $1/s$ could be combined to a single block, g/Ms. This would, however, eliminate the intervening acceleration variable, $\ddot{y}$, from the problem and this variable no longer would be indicated by the simulation procedure. Such block-diagram simplifications are more appropriate for purposes of pencil-and-paper analyses than for simulation models.

1-4   State-Variable Viewpoint

Relations (1-1) to (1-8) could have been combined into a single differential equation. This would have been the usual procedure for a pencil-and-paper analysis of the system but is not required when computer-simulation techniques are to be employed. For this example, such a differential equation would have been of second order. Hence, the system being considered here would be described as a *two-state* system. From the simulation viewpoint, this fact is of interest for a number of reasons. Among them are the facts that

    1. The minimum number of time-integration operations to be performed is two. [Use of more integrating operations would not only

be wasteful of equipment or (with a digital simulator) of execution time, but could also introduce errors or convergence difficulties.] This minimum number does not include additional integrators sometimes required to generate the stipulated independent variables; these integrators are not part of the system simulation proper.

2. The relations given do not describe the system completely. As many *boundary values* must also be stated as there are system states, in this case two.

The boundary values are frequently, but not necessarily, *initial conditions* of the system. Cases of stipulated boundary values other than initial conditions represent more difficult simulation problems and will be referred to as *boundary-value problems*. For this example, it will be assumed that there are two known initial conditions, the initial displacement $y(0)$, and the initial velocity $\dot{y}(0)$. These, plus a definition of the independent variables x and $\dot{x}$ as functions of time, will be sufficient to describe the disturbance situation to which this spring–mass system is being subjected. Two such initial conditions are sufficient since this is a two-state system; as a matter of fact, the statement of a third initial condition would simply be contradictory or ambiguous.

Almost any two of the variables appearing in the preceding block diagram could have been chosen as *state variables*, to be employed when writing the two *state equations* of the system. However, the most logical choice of state variable is y itself, which for state-variable purposes will be designated as y_0. The second most logical choice is the velocity $\dot{y}$, which will be designated in state-variable notation as y_1.

In general, the state equations for any linear system will have the form

$$\frac{d}{dt}[y_i] = [A][y_i] + [D][u_i] \tag{1-9}$$

where, for an *n*-state system, $[y_i]$ is the column matrix or "vector"

$$\begin{bmatrix} y_0 \\ y_1 \\ \cdot \\ \cdot \\ \cdot \\ y_n \end{bmatrix}$$

$[A]$ will be an $n \times n$ matrix, $[u_i]$ will be an *m*th-order vector [where m is the number of independent variables (other than time) that might affect the system], and $[D]$ is an $n \times m$ matrix describing the assumed linear effect of these disturbances.

In this example, $n = 2$, and $[y]$ is a two-element vector. There are three disturbances (independent variables other than time): $x = x_0$; $\dot{x} = x_1$;

and the acceleration of gravity, g, related to the weight force; hence $m = 3$.

The state equations may be obtained directly from inspection of the block diagram or by combining relations (1-1) to (1-8); they are

$$\frac{dy_0}{dt} = y_1 \tag{1-10}$$

$$\frac{dy_1}{dt} = -\frac{k}{M}y_0 - \frac{B}{M}y_1 + \frac{k}{M}x_0 + \frac{B}{M}x_1 - g \tag{1-11}$$

or, in matrix notation,

$$\frac{d}{dt}\begin{bmatrix} y_0 \\ y_1 \end{bmatrix} = \begin{bmatrix} 1 & 0 \\ -\dfrac{k}{M} & -\dfrac{B}{M} \end{bmatrix}\begin{bmatrix} y_0 \\ y_1 \end{bmatrix} + \begin{bmatrix} 0 & 0 & 0 \\ \dfrac{k}{M} & \dfrac{B}{M} & -1 \end{bmatrix}\begin{bmatrix} x_0 \\ x_1 \\ g \end{bmatrix} \tag{1-12}$$

Hence, with reference to relation (1-9),

$$[y] = \begin{bmatrix} y_0 \\ y_1 \end{bmatrix} \qquad\qquad [u] = \begin{bmatrix} x_0 \\ x_1 \\ g \end{bmatrix}$$

$$[A] = \begin{bmatrix} 1 & 0 \\ -\dfrac{k}{M} & -\dfrac{B}{M} \end{bmatrix} \qquad [D] = \begin{bmatrix} 0 & 0 & 0 \\ \dfrac{k}{M} & \dfrac{B}{M} & -1 \end{bmatrix}$$

The vector block diagram describing relation (1-9) is shown in Figure 1-4.

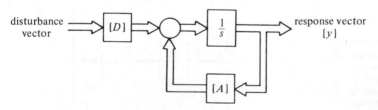

FIGURE 1-4

Such a vector diagram is useful for the purpose of generalized analyses relating to questions of system stability and control but normally would not be applied for the purpose of programming a simulation technique. The state-variable viewpoint does tell one that this example relates to a two-state system and, therefore, that a well-designed simulation system would involve no more than two integrators.

1-5 Alternative Block Diagrams

The following system of equations could have been written for this example and would have furnished an equally valid description of the dynamics of this system:

$$y = x - (x - y) \qquad (x - y) = \frac{1}{k}f_k$$

$$f_k = f_M + M - f_B \qquad\qquad f_M = \frac{M}{g}y \qquad\qquad (1\text{-}13)$$

$$f_B = B(\dot{x} - \dot{y}) \qquad\qquad (\dot{x} - \dot{y}) = \dot{x} - \dot{y}$$

$$\ddot{y} = s\dot{y} \qquad\qquad\qquad \dot{y} = sy$$

This will lead to the block diagram of Figure 1-5. This block diagram is equally useful for the purpose of pencil-and-paper analysis of the system. However, for the purpose of simulation, it involves "s boxes," implying time differentiation rather than integration. With analog simulation the process of differentiation is best avoided, because of the tendency for it to accentuate noise difficulties. With digital simulation differentiation is more prone to cumulative errors associated with the iterative techniques that must be used, as well as leading to convergence difficulties associated with the finite increments (of time) necessary with any digital-simulation method. For this reason the block diagram of Figure 1-5 is not as well suited for system simulation as is that of Figure 1-3.

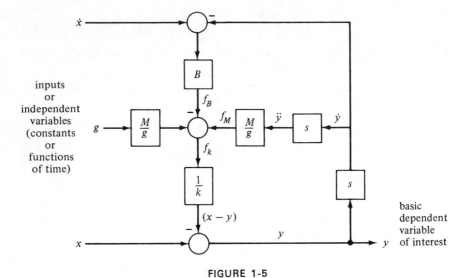

inputs
or
independent
variables
(constants
or
functions
of time)

basic
dependent
variable
of interest

FIGURE 1-5

1-6   Configuration of the Analog-Computer Program

In an electronic analog computer, the only true independent variable of the machine is *time*. Hence it is necessary to relate *machine time*, t_m, to the value of the basic independent variable of the problem being simulated. This basic variable will not be time in all problems, but in problems of *dynamics* it ordinarily will be. (For example, when using the computer to simulate the static bending of a beam, the basic independent variable is distance along the beam.) In this Figure 1-1 example, the basic independent variable does happen to be time, measured from an arbitrary initial instant defined as $t = 0$. However, there still need not be a $1 : 1$ relationship between *problem time*, t, and machine time, t_m. Sometimes, various scale conversion factors will be employed so that the speed of the simulation process is convenient for the means employed to observe or record the results. Of course, there are applications, particularly in control and in training simulators, where machine time must correspond to problem time; this is referred to as *real-time simulation*.

With electronic analog computers, all variables other than the basic independent variable are represented as electrical *voltages*. For example, the major dependent variable of interest in this example is the displacement y. This will be represented on the machine as a voltage y_m equal to y times a scale factor. Similarly, an independent variable of interest other than time t is the displacement of the support x. This will also be represented by a related voltage, x_m. The *scale factors* used in this example, relating the problem variables to the machine variables, are established by methods to be discussed later. By such methods the following scale factors are chosen for the example treated here:

$$y = 0.1y_m \qquad \text{cm}$$

That is, 1 V on the computer will represent 0.1 cm of displacement, where y_m is the voltage representing y on the computer. Similarly,

$$t = 0.01t_m \qquad \text{sec}$$

meaning the 0.01 sec of time in the actual problem being simulated will be represented by 1.0 sec of computer running time. Completing this scaling list,

$$\dot{y} = 20\dot{y}_m \qquad \text{cm/sec}$$
$$x = 0.1x_m \qquad \text{cm}$$
$$\dot{x} = 20\dot{x}_m \qquad \text{cm/sec}$$
$$\ddot{y} = 5000\ddot{y}_m \qquad \text{cm/sec}^2$$
$$f = 2f_m \qquad \text{kg (applicable to } f_B, f_k, f_M, \text{ and } M)$$

One of the summing points in Figure 1-3 develops the relation

$$(\dot{x} - \dot{y}) = \dot{x} - \dot{y}$$

Substituting from the above list, there results

$$20(\dot{x}_m - \dot{y}_m) = 20\dot{x}_m - 20\dot{y}_m$$

or

$$(\dot{x}_m - \dot{y}_m) = \dot{x}_m - \dot{y}_m \qquad (1\text{-}8\text{m})$$

Therefore, it is necessary merely to employ a summing amplifier (or "summer"), which is capable of adding and/or subtracting, in order to perform this operation. The summing symbol in the block diagram of Figure 1-3 is therefore replaced in the manner shown in Figure 1-6. The triangular shape shown is conventionally employed to represent such a summing amplifier.

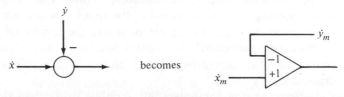

FIGURE 1-6

The other summing junctions of Figure 1-3 are similarly replaced by summing amplifiers, as shown in Figure 1-7. It should be noted in Figure 1-7 that the constant gravity force, M, or 0.5 kg, becomes represented by a

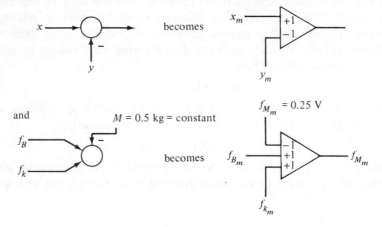

FIGURE 1-7

machine voltage of 0.25 V, consistent with the relationship $f = 2f_M$. This constant source of voltage will be obtained from a device called a *potentiometer*, which can reduce fixed *reference voltages* available within the computer to lower specific values, which might be required in instances such as this. The inclusion of such a potentiometer might be shown in the analog-program diagram as illustrated in Figure 1-8.

A potentiometer connection such as that used in Figure 1-8 might be used in those analog computers where a 100 V reference supply is available. The notation 0.0025 next to the potentiometer symbol (circle) indi-

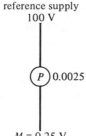

reference supply
100 V

P 0.0025

FIGURE 1-8 $M = 0.25$ V

cates that the mechanical setting is such that the output voltage is 0.0025 times the 100 V available from the reference supply.

Therefore, such potentiometers are the devices most appropriately used when a voltage is to be multiplied by a factor less than unity. They also find application for representing the simple multiplications indicated by the blocks B, k, and g/M in Figure 1-2.

From Figure 1-3 or relation (1-2), $f_B = B(\dot{x} - \dot{y}) = 0.05(\dot{x} - \dot{y})$. Substituting the scale relations $f_B = 2f_{B_m}$, etc., in terms of the machine voltages, this relation becomes $2f_{B_m} = 0.05(20\dot{x}_m - 20\dot{y}_m)$, or

$$f_{B_m} = 0.5(\dot{x}_m - \dot{y}_m) \qquad (1\text{-}2m)$$

and the configuration shown in Figure 1-9 is established.

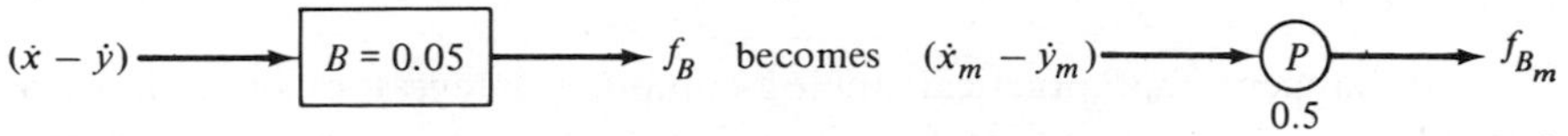

$(\dot{x} - \dot{y}) \longrightarrow \boxed{B = 0.05} \longrightarrow f_B$ becomes $(\dot{x}_m - \dot{y}_m) \longrightarrow P \longrightarrow f_{B_m}$
                                                                          0.5

FIGURE 1-9

From Figure 1-3 or relation (1-1), $f_k = k(x - y) = 20(x - y)$; or from the scale conversion table, $2f_{k_m} = 20(0.1x_m - 0.1y_m)$, or

$$f_{k_m} = 1.0(x_m - y_m) \qquad (1\text{-}1m)$$

Thus it happens that the potentiometer factor required is unity, and in actuality, no potentiometer is required at all. This is shown in Figure 1-10.

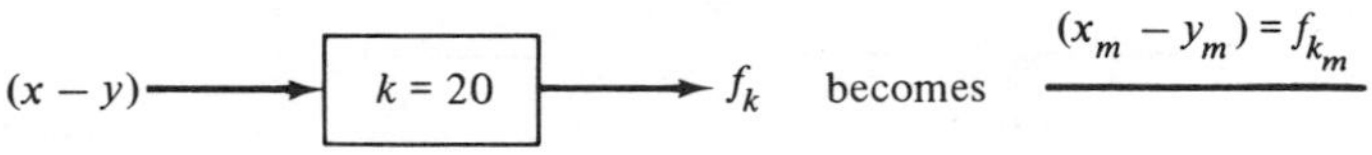

$(x - y) \longrightarrow \boxed{k = 20} \longrightarrow f_k$ becomes $\dfrac{(x_m - y_m) = f_{k_m}}{}$

FIGURE 1-10

From Figure 1-3 or relation (1-4), $\ddot{y} = (g/M)f_M = (980/0.5)f_M = 1960f_M$. From the scale conversion table, $5000\ddot{y}_m = 1960(2f_{M_m})$, or

$$\ddot{y}_m = 0.784f_{M_m} \qquad (1\text{-}4m)$$

This is shown in Figure 1-11.

The only remaining blocks to be represented are those involving

$$f_M \longrightarrow \boxed{\dfrac{g}{M}} \longrightarrow y \quad \text{becomes} \quad f_{M_m} \longrightarrow \!\!\underset{0.784}{\bigcirc\!\!P}\!\! \longrightarrow y_m$$

FIGURE 1-11

integration of the $1/s$ type. For example, from Figure 1-2 or relation (1-5), $\dot{y} = (1/s)\ddot{y}$, or $\dot{y} = \int \ddot{y}\, dt$. With the scale conversion factors given, $20.0\dot{y}_m = \int (5000\ddot{y}_m)\, d(0.01t_m)$, or $\dot{y}_m = 2.5 \int \ddot{y}_m\, dt$, or

$$\dot{y}_m = \frac{2.5}{s_m}\ddot{y}_m \tag{1-5m}$$

where s_m represents the operation d/dt_m. This operation is shown in Figure 1-12. Note the shape of the symbol used for the electronic *integrating amplifier* (or simply *integrator*). The notation within this symbol, 2.5, relates to the same numerical coefficient in relation (1-5m) and sometimes is referred to loosely as the *integrator gain*. It means that this type of amplifier will function so that the output will increase at a rate of 2.5 V/sec for every volt applied to its input.

$$\ddot{y} \longrightarrow \boxed{\dfrac{1}{s}} \longrightarrow \dot{y} \quad \text{becomes} \quad \ddot{y}_m \longrightarrow \!\!\triangleright\!\!\overline{2.5}\!\!\triangleright\!\! \longrightarrow \dot{y}_m$$

FIGURE 1-12

It happens that practical analog-computer integrators often have a limited number of gains that may be utilized (the particular gain obtained depending on a choice of input connections or switch positions). In a typical case those values might be 1, 2, 3, 10, 20, and 30, none of which corresponds to the gain of 2.5 required here. The most practical solution would be to use some higher value of gain than is required and then reduce this effective gain by the addition of a potentiometer. For example, the modified integrator for effecting relation (1-5m) might be as shown in Figure 1-13.

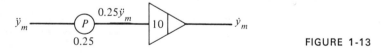

$$\ddot{y}_m \longrightarrow \!\!\underset{0.25}{\bigcirc\!\!P}\!\! \xrightarrow{\;0.25\ddot{y}_m\;} \!\!\triangleright\!\!\overline{10}\!\!\triangleright\!\! \longrightarrow \dot{y}_m$$

FIGURE 1-13

Similarly, relation (1-6), $y = (1/s)\dot{y}$, is converted to machine variables by the operations $y = \int \dot{y}\, dt$, $0.1y_m = \int (20\dot{y}_m)\, d(0.01t_m)$, $y_m = 2 \int \dot{y}_m\, dt_m$, or

$$y_m = \frac{2}{s_m}\dot{y}_m \tag{1-6m}$$

and an integrator gain of 2 is required. The block of Figure 1-3 corresponding to relation (1-6) is then converted as shown in Figure 1-14.

FIGURE 1-14

Employing all the problem-to-machine conversions described above, Figure 1-3 may now be changed to an analog-computer-program diagram as in Figure 1-15.

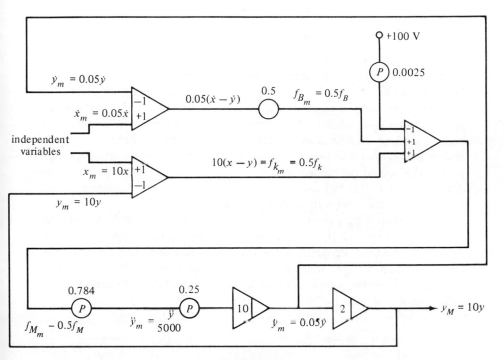

FIGURE 1-15

1-7 Introducing Initial Conditions in the Analog Program

Figure 1-15 is still incomplete in a number of respects:

1. It does not provide for initial conditions of the basic variables.
2. It does not provide for the independent variables x and $\dot{x}$.
3. It does not provide for output (i.e., the display of the results).

The first of these matters will be discussed in this section.

Since this example constitutes a two-state problem, its response cannot be determined until two boundary conditions are specified. As mentioned previously, the two to be used are the initial value of the displacement, y, or $y(0)$, and the initial value of the velocity, $\dot{y}$, or $\dot{y}(0)$. This will determine the initial values of the output voltages of the two integrators shown in Figure 1-5.

Suppose, for example, that the initial displacement y is 1.0 cm, and the initial velocity is zero. The corresponding initial machine values would be

$$y_m(0) = \frac{y(0)}{0.1} = 10 \text{ V}$$

$$\dot{y}_m(0) = 0$$

All analog computers have some method for establishing the initial outputs of integrators, the technique differing considerably from one computer design to the other. (These techniques will be discussed later.) The most common method consists of applying the desired initial-condition voltage to an initial-condition (IC) terminal at the integrator. The integrator will then adjust itself to that value of output prior to switching the operation of the computer to the operate or compute mode. Hence, in the example given, 10 V would be applied to the IC terminal of the integrator that produces y_m. First, this voltage must be developed by a potentiometer connected to the reference supply (unless this required voltage should happen to be available). Then, the connection to that integrator would be modified as shown in Figure 1-16a. The other, the $\dot{y}$-producing integrator, requires zero initial voltage. Properly speaking, this is accomplished by grounding the IC terminal of that integrator, as shown in Figure 1-16b. With many computers, however, simply leaving the IC terminal disconnected will also suffice to assure zero initial condition.

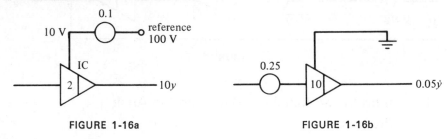

FIGURE 1-16a   FIGURE 1-16b

1-8   Introducing the Independent Variables
in the Analog Program

The description of the problem is not complete until the manner in which x and $\dot{x}$ vary with time is specified. In different types of problems many possibilities exist. x might vary sinusoidally in a random fashion or follow any arbitrary pattern, perhaps only once or perhaps repetitively. One of the simplest cases is when x varies in a *ramp* fashion, as shown in Figure 1-17a. Its time derivative $\dot{x}$ would then be a *step function*, as shown in Figure 1-17b. [Note that in this problem the computer cannot handle the case of x itself being a step function, because then $\dot{x}$ would be an impulse with an infinite amplitude for an infinitesimal time. This, however, is not a weakness of the computer; in the actual physical problem, x could not be a step function because this would imply an infinite force available to overcome the damping force $f_B = B(\dot{x} - \dot{y})$.]

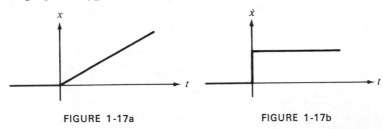

FIGURE 1-17a   FIGURE 1-17b

The simple example of x being such a ramp function will be considered here. Means are also available within analog computers for producing other functions of time as independent variables, but they are more complicated and their discussion will be deferred.

Let it be supposed that x varies as such a ramp function with a slope of 100 cm/sec or

$$x = 100tu(t) \qquad \text{cm} \qquad (1\text{-}14)$$

Hence

$$\dot{x} = 100u(t) \qquad (1\text{-}15)$$

and of course

$$x = \int_0^t \dot{x}\, dt = \frac{1}{s}\dot{x} \qquad \text{with } x(0) = 0 \qquad (1\text{-}16)$$

In machine language the corresponding values of x_m and $\dot{x}_m$ are substituted for x and $\dot{x}$ from the scaling relationships already listed; then

$$\dot{x} = 20\dot{x}_m = 100u(t)$$

or

$$\dot{x}_m = 5u(t) \qquad \text{V} \qquad (1\text{-}15\text{m})$$

and

$$x = 0.1x_m = \int_0^t \dot{x}\, dt = \int_0^{t_m} m(20\dot{x}_m)\, d(0.01t_m) = 0.2\int_0^{t_m} x_m\, dt_m$$

or

$$x_m = 2\int_0^{t_m} \dot{x}_m\, dt_m = \frac{2}{s_m}\dot{x}_m \qquad (1\text{-}16\text{m})$$

The step function x can be produced by simply closing a switch at time $t_m = 0$. This switch applies a voltage of $\dot{x}_m = 5$ V to the $\dot{x}_m$ terminals. The 5 V signal is produced by a potentiometer connected to the 100 V reference supply and set for a factor of 0.05. The program for producing x and $\dot{x}$ therefore appears as shown in Figure 1-18.

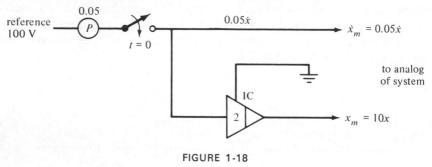

FIGURE 1-18

1-9   Provision for Output Display with the Analog Program

In a program of this sort, the outputs of interest might be x, $\dot{x}$, y, $\dot{y}$, $\ddot{y}$, and f_k. Various methods of output display could be used. In more elaborate installations, the solution could be interrupted at specified time intervals (machine time could be brought to a halt) by putting the computer in a hold mode; the voltages corresponding to these quantities could then be read by a digital voltmeter and tabulated by a digital printer. A different technique would be to present displays of the output response plotted versus time on a cathode-ray oscilloscope. This is accomplished by utilizing such a time scale that the problem is solved in lengths of machine time on the order of milliseconds; this solution is repeated at a rapid rate by repetitive switching means that periodically place the computer in alternate operate and initial condition (also called reset) modes. If the linear-sweep rate of the cathode-ray oscilloscope is synchronized with such switching periods, time plots of the response can be observed. Either of these two methods would require radically different time-scale factors than the one chosen here ($t = 0.01t_m$). These methods of output display will be discussed in more detail later.

The method of output display to be considered here, involving a recording oscillograph, is one of the most popular. If the oscillograph available has at least six channels, then all the output voltages corresponding to the six quantities listed above, x_m, $\dot{x}_m$, y_m, $\dot{y}_m$, $\ddot{y}_m$, and f_{k_m}, may be recorded as plotted functions of time. This procedure simply requires connecting these output voltages to the associated input channels of the oscillograph. The gains of the internal amplifiers for each oscillograph channel are adjusted separately, generally on a trial-and-error basis, so that each output will be displayed with the maximum possible scale deflection not exceeding the range of the record. The paper speed is adjusted to give a record of reasonable length (in a problem such as this usually of no more than 13 cm to permit posting in a notebook) during the time of interest. In this example, all transient phenomena will have died out in about 0.05 sec of problem time, corresponding to 5 sec of machine time. It can be seen that the execution time of an analog computer is almost negligible compared with the time required to establish the programming, and that repeated runs can be made readily with no significant additional cost. For this reason, trial-and-error adjustments constitute an acceptable procedure. (This also applies to trial-and-error adjustment of scale factors used in problem-to-machine conversion.) This advantage will not apply as well with digital simulation since the execution time normally is longer and more expensive.

[It might appear trivial to mention the following precaution here except for the many useless oscillograph records that have been obtained because it was ignored. After the oscillograph gain factors are adjusted satisfactorily, it is important to record these factors for each channel (e.g., the volts corresponding to full-scale deflection). It is then important that ordinate scales be added immediately after each record is run, with the problem–machine scale factors taken into account. This precaution also applies to recording paper speed, except that in many cases a timing marker will be utilized that produces a pip once every second (machine time). When this is the case, a record of the paper speed used is not required.]

1-10 Actual Computation and Results

There is no intention here to go into the details of computer operation or construction. There will be some brief mention of this later in regard to those details necessary to understand the computer's limitations and to recognize causes of computer malfunction. From the standpoint of applying a program, as in this example, it is merely necessary to establish the interconnections between computer elements, as shown in Figure 1-19. The procedure for doing so depends upon the computer used, but, in any event, no electronic-technician ability is required. After this is done, the potentiometers employed are all set to the values indicated in the program. Then the computer-mode switch is thrown to the IC (initial condition) or reset mode so that the outputs of all integrators will be brought to their desired initial values. This mode must be maintained for about 1 sec for normal operation (and less for the repetitive form of operation described previously with oscilloscope

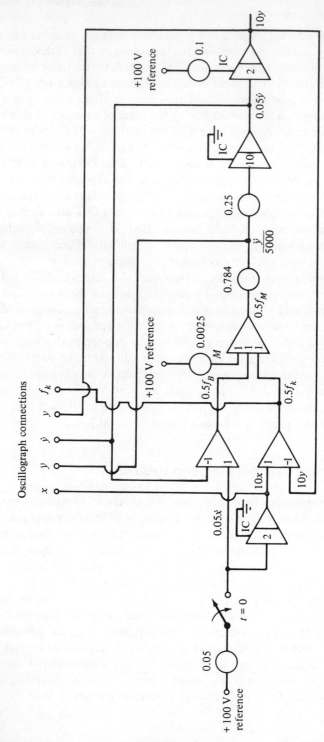

FIGURE 1-19

18

display of output). Then the mode switch is thrown to the operate or compute position and the results are recorded on an oscillograph.

In this particular problem, some of the voltages (specifically x_m and y_m) will exceed the voltage range of the computer after a certain time has elapsed; subsequent results will be erroneous and should be ignored. This overload condition will be indicated by some sort of warning signal but (in any properly designed computer) does not damage the equipment. The scale factors listed previously were selected for a computer designed for operation within the ranges of -100 to $+100$ V, and such an overload condition would not occur until the transient portion of the response had died out and only the steady-state response remained; hence all pertinent information related to the problem would have been obtained before this con-

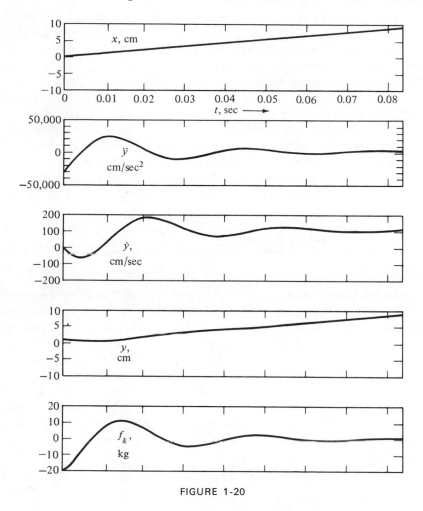

FIGURE 1-20

dition arose. Figure 1-20 is a diagram of the specific results obtained for this example.

1-11   Modification of the Program with Inverting Types of Amplifiers

The program shown in Figure 1-19 is based on the premise that summers and integrators are available that can accept inputs and provide gains in either the positive or negative sense by either positioning a sign switch or by an appropriate input connection. Such provisions are available in a minority of the analog computers used in practice.

More often, however, the amplifiers used for summing or integrating do not present such an algebraic choice; their inputs are always changed in algebraic sign (i.e., inverted) when the corresponding output appears. This is not as serious a limitation as it might first seem, as a negative signal can always be introduced in the positive sense, when needed, by applying it through an *inverter* (i.e., an amplifier of unity gain that merely changes the algebraic sign). The symbol for an inverter is shown in Figure 1-21. Consequently, programs will normally include more amplifiers when only inverting types of amplifiers are available because of needs that may arise for algebraic-sign conversion. This disadvantage is said to be overcome by the fact that inverting types of amplifiers (summers and integrators) are less expensive and complicated than those that permit a choice of sign.

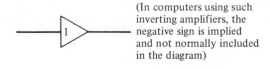

(In computers using such inverting amplifiers, the negative sign is implied and not normally included in the diagram)

FIGURE 1-21

In any event, when a computer having such sign-inverting amplifiers is being used, the program of Figure 1-19 will require some modification. The number of inverting amplifiers needed can be minimized by permitting some of the variables of interest to appear in their negative sense. Figure 1-22 shows such a modification. It should be noted that it was necessary to add four inverters. [Figure 1-22 represents the actual program employed to obtain the results shown in Figure 1-20. It should also be noted that all amplifiers (summers, integrators, and inverters) and all potentiometers have been numbered. This was for identification purposes. These numbers have significance only in regard to the particular computer employed to obtain these results.]

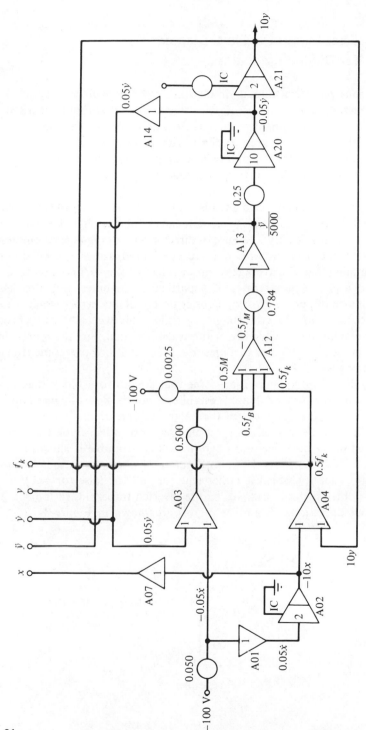

All amplifiers (integrators and summers) are of inverting type.

FIGURE 1-22

1-12   Establishing the Flow Diagram
for Digital Simulation

Discussions regarding digital simulation programs will be conducted here on a general basis, in terms of *flow* diagrams, and without regard to any particular computer language such as Fortran or Algol. This policy is being followed because of the great rapidity with which these languages are being modified. However, for this particular example only, an example will be given in Appendix 1A of the Fortran IV program used to obtain the results described.

It might be mentioned at this point that some scientifically oriented computer language is usually recommended for the digital simulation of dynamic systems. Rarely is the use of direct machine language recommended. The latter not only requires a more specialized knowledge of computer programming than the average engineer is likely to have, and a more specific knowledge of the peculiarities of a particular computer, but also has the disadvantage of poorer error diagnosis; programming errors would be more likely to occur. Machine language is justified only when the same program is to be employed so frequently, without modification, that the more efficient utilization of the computer facilities that it might afford overcomes the other disadvantages.

A flow diagram may look somewhat similar to a block diagram but is a very different sort of thing. It establishes not the flow of cause and effect, but the actual time sequence of the computer operations.

The basic flow-diagram symbols used here will include the rhombus, employed to indicate decision operations. One example is shown in Figure 1-23. Another example is shown in Figure 1-24 where the variable is a logical (Boolean) quantity which is either true (or = 1) or false (or = 0).

Another symbol used will be the inverted trapezoid, to indicate input or output operations. Examples of this are shown in Figure 1-25.

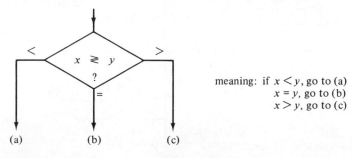

meaning: if $x < y$, go to (a)
$x = y$, go to (b)
$x > y$, go to (c)

FIGURE 1-23

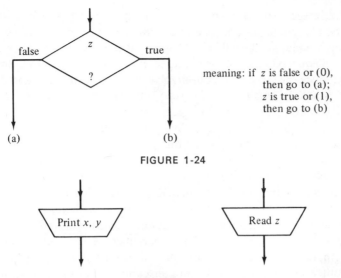

meaning: if z is false or (0),
then go to (a);
z is true or (1),
then go to (b)

FIGURE 1-24

FIGURE 1-25

Often the computer program will require format instructions along with such input or output statements; these will not be discussed here.

The most common symbol will be a simple rectangle, used for ordinary arithmetic operations, as shown in Figure 1-26. The significance of the equal

$$y = y + x \qquad\qquad y = ay$$

FIGURE 1-26

sign in an arithmetic statement should be noted. It does not mean equality in the algebraic sense (the digital computer cannot do algebra directly), but rather the replacement of the quantity assigned to a given variable. For example, $y = y + x$ means that the old value of y is to be replaced by a new one equal to the old value plus x. The statement $y = ay$ instructs the computer to replace the old value of y by a new value equal to a times the old.

The computer will handle differently those variables that are designated as integers (*fixed-point variables*) and those that are real (*floating-point variables*). For example, if x and y are integers and $x = 6$ while $y = 4$, then x/y would be computed as 1, the correct quotient when truncated to the next lower integer. But if x and y are real with $x = 6.0$ and $y = 4.0$, then x/y will be computed as 1.5. The exponential operation x^y, where, say, y is an integer equal to 3, will be executed by the multiplication $x \cdot x \cdot x$; if y is real and equals 3.0, it will be executed as $x^y = \log^{-1}(3 \log x)$. Both procedures produce the same result but involve different operations and different execution times. In this example the second procedure would be a slower one, but if y were a much higher integer, it would be a faster one. Naturally, the second procedure is necessary when y is not an integer.

There are many more distinctions between the manner in which the computer handles real and integer quantities. These ordinarily will be known by anyone who has had elementary programming experience. Most variables to be discussed in the simulation programs here must necessarily be real, since they represent analog-type quantities for the most part; when a variable used in a computation is to be treated as an integer, this will be stated.

Depending on the programming language used, the mathematical symbols employed here may require modification before they can be used in a computer source program. Computer compilers in most Western countries can normally accept only letters from the Roman alphabet as symbols for variables; hence Greek symbols such as Δ will require conversion. Nevertheless, the flow diagrams used here to illustrate simulation methods will employ the conventional mathematical symbols, it being understood that these will be modified as necessary in the source program.

Other restrictions might also apply regarding the choice of symbols used in the source program. Some languages restrict the usage of the first alphabetical character of a symbol in the sense that symbols beginning with alphabetical characters from I to N must apply to quantities that are only integers, while symbols starting with some other letter must apply to real, or floating-point, quantities. In the more modern languages the programmer may take exception to this restriction. For that reason the restriction will not be observed when presenting flow diagrams here. For example, the symbol M will be used to designate the mass in the example being treated, even though the quantity, mass, must be represented by a real number. It is assumed that a user employing a language in which this restriction applies (as Fortran II) will make the necessary modification, such as by changing the symbol to AM.

The second restriction applies to the length of symbols. Symbols such as CALIBRATE and FIRSTCALL will be employed here even though some languages will not permit symbol lengths in excess of six characters. It is assumed, again, that the user will make the necessary modifications when this is necessary.

As all simulation programs of the type with which we are concerned will involve integration with respect to some basic independent variable, and as digital integration normally must be performed in a stepwise, or *iterative* manner, it is necessary to select an *iteration interval* to be designated (when time is the independent variable) as Δt. It will be necessary to recompute all variables at every time increment Δt. (Some exceptions to this will be discussed in Chapter 3.) This procedure will be discussed in more detail in Chapter 3, and it will be shown that exact results of integration can be obtained only as $\Delta t \rightarrow dt \rightarrow 0$. Hence accuracy of simulation improves with decreasing size of Δt; execution time, however, will increase by the same proportion. Therefore, one of the major problems associated with digital simulation will be the selection of an appropriate interval Δt. This selection will be done here on a trial-and-error basis, but a more quantitative and analytic approach to this problem of *sampling error will be considered later*.

The digital-computer flow diagram indicates the *time sequence* of the operations to be performed. Within one given integration interval, the following operations are required:

(a) The outputs of all integrators will be known for the present time instant from the integration operations performed over the preceding time interval.

(b) The new values of the time-dependent inputs to the system (e.g., x and $\dot{x}$ in the example) are established.

(c) The block diagram is traced to establish the inputs to all integrators as they will now apply at the present time instant. This is a purely arithmetic operation involving the summing junctions and transfer constants (such as B, k, g/M).

(d) Time is updated (i.e., t is replaced as $t + \Delta t$).

(e) One iteration of numerical integration is performed so that the new integrator outputs (e.g., y and $\dot{y}$ in the example) applicable at the new time instant may be established.

The operation then returns to step (a). This is illustrated in Figure 1-27. Each traversal of this loop advances time by the amount Δt.

The procedure described, which starts with the block diagram and establishes the desired sequence of digital operations (as represented by the flow diagram), is known as *sorting*. A user acquainted with the principles described here may readily do his own sorting when preparing the program. For the benefit of those who lack this knowledge, *macroscopic simulation programs*, such as MIDAS, MIMIC, and IBM-CSMP, will permit one unfamiliar with digital procedures to load his own program on a computer, starting only with the block diagram and following various specific instructions [1, 2].

Figure 1-28 is a flow diagram showing the application of the general procedure of Figure 1-27 to the specific problem treated as an example in this chapter. It should be noted that step (a) is not actually executed, except

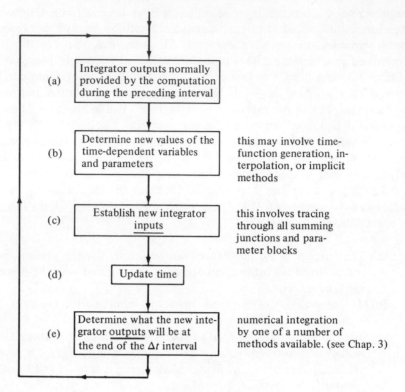

(a) Integrator outputs normally provided by the computation during the preceding interval

(b) Determine new values of the time-dependent variables and parameters

this may involve time-function generation, interpolation, or implicit methods

(c) Establish new integrator <u>inputs</u>

this involves tracing through all summing junctions and parameter blocks

(d) Update time

(e) Determine what the new integrator <u>outputs</u> will be at the end of the Δt interval

numerical integration by one of a number of methods available. (see Chap. 3)

FIGURE 1-27

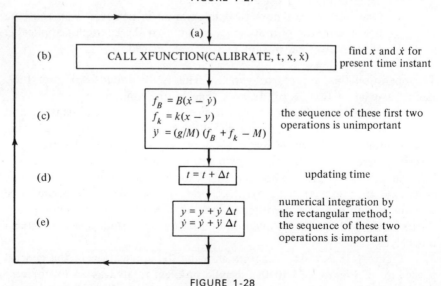

(a)

(b) CALL XFUNCTION(CALIBRATE, t, x, $\dot{x}$)

find x and $\dot{x}$ for present time instant

(c) $f_B = B(\dot{x} - \dot{y})$
$f_k = k(x - y)$
$\ddot{y} = (g/M)(f_B + f_k - M)$

the sequence of these first two operations is unimportant

(d) $t = t + \Delta t$

updating time

(e) $y = y + \dot{y}\,\Delta t$
$\dot{y} = \dot{y} + \ddot{y}\,\Delta t$

numerical integration by the rectangular method; the sequence of these two operations is important

FIGURE 1-28

as a transfer operation returning the iterative loop. Step (b) is handled by a procedure or subroutine that can be prepared as an independent program. This would permit a number of input time functions to be used by changing the choice of subroutine, called here XFUNCTION, without requiring alterations of the main program.

It should be noted that the actual integration operation, designated by $1/s$ in two blocks of Figure 1-3, has now been replaced by a *rectangular integration* operation, illustrated in Figure 1-29. As Δt becomes sufficiently small, the approximation error becomes insignificant. Other integration techniques discussed later will permit the size of the integration interval Δt to be increased without impairing the integration accuracy.

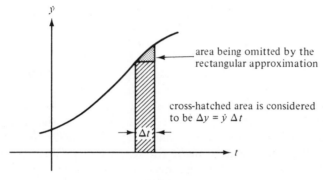

FIGURE 1-29

Referring to Figure 1-28, it should be noted that if the two operations of step (e) had been interchanged, the integration for obtaining Δy would have been based on the future, rather than past, value of the integrand $\dot{y}$. This is not necessarily less desirable, but it does represent a different method of numerical integration.

1-13 Additions to Provide a Workable Program

The program development shown in Figure 1-28 is incomplete, as was the preliminary analog program of Figure 1-15, for the following reasons:

1. It does not provide for initial output values of the integrators.
2. The subroutine that provides the values of x and $\dot{x}$ must still be furnished.
3. It does not provide for the display of output.

Furthermore,

4. It does not provide for establishing the values of constants or parameters such as B, k, or M (corresponding to setting the potentiometers in the analog program).
5. It does not provide for the termination of a run.

The logical place to *enter* the program for the purpose of starting the simulation and to overcome the first deficiency is at the point called (a) in Figures 1-27 and 1-28. At that point the initial values of all integrator values must be furnished. It is also necessary to designate the initial value of time at this point—most frequently by the operation $t = 0$.

Deficiency 2 is handled by the subroutine XFUNCTION, to be discussed further. The logical place to branch from the program temporarily for the purpose of listing (or storing) output results is after step (c), since then the new values of all variables of interest will have been calculated.

An arbitrary terminology distinction will be made between what are called constants and what are called parameters that does not correspond to normal mathematical usage. As some of these quantities may maintain the same value from one run to another, these will be designated *constants*. Others, which may be changed from one run to the other, will be designated *parameters*. Provisions will be made for reading in parameters more than once; constants will be read in only once, at the beginning of the program.

Deficiency 5 related to the necessity of terminating a run, either when t has reached some particular value or when some other stipulated criterion has been met. In the example, it will be assumed that the former criterion applies and that the run is to be terminated when t equals or exceeds a specific value designated as t_{max}. Such tests for termination will normally be made only after a listing (or recording) of output results has been executed.

Figure 1-30 is a flow diagram that describes the complete program (except for such input subroutines as XFUNCTION) with the previously described deficiencies removed. It is merely an extension of Figure 1-27. It should be noted that the first step consists of reading in all constants and instructions. The latter refers to such things as the prescribed size of the interval, Δt, the time interval between printout of results, Δt_p, and the intended duration of the run (in terms of problem, not machine time), t_{max}.

Figure 1-31 is a flow diagram that follows the general scheme of Figure 1-30 but applies specifically to the example problem being treated in this chapter. It is assumed here that a number of runs are intended for various trial values of the damping constant B; hence B is considered as a *parameter*. It is read in again every time the program returns to the second step (read-in parameters). It is also necessary to state at this time whether still another run is to follow. This is done by reading in, along with the value of B, the

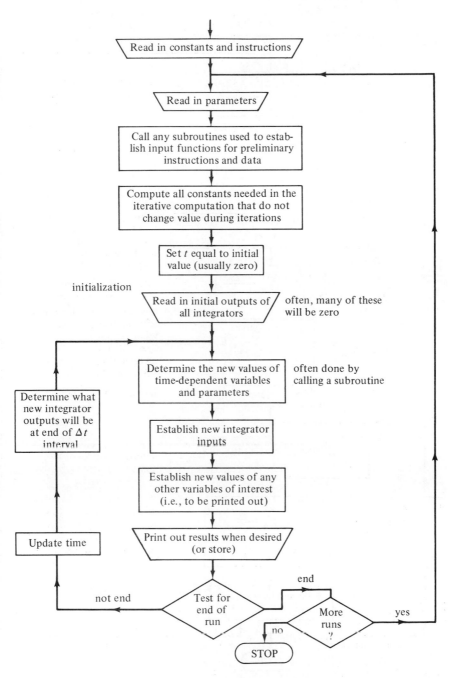

FIGURE 1-30

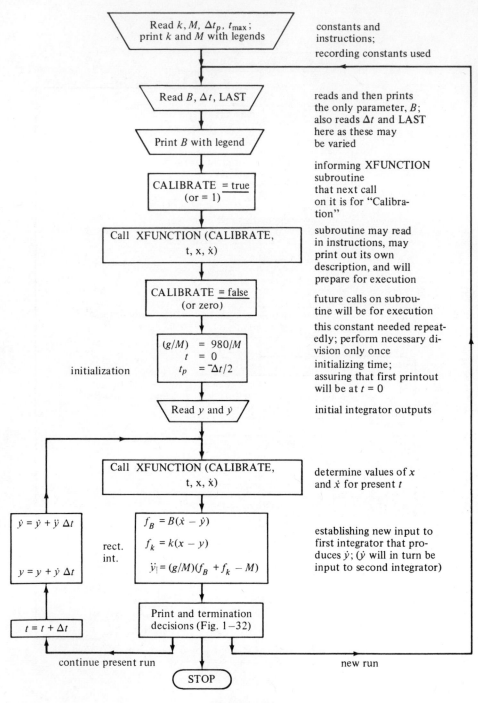

Read $k, M, \Delta t_p, t_{max}$;
print k and M with legends — constants and instructions; recording constants used

Read $B, \Delta t$, LAST — reads and then prints the only parameter, B; also reads Δt and LAST here as these may be varied

Print B with legend

CALIBRATE $= true$ (or $= 1$) — informing XFUNCTION subroutine that next call on it is for "Calibration"

Call XFUNCTION (CALIBRATE, t, x, ẋ) — subroutine may read in instructions, may print out its own description, and will prepare for execution

CALIBRATE $= false$ (or zero) — future calls on subroutine will be for execution

initialization

$(g/M) = 980/M$
$t = 0$
$t_p = {}^-\Delta t/2$ — this constant needed repeatedly; perform necessary division only once / initializing time; assuring that first printout will be at $t = 0$

Read y and $\dot y$ — initial integrator outputs

Call XFUNCTION (CALIBRATE, t, x, ẋ) — determine values of x and $\dot x$ for present t

$\dot y = \dot y + \ddot y \, \Delta t$

$y = y + \dot y \, \Delta t$

rect. int.

$f_B = B(\dot x - \dot y)$

$f_k = k(x - y)$

$\ddot y_| = (g/M)(f_B + f_k - M)$ — establishing new input to first integrator that produces $\dot y$; ($\dot y$ will in turn be input to second integrator)

$t = t + \Delta t$

Print and termination decisions (Fig. 1–32)

continue present run   new run

STOP

FIGURE 1-31

30

logical variable, LAST. If LAST is designated as true, or 1, this indicates that this is the last run and that the program should terminate at its completion. Otherwise, LAST will be read in as zero or false and the program will return to the parameter-read statement again after the run is completed. In Figure 1-31, the details of the printout decision and execution, and the termination decision, are not shown. These details are shown in Figure 1-32.

It would have been possible to arrange this printout decision, execution, and termination decision as a subroutine; this is pretty much a matter of programmer preference. It should be noted that the variable t_p, meaning time to print, controls the printout decision. Normally, t_p would be set to zero initially so that a printout at $t = 0$ would be obtained. Actually, in Figure 1-32, it should be noted that t_p is set initially to $-\Delta t/2$. This has the same effect, but often is preferable because it eliminates the danger of round-off errors causing the printout to occur after (when $t = \Delta t$) the first iteration.

The generation of the time-dependent inputs x and $\dot{x}$ by the subroutine described as XFUNCTION is still to be described. As in the analog example,

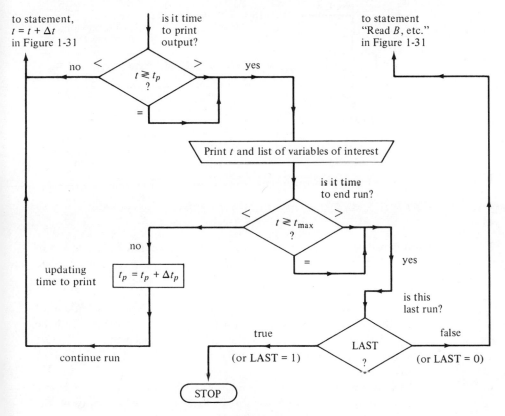

FIGURE 1-32

the simple case of $x(t)$ being a ramp function will be used for illustration. The subroutine then becomes so absurdly simple that the question might arise as to why a subroutine is necessary: Why not handle it by a few simple statements in the main program? The answer is, of course, the desire for flexibility. Other inputs might also be considered and it would be more convenient to change to a new subroutine than to alter the main program. For example, $x(t)$ or $\dot{x}(t)$ might be generated from tabulated data with interpolation procedures to provide intermediate points. The ramp-generation subroutine used for this example is shown in Figure 1-33. It should be noted that provisions are made for printing the information that the input is a ramp with a slope of r, with the value of r also printed.

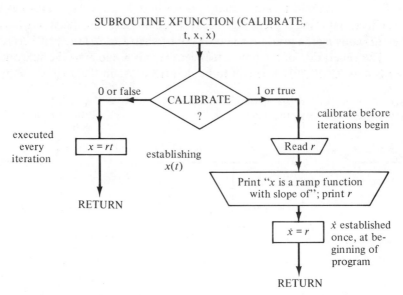

FIGURE 1-33

Data cards or other sources of input will be required for such a program as follows:

1. The values of the constants, k and M.
2. The value of the parameters, in this case B. Also, the values of Δt, the print interval Δt_p, the time range of the run t_{max}, and the logical information as to whether this run is to be the last (LAST is *true* or 1) or whether another run is to follow (LAST is *false* or zero).
3. The numerical characteristics of the x function. When the simple ramp subroutine is used, as shown here, this would simply be the slope of the ramp function r in cm/sec.

4. The initial values of y and $\dot{y}$ in cm and cm/sec.

Card 1 is used only once, at the beginning of the program; cards 2 to 4 must be fed into the program for each run.

Appendix 1A shows a Fortran IV version of the program represented by these flow diagrams.

1-14   Results of the Digital Simulation Program

The program shown in Figures 1-31 and 1-32, along with the subroutine of Figure 1-33, was executed on an IBM 360, Model 65 computer after being compiled by a Fortran IV compiler. The conditions represented were identical with those of the analog program of Figure 1-22, and results identical with those plotted in Figure 1-20 should be expected. The duration of problem time chosen was 0.100 sec ($t_{\max} = 0.100$) with printouts of response obtained every 0.002 sec. This is a sufficient time range for this particular problem, since the transient portion of the response will have essentially died out by the end of this period.

The results of a typical run employing such a program are shown in Figure 1-34. (There, owing to printer limitations, YDD denotes $\ddot{y}$ and YD indicates $\dot{y}$.) The iteration interval Δt chosen was 0.0002 sec; hence 500 iterations were necessary to cover the time range. The execution time of the iterative portion of the program, including the output operation of transferring output data for later off-line printout, was 16 sec with this particular computer. The program shown in Appendix 1A was used, with statements added to accomplish execution-time measurement.

It is not fair, however, to include output execution time when comparing various methods of simulation. Hence, for a more indicative measurement of execution time, the program shown in Appendix 1A was modified to place the output data in a storage array for later printout after the iterative cycles are completed. The execution time then noted, for the iterative portion of the program only, was 3.6 sec. As this represented a problem time of 0.100 sec, it may be seen that even with the relatively fast computer employed nothing approaching real-time simulation was obtained.

The problem used as an example in this chapter is, of course, readily solved analytically; hence the percentage of computation error may be established directly. Percentage of error is defined as

$$100 \frac{(\text{computed value}) - (\text{correct value})}{\text{range of the variable}}$$

On this basis and with the Δt of 0.0002 sec used to obtain the results tabulated in Figure 1-34, the computed values of the variables of interest have *maximum* errors as follows during the course of the run:

K= 20.000 KG/CM M= 0.500 KG
B= 0.050 KG/CM/SEC
ITERATION INTERVAL, DT= 0.00020 SECS
X IS RAMP FUNCTION WITH SLOPE OF 100.000 CM/SEC

TIME SECS	X CM	YDD CM/SEC2	YD CM/SEC	Y CM	FK KG
0.0	0.0	-30380.	0.0	1.000	-20.00
0.002	0.200	-15962.	-47.96	0.952	-15.04
0.004	0.400	-1663.	-66.81	0.834	-8.69
0.006	0.600	10494.	-58.71	0.704	-2.08
0.008	0.800	19130.	-29.29	0.610	3.80
0.010	1.000	23598.	13.70	0.589	8.22
0.012	1.200	23953.	61.85	0.659	10.81
0.014	1.400	20828.	107.44	0.825	11.50
0.016	1.600	15250.	144.39	1.075	10.50
0.018	1.800	8422.	168.85	1.388	8.24
0.020	2.000	1527.	179.41	1.738	5.25
0.022	2.200	-4438.	176.87	2.096	2.08
0.024	2.400	-8778.	163.78	2.439	-0.79
0.026	2.600	-11142.	143.76	2.750	-3.00
0.028	2.800	-11521.	120.82	3.017	-4.34
0.030	3.000	-10193.	98.73	3.238	-4.76
0.032	3.200	-7630.	80.49	3.418	-4.37
0.034	3.400	-4404.	68.08	3.567	-3.34
0.036	3.600	-1085.	62.28	3.697	-1.94
0.038	3.800	1836.	62.84	3.821	-0.42
0.040	4.000	4009.	68.61	3.951	0.98
0.042	4.200	5248.	77.90	4.096	2.07
0.044	4.400	5531.	88.81	4.262	2.76
0.046	4.600	4978.	99.49	4.449	3.01
0.048	4.800	3806.	108.48	4.657	2.87
0.050	5.000	2285.	114.75	4.880	2.40
0.052	5.200	691.	117.88	5.113	1.75
0.054	5.400	-736.	117.93	5.349	1.02
0.056	5.600	-1821.	115.42	5.583	0.34
0.058	5.800	-2465.	111.12	5.810	-0.20
0.060	6.000	-2650.	105.95	6.028	-0.55
0.062	6.200	-2426.	100.79	6.235	-0.70
0.064	6.400	-1894.	96.38	6.432	-0.65
0.066	6.600	-1180.	93.21	6.622	-0.44
0.068	6.800	-416.	91.54	6.807	-0.14
0.070	7.000	280.	91.36	6.989	0.21
0.072	7.200	821.	92.43	7.173	0.54

0.074	7.400	1154.	94.41	7.359	0.81
0.076	7.600	1267.	96.86	7.550	0.99
0.078	7.800	1180.	99.34	7.746	1.07
0.080	8.000	939.	101.51	7.947	1.05
0.082	8.200	605.	103.09	8.152	0.96
0.084	8.400	239.	103.97	8.359	0.82
0.086	8.600	-100.	104.14	8.567	0.66
0.088	8.800	-368.	103.68	8.775	0.50
0.090	9.000	-539.	102.78	8.981	0.36
0.092	9.200	-605.	101.62	9.186	0.27
0.094	9.400	-573.	100.43	9.388	0.23
0.096	9.600	-465.	99.37	9.588	0.23
0.098	9.800	-308.	98.57	9.786	0.27
0.100	9.999	-134.	98.11	9.983	0.34

FIGURE 1-34

displacement, y	0.1%
velocity, $\dot{y}$	0.7%
acceleration, $\ddot{y}$	1.6%
force, f_k	1.0%

Whether such degrees of accuracy are adequate will depend upon the application of the simulation procedure. Quite possibly this degree of accuracy is better than is really required in view of the approximation errors when establishing the mathematical description of the problem, such as the neglecting of nonlinear effects and of the distributed mass and resilience of the spring (as discussed in Chapter 10). It would also be questionable, in most practice, whether the parameters M, k, and especially B are really known more closely than a few per cent.

In any event, the computation error caused by finite iterations (i.e., the sampling error) can always be improved by reducing the size of the iteration interval. This will, of course, be at the cost of additional execution time. A more practical way for both improving accuracy and reducing the required execution time is by employing one of the more sophisticated methods of numerical integration described in Chapter 3. The relatively crude method described in this chapter, rectangular integration, was introduced simply because it is the easiest to explain.

Frequently, a graphical description of the output is desired, as in Figure 1-20, rather than the tabulated digital results shown in Figure 1-34. In an increasing number of digital-computer installations, plotters are available that can convert the output to a specified plotted form; this usually is an off-line operation. Another alternative consists of the relatively crude output plots that can be executed by the printer. Program modules for this purpose are available in many packaged simulation programs such as CSMP. However, it is relatively simple for the user who has some elementary programming experience to prepare a subroutine that will produce such an output plot. Such crude printed plots are especially useful in that they permit faster inspection of the output results than is possible by a visual scanning of tabulated output data.

1-15   Relative Advantages of Analog
and Digital Simulation

It is difficult to reach any general conclusions concerning the relative advantages of analog and digital simulation from the simple problem used in this chapter. Because of the simplicity of the problem, no unusual programming difficulties are encountered with either method. The analog simulation will prove to be faster, but whether this is a significant advantage will depend upon the application of the simulation procedure. If real-time simulation is required, particularly of a problem involving more dynamics, analog techniques of integration may be necessary to meet the execution-speed requirements. On the other hand, discontinuous-type problems requiring extensive logic may require digital procedures. In a number of practical simulation problems, the only really satisfactory answer may be the use of a hybrid computer that possesses both analog and digital features. These are discussed later.

When determining whether an analog or digital approach is to be employed in a given simulation application, the question of relative cost will always be important. Determination of the expenses involved will include not only the equipment cost and the cost of the operating time, but also the cost of the time of the associated personnel. Urgency of the results also may be a factor. Analog simulation is fast, but considerable time may have been spent preparing the program and making the necessary interconnections. Digital programming also requires program-preparation time, which, depending on the problem, the programmer's knowledge and experience, and the possibility of using standard program modules, may be greater or less than that required to get the analog program working. Prepackaged simulation programs, such as CSMP, will shorten the programming time and reduce the amount of knowledge and skill required of the programmer (however, only after he has learned the special language that is employed). It may result in less flexibility and possibly longer execution times than a program prepared specifically for a given simulation problem.

When a simulation problem is to be prepared that will be subject to many trial-and-error parameter adjustments that cannot be foreseen at the outset, analog procedures may be preferred because the procedure of reset-ting a coefficient potentiometer is generally simpler and less expensive than calling for a repeat run with revised data. The extent to which this is the case will depend upon the convenience of operation of the digital-computer facility. One that has a turn-around time (time elapsed from when the pro-gram is submitted to when the results are received) of, say, 24 hours certainly will encourage the use of analog simulation instead. As more and more digital-computer facilities adopt such schemes as remote consoles and time sharing, the turn-around time decrease to the point where analog computers lose much of this advantage. Furthermore, some parameter changes may necessitate rescaling when analog computers are used. This difficulty does not occur with digital simulation.

In summary, when a choice between analog and digital simulation is to be made, no specific rules can be formulated. The answer will depend upon the form of the simulation problem, the use to which the simulation model is to be put, the type of analog and digital equipment available, and the relative ease of access to each facility.

Suggested Problems

Both analog and digital programs should be prepared for the following simulation problems employing techniques shown in this chapter. If the equipment is available, it is suggested that the resulting programs be tested by actual computer runs with proper provisions made for the handling of input and output data. (*Note*: Suggested analog-computer scaling factors are based on using a computer of 100 V range. If a 10 V computer is used, all machine variables should, of course, be only one tenth as great.)

1-1. Five hundred dollars invested in a certain type of bond becomes worth $1000 10 years later. The applicable compound interest rate is to be deter-mined by trial-and-error simulation with different rates. (Later, when boun-dary-value problems are discussed, techniques for eliminating the trial-and-error procedure will be introduced.)

(a) Develop an analog-computer program to represent this problem and to find R, the rate of interest, based on the assumption that interest is compounded continuously. The following scale factors are suggested:

        rate R is a potentiometer setting to be adjusted by trial and error

        principal $P = 10P_m$ dollars, where P_m is the machine variable in volts

        time $t = t_m$ years, where t_m is machine time in seconds

(b) Develop a digital program to simulate the same situation as in (a).

(c) Modify the program of (b) to represent the interest being compounded quarterly. (*Note*: To handle this with an analog computer would require methods beyond the scope of this chapter's discussion.)

1-2. Two streams, A and B, of dissolved chemical flow continuously into a stirred tank and react almost immediately, producing 400 Btu of heat per pound of the solution A. The result is drawn off as stream C. The solution is cooled in the tank by means of cooling coils containing water at a temperature of $\theta_0 °F$; presumably the rate of coolant flow is fast enough so that there will be negligible rise in this cooling-water temperature. The following numerical values are given:

rate of flow of A is $F_a = 500$ lb/hr
rate of flow of B is $F_b = 800$ lb/hr
rate of flow of C if $F_c = 1300$ lb/hr
temperature of A is $\theta_a = 75°F$
temperature of B is $\theta_b = 85°F$
temperature of C is θ_c—variable
temperature of coolant is $\theta_0 = 60°F$
specific heats of A, B, and C are $c_p = 1$
θ_c is initially 60°F.
conductivity of the cooling-tube walls conducting heat from the tank solution to the coolant is $G = 10,000$ Btu/hr/°F
solution *stored* in tank is W, where, at $t = 0$, $W(0) = 3000$ lb

Prepare both analog- and digital-computer programs that will indicate θ_c as a function of time. For the analog program, the following scale factors are suggested:

heat flows: $R = 2500R_m$ Btu/hr, where R_m is corresponding machine volts
temperature: $\theta = \theta_m °F$
time: $t = 0.1t_m$ hr

1-3. Figure P1-3 is a schematic diagram of an electronically controlled variable-speed drive capable of reversal in direction. (With additional equipment, it can be made a servomechanism capable of precise control of angular position of the load.) The pertinent mathematical relations describing its performance are

generator field
   current relation:
$$(R_o + R_f + L_f s)i_f = e_o \quad \text{V} \qquad (i_f \text{ in amperes})$$
generated voltage:
$$e_g = k_f i_f \qquad \text{V}$$
terminal voltage:
$$V = e_g - R_g i \qquad \text{V}$$
motor back-emf:
$$e_1 = V - R_1 i \qquad \text{V}$$

motor and generator armature inductance negligible

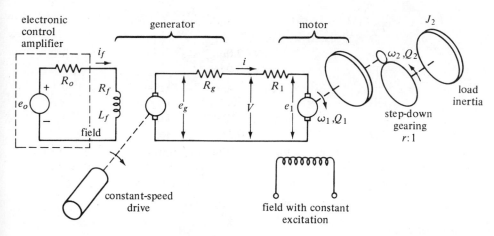

FIGURE P1-3

motor speed:
$$\omega_1 = k_\omega e_1 \qquad \text{rad/sec}$$
developed torque:
$$Q_1 = k_Q i \qquad \text{kg-cm}$$

$\left.\begin{array}{l}\\\\\\\end{array}\right\}$ assumes constant magnetic flux

torque at gearing:
$$Q_g = Q_1 - J_1 s\omega_1 \qquad \text{kg-cm} \qquad \text{neglects motor friction}$$
gear output speed:
$$\omega_2 = \omega_1/r \qquad \text{rad/sec} \qquad \text{neglects gear backlash}$$
gear output torque:
$$Q_2 = rQ_g \qquad \text{kg-cm} \qquad \text{neglects gear friction losses}$$
load inertia effect:
$$Q_2 = J_2 s\omega_2 \qquad \text{kg-cm} \qquad \text{neglects load friction}$$

(*Hint:* The last four relations may be combined to obtain one first-order differential equation.) Numerically,

$R_o = 2000\ \Omega$ (effective source resistance)
$R_f = 500\ \Omega$
$L_f = 100\ \text{H}$
$k_f = 4000\ \text{V/A}$
$R_g = 1.0\ \Omega$
$R_1 = 1.0\ \Omega$
$k_\omega = 0.5\ \text{(rad/sec)/V}$
$k_Q = 20.4\ \text{kg-cm/A}$
$J_1 = 0.8\ \text{kg-cm/(rad/sec}^2)$
$r = 50\ \text{(gear ratio)}$
$J_2 = 2000\ \text{kg-cm/(rad/sec}^2)$

(a) Prepare an analog-computer program to simulate the variation of i, V, ω_1, and ω_2 as functions of time when e_o is some prescribed function of time. Observe and record results for specifically: $e_o = 100u(t)$ V

(100 V step function) with initial conditions of $i_f(0) = V(0) = \omega_1(0) = \omega_2(0) = 0$. Suggested scaling is

$e_o = 2e_{o_m}$	V	$\omega_1 = 2.0\omega_{1_m}$	rad/sec
$i_f = 10^{-3}i_{f_m}$	A	$\omega_2 = 0.04\omega_{2_m}$	rad/sec
$e_g = 4e_{g_m}$	V	$Q_1 = 50Q_{1_m}$	kg-cm
$V = 4V_m$	V	$Q_g = 50Q_{g_m}$	kg-cm
$e_1 = 4e_{1_m}$	V	$Q_2 = 2500Q_{2_m}$	kg-cm
$i = 2i_m$	A	$t = 0.1t_m$	sec

(b) Prepare a corresponding digital-computer program including appropriate input and output statements and execute for the same specific $e_o(t)$ example as in (a) with a Δt adequate for 1 per cent accuracy.

References

1. Geoffrey Gordon, *System Simulation* (Englewood Cliffs, N.J.: Prentice-Hall, Inc., 1969).

2. Yaohan Chu, *Digital Simulation of Continuous Systems* (New York: McGraw-Hill, Inc., 1969).

3. D. B. Suits, Forecasting and Analysis with an Econometric Model, *American Economic Review*, Vol. LII (1962), 104–132.

Appendix 1A

```
C      SIMULATION OF SPRING-MASS SYSTEM - CHAPTER 1
      1EXAMPLE
       REAL K,M
       LOGICAL CAL,LAST
    1  READ 100,K,M
       PRINT 101,K,M
    2  READ 103,B,DT,DTP,TMAX,LAST
       PRINT 104,B
       PRINT 105,DT
       CAL=.TRUE.
       CALL XFUNC(CAL,T,X,XD)
       CAL=.FALSE.
       GOVERM=980./M
       T=0.
       TP=-.5*DT
       TMAX=TMAX-.5*DT
       READ 100,Y,YD
C      PRINTING LEGEND FOR OUTPUT LIST
       PRINT 102
       PRINT 106
       PRINT 107
C      ITERATIVE PROGRAM BEGINS
    3  CALL XFUNC(CAL,T,X,XD)
       FB=(XD-YD)*B
       FK=(X-Y)*K
       YDD=GOVERM*(FB+FK-M)
C      PRINTOUT DECISION
```

```
      IF(T.LT.TP) GO TO 5
      PRINT 108,T,X,YDD,YD,Y,FK
C     TERMINATION DECISION
      IF(T.LT.TMAX) GO TO 4
      IF(LAST) STOP
      GO TO 2
  4   TP=TP+DTP
  5   T=T+DT
C     RECTANGULAR INTEGRATION
      Y=Y+YD*DT
      YD=YD+YDD*DT
      GO TO 3
100   FORMAT(2F10.3)
101   FORMAT(1H1,20X,2HK=,F10.3,6H KG/CM,5X,2HM=,
     1F10.3,3H KG)
102   FORMAT(1H )
103   FORMAT(F10.3,F10.5,2F10.3,L2)
104   FORMAT(26X,2HB=,F10.3,10H KG/CM/SEC)
105   FORMAT(20X,23HITERATION INTERVAL, DT=,F10.5,5H
     1SECS)
106   FORMAT(16X,4HTIME,7X,1HX,7X,3HYDD,8X,2HYD,9X,
     11HY,8X,2HFK)
107   FORMAT(16X,4HSECS,6X,2HCM,5X,7HCM/SEC2,4X,
     16HCM/SEC,6X,2HCM,8X,12HKG)
108   FORMAT(10X,2F10.3,F10.0,F10.2,F10.3,F10.2)
      END
```

FIGURE 1A-1

```
C     RAMP FUNCTION SUBROUTINE
      SUBROUTINE XFUNC(CAL,T,X,XD)
      LOGICAL CAL
      IF(CAL) GO TO 1
      X=R*T
      RETURN
  1   READ 300,R
300   FORMAT(F10.3)
      PRINT 301,R
301   FORMAT(15X,32HX IS RAMP FUNCTION WITH SLOPE OF,
     1F10.3,7H CM/SEC
      XD=R
      RETURN
      END
```

FIGURE 1A-2

Basic Principles
of Analog Computers

2

2-1 General Comments

Routine programming and operation of general-purpose analog computers is possible with modern equipment simply by following the manufacturer's instructions. Then no electronic knowledge is required. There is, however, value in the user's having some appreciation of the simpler electronic principles that are involved. He will then have a greater understanding of both the limitations and potentialities of these devices. This will permit more reliable programming and also the establishment of the more unusual programs that often are called for in simulation problems and might not have been anticipated by the computer manufacturer.

There is another reason why the understanding of the basic electronic principles might be of particular interest to *some* readers. Often the need arises for a *special-purpose* analog simulator. It is often practical and desirable to assemble such a simulator from the basic electronic module elements available commercially. This procedure might be preferable to tying up a more extensive general-purpose analog computer for a long-range problem. Such special-purpose simulators can be programmed and assembled only with some knowledge of the basic principles that are described here. On the other hand, knowledge of the intimate details of the internal circuitry involved in each electronic component will not be necessary.

2-2   Operational Amplifier

The most basic element of the analog computer is the *operational amplifier*, represented by the schematic diagram of Figure 2-1. This is a high-gain electronic amplifier that might employ vacuum tubes or, more likely with

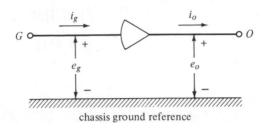

chassis ground reference   FIGURE 2-1

modern units, transistors. An input voltage is applied, e_g, commonly called the *grid voltage*. (This term arises from the historic fact that this voltage originally was applied to the grid of the first amplifier stage's vacuum tube, and sometimes still is. In more modern units it is more likely to be applied to the base of the first stage transistor or to some other element.) The output voltage, e_o, will then be some amplified version of e_g. An acceptable operational amplifier will have the following characteristics:

1. When $e_g = 0$, then $e_o = 0 \pm e_\epsilon$, where the *null voltage*, e_ϵ, should be some very small fraction (e.g., 0.05 per cent) of the range of e_o.
2. $e_o/e_g = -\mu$, where $\mu \gg 1$; μ, the *gain*, may be a function of e_g but should be at least 5000 in simpler computers intended for less accurate work and 100,000 or more with more accurate installations.
3. The grid current, i_g, that flows should be almost negligible so that it does not constitute any significant electrical load that might affect e_g in consideration of the impedance of the electrical elements (e.g., feedback and input resistors) that will be connected to the grid.
4. The amplifier should be capable of supplying output current i_o to the other computer elements that normally might be connected to it without having the gain μ reduced to the extent that condition 2 no longer applies.
5. The ability of the operational amplifier to handle time-varying signals, such as transient and random signals, may be expressed in terms of its ability to handle sinusoidal signals of various frequencies (i.e., in terms of the *frequency response*). This is described by the lower and upper limits of sinusoidal frequency, beyond which there will be an excessive distortion of either signal amplitude or phase. Just what this frequency range should be will be discussed.

Specification 1 relates to the *zero-balance* problem, where zero volts in should mean essentially zero volts out. This is handled in one of two ways:

1. By manual control of zero balance, with appropriate meter indications. The zero balance is then checked and readjusted occasionally for each amplifier. This is a common practice in the less expensive and less accurate types of computers.
2. By an auxiliary automatic balancing circuit that repetitively checks and readjusts the zero balance. This is the technique used in the more precise and elaborate computers.

Specification 2 refers to the high-gain requirements of the operational amplifier. The need for such a high gain will be obvious when the use of these amplifiers as summers and integrators is discussed in this chapter. It should be noted that the *linearity* of the relationship between e_o and e_g is not essential as long as the incremental gain, $\partial e_o/\partial e_g$, as well as μ, remains high over the entire voltage range of operation.

The need for specifications 3 and 4 will also be obvious when the use of operational amplifiers as summers and integrators is discussed.

Specification 5 depends upon the application of the computer. The computer should be capable of slow problem solution, which may involve runs of many minutes; this is particularly necessary with *real-time simulation* of process-control problems. Therefore, the lower frequency limit should be *zero;* direct-coupled amplifiers capable of amplifying d.c. as well as a.c. are required. The computer should also be able to handle high-frequency variations without distortion up to, perhaps, 100 Hz. An upper-frequency limit of about 5 kHz might be adequate for computers intended for such applications.

It is, however, desirable to permit, as well, operation on a high-speed-repetitive basis.[1] (This capability is particularly necessary in connection with the *dynamic-storage techniques* discussed in Chapter 4.) This would involve only short solution times (e.g., 0.05 sec) but features a continuous repetition of the solution at a repetition frequency, such as 10 Hz. The results then are normally displayed on a cathode-ray oscilloscope. Because of the fast solution time required with such applications (a greatly sped-up time base), the required high-frequency response limit is greatly increased, possibly to as high as 1.0 MHz.

Today's many successful applications of analog computers are due to the ingenuity and perseverance of many people engaged in operational-amplifier design over a long period of time. A knowledge of the electronic

---

[1] Many analog computers have been manufactured in the past that have been capable of *only* repetitive operation. This type is now becoming obsolete.

circuit details is not, however, essential to their successful utilization in simulation problems. This subject, therefore, will not be covered here.

All operational amplifiers have a limited useful range of output voltage, V_R. Standard ranges are 50 and, more commonly, 100 V for amplifiers using vacuum tubes, and usually 10, but also 25, 50, and 100 V, for those using transistors. In the newer installations the tendency is toward transistorized amplifiers with a 10 V nominal range.

In any event, if the output of any operational amplifier is driven substantially beyond its design range, this output will level off and eventually limit itself. This is accompanied by some type of warning indication to alert the operator. Such an *overload* condition does no damage other than providing erroneous results. (A properly designed operational amplifier should tolerate such overloads for sustained periods.) One of the functions of problem-machine scaling is the avoidance of such an overload condition.

In the discussion to follow, reference will often be made to an "ideal" operational amplifier. Referring to specifications 5 above, this is a hypothetical amplifier in which

1. when $e_g = 0$, $e_o = 0$.
2. $\mu = -e_o/e_g$ with $\mu \to \infty$.
3. $i_g = 0$.
4. μ is unaffected by i_o.
5. the frequency range is from zero to ∞ Hz.

2-3 General Input–Output Relations with an Ideal Operational Amplifier

When employed in linear operations, the e_o and e_g terminals are connected to each other through a linear *feedback impedance*, z_f, and one or more input terminals are connected to the e_g terminal through *input impedances* designated as z_1, z_2, etc. The result is shown in Figure 2-2. Since $i_g = 0$, from the law of continuity of current flow (Kirchhoff's current law),

$$i_f = i_1 + i_2 + i_3 + \cdots + i_n$$

but

$$i_f = \frac{e_g - e_o}{z_f}$$

and

$$i_1 = \frac{e_1 - e_g}{z_1}, \quad i_2 = \frac{e_2 - e_g}{z_2}, \quad i_3 = \frac{e_3 - e_g}{z_3}, \quad \text{etc.}$$

Hence

$$\frac{e_o}{z_f} = \frac{e_g}{z_f} + \frac{e_g}{z_1} + \frac{e_g}{z_2} + \cdots - \left(\frac{e_1}{z_1} + \frac{e_2}{z_2} + \frac{e_3}{z_3} + \cdots + \frac{e_n}{z_n} \right)$$

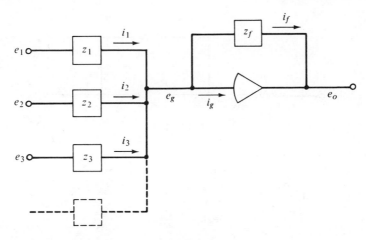

FIGURE 2-2

or

$$e_o = e_g\left(1 + \frac{z_f}{z_1} + \frac{z_f}{z_2} + \frac{z_f}{z_3} + \cdots + \frac{z_f}{z_n}\right)$$
$$- \left(\frac{z_f}{z_1}e_1 + \frac{z_f}{z_2}e_2 + \frac{z_f}{z_3}e_3 + \cdots + \frac{z_f}{z_n}e_n\right)$$

But $e_g = -e_o/\mu$; therefore,

$$e_o = -\frac{e_o}{\mu}\left(1 + \frac{z_f}{z_1} + \frac{z_f}{z_2} + \frac{z_f}{z_3} + \cdots + \frac{z_f}{z_n}\right)$$
$$- \left(\frac{z_f}{z_1}e_1 + \frac{z_f}{z_2}e_2 + \frac{z_f}{z_3}e_3 + \cdots + \frac{z_f}{z_n}e_n\right)$$

(2-1)

For the ideal operational amplifier, as $\mu \to \infty$ the first term in parentheses becomes negligible and

$$e_o = -\frac{z_f}{z_1}e_1 - \frac{z_f}{z_2}e_2 - \frac{z_f}{z_3}e_3 - \cdots - \frac{z_f}{z_n}e_n$$

(2-2)

This is the important relation upon which most analog-computer programming is based. The output voltage e_o is the weighted sum of all input voltages, the weighting factors being the ratios of the feedback impedance to the particular input impedances. Only these impedances, not the amplifier itself, determine the input–output or *transfer* relationship. Hence a practically perfect linear relationship between input and output voltages can be expected.

2-4 Simple Amplifier

Figure 2-3 shows the connection of elements for a simple amplifier. Here only one input signal is employed, e_1, and the input and feedback impedances

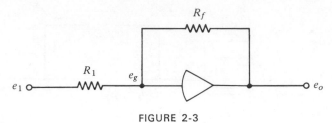

FIGURE 2-3

are pure resistances; i.e.,

$$z_1 = R_1 \qquad z_f = R_f$$

Then, from (2-2),

$$e_o = -\frac{R_f}{R_1}e_1 \tag{2-3}$$

The alternative diagram more often used in programming, rather than Figure 2-3, is the one shown in Figure 2-4, where k is a stated numerical value equal to the ratio R_f/R_1 and is called the *amplifier gain* (as contrasted to the much higher operational-amplifier gain, μ). The change in algebraic sign is not indicated in Figure 2-4 but is implied.

FIGURE 2-4

R_f and R_1 may be chosen (within reason) in any combination of values in order to multiply an input voltage by any constant greater or less than unity. (To multiply by less than unity, potentiometers, discussed later, may also be employed.) There usually are practical limits to the values of R_1 and R_f. Minimum permissible values are between 10,000 and 100,000 Ω (with vacuum-tube operational amplifiers) in order to prevent errors caused by excessive loading of the amplifier (with reference to specification 1 in Section 2-1).[2] Maximum permissible values are about 10 MΩ; use of higher resistances can cause errors because of voltage drops caused by the grid current flow (recalling that the actual amplifiers will not be ideal). Hence amplifier gains as high as 1000 are obtainable but are rarely required in most computer applications if proper scaling is employed. With transistor-type operational amplifiers the same general limitations apply, except that the upper and lower limits of the resistances that may be employed will normally be smaller.

When unusually high gains are required without resorting to unreasonably high ratios of resistance, the method to be described in Section 2-12 may be employed.

---

[2]These values of resistance are about one-tenth as much for transistor type operational amplifiers.

The most frequent use of a simple amplifier is as an *inverter*, where $R_1 = R_f$; this merely accomplishes a change in algebraic sign.

2-5   Summers

Summers are simply an extension of the above principle where a number of input resistances are used. Figure 2-5 shows the arrangement. Here

$$e_o = -\left(\frac{R_f}{R_1}e_1 + \frac{R_f}{R_2}e_2 + \frac{R_f}{R_3}e_3 + \cdots + \frac{R_f}{R_n}e_n\right) \tag{2-4}$$

The alternative diagram, used more often in programming, is shown in Figure 2-6, where k_1, k_2, k_3, etc., are the specific numerical values of the ratios R_f/R_1, R_f/R_2, etc. Again, algebraic sign inversion is implied.

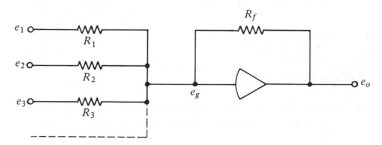

FIGURE 2-5

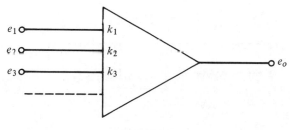

FIGURE 2-6

2-6   Integrators

If the feedback impedance element z_f is made a capacitor so that $z_f = 1/C_f s$, with the input impedance z_1 remaining a resistance R_1, an integrator results. Figure 2-7 illustrates this. Here, from (2-2),

$$e_o = -\frac{1}{R_1 C_f s}e_1 \tag{2-5}$$

The factor $1/R_1 C_f$ has the dimensions of seconds^{-1} and is described as the

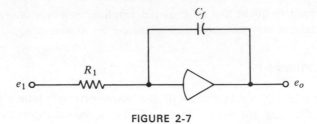

FIGURE 2-7

integrator gain (i.e., the volts per second rate of output change per volt of input). In Chapter 1 the type of diagram shown in Figure 2-8 was used to represent such an integrator, where k is the specific numerical value of the integrator gain.

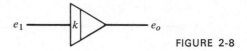

FIGURE 2-8

2-7   Summer–Integrators

From the preceding discussion it should be obvious that the arrangement of Figure 2-9 combines the functions of summing and integrating in a single amplifier and that

$$e_o = -\frac{1}{s}(k_1 e_1 + k_2 e_2 + k_3 e_3 + \cdots + k_n e_n) \qquad (2\text{-}6)$$

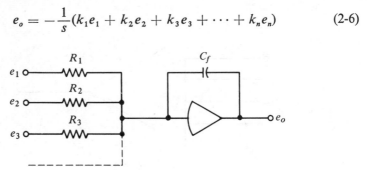

FIGURE 2-9

where $k_1 = 1/R_1 C_f$, $k_2 = 1/R_2 C_2$, etc. Another diagram for this is pictured in Figure 2-10.

The program shown in Figure 1-22 did not employ such combined summer–integrators. It would have been possible to employ them; for example, the functions of amplifiers A12, A13, and A20 could have been performed by one summer–integrator (using two less amplifiers as a result). However, if this had been done, the intermediate signal $\ddot{y}$ would not have been available as an indication.

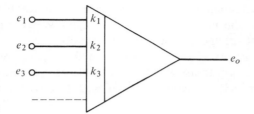

FIGURE 2-10

2-8   Differentiators

Referring to Figure 2-7 it becomes obvious that the functions of the capacitor and resistor shown could have been reversed, as in Figure 2-11. Then

$$e_o = R_f C_1 s e_1 \qquad (2\text{-}7)$$

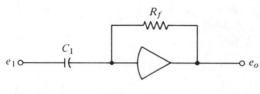

FIGURE 2-11

The output is now proportional to the time derivative of the input. This might at first appear to offer opportunities for using alternative forms of block diagrams in programming, as in Figure 1-5. Actually, such differentiating circuits are best avoided whenever possible. The reason for this can be explained by a *Bode diagram* relating the output and input amplitudes when signals of sinusoidal form of frequency ω are assumed applied. Such a diagram is shown in Figure 2-12. It may be noted that the gain increases without limit as the frequency is increased. There will always be some high-frequency noise present in analog computers from stray pickup from other equipment, power supply and vibrator hum, etc. Ordinarily, this is not at all noticeable. However, when such differentiating amplifiers are employed,

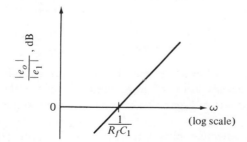

FIGURE 2-12

these signals are accentuated and not only become noticeable but might even be excessive to the point of driving the amplifiers beyond the normal range of their output voltage into an overload condition. It is for this reason that the use of differentiating amplifiers is avoided whenever possible.

When it is necessary to use a differentiating circuit, an imperfect form, as shown in Figure 2-13, generally is employed to avoid this problem. Here, for circuit (a),

$$e_o = \frac{R_f C_1 s}{1 + R_1 C_1 s} e_1 \qquad (2\text{-}8a)$$

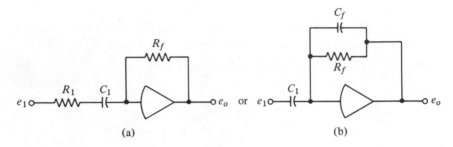

(a)   (b)

FIGURE 2-13

For circuit (b),

$$e_o = \frac{R_f C_1 s}{1 + R_f C_f s} e_1 \qquad (2\text{-}8b)$$

This no longer is a perfect differentiating circuit but has a *response lag* of $R_1 C_1$ or $R_f C_f$ sec. For example, if a rate of change of e_1 is suddenly applied, e_o would not immediately attain the new value of the time derivative but would approach this value with an exponential lag. Figure 2-14 illustrates this.

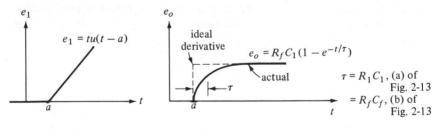

FIGURE 2-14

This circuit, however, has the advantage that the gain at high frequencies, and the consequent accentuation of noise, can be kept under reasonable control. The Bode diagram in Figure 2-12 is now modified to the form shown in Figure 2-15.

In general, the effective programming of simulation problems will

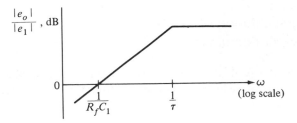

FIGURE 2-15

avoid the use of differentiating elements when either analog or digital techniques are employed.

2-9 Representation of Response Lag

Frequently, two variables will be related as follows:

$$y_m = \frac{k}{1 + \tau s} x_m \qquad (2\text{-}9)$$

Under these circumstances, the relation could be written as

$$\dot{y}_m = \frac{1}{\tau}(k x_m - y_m) \qquad (2\text{-}10)$$

The program for generating the y_m indication would be as shown in Figure 2-16 if a summer–integrator were employed.

An alternative viewpoint would involve the circuit of Figure 2-17.

A comparison of the arrangements of Figures 2-16 and 2-17 would show that they are equivalent in all respects.

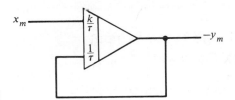

FIGURE 2-16

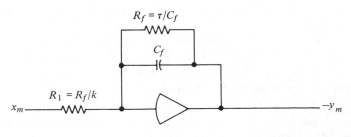

FIGURE 2-17

2-10   Representation of Lead–Lag
         Transfer Functions

Particularly in the field of control, it will often be found desirable to add elements with the following type of transfer function to improve the control system:

$$y_m = k \frac{1 + \tau_n s}{1 + \tau_d s} x_m$$

Depending upon the control problem encountered, τ_n may be greater or less than τ_d. The term *lead–lag* is applied to such transfer elements because the numerator produces a phase lead (when considered with respect to the response to sinusoidal signals) and the denominator produces a phase lag. Such a transfer function is accomplished by a number of different techniques in actual control problems; sometimes operational amplifiers are used just as with analog simulation. This relation may be simulated as in Figure 2-18.

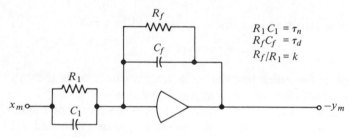

FIGURE 2-18

2-11   More Complicated Types of Input
         and Feedback Circuits[3]

With some very special problems, input and feedback impedances are constructed which are more complicated than those shown above. An understanding of them requires some knowledge of electrical-circuit theory. The circuit of Figure 2-19 is an example. Here the feedback impedance is not of a simple series or parallel type but has an intermediate ground connection. It may be treated by means of Thévenin's theorem. This is illustrated in Figure 2-20. Relation (2-2) may be employed if $e_o{'}$ is substituted for e_o and the equivalent z_f is as shown in Figure 2-20.

---

[3]This section may be skipped by readers interested only in standard programming with "closed" general-purpose computers.

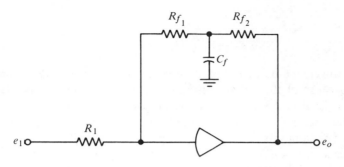

FIGURE 2-19

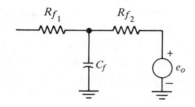

is equivalent to

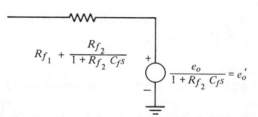

FIGURE 2-20

$$z_f = R_{f_1} + \frac{R_{f_2}}{1 + R_{f_2} C_f s} = \frac{R_{f_1} + R_{f_2} + R_{f_1} R_{f_2} C_f s}{1 + R_{f_2} C_f s}$$

$$= R_f \frac{1 + R_p C_f s}{1 + R_{f_2} C_f s} \qquad (2\text{-}11)$$

where

$$R_f \triangleq R_{f_1} + R_{f_2}$$

$$R_p \triangleq \frac{R_{f_1} R_{f_2}}{R_{f_1} + R_{f_2}}$$

Hence

$$e_o{}' = -\frac{R_f}{R_1}\left(\frac{1 + R_p C_f s}{1 + R_{f_2} C_f s}\right) e_1$$

However, from Figure 2-20,

$$e_o = (1 + R_{f_2} C_f s) e_o{}'$$

Hence

$$e_o = -\frac{R_f}{R_1}(1 + R_p C_f s)e_1 \qquad (2\text{-}12)$$

This arrangement be described as producing a *proportional-plus-derivative effect*. Because of the differentiating term, it has all the disadvantages discussed in Section 2-8 as far as noise accentuation is concerned.

The circuit shown here was used only to illustrate the general method employed for analyzing such more complicated arrangements. Such arrangements generally are not employed in ordinary simulation problems but rather for special purposes, as when analog circuits are to be used as part of the control equipment and the number of amplifiers to be employed is to be kept a minimum. Such arrangements are practical only when the type of operational amplifier is of the form to be described later as the *open type*, not found normally in general-purpose precision-type analog computers.

A more general procedure that might be employed to obtain various desired transfer functions without resorting to such complicated feedback circuits is discussed in Appendix 2A. These methods will be applicable to closed as well as open-type computers.

2-12   Increasing the Gains of Amplifiers by Reducing the Amount of Feedback

The principles discussed in Section 2-11 do suggest one simple way of obtaining high values of amplifier gain without using unreasonably high ratios of the feedback resistance to the input resistance. The feedback signal is simply reduced by a potentiometer before being applied to the feedback resistor; this is equivalent to the use of a larger resistor. The scheme is shown in Figure 2-21 as it would be applied to a summer. The gains will now be expressed by the relation

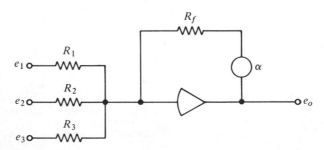

FIGURE 2-21

$$e_o = -\frac{R_f}{\alpha R_1}e_1 - \frac{R_f}{\alpha R_2}e_2 - \frac{R_f}{\alpha R_3}e_3$$

where α is the potentiometer setting (see Section 2-17).

This method for increasing gain may generally be applied with closed types of computers as well, as these usually have some provision for opening the circuit that normally connects the feedback resistor to the output and interposing a potentiometer.

This principle might also be applied to an integrator for the purpose of increasing its gain, but it would operate in an imperfect sort of way. The method is illustrated by Figure 2-22, where α is the potentiometer setting. The potentimeter may be considered as a circuit element, as described in Section 2-17, and a circuit equivalent to those discussed in Section 2-11 will then result. If this, in turn, is analyzed, it will be found that the input–output relationship will be given by the relation

$$\frac{e_o}{e_1} = -\frac{1}{\alpha R_1 C_f s} - (1-\alpha)\frac{R}{R_1} \tag{2-13}$$

The first term represents the pure integration effect, as desired, augmented by the factor $1/\alpha$. However, the second term indicates that a normally un-desired proportional effect has been added as well, proportional to the value of the potentiometer's total resistance R.

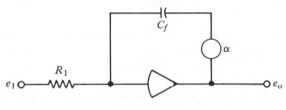

FIGURE 2-22

2-13 Establishing Initial Conditions

The discussion of integrators in Section 2-6 is not complete because it pro-vides for no method for establishing the initial condition of the output volt-age at time $t_m = 0$ (i.e., at the beginning of the computation period). This statement also applies to the arrangements shown in Figures 2-11, 2-13, 2-17, 2-18, and 2-19. In all cases, all initial conditions, as determined by the initial charges on all capacitances used in either feedback or input circuits, must be established.

The simplest method for accomplishing this is by means of a number of *floating* initial-condition power supplies. Such power supplies are called

$$V_i$$

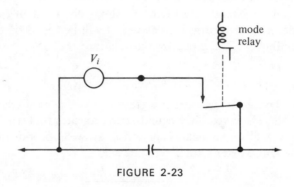

FIGURE 2-22a

floating because, unlike most other supplies, there can be no definite connection to the computer ground. The symbol denotes such a supply. Normally, it may be manually adjusted to any value of voltage within the operating range of the computer.

The procedure for employing such supplies is quite simple. They are connected through relay contacts to the capacitor involved, as shown in Figure 2-23. During what is called the initial condition (IC), or else the

FIGURE 2-23

reset mode, the relay contacts shown are closed. Each initial condition supply is then adjusted separately to the appropriate magnitude and polarity corresponding to the initial conditions of the problem. This adjustment is quite simple and the results are observed through a meter while it is being made. After all the initial conditions are established, the computer is switched to the operate or compute mode. At the instant of starting this mode, all mode relays open their contacts and disconnect the initial-condition supplies. The capacitors then are all released and computation results. In instances where the proper initial condition happens to be zero volts, the initial-condition supply shown in Figure 2-23 is simply replaced by a short circuit.

The technique described is used most often with those simpler forms of analog computer to be described later as the open type. With the more elaborate and precise closed type of computer, the accuracy requirements do not permit the use of such floating power supplies and a different technique is used. It should be pointed out that the closed type of computer does not employ capacitors in any function other than as the feedback element of an integrator. (Other functions, such as those shown in Figures 2-11, 2-13, 2-17, 2-18, and 2-19, may always be performed with integrators and summers alone.) Hence the problem of initial conditions becomes simply that of establishing the proper initial value of output voltage e_o for all such integrators. This may be accomplished by a scheme as shown in Figure 2-24. In the normal operate position, the mode-relay contact is in the b position and the circuit is a normal summer–integrator similar to that of Figure 2-9 (or is a simple integrator, as shown in Figure 2-7, if only one input resistance is connected to the summing junction). When initial conditions are being set, (i.e., operation is in the IC or reset mode), the relay contact moves to position a. The circuit then has the form shown in Figure 2-17 with the initial-condition voltage corresponding to the input. As the two R_r's are equal, the operation is that of a simple inverter with lag, and the output voltage e_o approaches a value equal in magnitude and opposite in sign to the value of voltage applied to the IC terminal. The response lag associated with the attaining of this initial condition is R_rC sec. (For this reason, the computer should be maintained in the reset mode for at least $5R_rC$ sec so that the proper initial conditions will be reached. In a real-time computer, R_rC might typically be 0.1 sec; the reset mode then should be maintained for at least 0.5 sec.)

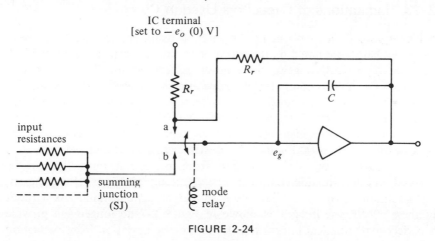

FIGURE 2-24

In Chapter 1 the question of establishing the initial conditions was disposed of rapidly by simply stating that the appropriate voltages be connected to the IC terminal of each integrator. The above discussion was for the purpose of explaining more completely what this procedure actually does.

2-14   Hold Operation

Referring to Figure 2-24, a third midposition of the mode relay could have been introduced where the e_g terminal is connected to neither position a nor b, but remains disconnected. The equivalent situation may be created by simply disconnecting all inputs to the integrators except that of the feedback capacitor itself. In either case, when this is done during computation, the associated integrator will lock or *hold*, maintaining its output value. When returned to the operate mode, integration will continue from this point.

Such a *hold mode* is convenient when it is desired that a computation be halted temporarily while all signals are being observed by some device such as a digital voltmeter. Operation continues again when the mode is returned to compute (or operate).

It should be noted from the above that an integrator in the hold position functions as a data-storage device, storing the one particular value of a signal voltage. Compared to digital-storage techniques, it will have limits in regard to the duration of time during which such storage may be maintained reliably. The reason for this is discussed next.

2-15   Limitations of Capacitors Used in Computers

All analyses of the performance of circuits using capacitances that were described here were based on the assumption that the capacitance was ideal. In reality, physical capacitors are never perfect, although those used in high-precision analog computers do come as close to perfection as is possible (hence their cost). Nevertheless, all capacitors will possess some leakage, equivalent to a high resistance in parallel with the actual capacitance parameter, and also some dielectric hysteresis, represented very approximately by a resistance in series. Figure 2-25 illustrates this. (For an ideal capacitor, $R_{cp} \rightarrow \infty$; $R_{cs} \rightarrow 0$.) This deviation from perfection normally can be ignored in most analog-computer programming problems. Nevertheless, the limitations that it does introduce should be kept in mind. As a result of these effects, the integrator shown in Figure 2-7 no longer will provide a perfect mathematical integration. However, the deviation from perfection will be obvious only under unusual circumstances, as when a computer solution is to be obtained over a long period of time (order of 10 min or more for precision computers, 1 min or more for less precise ones).

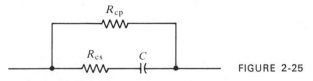

FIGURE 2-25

It is this limitation of capacitances that prevents an integrator being operated in the hold position from being an almost ideal storage device. If the initial output voltage of such an integrator is $e_o(0)$, the voltage t sec later, after being placed in the hold position, will be

$$e_o = e_o(0) \exp\left(\frac{-t}{R_{cp}C}\right)$$

In other words, the voltage being held will eventually drift toward zero. However, in a high-precision computer reliable holding action can be maintained for several minutes.

2-16 Open Versus Closed Computers

The terms open and closed computers have been used in discussions up to this point and should be clarified. To a limited extent these two types might also be referred to, respectively, as cheap and expensive computers—however, this point should not be overemphasized, as the first type often is admirably suited for the solution of many problems.

In general, the term *open computer* refers to computers in which the operational amplifiers are directly available to the user, having only e_g and e_o terminals. As they are generally intended for less precise work, they normally employ manual rather than automatic null-balancing techniques. This feature, which helps make the computer less expensive, may seem to detract from convenience of operation. In fairness it might also be stated that the avoidance of automatic-balancing circuits also avoids one possible item of troublesome maintenance.

With such open computers the feedback- and input-impedance elements are normally external components that are "plugged in." Often they are not even supplied by the computer manufacturer but must be obtained separately; any reasonably precise line (± 1 per cent) of resistors and capacitors will do. A large collection of various sizes of each are stored and hence combinations are possible far beyond those available with the closed units. Obviously, this technique does not permit the use of temperature-controlled environments for such elements and, as a result, such open computers are considerably less accurate.

One advantage that open computers possess is flexibility, as it is quite easy to connect various complicated types of input and feedback impedances. However, this flexibility is of no particular value unless the person doing the programming has a reasonable knowledge of electrical-circuit theory (not a requirement with closed computers). Because of this, such computers are often preferred for educational purposes, where very precise solutions are not necessary but where it is desired that the users obtain a full understanding of the principles, rather than simply learning the routine procedures, for establishing a program.

In his own consulting experience with industrial organizations contemplating the use of analog computers for the first time, the author has usually recommended that the first investment be in such an open-type of computer. In addition to the obvious advantage of relatively low expense, it has the additional advantage of educating the users to basic analog-computer principles. In some instances, where the degree of complication of the problems being handled was not too severe and where the accuracy requirements were only moderate, it was found that such open-type computers were adequate for all demands made by such organizations.

With more complicated problems, or where a higher degree of accuracy is necessary, *closed computers* are required. Such computers are described as closed because the elements for feedback input impedances must be held precisely to their nominal values if the expected accuracy (normally 0.1 per cent) is to be maintained. This can be accomplished only if they are of precise design and if they are maintained in a temperature-controlled environment. Such environments are thermostatically controlled ovens.

With the use of such oven-enclosed components (resistors and capacitances), obviously only a limited number of such elements can be accommodated. In a typical instance with a vacuum-tube type of computer, six input resistances are available for each summer or integrator amplifier furnished, three of 0.1 MΩ value and three of 1.0 MΩ value; only one feedback element is provided, 1.0 MΩ for summers and 1.0 μF for integrators. For such a typical case, the summer circuit would appear as shown in Figure 2-26. An input applied to any of three upper resistors results in an amplifier gain of 10; one applied to any of the three lower resistors, a gain of unity. Hence the markings to the left of the input terminals indicate the gain obtained. Of course, an input signal may be applied to more than one input terminal, effectively placing the associated input resistors

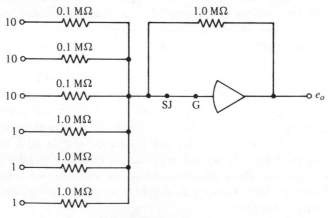

FIGURE 2-26

in parallel. Therefore, with the example shown in Figure 2-26, gains of 1, 2, 3, 10, 11, 12, 13, 20, 21, 22, 23, 30, 31, 32, and 33 are all possible. Frequently, the amplifier gain required will not correspond to any of these values; the next higher gain of 1, 2, 3, 10, 20, or 30 then is generally chosen and a potentiometer is added to the input to reduce the actual gain to the exact value desired.

The common tie point of the input and feedback elements is called the *summing junction* (SJ) in Figure 2-26 and in many computer layouts. As shown, it is normally connected to the grid terminal (G) of the operational amplifier. However, there is usually a provision for removing the connection between the SJ and G terminals to free the amplifier for less orthodox applications.

Typical integrator connections in a closed type of computer are similar to Figure 2-26, the only exception being the substitution of a 1.0-mF capacitor (for real-time computers) for the 1.0-MΩ feedback resistor, and the addition of an initial-conditions arrangement such as is shown in Figure 2-24. The same input provisions usually prevail with the input-gain values, such as 1 or 10 now applying to the integrator gains (volts per second output rate per volt input).

All the input and feedback elements shown are permanently associated with a given amplifier and are enclosed in temperature-controlled ovens. Frequently, some additional resistive and capacitive elements are also enclosed in such ovens with free connections so that they may be added to computer circuits in various ways. In any event, the degree of complication permitted of the input and feedback capacitances will definitely be limited. This is one of the prices that must be paid for the greater accuracy obtainable with closed computers.

2-17 Potentiometers

A potentiometer provides a method for multiplying a voltage by a prescribed factor, β (β is always less than unity), based on the voltage-divider principle shown in Figure 2-27. *If* there is negligible current drawn from the e_2 output

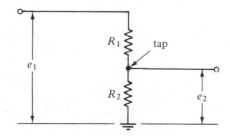

FIGURE 2-27

terminals, then

$$e_2 = \frac{R_2}{R_1 + R_2} e_1 = \alpha e_1 \tag{2-14}$$

where $\alpha = R_2/(R_1 + R_2)$ is the *potentiometer setting*. Hence here, with no output load, $\beta = \alpha$, where β is the *potentiometer factor*. In a potentiometer the sum of the resistances, $R = R_1 + R_2$, is constant but the separation between R_1 and R_2 is variable by a movable tap (i.e., α is variable and will be a function of the mechanical angle of the potentiometer, θ). This is illustrated in Figure 2-28.

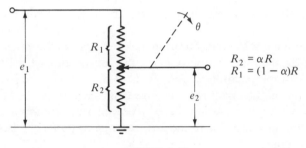

FIGURE 2-28

In this chapter we are concerned with *linear potentiometers* where $\alpha = k\theta$ and hence where, at least under conditions of no output load,

$$e_2 = k\theta e_1 \tag{2-15}$$

Hence the potentiometer setting will be a linear function of the mechanical angle. Such potentiometers are normally rotated by a calibrated-dial mechanism with micrometer indications by which the potentiometer setting α is indicated to about three decimal places.

Relations (2-14) and (2-15) apply only when no current is being drawn from the e_2 output terminal. If, as is usual, a load is connected to the output terminal of the potentiometer because of the elements that follow it in the program, these relations no longer apply exactly. The potentiometer factor β will no longer be exactly equal to the setting α indicated by the dials. It is possible to compute the error produced by a given load and to prepare charts that will permit a compensation of this error. These are, however, tedious to use.

The most reliable and easiest way to set the potentiometer factor β is by applying a fixed reference voltage V_R to the potentiometer's input terminal. The output voltage is then observed, usually by a digital voltmeter, and the potentiometer setting varied until this voltage equals βV_R. As V_R generally is 10 or 100 V in most computers, this adjustment is very easy to make. The necessary connections for this potentiometer-setting mode are usually established automatically by the simple throwing of a master switch on the computer console.

In view of this convenient method for setting potentiometers, little electrical knowledge is required of the programmer. He should, however, be aware of the fact that the potentiometer factor is affected by load and that all elements that establish this load should be connected to the potentiometer *before* the setting of potentiometers is attempted. If a change of program calls for a change in any of these output elements, a resetting is necessary.

In some analog-computer programs (as described in Chapters 4 and 6) the potentiometer may supply elements presenting electrical loads that change during the course of program operation. (Examples are diodes and comparator switches.) Then a potentiometer setting that may be correct during some parts of the operation may cease to be correct during other parts. When this presents a problem, the use of unloading circuits, discussed in the next section, may prove necessary.

2-18 Unloading Circuits

There will be circumstances, such as those mentioned in Section 2-17, in which it will be important that absolutely no current be drawn from an element in a computer, such as a potentiometer. In these instances the output of the element first is fed to an *unloading circuit*, and from this circuit in turn to whatever elements are to be supplied. Such an unloading circuit is simply a modified form of an inverting amplifier that has essentially infinite input impedance. Figure 2-29 is one example of such a circuit.

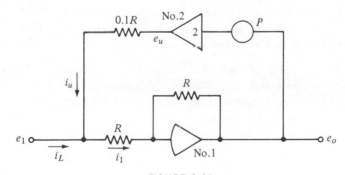

FIGURE 2-29

In this circuit the voltage e_1 is supplied by some source (such as a potentiometer), but the load current i_L that is drawn from that source must be zero. As amplifier 1 has identical feedback and input resistances, it serves as a simple inverter and $e_o = -e_1$. The current through the input resistor R, or i_1, must be e_1/R (since the grid terminal of amplifier 1 is at the potential $-e_o/\mu$, or essentially zero).

The voltage out of amplifier 2, or e_u, is $-2Pe_o$, or $2Pe_1$, where P is the potentiometer factor of the potentiometer P shown in the diagram. The unloading current i_u, therefore, is

$$i_u = \frac{e_u - e_1}{0.1R} = \frac{2P - 1}{0.1R}e_1$$

If i_u equals i_1, then no load current i_L will flow. The condition for this is

$$\frac{2P - 1}{0.1R}e_1 = \frac{e_1}{R}$$

or

$$P = 0.55$$

Hence, with such a potentiometer factor, the circuit of Figure 2-29 will function as an inverter but will have the special property of drawing no current from whatever source supplies it. If the inverter action that occurs incidentally is not desired, it is simply necessary to follow this circuit by another conventional inverter.

2-19 Ungrounded Potentiometers

With all the applications discussed up to now, the function of a potentiometer has been simply to multiply some voltage by a factor β, where β is less than unity. In such applications the conventional potentiometer connection is used, where one side of the resistance element is connected to the computer's chassis ground.

There will be other applications where the function of the potentiometer will be to combine two voltages, e_1 and e_2, in some adjustable proportion according to the relation

$$e_o = \alpha e_1 + (1 - \alpha)e_2 \tag{2-16}$$

This can be done as shown in Figure 2-30, utilizing what is known as an *ungrounded* or *floating potentiometer*. The Figure 2-30 arrangement is indicated symbolically in Figure 2-31.

Any conventional potentiometer may be used in such an application

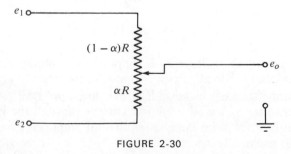

FIGURE 2-30

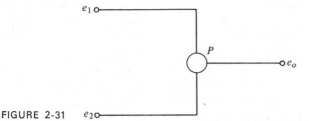

FIGURE 2-31 e_2

if there are provisions for ungrounding the normally grounded bottom lead so that the voltage designated as e_2 may be applied to it. In most computers a limited number of potentiometers are furnished that do have such provisions.

Relation (2-16) will apply to such an arrangement only if there is no output load. Unlike conventional grounded potentiometers, the effect of loading cannot be compensated by offsetting α. With a fixed load resistance R_L, an analysis similar to that in Section 2-17 will develop the relation

$$e_o = \frac{\alpha e_1 + (1 - \alpha)e_2}{1 + (1 - \alpha)\alpha R/R_L} \tag{2-17}$$

Hence loading does not change the proportion by which e_1 and e_2 are combined, but it does reduce the signal-transmission factor of the combined voltages. In a number of applications of floating potentiometers, only the relative proportion of e_1 and e_2 transmission is important. However, in applications where this loading effect does constitute a problem, either an unloading circuit should be used or a summer should be employed in place of the potentiometer.

2-20   Reference-Voltage Supplies

Chapter 1 showed instances where a specific voltage has to be provided for the purpose of (1) applying the correct initial condition voltage to an integrator, or (2) applying an input or disturbance voltage (independent variable) such as a step function. There will be other instances when such reference voltages are required.

Normally, the references voltages available are $\pm V_r$, where V_r is the nominal voltage range of the computer (e.g., 10, 50, or 100 V). Sometimes additional values of reference voltage will be available as well. In any event, other values of fixed voltage that may be needed can be obtained by connecting potentiometers to the reference supply.

In some instances a switch is made available that simultaneously reduces all reference-voltage supplies by a given factor, such as 10. As will be obvious from the discussion of scaling to follow, this will be useful when first investigating a program to see whether the proper scale factors have been selected. Suppose, for example, that the computer's voltage range V_R is 10 V. A test run is made with the reference voltage reduced by a factor of 10 and it is found that the output of one amplifier reaches a value of 1.5 V during a portion of the run. With the normal reference voltage, this would have corresponded to 15 V and an overload condition would have resulted. The scale factors selected obviously are incorrect and will have to be modified on the basis of the information thus obtained.

2-21   Mechanics of Establishing the Program Connections

In the open type of analog computer likely to be used for instruction in basic analog-computer principles, the connections of the actual physical elements are likely to be made directly through terminals or jacks located on the front panel. With the more precise closed type of computer, *patchboards* that establish the interconnections between elements normally are used instead. The actual elements are enclosed within the computer, their connections being brought to the patchboard terminals through trunk wiring. A variety of leads and jumpers are inserted in the patchboard to establish the program. As such patchboards generally are removable, a program may be stored and a different program employed with the computer by the substitution of another board.

Still another possible method for establishing the program connections is by means of electrical relays. This procedure is most likely to be used in hybrid analog–digital installations and would permit the analog program description to be stored in digital form. The associated digital computer then establishes the necessary program connections on the basis of a digital record. Still more refinement, extending the automation of establishing the digital program further, is the use of servo-driven potentiometers that may also be adjusted in accordance with digital instructions. A computer so equipped represents the ultimate in operational convenience but, unfortunately, also in initial expense.

2-22   Selection of Analog-Computer Scale Factors

The first point that should be made in regard to the selection of scale factors is that, for intelligent scaling, some idea of the results to be expected should be known. This can be possible only if the person planning the program is trained and experienced in the analysis of the particular phenomena being studied.[4]

The second point to be made is that scaling errors in programming are not "fatal," and in any complicated program being run for the first time, some errors, but not gross errors, are to be expected. After all, if the person doing the programming could predict exactly the response of the system being simulated, there would often be no point at all in performing the simulation. As the cost of executing an analog program is often negligible, no great inconvenience is involved in changing one, or at the most, several scale factors after inappropriate scaling has been observed by means of trial runs.

The scaling problem is subdivided into two parts: time scaling and voltage scaling. Time scaling consists of selecting the factor k_t in the relation

$$t = k_t t_m \tag{2-18}$$

When slow solutions are desired for convenience or are required because of response-speed limitations of the output equipment, k_t will be small. With rapid solutions, as with the oscilloscope display of the output, k_t will be large. For an important type of simulation, called *real-time* simulation, when the computer represents a model of the system that is undistorted in the time scale, k_t must be unity.

Voltage scaling is based on two considerations. None of the voltage variables should be permitted to go beyond the nominal voltage range of the computer (e.g., 10, 50, 100 V). On the other hand, the voltage range of the machine variable should be some appreciable fraction of the total nominal range so that these voltages may be measured readily and will not be masked by drift or noise. When nonlinear functions or multipliers are treated later, it will be found that their percentage of accuracy deteriorates rapidly as the voltage becomes small; these will present additional reasons for having as large a voltage "swing" as is possible and permissible. In other words, there are the possibilities of either too much or too little.

Finally, before going into specific details of selecting scale factors, the point should be made that these factors should always be convenient round numbers, usually decimal multiples of 1, 2, or 5. If this is done, it becomes relatively simple to observe the machine results in terms of voltages, and to interpret them directly in terms of the actual units of the problem.

[4] This comment brings up an important consideration regarding the choice of personnel involved in preparing a simulation program. It is sometimes believed that simulation programs may be prepared by programmers who are not acquainted with the field related to the application being simulated. As far as the initial program planning is concerned, this is not the case with either digital or analog simulation. However, after the basic simulation arrangement has been established, a trained programmer may be able to suggest methods of greater improvement.

2-23   Time Scaling

No choice of time scale is available, of course, with real-time simulation; k_t must be unity. In other instances, the first consideration must be given to the *maximum* value of k_t that is permissible in view of response-speed limitations of components used in the computer and of the output equipment.

Next, consideration is given to the *minimum* value of k_t permissible in consideration of the storage capability of integrators and the method of output display or recording. If a repetitive oscilloscope display is desired, as described later in this chapter, the limits of screen persistence dictate a total solution time that normally does not exceed 0.100 sec (for each solution repetition). In the problem of the example of Chapter 1, a solution time of 0.100 sec (actual problem time) was desirable in order to describe the response transient completely; hence a k_t of 0.100/0.100, or unity (which happens to correspond to real-time simulation), would be appropriate.

However, in the example of Problem 1-1 a recording oscillograph was selected for output display. Here consideration should be given to the maximum frequency-response limitations of such a device. A preliminary study of the problem involved (referring back to Section 1-2) shows that there should be a dominant resonant frequency of

$$\omega_n = \sqrt{\frac{kg}{M}} = \sqrt{\frac{(20)(980)}{0.5}} = 198 \text{ rad/sec}$$

or $198/2\pi = 32$ Hz. The oscillograph used has a frequency response ranging to 80 Hz; hence, for recording the results of this problem solution, a k_t of unity would not have been excessive from the standpoint of oscillograph capability. This, however, would have meant a solution time of 0.100 sec of machine time; a fast paper speed would have been required of the oscillograph, and considerable paper wastage would have resulted when manually controlling the starting and stopping of each run. Ordinarily, the speed of solution is not so urgent an item that a 10 sec solution time would not be more convenient. The actual time scale used was selected on this basis, with a k_t of 0.01. It was this value that was used when producing the results shown in Figure 1-20.

For other methods of output display, even smaller k_t's (slower solutions) might be advisable. Suppose, for example, that the results are to be observed visually on a digital voltmeter with the intention of interrupting the solution periodically (by placing all integrators in a hold mode—see Section 2-14) so that the pertinent response values might be recorded, possibly by a digital printer. For such purposes a k_t of 0.0001, corresponding to a solution time of 1000 sec, might be desirable. For reasons to be mentioned below, this would represent close to the upper limit of solution time with a typical precision-type analog computer.

In Section 2-15, the limitations of the capacitors used with integrators were discussed. Because of the inevitable leakage of even the best capacitors, there are definite limitations to their ability to store voltages for extended periods of time. With some computers the solution time of 1000 sec, suggested above for visual observation of the output, might be excessive, and a solution time not exceeding 100 sec might be necessary to guarantee reasonably accurate results.

When selecting the time scale k_t, thought should also be paid to the limitations of the computer elements as well as the output equipment. The minimum limitation of k_t is generally caused by capacitor leakage, as was discussed above. There also is a maximum limitation of k_t imposed by the high-frequency-response limits of the equipment. The program associated with the example of Chapter 1 required only conventional linear elements (amplifiers, summers, integrators, and potentiometers); all these have frequency-response ranges up to about 100,000 Hz for a high-quality computer. In consideration of the dominant resonant frequency of the problem in the example (computed above as 32 Hz), this limit is not a significant factor when selecting the time scale. However, in more complicated problems, computer elements may be employed that have considerably slower responses. For example, electromechanical servo-driven multipliers or resolvers[5] might have been used. Such devices have upper frequency-response limits that sometimes are as low as 1 Hz. If this were the case, then in a problem such as this where the dominant response frequency is 32 Hz, a k_t of $\frac{1}{32}$, or 0.03, would represent the maximum permissible time-scale factor.

2-24   Change of Time Scale

In some instances it is desired to change the time scale of a problem after the programming has been completed. One way of doing this is by changing the values of *all* capacitors involved by the *same* factor—increasing the capacitance values reduces k_t (lengthens the time required for a solution) by the same factor.

In many problems such as that of the example of Chapter 1, the only computers used were those associated with integrators. In this event, time scale could also be changed by changing *all* integrator gains by the same factor. Here an increase of integrator gain results in a faster solution (i.e., a higher k_t by a factor equal to the change in gain value).

The above principle is often used when revising a program after it is

[5] These devices are now becoming obsolete but are still in extensive use.

decided that a change of time scale is desired. Simple provisions for such a change are also included in some computers. For example, the standard feedback capacitor used with all integrators might be 1.0 mF for normal-time operation. Throwing a master switch to a "fast" position effects a substitution of 0.01-mF capacitors. Operation then is 100 times faster than in the normal position. Sometimes, a "slow" position is also provided where 10-mF capacitors are substituted instead.

2-25   Determination of the Voltage-Scale Factors

To select a scale factor for each variable to be represented in a given simulation problem, it is first necessary to estimate the maximum range of variation of each of these variables. This procedure is demonstrated best by using again the example of Chapter 1. As in Chapter 1, it will be assumed here that an analog computer is being used that has a nominal voltage range of ± 100 V.

Referring to Figure 1-3, the variables to be represented are seen to be $x, \dot{x}, y, \dot{y}, \ddot{y}, f_k, f_B,$ and f_M. Of these, the *independent* variables should be considered first. A knowledge of their range of variation requires some understanding of the application of the mechanism being simulated. It will be assumed here that the input displacement, x, may attain magnitudes as great as 6 cm, and the associated input velocity, $\dot{x}$, magnitudes as great as 1500 cm/sec. Now, considering x, a magnitude of $|x| = 6$ cm should result in a machine-voltage magnitude $|x_m|$ that equals, or is somewhat less than, 100 V. The factor $\frac{6}{100}$, or 0.06, would make $|x_m|$ exactly 100 V. However, such a factor is not sufficiently round to be convenient and the next *higher* round factor, or 0.1, is chosen instead; i.e.,

$$x = 0.1 x_m \qquad \text{cm}$$

and the maximum range of 6 cm would cause a voltage range of 60 V.

Similarly, considering $\dot{x}$, a magnitude of $|\dot{x}| = 1500$ cm/sec would call for an exact scale factor of 1500/100 or 15. The next higher round conversion factor of 20 is employed and

$$\dot{x} = 20 \dot{x}_m \qquad \text{cm/sec}$$

This completes the scaling of the independent variables.

Among the dependent variables, y and $\dot{y}$ normally would be expected to employ the same scale factors as x and $\dot{x}$, respectively. In the problem of this example, this is a reasonable procedure since, with constant x, y would approach the same steady-state value and, with constant $\dot{x}$, $\dot{y}$ would approach the same value of velocity if $\dot{x}$ could be maintained for a long enough time. (Furthermore, it is usually desirable to observe the variations of x and y together as they appear in the output display, and this is most convenient if they are shown with the same relative scale.) Hence

$$y = 0.1y_m \quad \text{cm}$$

$$\dot{y} = 20\dot{y}_m \quad \text{cm/sec}$$

The remaining dependent variables may now be considered by tracing through the block diagram of Figure 1-3. The maximum magnitude of $(x - y)$ would result from a step change of x by the maximum expected value of 6 cm; this would result in an f_k of $k|x - y| = (20)(6) = 120$ kg. The maximum value of $(\dot{x} - \dot{y})$ would be 1500 cm/sec (resulting from a suddenly applied ramp change of x); then the maximum value of f_B would be $B|\dot{x} - \dot{y}| = (0.05)(1500) = 75$ kg. Now, considering the summation shown in Figure 1-3 that produces f_M and assuming the most extreme case of these maximum values adding directly, a maximum f_M of $120 + 75$ kg might be considered (the effect of the gravity force M, also added, is negligible for the purpose of these scaling computations). Hence it is estimated that $|f_M|$ is 195 kg, and it is considered that this should not result in a machine voltage of greater than 100 V. The exact conversion factor then is $\frac{195}{100}$, or 1.95, and the next higher round number is used (i.e., $f_M = 2f_{M_m}$ kg). It will be convenient to employ the same factor for all forces, so, in general,

$$f = 2f_m \quad \text{kg}$$

The above applies to all the forces, f_k, f_B, f_M, and M.

In the above a possible peak magnitude of f_M equal to 195 kg was estimated. This, in turn, would cause an acceleration magnitude of $\ddot{y}$ equal to $(195/M)g = (195)(980)/0.5 = 382,000$ cm/sec². For this to correspond exactly to 100 machine volts, the exact scale factor would be $382,000/100 = 3820$; in practice the next higher round factor of 5000 was employed:

$$\ddot{y} = 5000\ddot{y}_m \quad \text{cm/sec}^2$$

All the voltage-scale factors have now been established for the variables shown in Figure 1-3. These correspond to those listed in Section 1-6.

One additional comment might be made regarding a scaling problem that occurs frequently, although it did not arise in the example just treated. Let a different type of problem be considered where the variable concerned is, say, N, the rpm of an engine, with N varying between the limits of 2300 and 2500 rpm. If the procedure described above were used, $|N|$ would be 2500 rpm and would be made to correspond to 100 V on the machine. Then $N = 25 N_m$ rpm and the actual variation of N_m would be between $+92$ and $+100$ V. Only 4 per cent of the ± 100 V range of the computer would be utilized. To make better use of this range, it would be preferable to simulate, instead, the *increment* of N, or ΔN, defined as, say,

$$\Delta N = N - 2400$$

The magnitude $|\Delta N|$ is now merely 100 rpm and the appropriate conversion factor would be unity, indicated by the relation $\Delta N = \Delta N_m$. The full voltage range of the computer would now be utilized with a resulting improvement in accuracy (particularly if nonlinear elements should be required in the program).

2-26   Odd-Amplifier Rule

When preparing an analog program, it is quite easy to lose track of the algebraic sign, especially considering the sign inversion usually occurring with each amplifier. To provide a final check on errors of sign, the *odd-amplifier rule*, applicable when the amplifiers are of the inverting type, is often proposed. To apply this rule, every *closed loop* in the computer program is traced; each of these should involve an *odd* number of amplifiers. There are only two such loops in the example shown in Figure 1-22. (In more complicated programs, many more would appear.) These loops include an upper loop (as drawn in the diagram) involving amplifiers A12, A13, A20, A14, and A30, and a lower loop involving amplifiers A12, A13, A20, A21, and A04. The rule is satisfied here because in both cases the number of amplifiers involved is odd. The value of this rule is pointed out by the fact that in such a program construction it would have been very easy to have omitted the inverter, A14, by error; this rule would have spotted such an error.

The rule is a useful one, but note should be taken of the fact that *it is not always applicable*. It is based upon the fact that in most situations of system dynamics closed loops normally will be associated with *negative* feedback. As the block diagram of Figure 1-3 shows, this is the case for the example treated there that led to the Figure 1-15 program. However, there will be exceptions to this negative-feedback rule, many of them important. Many problems do arise where positive feedback will exist. Examples are statically unstable aircraft, mechanical toggles, the compound-interest problem of Chapter 1, etc. Whenever such positive feedback is the case, this fact should be recognized and an *even* number of amplifiers should be expected in the associated loop.

2-27   High-Speed-Repetitive Operation

In Section 2-23 it was mentioned that in many cases an oscilloscope display of the output variables is desired, and that such a method of display requires a fast and repeated solution. Many computers have provisions for such a repetitive solution and there are some that can operate *only* in such a mode. To adapt a computer ordinarily intended for real-time solutions to such a high-speed-repetitive (HRO) operation, it is of course first necessary that the frequency range of the computer's functional amplifiers be adequate. The computer is then operated in a fast mode; that is, a procedure as described in Section 2-24 is used to increase k_t, such as by having a master switch and relay change all integrator capacitors to some lower value of capacitance. The repetitive feature is introduced by alternately returning the computer to the initial condition, or reset, mode long enough for initial conditions to be reestablished, and then to the operate, or compute, mode long enough to accommodate the desired solution time. Computers equipped for this type of operation have timing devices that establish such a cycle; the appropriate relays, as shown in Figure 2-24, one for each integrator, are simultaneously actuated. The rate of repetition is usually adjustable, either continuously or in steps.

In a typical problem where the variable of interest, say y, might have a response as shown in Figure 2-32a, the resulting response with such repetitive operation would be as shown in part b. It should be noted that only the portion of the response occurring during the compute periods has any significance as far as results are concerned.

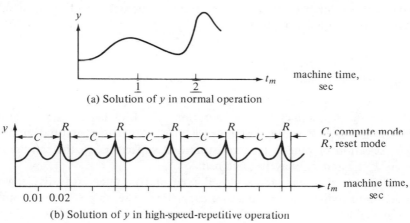

(a) Solution of y in normal operation

(b) Solution of y in high-speed-repetitive operation

FIGURE 2-32

When such a repetitive solution is to be displayed on a cathode-ray oscilloscope, the horizontal sweep on the CRO, representing time, should be synchronized with this switching operation. If the high-speed switching is done within the computer itself, this may be accomplished by also developing the sweep voltage within the computer as well as by means of an integrator amplifier.

In some more elaborate installations, a cathode-ray oscilloscope (usually of the multichannel type using an electronic switch) is furnished that develops its own sweep voltage and also controls, synchronized with this time sweep, the repetitive switching of the computer. In such instances the repetition frequency is controlled at the oscilloscope, not at the computer itself.

It may be noted from Figure 2-32b that there is a response during the reset mode that is not of interest in the problem solution and preferably should be omitted from the oscilloscope display. With the oscilloscope-controlled type of repetitive operation described above, provision is usually included for blanking the oscilloscope screen during this reset period.

Such high-speed-repetitive procedures, associated with oscilloscope displays, are especially convenient when a trial-and-error adjustment of some parameter should be made to achieve desired results. It is merely necessary to observe the results on such a display while adjusting the potentiometer associated with the variable parameter until the results desired are obtained.

The application of high-speed-repetitive operation to dynamic-storage techniques will be described later. This technique is used when the major part of the problem is being solved with normal operation, but certain auxiliary computations must be made repeatedly and rapidly. It will be found that this latter technique will be roughly analogous to the use of subroutines with digital computers.

Suggested Problems

2-1. Section 2-10 shows the configuration of a lead–lag transfer-function simulation using an analog computer having open amplifiers and an adequate selection of plug-in type resistors and capacitors so that any parameters k, τ_n, and τ_d, may be obtained.

Suppose that, instead, a closed type of computer is available with no access to individual resistors and capacitors. The only summing amplifiers available have two sets of input terminals, a set of three providing a gain of unity, and a set of three providing a gain of 10. Integrators are identical to summers except that the 1.0-MΩ resistor used in the summer is replaced with a 1.0-μF capacitor when the amplifier is used as an integrator. Potentiometers also are available.

Devise a program with such components that will accomplish the same operations as in Figure 2-18 and that will

(a) employ a minimum number of amplifiers, or

(b) employ a minimum number of amplifiers with the added stipulation that k, τ_n, and τ_d can be set individually and independently with separate potentiometers.

2-2. Figure 2-16 shows a technique for representing a simple response lag of τ sec by means of closed amplifiers. Of course, potentiometers will also be required, as it is unlikely that the exact gains, k/τ and $1/\tau$, shown in that diagram will be available in a closed amplifier. However, a direct adaptation of the Figure 2-16 arrangement would require that both potentiometers be adjusted in order to adjust the time constant τ.

Assume a closed computer as in the previous problem. Develop an arrangement for representing such an operation so that only one potentiometer is required to adjust the value of k, and only one to adjust, separately, the value of τ.

2-3. The analog-computer circuit of Figure P2-3 is sometimes employed. what will this circuit accomplish?

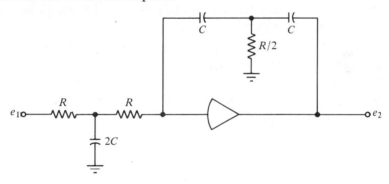

FIGURE P2-3

2-4. Frequently, particularly when simulating some types of system controllers, it is necessary to perform the operation

$$y_m = kx_m = \frac{k}{\tau} \int x_m \, dt$$

(a) Using closed amplifiers only, as described in the previous problems, devise an analog-computer arrangement to simulate this operation with two potentiometers, one controlling the factor k, and the other the factor k/τ.

(b) Repeat (a) with the new proviso that the second potentiometer control is simply τ, instead.

(c) Devise an arrangement using open-computer construction for accomplishing the simulation of the above function with only one amplifier.

2-5. Develop an analog-computer program to develop simultaneously the machine variables $x = 10 \cos \omega t$ V and $y = 10 \sin \omega t$ V. (*Hint:* Determine the differential equations where these expressions will constitute the time solutions; construct the block diagram corresponding to these equations; proceed from there.)

2-6. The program constituting the solution to Problem 2-5 has been developed. However, the actual operational amplifiers employed cannot be considered as ideal; their finite gain μ of only 100,000 must be considered. As a result, the amplitude of the sinusoidal signal produced will be found to decay with time. How rapidly will it decay to one half the original amplitude? Will it do this in a specific length of time, regardless of frequency, or will it do this after a specific number of cycles?

2-7. As in Problem 2-6, this again refers to the program for the solution of Problem 2-5. Here the operational amplifiers may be considered as ideal. However, the integrators each employ a 1.0-mF feedback capacitor that has a shunting leakage resistance of 100-MΩ. Again, as a result, the amplitude of the signals will decay with time. How rapidly will they now decay to one half the original amplitude? Again, will they do this in a specific length of time or after a specific number of cycles?

2-8. In the statements of the three problems of Chapter 1, the suggested scaling factors were given. Had they not been given, show how the techniques described in this chapter could have been used to establish them.

2-9. In Figure P2-9, x is the displacement of the mass as measured from its normal position with zero force f.

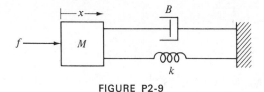

FIGURE P2-9

$$M = 0.1 \quad \frac{\text{lb}}{\text{in./sec}^2} \quad \text{(equivalent to 38.6 lb of weight)}$$

$$k = 40 \quad \frac{\text{lb}}{\text{in.}}$$

$$B = 2.0 \quad \frac{\text{lb}}{\text{in./sec}}$$

At $t = 0$, a step function of f equal to 50 lb is applied. Prepare a properly scaled program to represent this case on a real-time basis. Assume a reference voltage of either 10 or 100, whichever is preferred. State which you are using.

2-10. This is a laboratory problem to be performed if an analog computer is available that can be operated in a high-speed-repetitive mode and with an oscilloscope display. Use such a method of operation to simplify the trial-and-error determination of the interest rate in part (a) of Problem 1-1.

2-11. (a) What are the time relations for the signals x and y as developed by the program in Figure P2-11, and (b) why does the odd-amplifier rule not apply?

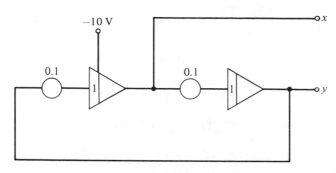

FIGURE P2-11

2-12. Derive relation (2-13).

Suggested Reading

(The following books treat analog computers in considerably more detail than has been attempted here.)

1. A. S. Jackson, *Analog Computation* (New York: McGraw-Hill, Inc., 1960).

2. Z. Nenadel and B. Mirtes, *Analogue and Hybrid Computers* (London: Iliffe Books Ltd. and New York: American Elsevier Publishing Co., 1968) (translated from Czech).

Appendix 2A:
Developing Linear
Transfer Functions[6]

In problems of simulation, it is generally not the object to develop specific transfer functions, but to model the system being simulated as closely as is possible. That is, many block-diagram configurations and resulting computer programs may be developed to represent a given transfer function; the one that should be used in the simulation program is the particular one that follows the cause-and-effect relationship existing in the system being simulated. This is not necessarily the simplest or "canonic," form.

There are some instances, however, when direct modeling is not required and a particular transfer function is to be represented. If the transfer function is linear and rational (does not involve distributed parameters), it can be expressed as a ratio of polynomials in s of the form

$$\frac{y(s)}{x(s)} = \frac{a_n s^n + a_{n-1} s^{n-1} + \cdots + a_1 s + a_o}{s^n + b_{n-1} s^{n-1} + \cdots + b_1 s + b_o} \qquad (2A\text{-}1)$$

(It should be noted that the highest power of s in the numerator cannot be higher than that of the denominator. If it were, the system would have an amplitude response that approached infinity as the frequency approached

[6]Acknowledgement is due to Mr. Frank J. Hannigan, a graduate student at the University of Connecticut and an engineer with the General Dynamics Corp., who suggested the inclusion of this material and the particular tutorial approach that has been followed.

infinity. This does not occur in physical systems, and such a transfer function would indicate that some response lags had been neglected. It could not be simulated without noise problems—the "pure" derivative program of Section 2-7 is an example. In many instances, the a coefficients of higher order will be zero.)

A new variable is defined as

$$z(s) = \frac{1}{s^n + b_{n-1}s^{n-1} + \cdots + b_1 s + b_0} x(s) \qquad (2A\text{-}2)$$

This may be rewritten in the time domain as

$$\frac{d^n}{dt^n}z(t) = x(t) - \left(b_{n-1}\frac{d^{n-1}}{dt^{n-1}} + \cdots + b_1\frac{d}{dt} + b_0\right)z(t) \qquad (2A\text{-}3)$$

The block diagram for developing $z(t)$ is shown in Figure 2A-1. By combining relations (2A-1) and (2A-2), it may be determined that

$$y(s) = (a_n s^n + a_{n-1}s^{n-1} + \cdots + a_1 s + a_0)z(s) \qquad (2A\text{-}4)$$

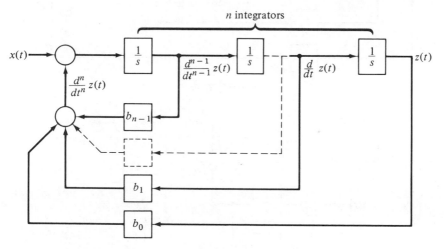

FIGURE 2A-1

or, in the time domain,

$$y(t) = \left(a_n\frac{d^n}{dt^n} + a_{n-1}\frac{d^{n-1}}{dt^{n-1}} + \cdots + a_1\frac{d}{dt} + a_0\right)z(t) \qquad (2A\text{-}5)$$

All the derivatives of $z(t)$ appearing in relation (2A-5) are available in the block diagram of Figure 2A-1; hence the complete block diagram for obtaining $y(t)$ is as shown in Figure 2A-2. The analog or digital program used for simulating the transfer function may be based on this block diagram. Note that n integration operations are required for this n-state system.

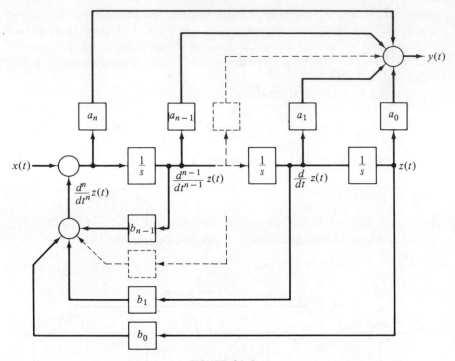

FIGURE 2A-2

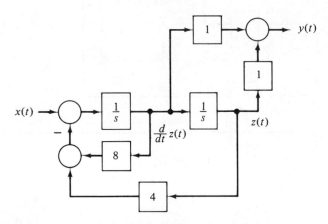

FIGURE 2A-3

As an example, consider the function

$$\frac{y(s)}{x(s)} = \frac{s + 1}{s^2 + 8s + 4}$$

Here $n = 2$ and

$$a_2 = 0 \qquad a_1 = 1 \qquad a_0 = 1$$
$$b_1 = 8 \qquad b_0 = 4$$

The block diagram for this relation that corresponds to Figure 2A-2 is Figure 2A-3. The analog program would be as shown in Figure 2A-4. However, it should be noted that entirely different block diagrams, shown in Figure 2A-5, could also have represented this transfer function.

Ordinarily, the configuration selected for developing a simulation program will be the one that matches most closely the actual cause-and-effect relationship in the system being simulated.

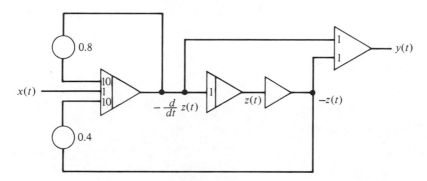

FIGURE 2A-4

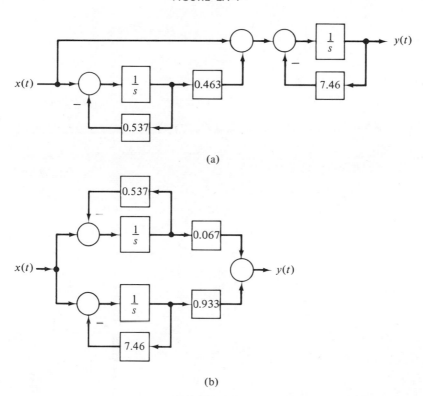

(a)

(b)

FIGURE 2A-5

Linear Simulation Operations with Digital Computers $\quad$ 3

3-1 Computer Languages Used for Simulation

When establishing a digital computer program, a choice always exists between (1) direct machine languages, and (2) a user-oriented language such as Fortran or Algol. The latter alternative may prove somewhat less efficient in the use of the computer from the standpoint of both economy of elements and speed of execution. It is, however, simpler, as far as the preparation of the program is concerned, in the sense that there is a smaller likelihood of programming errors and (in consideration of compiler error-detecting features) a better chance to detect such errors in the initial programming.

When a simulation program is to be used frequently, as when it is to be part of a working system rather than simply for the purpose of system analysis and synthesis, machine language generally is justified. The construction of such a program requires the services of an expert programmer fully acquainted with the *particular* computer to be employed. In such applications, special-purpose computers designed for this particular type of program are often used. Even when this is the case, the preliminary runs of the prototype program would probably be conducted in terms of a user-oriented language, because such a language is not only easier to devise but also easier to modify. It will not be assumed here that the reader is acquainted with machine-language programming.

In this book, a knowledge of some user-oriented language will be assumed instead. Such languages are applicable to general-purpose computers that employ a *compiler* to translate the user-oriented language into the language of the machine in the form called an *object program*. As such object programs may be stored on cards, tape, disk, or magnetic drum, they can be reemployed at various times with various data. Therefore, in a sense, the slower execution time when a user-oriented language is employed results partly from the time required for compilation and assembly. This time, however, applies only to the first run of a given program; compilation and assembly need be repeated only if the program instructions should be modified. For repeated runs after the compilation is performed, the computer operates directly from the stored object program, and the only time required in addition to actual execution time is that required to place the object program in storage (i.e., to load it). This loading time need be repeated only if the object program has been removed from the computer to free it for other work. As far as actual execution time is concerned, the program arranged from a user-oriented language is only slightly less efficient than a machine-language program prepared by a highly skilled programmer and is likely to be more efficient than one prepared by a programmer who is less skilled.

The discussion here, therefore, will be on the basis of user-oriented languages, but no specific language will be referred to except for a few isolated examples. When methods are compared on the basis of execution times, these times will not include the times required for compilation or loading.

The current most well-known user-oriented languages are Fortran and Algol in their various varieties and levels of sophistication. However, new and more versatile languages, such as PL/1, are being introduced. Hence, for the sake of generality and to guard against obsolescence, discussions here will be in terms of general flow diagrams rather than in terms of specific languages.

3-2 Basic Linear Operations

In linear simulation problems to which we have been confined up to now, the only computation operations (as distinguished from input and output operations and decisions concerning them) that need be performed are

1. Addition and subtraction.
2. Multiplication and division by a constant.
3. Integration with respect to the basic independent variable.
4. Differentiation with respect to the basic independent variable.

The first two of these operations are straightforward and require no explanation. In general, the numerical quantities representing either program parameters or variables will be expressed in floating-point (real) rather than integer (fixed-point) form. Only in those special instances where variables are quantized will integer forms be employed.

Integration and differentiation with respect to the independent variable are not straightforward operations with digital computers; their implementation is more complicated than with analog computers and will require special treatment in this chapter.

3-3 Methods of Integration with Respect to the Independent Variable

Many methods of digital integration have been proposed and employed, this being one of the subjects treated within the field of *numerical analysis* and specifically within the area of the subject, *numerical integration*. The reader is warned, however, not to become confused or misled when examining this area. A tremendous number of numerical-integration techniques have been proposed; in many instances the same technique is given a number of different names. For example, what has been described in Chapter 1 as simple rectangular integration is also called Euler's method, the point-slope method, and the first-order Runge–Kutta method.

The reader is also warned that many proposed techniques of numerical integration, convenient though they might be for other computational purposes, are not suitable for simulation. In simulation problems each iterative step of the independent variable, Δt,[1] requires a computation of the integral over the range Δt. However, the integrand is known only at the *beginning* and *before* the beginning of this range. The value of the integrand at the end of the range can be determined only after the integral itself has been established.

To facilitate this explanation the general problem is considered where the integration to be performed is, for example,

$$y(t) = \int x(t)\, dt \qquad (3\text{-}1)$$

The integrand $x(t)$ is, in turn, a function of $y(t)$ and other functions of time, i.e.,

$$x(t) = f[y(t), t] \qquad (3\text{-}2)$$

---

[1] The discussion of this chapter is conducted on the basis of time, t, being the basic independent variable. Of course, there will be simulation problems in which the basic independent variable will be some other quantity.

The functional relationship described by (3-2) is not generally analytic or algebraic. It is obtained by tracing the feedback loop of the block diagram to determine how $y(t)$ affects $x(t)$.

Since it will be necessary to work in terms of finite Δt's when a digital computer is used, it is convenient to express $y(t)$ as $y(n)$, where

$$t = n \, \Delta t \qquad (3-3)$$

This obviously implies that y will be known only at discrete instants of time, at the end of the Δt intervals. Similarly, $x(t)$ is described as $x(n)$. The integration problem presented by relation (3-1) may then be restated as

$$y(n + 1) = y(n) + \int_{t=n \, \Delta t}^{t=(n+1) \, \Delta t} x(t) \, dt \qquad (3-4)$$

when being carried out over a single interval, Δt.

In simulation the difficulty arises from the fact that $x(t)$ is known only for values of t less than $n \, \Delta t$ [*i.e.*, $x(n)$, $x(n - 1)$, $x(n - 2)$, etc., are known, but $x(n + 1)$, $x(n + 2)$, etc., are not]. Therefore, for simulation applications only those techniques that do not depend upon a knowledge of $x(n + 1)$ may be employed. A number of such schemes of numerical integration have been described in the literature. [1–4].

In general, these schemes may be classified in the manner shown in Table 3-1. For ease of classification these methods will be grouped in categories designated as 1a, 1b, 2a, 2b, 3a, etc. Before proceeding with a description of the various schemes, the terms used in Table 3-1 will be clarified.

TABLE 3-1

Techniques	(a) Nonextrapolating	(b) Extrapolating
1. Single pass	1a. Examples: rectangular integration; Euler's methods	1b. Examples: backward-difference methods
2, 3, etc. Multipass (class number refers to number of passes)	2a, 3a, 4a, etc. Examples: predictor–corrector; Simpson's rule; Runge–Kutta methods	2b, 3b, etc. Examples: Milne methods

In general, when proceeding with numerical integration, the integrand values $x(n - 1)$, $x(n - 2)$, etc., will have been evaluated; similarly, $y(n)$, $y(n - 1)$, $y(n - 2)$, etc., will have been established during previous iterations. The integrand $x(n)$ has just been established from a knowledge of $y(n)$ by traversing the feedback loop (of the block diagram) that relates them. The integration procedure now is to determine the value of $y(n + 1)$.

In a *single-pass technique* (1a or 1b), $y(n + 1)$ will be determined directly from a knowledge of the previous y's and the previous x's. The loop will not then be retraversed to determine the resulting value of $x(n + 1)$ for the purpose of correcting the value of $y(n + 1)$ that was just computed. That is, there are no first guesses followed by subsequent corrections.

In a *single-pass, nonextrapolating technique* (1a), only one value of the integrand x and one previous value of the integral y will be used to determine $y(n + 1)$. Rectangular integration as described in Chapter 1 is an example of this.

In a *single-pass extrapolating technique* (1b), more than one value of the integrand x [e.g., $x(n)$ and $x(n - 1)$] will be employed in connection with some extrapolating formula in order to make a guess as to what $x(n + 1)$ might be. This is used, in turn, to establish a better value of the mean value of the integrand over the range of integration in order to improve the integration accuracy.

In a *multipass technique* (2a or 2b), a first guess will be made of the value of $y(n + 1)$ using one of the single-pass techniques. Then the *feed-back loop will be traced again*, to determine the corresponding first guess of $x(n + 1)$. This may then be used for a second more accurate integration, more accurate because at least an estimate of $x(n + 1)$ has been established and the accuracy of the integrand may be improved. If the procedure is terminated at this point, it would be called a *two-pass technique*. If repeated to obtain still greater accuracy, it would be described as three-pass, four-pass, etc.

In a *multipass nonextrapolating technique* (2a, 3a, etc.), the procedure just described is employed without making use of the extrapolated values of x based on $x(n - 1)$, $x(n - 2)$, etc. These techniques are generally referred to as *Runge–Kutta methods*.

In general, the more complicated the method, the greater the accuracy that will be obtained for a given iteration interval; conversely, a larger iteration interval will be permissible for a required degree of accuracy. However, the more complicated the technique, the greater the time required *per* iteration interval. Hence it does not always follow that the more sophisticated techniques will lead to the shortest total execution time. This question will be discussed further, but first the details of the various numerical-integration techniques adapted to problems of simulation will be explained.

3-4 Type 1a—Single-Pass Nonextrapolating Numerical Integration

Only two techniques within this category are of particular interest in simulation problems. The first is the simple rectangular-integration procedure described in Chapter 1, where

$$y(n + 1) = y(n) + x(n)\,\Delta t \qquad (3\text{-}5)$$

This will be referred to here as method 1a-1. It has been explained in geometric terms in Figure 1-29.

The second technique is similar, but it is based on using the previous
value of the integral, or $y(n-1)$, rather than $y(n)$. The relation employed is

$$y(n+1) = y(n-1) + 2x(n)\, \Delta t \qquad (3\text{-}6)$$

This will be referred to as method 1a-2. Its geometric significance is shown
in Figure 3-1. This method has the apparent advantage that the value of the
integrand employed is that at the middle of the interval rather than at the
beginning. It often is referred to as the *modified Euler method*. It does present
starting difficulties since, to determine $y(1)$, $y(-1)$ will not be known. Hence,
in the first iterative step only, method 1a-1 is employed. However, it can
be shown that when used in the simulation of a component in a feedback
loop, an unstable solution will always result. Therefore, it is mentioned as
a matter of record; its use is not advocated.

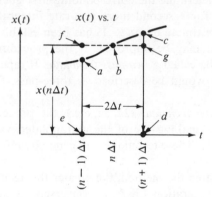

Correct integral is the area *abcde*;
computed integral is the area of the
rectangle *fbgde;* error is (area *bcg*
area *baf*)(no error when area *bcg*
equals area *baf*)

FIGURE 3-1

3-5   Type 1b—Single-Pass Extrapolating
Numerical Integration

Because in simulation problems future values of the integrand will not be
known prior to the integration's being completed, any estimate of these
future values that might be obtained by means of extrapolating techniques
must depend only upon the present and previous values of the integrand;
hence such extrapolating procedures depend upon *backward differences*.
Such backward differences are defined by the following relations and symbolism:

$$\nabla x(n) \triangleq x(n) - x(n-1)$$

$$\nabla^2 x(n) \triangleq \nabla x(n) - \nabla x(n-1)$$
$$= x(n) - 2x(n-1) + x(n-2) \tag{3-7}$$

etc.

Two widely employed extrapolating techniques are based on the assumption that the integrand x can be represented approximately by a polynomial in t of order m. Then, if values of x are known at $(m+1)$ values of t, the polynomial relationship can be established. This may be used in turn to establish an integral over the iteration interval based on this analytic relationship. The details have been developed in a number of textbooks dealing with numerical integration. In general, these are based on Simpson's rule. One of the most basic techniques, related to method 1a-1, is as follows:

$$y(n+1) = y(n) + \Delta t \, [x(n) + \tfrac{1}{2} \nabla x(n) + \tfrac{5}{12} \nabla^2 x(n)$$
$$+ \tfrac{3}{8} \nabla^3 x(n) + \tfrac{251}{720} \nabla^4 x(n) + \cdots] \tag{3-8}$$

This technique, also described as Adams' method, will be described as method 1b-1. The extrapolation may be carried out to any order desired, the order being described as the highest order of ∇ employed. Ordinary rectangular integration, method 1a-1, is simply the zeroth-order version of this method. Figure 3-2 explains this technique geometrically for the first- and second-order cases.

Just as with the type 1 technique, a modified version has been proposed based on starting form $y(n-1)$ rather than from $y(n)$. The relation is

$$y(n+1) = y(n-1) + 2 \, \Delta t \, x(n)$$
$$+ \frac{\Delta t}{3} [\nabla^2 x(n) + \nabla^3 x(n) + \nabla^4 x(n) + \cdots]$$
$$- \frac{\Delta t}{90} [\nabla^4 x(n) + 2\nabla^5 x(n) + 3\nabla^6 x(n) \mid \cdots] \tag{3-9}$$

This technique will be described as 1b-2. It has the apparent advantage common with 1a-2 that the integrand over the middle of the interval is employed. However, as was the case with method 1a-2, this method also "blows up" when it is used for the simulation of an element appearing in a feedback loop. The addition of the extrapolation feature causes this instability to appear sooner and to be more extreme than with 1a-2. The use of this method is therefore not advocated.

Extrapolating techniques will introduce starting difficulties as, for low values of n, not all the necessary backward differences, or ∇ terms, can be established. Hence, when employing method 1b-1, it is necessary to use a zeroth-order version (simple rectangular integration) for the first iteration, a first-order version for the second, etc., until enough iterations have been executed to accommodate the order of extrapolation desired.

These extrapolating methods are suspect when simulating systems

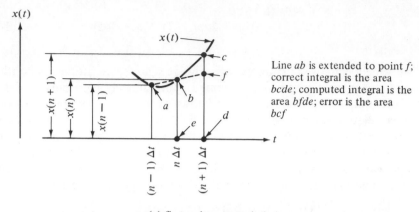

Line *ab* is extended to point *f*; correct integral is the area *bcde*; computed integral is the area *bfde*; error is the area *bcf*

(a) first-order extrapolation

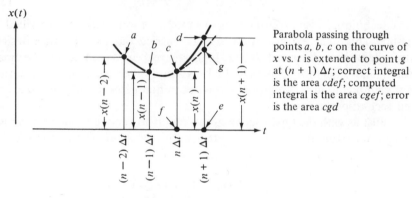

Parabola passing through points *a*, *b*, *c* on the curve of *x* vs. *t* is extended to point *g* at $(n + 1) \Delta t$; correct integral is the area *cdef*; computed integral is the area *cgef*; error is the area *cgd*

(b) second-order extrapolation

FIGURE 3-2

where sharp discontinuities of the $x(t)$ versus t relationship might occur. This can be the case, for example, in mechanical systems when backlash and friction are present, or in any type of system subject to sharp limiting, as in linear-programming problems. In such instances, previous values of the integrand are better ignored. If improved accuracy per iteration is required, going to one of the multipass nonextrapolating techniques (types 2a, 3a, etc.) might be preferred.

3-6   Type 2a, 3a, etc.—Multipass Nonextrapolating Techniques of Integration

These methods generally are called *predictor–corrector* or Runge–Kutta methods. Their general philosophy is illustrated by a two-pass technique described here as method 2a-1. The steps are as follows:

$$y_p(n + 1) = y(n) + x(n)\,\Delta t \tag{3-10a}$$

$$x_p(n + 1) = f[y_p(n + 1), t(n + 1)] \tag{3-10b}$$

$$y(n + 1) = y(n) + \tfrac{1}{2}\,\Delta t\,[x(n) + x_p(n + 1)] \tag{3-10c}$$

$$x(n + 1) = f[y(n + 1), t(n + 1)] \tag{3-10d}$$

Of the four basic steps represented by these equations, the first is simply method 1a-1, or simple rectangular integration; it is used to obtain the first guess or predicted value of $y(n + 1)$, hence the p subscript. This first guess is then employed in a second traversal of the feedback loop to obtain the corresponding predicted integrand value, $x_p(n + 1)$. This second step is represented by the functional relationship (3-10b). Then, corresponding to relation (3-10c), a second, final evaluation of $y(n + 1)$ is made by using the *trapezoidal formula* for integration. This formula is similar to rectangular integration with, however, the value of the integrand employed being the mean of the initial, $x(n)$, value and the predicted, $x_p(n + 1)$, final value. Finally, corresponding to the functional relationship (3-10d), the feedback loop is traversed the second time for this iteration (the second pass) to determine the corrected value of $x(n + 1)$ so that it may be available for the next iterative step. In general, it may be noted that twice as many relations are needed to describe the process as there are iterative passes.

This technique has been variously referred to as the *improved Euler method*, the *predictor–corrector method*, and the *trapezoidal method*. Another two-pass method has also been proposed that commences by progressing only one half of a Δt interval during the first pass, and then the second half of the interval during the second pass. Just as other techniques have sometimes been named, this is also frequently referred to as the *modified Euler method*. The steps employed in this method, to be referred to here as method 2a-2, utilize the predicted value of the integrand at the *middle* of the iteration interval. The steps are

$$y_p(n + \tfrac{1}{2}) = y(n) + x(n)\frac{\Delta t}{2} \tag{3-11a}$$

$$x_p(n + \tfrac{1}{2}) = f[y_p(n + \tfrac{1}{2}), t(n + \tfrac{1}{2})] \tag{3-11b}$$

$$y(n + 1) = y(n) + x_p(n + \tfrac{1}{2})\,\Delta t \tag{3-11c}$$

$$x(n + 1) = f[y(n + 1), t(n + 1)] \tag{3-11d}$$

Methods 2a-1 and 2a-2 both employed two passes. More passes can be used for still greater accuracy for a specified interval Δt. Such procedures are generally described as Runge–Kutta methods. An example of a three-pass technique is the *Simpson's-rule method*, classified here as method 3a-1.

$$y_p(n + \tfrac{1}{2}) = y(n) + \frac{\Delta t}{2}\,x(n) \tag{3-12a}$$

$$x_p(n + \tfrac{1}{2}) = f[y_p(n + \tfrac{1}{2}), t(n + \tfrac{1}{2})] \tag{3-12b}$$

$$y_p(n + 1) = y_p(n + \tfrac{1}{2}) + \frac{\Delta t}{2} x_p(n + \tfrac{1}{2}) \qquad (3\text{-}12\text{c})$$

$$x_p(n + 1) = f[y_p(n + 1), t(n + 1)] \qquad (3\text{-}12\text{d})$$

$$y(n + 1) = y(n) + \frac{\Delta t}{6} [x(n) + 4x_p(n + \tfrac{1}{2}) + x_p(n + 1)] \qquad (3\text{-}12\text{e})$$

$$x(n + 1) = f[y(n + 1), t(n + 1)] \qquad (3\text{-}12\text{f})$$

What is generally called *the* Runge–Kutta method involves four passes. (It is often referred to as the fourth-order Runge–Kutta method, but it is preferable here to reserve the use of the word "order" to the order of extrapolation that might be employed.) It has the following steps:

$$y_{p1}(n + \tfrac{1}{2}) = y(n) + x(n) \frac{\Delta t}{2} \qquad (3\text{-}13\text{a})$$

$$x_{p1}(n + \tfrac{1}{2}) = f[y_{p1}(n + \tfrac{1}{2}), t(n + \tfrac{1}{2})] \qquad (3\text{-}13\text{b})$$

$$y_{p2}(n + \tfrac{1}{2}) = y(n) + x_{p1}(n + \tfrac{1}{2}) \frac{\Delta t}{2} \qquad (3\text{-}13\text{c})$$

$$x_{p2}(n + \tfrac{1}{2}) = f[y_{p2}(n + \tfrac{1}{2}), t(n + \tfrac{1}{2})] \qquad (3\text{-}13\text{d})$$

$$y_p(n + 1) = y(n) + x_{p2}(n + \tfrac{1}{2}) \Delta t \qquad (3\text{-}13\text{e})$$

$$x_p(n + 1) = f[y_p(n + 1), t(n + 1)] \qquad (3\text{-}13\text{f})$$

$$y(n + 1) = y(n) + [x(n) + 2x_{p1}(n + \tfrac{1}{2}) $$
$$+ 2x_{p2}(n + \tfrac{1}{2}) + x_p(n + 1)] \frac{\Delta t}{6} \qquad (3\text{-}13\text{g})$$

$$x(n + 1) = f[y(n + 1), t(n + 1)] \qquad (3\text{-}13\text{h})$$

Simpson's rule is employed to weight the effects of the various predicted values of the integrand, x_{p1}, x_{p2}, and x_p. The last pass, relation (3-13h), is necessary to find $x(n + 1)$ for use in the following iteration interval.

There are also Runge–Kutta methods involving still more passes. They are rarely employed in simulation applications because the increased execution time required is generally not justified in consideration of the accuracy that they afford.

3-7   Types 2b, 3b, etc.—Multipass Extrapolating Integration

Various combinations of type b (i.e., extrapolating) methods and multipass methods might be employed. These generally are referred to as *Milne methods*. Only one type will be discussed here, designated as method 2b-1 and often called the *modified trapezoidal method*. It combines a first-order version of extrapolating technique, 1b-2 [relation (3-9)], with the two-pass approach.

$$y_p(n + 1) = y(n) + \Delta t \left[\tfrac{3}{2}x(n) - \tfrac{1}{2}x(n - 1)\right] \tag{3-14a}$$

$$x_p(n + 1) = f[y_p(n + 1), t(n + 1)] \tag{3-14b}$$

$$y(n + 1) = y(n) + \frac{\Delta t}{2}[x(n) + x_p(n + 1)] \tag{3-14c}$$

$$x(n + 1) = f[y(n + 1), t(n + 1)] \tag{3-14d}$$

3-8　Summary of Methods

The methods mentioned here are summarized in Table 3-2. The ambiguous terminology used to describe these methods is apparent from this table.

TABLE 3-2　Methods of Numerical Integration

Type No.	Relation No.	Typical Name
1a-1	(3-5)	Simple rectangular integration Euler's method Point-slope method
1a-2	(3-6)	Modified Euler method Trapezoidal method
1b-1	(3-8)	Backward-difference method
1b-2	(3-9)	Modified backward-difference method
2a-1	(3-10)	Predictor–corrector method Trapezoidal method Improved Euler method
2a-2	(3-11)	Modified Euler method
2b-1	(3-14)	Modified trapezoidal method
3a-1	(3-12)	Simpson's-rule method
4a-1	(3-13)	*The* Runge–Kutta method

3-9　Numerical Differentiation

The same general objections arise with the use of differentiation rather than integration in digital-simulation problems as occur with analog computers. The noise problems arising in analog computers have their counterparts with digital simulation, such as oscillatory and often unstable response inherent in the simulation method rather than in the system being simulated. Work in the field of numerical analysis has established that numerical-differentiation techniques are poorly suited to the solution of differential equations; it follows for the same reasons that they are poorly suited to simulation as well. Furthermore, the use of derivatives will introduce starting difficulties at $t = 0$.

Hence numerical differentiation will rarely be employed in simulation. It will never be used in the applications discussed in this book when the operation is part of a closed loop (in the block diagram), since there the errors and convergence difficulties can be cumulative. Only when a derivative is required in an open-loop situation and cannot be obtained in any other convenient way will numerical differentiation be employed. Then the problem is to find

$$x(t) = \frac{d}{dt} y(t) \tag{3-15}$$

One way of finding this derivative is by working backward from relation (3-8). By rewriting this relation with the difference terms (∇ terms) expressed in the form of relation (3-7), the result is obtained:

$$y(n + 1) = y(n) + \Delta t \,\{x(n) + \tfrac{1}{2}[x(n) - x(n - 1)]$$
$$+ \tfrac{5}{12}[x(n) - 2x(n - 1) + x(n - 2)] + \cdots\} \tag{3-16}$$

If none of the difference terms in relation (3-16) is employed, the algebraic solution for $x(n)$ is simply

$$x(n) = \frac{y(n + 1) - y(n)}{\Delta t} \tag{3-17}$$

This is the simplest form of numerical differentiation.

If only the first difference term of relation (3-16) is retained, the algebraic solution for $x(n)$ will be

$$x(n) = \frac{1}{3}\left[2\frac{y(n + 1) - y(n)}{\Delta t} + x(n - 1) \right] \tag{3-18}$$

If the second difference term is retained as well, the algebraic solution for $x(n)$ will be

$$x(n) = \frac{1}{23}\left[12\frac{y(n + 1) - y(n)}{\Delta t} + 16x(n - 1) - 5x(n - 2) \right] \tag{3-19}$$

Obviously, in the first iteration only relation (3-17) could be used; in the second, relation (3-18) could be used, and in the third and subsequent iterations, relation (3-19).

3-10   The z Operator

When handling ordinary differential equations dealing with continuous functions, it is often convenient to employ the operator p to represent the operation d/dt; with discrete or difference equations it is similarly convenient to employ an operator, $\mathfrak{z}$,[2] to represent a time advance of one iteration. That is,

$$x(n+1) = \mathfrak{z}x(n) \tag{3-20}$$

Similarly,

$$x(n+2) = \mathfrak{z}x(n+1)$$
$$= \mathfrak{z}[\mathfrak{z}x(n)] = \mathfrak{z}^2 x(n)$$

and

$$x(n-1) = \mathfrak{z}^{-1}x(n)$$

On this basis, integration method 1a-1, simple rectangular integration, could be expressed in the following operational form, equivalent to relation (3-5):

$$\mathfrak{z}y(n) = y(n) + \Delta t\, x(n) \tag{3-21}$$

or

$$y(n) = \Delta t\, \frac{1}{\mathfrak{z}-1}x(n) \tag{3-22}$$

The above relations could be expressed in block-diagram form, as in Figure 3-3.

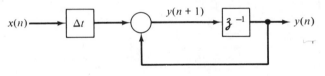

simplifies to

FIGURE 3-3

The operation ∇, or backward difference, is represented in this form as

$$\nabla x(n) = x(n) - x(n-1) = (1 - \mathfrak{z}^{-1})x(n)$$

or

$$\nabla = 1 - \mathfrak{z}^{-1} = \frac{\mathfrak{z}-1}{\mathfrak{z}} \tag{3-23}$$

Also, since $\nabla^2 x(n)$ is given by

$$\nabla^2 x(n) = [x(n) - x(n-1)] - [x(n-1) - x(n-2)]$$
$$= x(n) - 2x(n-1) + x(n-2)$$
$$= (1 - 2\mathfrak{z}^{-1} + \mathfrak{z}^{-2})x(n)$$

---

[2] The operator $\mathfrak{z}$ is not the z of the z transform; it bears the same relation to it that p does to the Laplace-transform variable s.

$$\nabla^2 = (1 - \mathbf{z}^{-1})^2 = \left(\frac{\mathbf{z} - 1}{\mathbf{z}}\right)^2 \tag{3-24}$$

Hence algebraic manipulation of $\mathbf{z}$ is permissible and, in general,

$$\nabla^m = \left(\frac{\mathbf{z} - 1}{\mathbf{z}}\right)^m \tag{3-25}$$

Method 1b-1, described by relation (3-8), also could have been written as

$$\mathbf{z}\,y(n) = y(n) + \Delta t \left[1 + \frac{1}{2}\left(\frac{\mathbf{z} - 1}{\mathbf{z}}\right) + \frac{5}{12}\left(\frac{\mathbf{z} - 1}{\mathbf{z}}\right)^2 \right.$$
$$\left. + \frac{3}{8}\left(\frac{\mathbf{z} - 1}{\mathbf{z}}\right)^3 + \frac{251}{720}\left(\frac{\mathbf{z} - 1}{\mathbf{z}}\right)^4 + \cdots \right] x(n) \tag{3-26}$$

or in block-diagram form, as in Figure 3-4. The block diagram of Figure 3-4 could also be simplified by the general principles of block-diagram algebra.

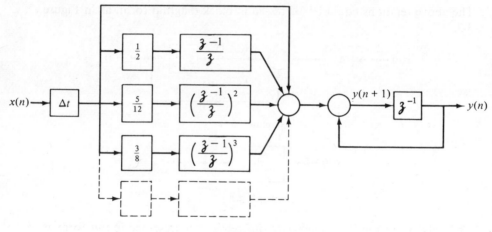

FIGURE 3-4

3-11   The *z* Transform

As is the case with operational methods applied to continuous functions, the use of the operator $\mathbf{z}$ presents certain difficulties, in that it does not automatically take into account the *boundary conditions*. As with operational calculus employing the operator p, the basic *modes of response* can be determined by these operational methods. Then, however, it is necessary to assign unknown coefficients to the terms concerned with each of these modes and later to find the values of these coefficients so that the stipulated boundary values can be met. This can be avoided by the transform approach.

When dealing with difference equations, as are involved when iterative methods of computation are employed, the z transform [5] is the most convenient.

In this chapter it will be assumed that the reader is acquainted with the z transform. However, for the benefit of those readers who are not, Appendix 3A presents a brief introduction; it should be read before proceeding.

When applying the z transform to difference equations (i.e., the type of equations that arise when describing iterative methods of computation), use is made of the *shifting theorem*, restated here: If $Z[f(n)] = F(z)$, then

$$Z[f(n + 1)] = zF(z) - zf(0)$$

and

$$Z[f(n + 2)] = z^2F(z) - z^2f(0) - zf(1) \qquad (3\text{-}27)$$

$$\text{etc.}$$

Hence, for example, relation (3-5), relating to numerical integration method 1a-1, can be transformed to

$$zY(z) - zy(0) = Y(z) + \Delta t\, X(z)$$

or

$$Y(z) = \frac{\Delta t\, X(z) + zy(0)}{z - 1} \qquad (3\text{-}28)$$

This is practically identical in form to relation (3-22), which handles this same relationship on the basis of the $\mathfrak{z}$ operator; the only difference is that now, with the transform, the one pertinent initial condition, $y(0)$, has also been included.

One application of this transform method is its use in determining the effects of numerical-integration techniques and comparing them with the performance of an ideal integrator. As an example, let simple rectangular integration, method 1a-1, again be considered. Its output (integral) has been described in z-transform form in relation (3-28). Two types of inputs (integrands) will be considered.

Case 1: $x(t) = k = $ constant. Then $x(n) = k$, and its z transform is (see Appendix 3A)

$$X(z) = \frac{kz}{z - 1}$$

Hence, from (3-28),

$$Y(z) = k\, \Delta t\, \frac{z}{(z - 1)^2} + \frac{z}{z - 1}y(0)$$

The inverse transform of this is (again from Table 3A-1 of Appendix 3A)

$$y(n) = kn\, \Delta t + y(0)$$

or, since $n \, \Delta t = t$,

$$y(t) = kt + y(0)$$

for $t = n \, \Delta t$ only, where n is an integer. On the other hand, the correct value of y_i (y ideal) is

$$y_i(t) = \int_0^t k \, dt + y(0) = kt + y(0)$$

and is identical to the computed value. This simply proves the obvious fact that simple rectangular integration produces a perfect result when the integrand in constant.

     Case 2: $x(t) = kt$. Then, $x(n) = kn \, \Delta t$ and its z transform is

$$X(z) = k \, \Delta t \, \frac{z}{(z-1)^2}$$

Hence, from (3-28),

$$Y(z) = k(\Delta t)^2 \frac{z}{(z-1)^3} + y(0) \frac{z}{z-1}$$

or

$$Y(z) = k(\Delta t)^2 \left[\frac{1}{2} \frac{z(z+1)}{(z-1)^3} - \frac{1}{2} \frac{z}{(z-1)^2} \right] + y(0) \frac{z}{z-1}$$

[The last form of $Y(z)$ is obtained from a partial fraction expansion, devised so that terms would be obtained matching those of Table 3A-1.] Hence, from Table 3A-1,

$$y(n) = k(\Delta t)^2 \left[\frac{n^2}{2} - \frac{n}{2} \right] + y(0)$$

or, since $n \, \Delta t = t$,

$$y(t) = \frac{kt^2}{2} + y(0) - \frac{k \, \Delta t}{2} t$$

for $t = n \, \Delta t$ only, with n an integer. On the other hand, the correct (ideal) value is

$$y_i(t) = \int_0^t kt \, dt + y(0) = \frac{kt^2}{2} + y(0)$$

Hence a cumulative error results, equal to

$$y_e(t) = y_i(t) - y(t) = \frac{k \, \Delta t}{2} t$$

A comparison of the ideal and actual integral computed is shown graphically in Figure 3-5.

     The same technique could be used to find the integral that results from other methods of numerical integration when the inputs (integrands) are polynomial, exponential, or trigonometric functions of time. However, since in problems of simulation, integrators appear most often in *closed-*

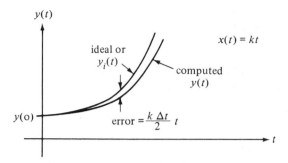

FIGURE 3-5

loop situations, the performance of the various numerical methods in such situations is of greater interest.

3-12 Comparing Numerical-Integration Methods in Closed-Loop Situations

The most useful comparison of the various methods of numerical integration would be based on the performance in the actual simulation situation being considered. Most such situations, however, will involve fairly complicated relationships, often with more than one integration operation in a loop; multiloop situations also are common. *If* the relations are all linear, analysis by means of the z transform is still theoretically possible, but it becomes impractically cumbersome for all but the most simple situations. If, as frequently is the case, nonlinear relationships are involved, the z-transform method is inapplicable. Hence any comparison of methods of numerical integration in an actual simulation situation must be done on an experimental basis.

A general comparison of numerical methods of integration, however, can be performed by using the same test method frequently employed when analog-computer integrators are being tested. Here the situation shown in Figure 3-6 is simulated, which is simply the block-diagram representation

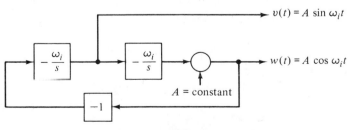

FIGURE 3-6

of a sine–cosine generator. In analog-computer tests, two supposedly identical integrators are employed in the configuration represented by the block diagram. Two response criteria are then noted:

1. How the frequency, ω, of the actual sinusoidal wave generated compares with the correct, or "ideal" value, ω_i.
2. The rate at which the amplitude increases or decreases with time. Ideally, the amplitude should remain constant at the value A.

This *sine-wave generator test* may be applied to the various methods of numerical integration that have been mentioned here for the purpose of comparing them. For the simplest example, method 1a-1 again is considered. Applying its relation, (3-5), to the block diagram of Figure 3-6 results in the relations

$$w(n + 1) = w(n) - \omega_i\,\Delta t\,v(n)$$
$$v(n + 1) = v(n) + \omega_i\,\Delta t\,w(n)$$

with $w(0) = A$ and $v(0) = 0$.

The z transform is obtained by applying the shifting theorem of relation (3-27),

$$zW(z) - zw(0) = W(z) - \omega_i\,\Delta t\,V(z)$$
$$zV(z) - zv(0) = V(z) + \omega_i\,\Delta t\,W(z)$$

or, after substituting the values of $w(0)$ and $v(0)$ and rearranging,

$$(z - 1)W(z) + \omega_i\,\Delta t\,V(z) = Az$$
$$-\omega_i\,\Delta t\,W(z) + (z - 1)V(z) = 0$$

It is adequate for the purposes of this test to determine the solution for only $w(t)$. Solving these simultaneous equations for $W(z)$ results in

$$W(z) = \frac{Az\,(z - 1)}{(z - 1)^2 + (\omega_i\,\Delta t)^2}$$

or

$$W(z) = \frac{Az\,(z - 1)}{z^2 - 2z + 1 + (\omega_i\,\Delta t)^2} \tag{3-29}$$

The pole locations for $W(z)$ in the z plane are established most conveniently in polar-coordinate form. In general, for a denominator polynomial of the form

$$D(z) = z^2 + bz + c \tag{3-30}$$

the poles will be located at

$$z_p = \sqrt{c}\,\underline{/\pm\cos^{-1}(-b/2\sqrt{c}\,)} \tag{3-31}$$

or at

$$z_p = \sqrt{c}\,\exp\!\left(\pm j\cos^{-1}\frac{-b}{2\sqrt{c}}\right) \tag{3-31a}$$

In other words, the constant coefficient c determines the radius of the pole location in the z plane and the ratio $-b/2\sqrt{c}$, the angle. This is shown in Figure 3-7.

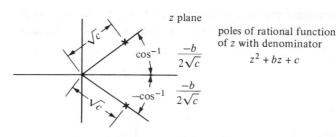

poles of rational function of z with denominator

$$z^2 + bz + c$$

FIGURE 3-7

For this example, referring back to relation (3-29) and employing relation (3-31a), the poles of $W(z)$ are found to be located at

$$z_p = \sqrt{1 + (\omega\,\Delta t)^2}\,\exp\left[\pm j\cos^{-1}\frac{1}{\sqrt{1 + (\omega\,\Delta t)^2}}\right] \qquad (3\text{-}32)$$

It would have been possible to express relation (3-29) in a partial-fraction-expansion form and then, by referring to pair (2) of Table 3A-1, determine $w(n)$ and, in turn, $w(t)$. This would be somewhat tedious and unnecessary; the pole locations just described are alone sufficient to establish the application of the test criteria.

If it is recalled (see Appendix 3A) that the variable z of the z transform is defined as

$$z = e^{s\,\Delta t}$$

and if s is described in terms of its real and imaginary parts,

$$s = \sigma + j\omega$$

then

$$z = e^{\sigma\,\Delta t}\,e^{j\omega\,\Delta t} = e^{\sigma\,\Delta t}\underline{/\omega\,\Delta t} \qquad (3\text{-}33)$$

In other words,

$$|z| = e^{\sigma\,\Delta t}$$

or

$$\sigma = \frac{1}{\Delta t}\ln z \qquad (3\text{-}34a)$$

and

$$\omega = \frac{1}{\Delta t}\underline{/z} \qquad (3\text{-}34b)$$

When the poles have been determined from a function having the denominator in the form of (3-30), this becomes

$$\sigma = \frac{1}{\Delta t}\ln\left(\sqrt{c}\right) \qquad (3\text{-}35a)$$

and

$$\omega = \frac{1}{\Delta t} \cos^{-1} \frac{-b}{2\sqrt{c}} \qquad (3\text{-}35\text{b})$$

For this particular example of method 1a-1, where the pole locations have been given by relations (3-32), the corresponding s plane location of these poles will be

$$\sigma = \frac{1}{\Delta t} \ln \sqrt{1 + (\omega_i \Delta t)^2} \qquad (3\text{-}36\text{a})$$

and

$$\omega = \frac{1}{\Delta t} \cos^{-1} \frac{1}{\sqrt{1 + (\omega_i \Delta t)^2}}$$
$$= \omega_i \frac{\tan^{-1} (\omega_i \Delta t)}{\omega_i \Delta t} \qquad (3\text{-}36\text{b})$$

The computed output, therefore, will be of the form

$$w(t) = K e^{\sigma t} \cos (\omega t + \phi) \qquad \text{for } t = n \Delta t \text{ only} \qquad (3\text{-}37)$$

The constants K and ϕ would have to be determined by finding the actual inverse transforms of the expression for $W(z)$ appearing in relation (3-29). For the purpose of this sine-wave-generator evaluation test, this is not necessary. The first test criterion is

1. The comparison of the actual frequency ω with the desired or ideal frequency ω_i. From relation (3-36b), their ratio is

$$\frac{\omega}{\omega_i} = \frac{\tan^{-1} (\omega_i \Delta t)}{\omega_i \Delta t}$$

   This ratio should be unity, but it is seen that the frequency of the computed signal will be somewhat lower than the ideal [the ratio $(\tan^{-1} x/x)$ is always less than unity]. Normally, in a practical computation instance, $(\omega_i \Delta t)$ will be sufficiently less than unity that the following approximation (based on the series expansion) may be used:

$$\tan^{-1} x \cong x - \frac{x^3}{3}$$

   so that, approximately,

$$\frac{\omega}{\omega_i} \cong 1 - \frac{(\omega_i \Delta t)^2}{3} \qquad (3\text{-}38)$$

2. The evaluation of the time decrement or increment of the amplitude of the generated sinusoidal wave. Here it is seen that σ will be positive and there will be an *increment* with time by the factor $e^{\sigma t}$. But

$$e^{\sigma t} = \exp\left[\frac{t}{\Delta t} \ln \sqrt{1 + (\omega_i \Delta t)^2}\,\right]$$

$$= \exp\{\ln[1 + (\omega_i \Delta t)^2]^{t/2\,\Delta t}\}$$

$$= [1 + (\omega_i \Delta t)^2]^{t/2\,\Delta t}$$

One period of oscillation will be $T = 2\pi/\omega$ or, approximately, $2\pi/\omega_i$. Substituting this for t yields the *perunit amplitude increment per period* as

$$e^{\sigma T} = [1 + (\omega_i \Delta t)^2]^{\pi/\omega_i \Delta t}$$

or, from the binomial expansion,

$$e^{\sigma T} = 1 + \frac{\pi}{\omega_i \Delta t}(\omega_i \Delta t)^2 + \frac{\dfrac{\pi}{\omega_i \Delta t}\left(\dfrac{\pi}{\omega_i \Delta t} - 1\right)}{2!}(\omega_i \Delta t)^4 + \cdots$$

$$= 1 + \pi(\omega_i \Delta t) + \frac{\pi}{2!}(\omega_i \Delta t)^2(\pi - \omega_i \Delta t) + \cdots$$

If Δt is sufficiently small so that $\omega_i \Delta t \ll 1$, the result is approximately

$$\text{per period increment ratio} = \frac{\text{amplitude in given period}}{\text{amplitude previous period}}$$

$$= 1 + \pi\omega_i \Delta t$$

or

$$= 1 + 2\pi^2 \frac{\Delta t}{T} \tag{3-39}$$

As a specific numerical example, let the case be considered where this per period increment ratio may be only 0.1 per cent. Then

$$2\pi^2 \frac{\Delta t}{T} \le 0.001$$

or

$$\frac{T}{\Delta t} \ge 2000\pi^2 = 19{,}800$$

That is, for this 0.1 per cent criterion to be met, approximately 20,000 iterations are required per period of the sinusoidal signal generated. This appears to be an excessive number of iterations and the use of more sophisticated methods of integration certainly would be expected to produce a more favorable result.

3-13   Use of $\mathfrak{z}$ Operator Rather than z Transform with Sine-Test Criteria

For this particular test criteria, the only analysis required was that to establish the poles of the $W(z)$ function. This could easily have been performed on an operational basis. In the preceding test of method 1a-1, Figure 3-3 could have been used as a substitute for the integration ($1/s$) operation of Figure 3-6; the resulting block diagram appears in Figure 3-8. The loop transfer function then is $[\omega_i \Delta t/(\mathfrak{z} - 1)]^2$ and the characteristic equation is

$$(\mathfrak{z} - 1)^2 + (\omega_i \Delta t)^2 = 0$$

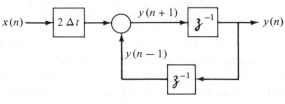

FIGURE 3-8

The roots of this equation produce the same poles on the $\mathfrak{z}$ plane as were located on the z plane by relation (3-29). The subsequent conclusions regarding the sine-wave-generator test criteria are the same. However, it was possible to avoid a number of steps by using this $\mathfrak{z}$ operator and it was no longer necessary to specify initial conditions.

When more sophisticated techniques of numerical integration are employed or when a more complicated feedback loop is involved, the technique is still applicable in theory, but the characteristic equation in $\mathfrak{z}$ becomes of a higher order, and more difficulty is encountered in finding the roots that lead in turn to the pole locations in the $\mathfrak{z}$ plane. As an example of this, this test criteria might be applied to method 1a-2. This method is based on relation (3-6) and might be portrayed in block-diagram form as shown in Figure 3-9.

$$x(n) \longrightarrow \boxed{2\,\Delta t} \longrightarrow \bigcirc \xrightarrow{\;y(n+1)\;} \boxed{\mathfrak{z}^{-1}} \longrightarrow y(n)$$
$$y(n-1) \qquad \boxed{\mathfrak{z}^{-1}}$$

FIGURE 3-9

The method may also be expressed as a transfer function employing the $\mathfrak{z}$ operator as

$$\frac{y(n)}{x(n)} = 2\,\Delta t\,\frac{\mathfrak{z}^{-1}}{1 - \mathfrak{z}^{-2}} = 2\,\Delta t\,\frac{\mathfrak{z}}{\mathfrak{z}^2 - 1} \tag{3-40}$$

Substituting this expression for the integration operation $1/s$ in Figure 3-6 results in the block diagram shown in Figure 3-10. The characteristic equation is based on

$$1 + \left(2\omega_i \, \Delta t \, \frac{\mathcal{z}}{\mathcal{z}^2 - 1} \right)^2 = 0$$

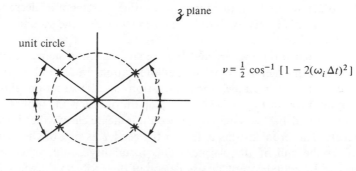

FIGURE 3-10

and is

$$\mathcal{z}^4 - [2 - (2\omega_i \, \Delta t)^2]\mathcal{z}^2 + 1 = 0 \tag{3-41}$$

Here a new operator is defined for ease in finding the roots:

$$\lambda = \mathcal{z}^2$$

The poles of this function, in terms of λ, are determined by analogy to relation (3-30) as

$$\lambda_p = \sqrt{1} \, \exp \{ \pm j \cos^{-1} [1 - \tfrac{1}{2}(2\omega_i \, \Delta t)^2] \}$$

and, since $\mathcal{z} = \pm \sqrt{\lambda}$, these poles are located in the $\mathcal{z}$ plane at

$$\mathcal{z}_p = \pm 1 \, \exp \{ \pm j \tfrac{1}{2} \cos^{-1} [1 - 2(\omega_i \, \Delta t)^2] \} \tag{3-42}$$

These pole locations are pictured in Figure 3-11. Since all these poles are on the unit circle of the $\mathcal{z}$ plane, $|\mathcal{z}_p| = 1$, it follows from (3-34a) that in the s plane they are located at $\sigma = 0$. Hence it may be concluded that the sine waves developed will have neither a decrement nor increment and the

$\mathcal{z}$ plane

unit circle

$$\nu = \tfrac{1}{2} \cos^{-1} [1 - 2(\omega_i \, \Delta t)^2]$$

FIGURE 3-11

second test criterion is met perfectly; a constant-amplitude sine wave is produced.

In Figure 3-11, the angle v may be expressed approximately in a series form as

$$v = \tfrac{1}{2} \cos^{-1} [1 - 2(\omega_i \, \Delta t)^2]$$
$$= \tfrac{1}{2} \{2[2(\omega_i \, \Delta t)^2] + \tfrac{1}{3}[2(\omega_i \, \Delta t)^2]^2 + \tfrac{4}{45}[2(\omega_i \, \Delta t)^2]^3 + \cdots \}^{1/2}$$
$$= \omega_i \, \Delta t \, \{1 + \tfrac{1}{6}[2(\omega_i \, \Delta t)^2] + \tfrac{4}{90}[2(\omega_i \, \Delta t)^2]^2 + \cdots \}^{1/2}$$
$$= \omega_i \, \Delta t \, [1 + \tfrac{1}{6}(\omega_i \, \Delta t)^2] \qquad \text{approximately}$$

Hence, from relation (3-34b), the actual frequency of the computed sine wave in this sine-wave-generator test based on the pairs of $\mathfrak{z}$-plane poles at the angles $\pm v$ will be approximately

$$\omega_1 = \frac{\big/\overline{\mathfrak{z}_p}}{\Delta t} = \omega_i [1 + \tfrac{1}{6}(\omega_i \, \Delta t)^2] \tag{3-43}$$

The other pair of poles are located at the angles $\pi \pm v$, or approximately at π. These will result in a spurious high-frequency oscillation of frequency

$$\omega_2 = \frac{\big/\overline{\mathfrak{z}_p}}{\Delta t} = \frac{\pi}{\Delta t} \tag{3-44}$$

This second, higher, frequency has a period $2\pi/\omega_2$ equal to $2\,\Delta t$ and shows that there will be a spurious oscillation of a period equal to twice the period of iteration. The magnitude of this oscillation depends upon how the computation is started (recalling that method 1a-2 is not self-starting). In any event, such oscillations will not die out.

The basic frequency is given by relation (3-43), and it may be seen to be related to the ideal frequency ω_i by the ratio

$$\frac{\omega_1}{\omega_i} = 1 + \tfrac{1}{6}(\omega_i \, \Delta t)^2$$

If this is compared with relation (3-38), based on the application of this same test criterion to method 1a-1, it may be seen that the frequency error is only one half as great with this second method. More important, when comparing it with the previous method, there is now no time increment or decrement in amplitude. In general, this test would seem to show that the second method, 1a-2, is far superior to 1a-1.

It can be shown, however, that for the simulation of many other feedback situations, this method of numerical integration, 1a-2, can lead to instability. Consider, for example, the simulation of the situation shown in block-diagram form in Figure 3-12. The $\mathfrak{z}$-operator criterion, applied for the case where method 1a-2 was employed, would indicate clearly that instability would result. The proof of this is left to the reader as one of the problems suggested at the end of the chapter. This instability could, of course, be demonstrated by actual computer simulation of the problem shown in Figure

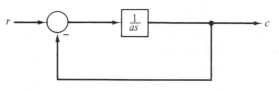

FIGURE 3-12

3-12, with method 1a-2 chosen for the numerical integration. It is because of this tendency toward instability that method 1a-2 is not recommended for simulation in feedback loops.

The sinusoidal test procedure described could be applied to still more sophisticated methods of numerical integration; however, the mathematical analysis becomes still more cumbersome. For this reason, the use of this criterion by actual simulation studies on a computer may be more feasible than z-transform or $\mathcal{z}$-operator methods of analysis. However, as the preceding example relating to Figure 3-12 showed, the sinusoidal criterion alone is not conclusive in regard to the predicted stability of the method.

3-14   Implementation of the Various Methods of Numerical Integration

Figure 1-27 showed a general flow diagram illustrating the procedures that might be employed in a simulation problem. Step (e) of that diagram represented the numerical-integration operation itself. This operation is handled most conveniently by calling a subroutine (procedure) that executes the desired integration operation for that interval. Different subroutines, corresponding to the various methods listed in Table 3-2, could be called to permit a change in the method selected without requiring any alteration of the main program.

Some of the more sophisticated numerical-integration methods will require more operations than were shown in Figure 1-27. With methods that present starting problems, the number of the iteration must be known. For example, with a fourth-order extrapolating technique it is necessary to use the zeroth-order version of integration for the first iteration, the first-order version for the second, etc., until finally, at the fifth iteration, all orders of backward differences are available and can be employed. Hence a quantity, labeled here ITERATIONS, must be set initially to unity by the main program and then progressively advanced by the integration subroutine itself. With multipass methods of integration a logical variable also should be used, called here LASTPASS, that informs the main program that the last pass of the integration procedure has been completed; only then would data be printed or stored for printout. Also, with multipass methods time is advanced (by amounts equal to Δt or $\Delta t/2$) only during some of the passes; following such time advances, then and only then should input functions (e.g., XFUNCTION in the Chapter 1 example) be looked up to determine the new values of the time-dependent input variables. For this purpose, another logical variable, called here NEWTIME, is introduced. For example, with the Runge–Kutta method 4a-1 and relation (3-14), time is advanced only during the first and third of the four passes; only after these passes is it necessary to call the subroutine(s) that provide the new inputs (e.g., x and $\dot{x}$ in the example of Chapter 1).

If there are a number of integration operations to be performed, the same integration subroutine may be employed for all; the input and output variables associated with each integration operation are identified by proper subscripts. When applied to the Chapter 1 example, the integration operation that develops $\dot{y}$ from $\ddot{y}$ could be called number 1 and that which develops y from $\dot{y}$, number 2 (the actual sequence of numbering is unimportant). With such a general-purpose integration subroutine, it will be necessary for the program to specify the number of states (i.e., the number of integration operations to be performed). This is done by the integer variable, called here STATES. For the Chapter 1 example, STATES $= 2$. Figure 1-31 is still applicable as a general flow diagram for the main simulation program provided the following steps are added to the initialization procedure:

STATES is established	($= 2$ in the Chapter 1 example problem)
ITERATIONS $= 1$	(to start the count of iterations)
LASTPASS $=$ true (or 1)	(to obtain a printout at $t = 0$)
NEWTIME $=$ true (or 1)	(so that independent input variables will be established at $t = 0$)
NEWDT $=$ true (or 1)	(needed with some types of integration; to be explained later)

The iterative program shown in Figure 1-31 would then be modified in the manner shown in Figure 3-13. Some of the symbols used in Figure 3-13 would, of course, require abbreviating if Fortran was used, because of limitations on symbol length. The symbols IN and OUT are arrays of as many elements as there are states; they represent the integrator inputs and outputs, respectively. These inputs and outputs will generally have other names in the main program that are more descriptive of their physical significance in the problem being simulated. (In the Fortran language, this is handled by EQUIVALENCE statements.) For example, with the Chapter 1 example, IN(1) is $\ddot{y}$, OUT(1) is $\dot{y}$, IN(2) is $\dot{y}$, and OUT(2) is y. Hence, in Fortran language, the following statement would be necessary at the beginning of the program:

```
EQUIVALENCE (IN(1),YDD),(OUT(1),YD),
            (IN(2),DYDT),(OUT(2),Y)
```

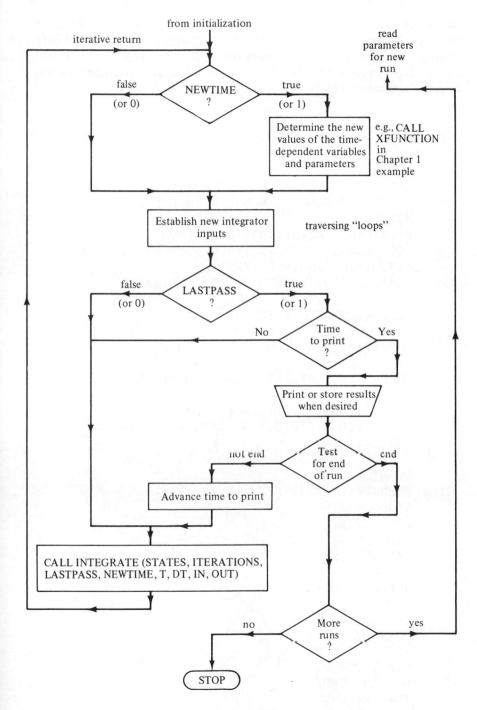

FIGURE 3-13

In the above, both YD and DYDT represent $\dot{y}$. However, it is necessary to assign different symbols (different core locations) to these to avoid over-lapping of arrays (a rather technical but important programming detail). In the iterative part of the program, prior to calling the integration subrou-tine, it therefore would be necessary to include the statement

$$DYDT = YD$$

Figure 3-14 is an example of a Fortran IV program used for the Chapter 1 example.

```
C      CHAPTER ONE EXAMPLE OF SPRING MASS SYSTEM
C      GENERAL PROGRAM FOR USE WITH ANY INTEGRATION
       MODULE
       DIMENSION INTIN(100),INTOUT(100)
       EQUIVALENCE(INOUT(1),Y),(INOUT(2),YD),(INTIN
      1(1),DYDT),(INTIN(2),YDD)
       LOGICAL NEWTIM,LSTPAS,LAST,CAL,NEWDT
       INTEGER STATE
       REAL K,M,INTIN,INTOUT
   1   READ 100,K,M
 100   FORMAT(3F10.3)
       PRINT 101,K,M
 101   FORMAT(1H1,10X,2HK=,F10.3,6H KG/CM,5X,2HM=,
      1F10.3,H KG)
   2   READ 103,B,DT,DTPT,TMAX,N,LAST
 103   FORMAT(10.3,F10.5,F10.4,F10.3,I10,L2)
       PRINT 104,B
 104   FORMAT(15X,2HB,=F10.3,10.H KG/CM/SEC)
       PRINT 105,DT
 105   FORMAT(10X,23HITERATION INTERVAL,DT =,F10.5,5H
      1SECS)
       CAL=.TRUE.
       CALL XFUNC(CAL,T,X,XD)
       CAL=.FALSE.
       STATE=2
       GOVERM=980./M
       T=0.
       TPT=-.5*DT
       TMAX=TMAX-.5*DT
       READ 100,Y,YD
       NEWDT=.TRUE.
       LSTPAS=.TRUE.
       NEWTIM=.TRUE.
       PRINT 102
```

```
 102   FORMAT(1H )
       PRINT 106
 106   FORMAT(15X,4HTIME,7X,1HX,8X,3HYDD,7X,2HYD,
      19X,1HY,8X,2HFK)
       PRINT 107
 107   FORMAT(15X,4HSECS,6X,2HCM,6X,7HCM/SEC2,3X,6HCM/
      1SEC,6X,2HCM,8X,2HKG)
C      ITERATIVE PORTION STARTS HERE
 3     IF(.NOT.NEWTIM) GO TO 4
       CALL XFUNC(CAL,T,X,XD)
 4     FB=(XD-YD)*B
       FK=(X-Y)*K
       YDD=GOVERM*(FB+FK-M)
       DYDT=YD
       IF(.NOT.LSTPAS) GO TO 6
       IF(T.LT.TPT) GO TO 6
       PRINT 108,T,X,YDD,YD,Y,FK
 108   FORMAT(10X,2F10.3,F10.0,F10.2,3F10.3)
       IF(T.LT.TMAX) GO TO 5
       IF(.NOT.LAST) GO TO 2
       STOP
 5     TPT=TPT+DTPT
 6     CALL INT(STATE,DT,T,NEWDT,LSTPAS,NEWTIM,INTIN,
      1INTOUT) GO TO 3
       END
```

FIGURE 3-14a

```
C      RUNGE KUTTA INTEGRATION METHOD 4A1
       SUBROUTINE INT(STATE,DT,T,NEWDT,LSTPAS,NEWTIM,
      1X,Y)
       DIMENSION X(100),Y(100),XLAST(100),YLAST(100),
      1XP1(100),1XP2(100),XP3(100)
       LOGICAL NEWTIM,LSTPAS,NEWDT
       INTEGER STATE
       IF(.NOT.LSTPAS) GO TO 205
C      FIRST PASS
       IF(.NOT.NEWDT) GO TO 203
       HALFDT=.5*DT
       DTOV6=.166667*DT
       NEWDT=.FALSE.
 203   T=T+HALFDT
       DO 204 J=1,STATE
       XLAST(J)=X(J)
       YLAST(J)=Y(J)
```

```
  204   IF(ABS(X(J)).GT.1.E-20)Y(J)=Y(J)+HALFDT*X(J)
        LSTPAS=.FALSE.
        NEWTIM=.TRUE.
        NXPASS=2
        RETURN
  205   IF(NXPASS-3)206,208,210
C       SECOND PASS
  206   DO 207 J=1,STATE
        XP1(J)=X(J)
  207   IF(ABS(X(J)).GT.1.E-20)Y(J)=YLAST(J)+HALFDT*X(J)
        NEWTIM=.FALSE.
        NXPASS=3
        RETURN
C       THIRD PASS
  208   T=T+HALFDT
        DO 209 J=1,STATE
        XP2(J)=X(J)
  209   IF(ABS(X(J)).GT.1.E-20)Y(J)=YLAST(J)+DT*X(J)
        NEWTIM=.TRUE.
        NXPASS=4
        RETURN
C       FOURTH (LAST) PASS
  210   DO 211 J=1,STATE
        XP3(J)=XLAST(J)+2.*XP1(J)+2.*XP2(J)+X(J)
  211   IF(ABS(X(J)).GT.1.E-20)Y(J)=YLAST(J)+DTOV6*X(J)
        NEWTIM=.FALSE.
        LSTPAS=.TRUE.
        RETURN
        END
C       RAMP FUNCTION SUBROUTINE
        SUBROUTINE XFUNC(CAL,T,X,XD)
        LOGICAL CAL
        IF(CAL) GO TO 1
        X=R*T
        RETURN
  1     READ 300,R
  300   FORMAT(F10.3)
        PRINT 301,R
  301   FORMAT(15X,32HX IS RAMP FUNCTION WITH SLOPE OF,
       1F10.3,7H CM/SEC)
        XD=R
        RETURN
        END
```

FIGURE 3-14b

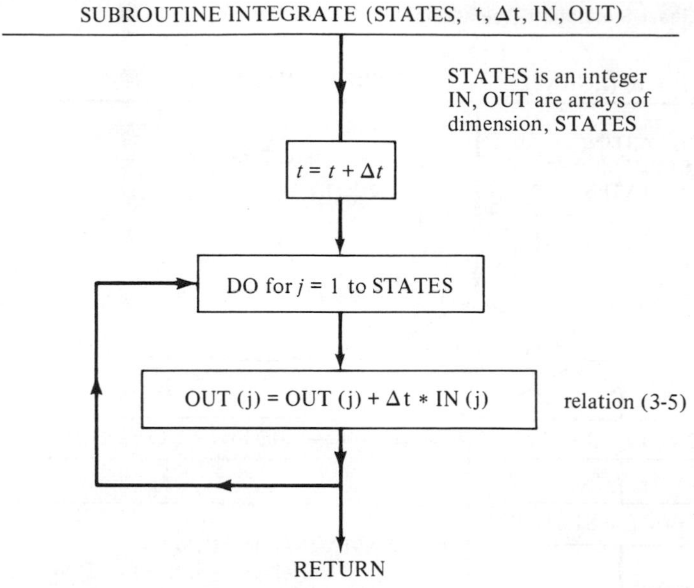

SUBROUTINE INTEGRATE (STATES, t, Δt, IN, OUT)

STATES is an integer
IN, OUT are arrays of
dimension, STATES

$t = t + \Delta t$

DO for j = 1 to STATES

OUT (j) = OUT (j) + Δt * IN (j)   relation (3-5)

RETURN

FIGURE 3-15

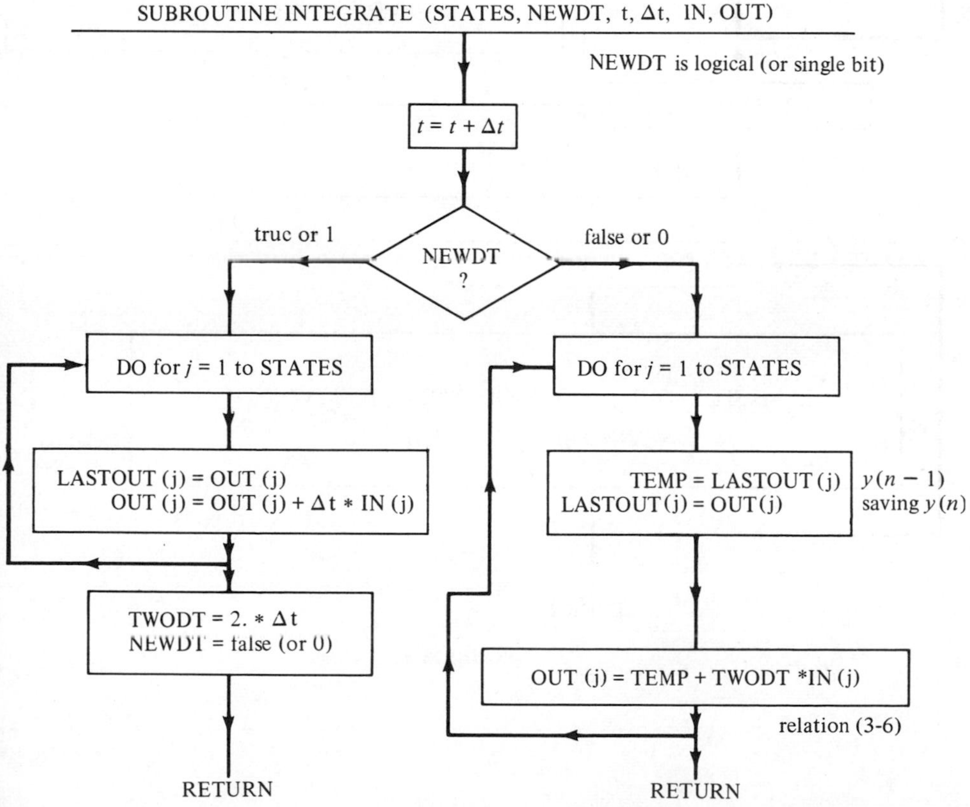

SUBROUTINE INTEGRATE (STATES, NEWDT, t, Δt, IN, OUT)

NEWDT is logical (or single bit)

$t = t + \Delta t$

true or 1   NEWDT ?   false or 0

DO for j = 1 to STATES

LASTOUT (j) = OUT (j)
OUT (j) = OUT (j) + Δt * IN (j)

TWODT = 2. * Δt
NEWDT = false (or 0)

DO for j = 1 to STATES

TEMP = LASTOUT (j) $y(n - 1)$
LASTOUT(j) = OUT(j)   saving $y(n)$

OUT (j) = TEMP + TWODT *IN (j)

relation (3-6)

RETURN   RETURN

FIGURE 3-16

SUBROUTINE INTEGRATE (STATES, ITERATIONS, Δt, t, IN, OUT)

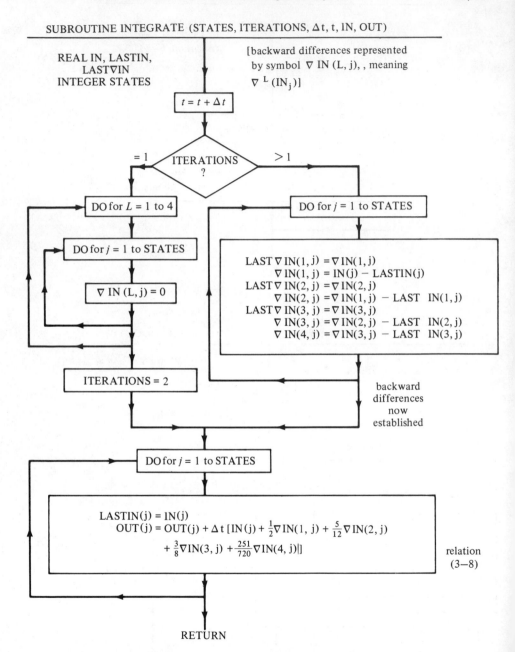

FIGURE 3-17

SUBROUTINE INTEGRATE (STATES, ITERATIONS, t, Δt, IN, OUT)

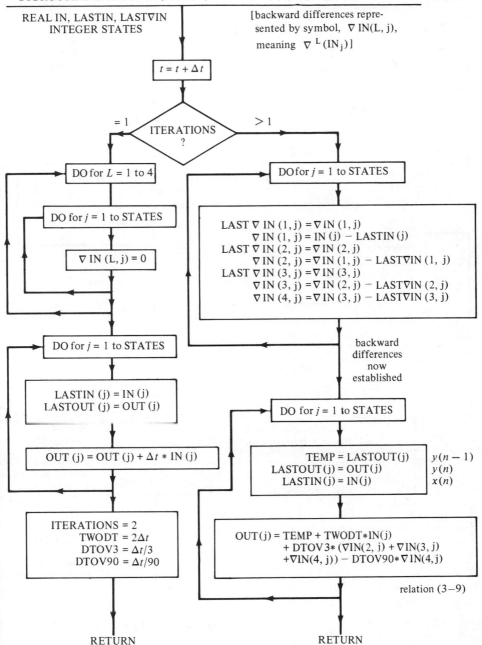

FIGURE 3-18

SUBROUTINE INTEGRATE (STATES, LASTPASS, NEWTIME, t, Δt, NEWDT, IN, OUT)

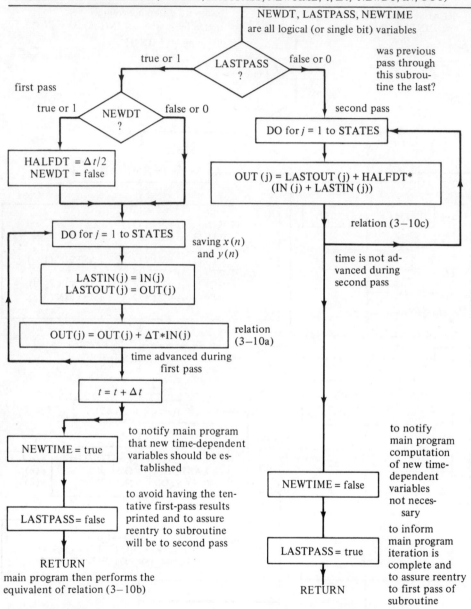

NEWDT, LASTPASS, NEWTIME
are all logical (or single bit) variables

was previous
pass through
this subrou-
tine the last?

relation (3−10c)

time is not ad-
vanced during
second pass

to notify main program
that new time-dependent
variables should be es-
tablished

to avoid having the ten-
tative first-pass results
printed and to assure
reentry to subroutine
will be to second pass

main program then performs the
equivalent of relation (3−10b)

to notify
main program
computation
of new time-
dependent
variables
not neces-
sary

to inform
main program
iteration is
complete and
to assure reentry
to first pass of
subroutine

[main program then performs the
equivalent of relation (3−10d)]

FIGURE 3-19

SUBROUTINE INTEGRATE (STATES, LASTPASS, t, Δt, NEWDT, IN, OUT)

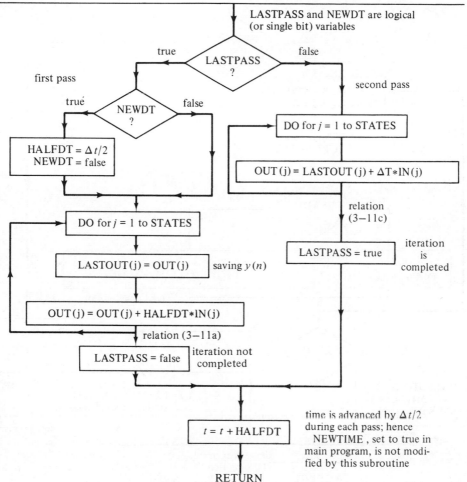

RETURN

[main program effects the equivalent of relation (3–11b) after
the first pass; the equivalent of (3–11d) after the second]

FIGURE 3-20

SUBROUTINE INTEGRATE (STATES, LASTPASS, NEWTIME, t, Δt, NEWDT, IN, OUT)

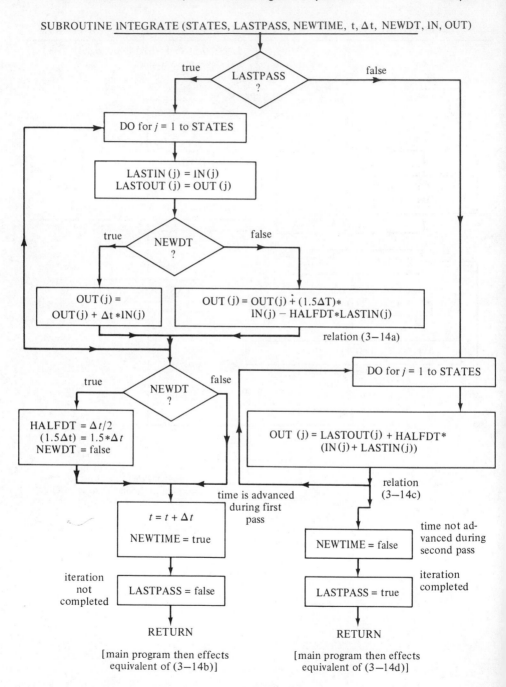

FIGURE 3-21

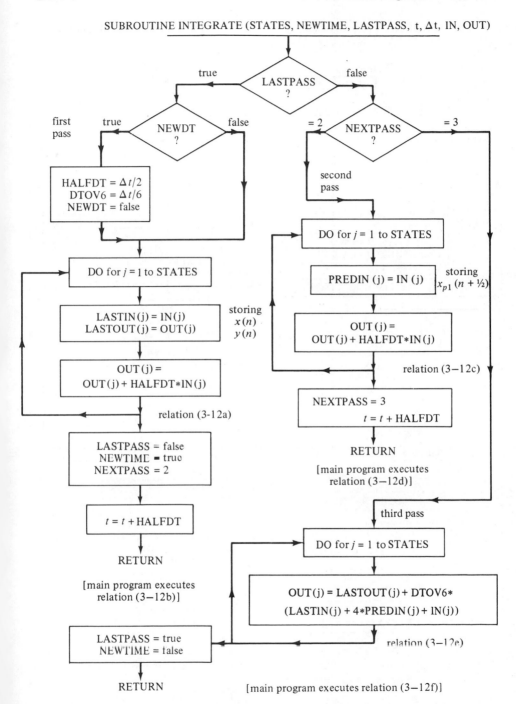

FIGURE 3-22

SUBROUTINE INTEGRATE (STATES, LASTPASS, NEWTIME, t, Δt, NEWDT, IN, OUT)

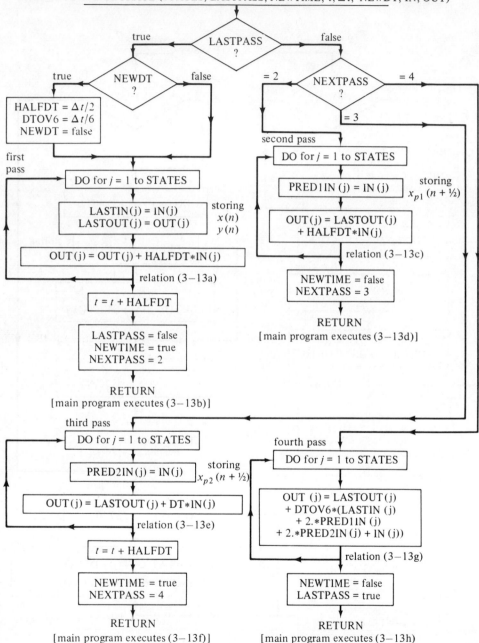

FIGURE 3-23

3-15   Integration Subroutines

Figures 3-15 to 3-23 are flow diagrams for the nine methods of numerical integration that have been discussed. These include two methods, 1a-2 (Figure 3-16) and 1b-2 (Figure 3-18), that have not been recommended because of unstable tendencies. Nevertheless, these have been included in the event that the reader may care to verify that these unstable tendencies exist.

3-16   Comparison of the Execution Times and Accuracies for the Various Methods of Numerical Integration

A comparison of the execution times associated with the various numerical-integration methods described here that is based on any one particular simulation example would not, of course, constitute a general comparison. However, it would be roughly indicative of the required execution times in general. For that matter, the relative speeds of execution, when comparing these methods of integration, will depend somewhat on the computer used and the type of compiler and assembler employed, as well as on the simulation program being handled.

The program shown in Figure 3-14 was executed on an IBM 360, Model 65 computer using a Fortran IVG compiler. The simulation covered a problem time (real time) of 0.100 sec. The various versions of the Subroutine INTEGRATE shown in Figures 3-15 to 3-23 were used, in turn, in connection with this main program. Results were obtained corresponding to those listed in Figure 1-34. The execution times measured did not, however, include time required for the actual printing of results (or of storing on output tape). Time was measured from when the repetitive iterations began up to when they ended before the actual listing of output results commenced. The results of such a test are shown in Table 3-3.

It should be noted that, along with this measurement of execution time, a measurement was also made of the root-mean-square (rms) error. For the purpose of this error measurement, the output variable $\dot{y}$ was chosen rather than y because it will, in general, display larger error percentages. It was possible for this error measurement to be made because the Chapter 1 example is so oversimplified that an analytic solution of the problem is easily derived and included in the program. (This program addition is not included in Figure 3-14.)

The computation of the rms error did not affect the execution times listed because the computation of the correct results from the analytic solu-

TABLE 3-3*

Method	Method No.	Execution Time, min	rms Error of $\dot{y}$, %
Rectangular	1a-1	0.07	3.8
Backward difference	1b-1	0.10	0.055
Trapezoidal (predictor–corrector)	2a-1	0.14	0.11
Predictor–corrector, modified	2a-2	0.13	0.11
Trapezoidal, modified	2b-1	0.13	0.054
Simpson's rule	3a-1	0.20	0.082
Runge–Kutta	4a-1	0.27	0.004

*Problem time $(t_{max}) = 0.100$ sec; $\Delta t = 0.0005$ sec; hence 200 iterations are involved.

tion and the error determination were made after the iterative program had been completed.

It is not possible to extrapolate the results of Table 3-3 to obtain the optimum interval Δt for any required degree of accuracy. This is because the relationship between accuracy and Δt is nonlinear. It is, however, possible to specify a given degree of accuracy, such as the permitted rms error in $\dot{y}$ and then adjust Δt by trial and error until this desired accuracy is obtained. The methods may then be compared on the basis of execution times after they each have had their associated iteration interval adjusted to meet the accuracy requirement. This was done with the same program, taken from the Chapter 1 example. The results obtained are summarized in Table 3-4 for rms error criteria of 0.1 and 0.01 per cent.

Methods 1a-2 and 1b-2 have not been included in these comparisons; because of their unstable tendencies it was found that they would have been unable to maintain any reasonable accuracy requirements regardless of the size of the iteration interval. It might be noted that the Runge–Kutta and

TABLE 3-4

Method	Method No.	rms Error of 0.1%		rms Error of 0.01%	
		Required Δt, sec	Exec. Time, min	Required Δt, sec	Exec. Time, min
Runge–Kutta	4a-1	0.0032	0.05	0.00046	0.28
Backward difference	1b-1	0.00057	0.10	0.00026	0.19
Trapezoid, modified	2b-1	0.00067	0.10	0.00021	0.30
Trapezoidal	2a-1	0.00047	0.13	0.00011	0.54
Predictor–corrector, modified	2a-2	0.00047	0.13	0.00006	1.12
Simpson's rule	3a-1	0.00055	0.18	0.00014	0.72
Rectangular	1a-1	0.000012	2.33	not observed— time excessive	

backward-difference methods share the honor of the shortest execution time; which of the two results in the fastest execution depends upon the accuracy specified.

The trial-and-error variation of Δt to obtain a specified accuracy was accomplished by the computer itself, employing an implicit program. Such programs will be discussed in Chapter 5. The resulting nonround values of Δt would not, of course, be employed in practice. Δt should always be some integer submultiple of the printout interval. For example, if printout is desired every 0.002 sec of problem time, as in the example that results in the listing shown in Figure 1-34, then Δt should be either 0.002 sec, 0.001 sec, 0.0005 sec, etc. Table 3-4 shows that when a 0.1 per cent accuracy is specified with the Runge–Kutta method, a Δt as great as 0.0032 would be permitted. This is, however, greater than the printout interval and hence Δt would have to be reduced to 0.002 sec. Execution time would then be increased from 0.05 to 0.08 min.

Although the Runge–Kutta and backward-difference methods appear to be roughly comparable with regard to speed of execution, the former is preferred whenever dealing with simulation problems involving discontinuities. Such problems occur quite frequently; they will be discussed in Chapter 6. The use of backward differences is always apt to introduce errors, rather than reduce errors, when the integrand is not a continuous function of time.

3-17 Use of Operational Modules in Place of Numerical Integration

Sections 2-9, 2-10, and 2-11 and Appendix 2A discuss, for the analog approach to simulation, the use of *modules* to represent transfer functions more complex than simple integration ($1/s$). This general principle can also be adapted to digital simulation. The block diagram representing some portion of the system being simulated might be simplified, by means of block-diagram algebra, to a more compact form. For example, the block diagram applicable to the Chapter 1 example, shown in Figure 1-3, could be simplified by means of block-diagram algebra to the form shown in Figure 3-24.[3]

This type of simplification is safe only if the user can be sure that there

[3] For the purpose of this chapter, the driving displacement in the Chapter 1 example, formerly called x, will now be referred to as x_1. Similarly, its rate of change will be $\dot{x}_1$. This is to avoid confusion with the use here of the symbol x as the *general* designation for the input to any transfer element. For this example, the input signal x would correspond to what is shown in Figure 3-23 as the force f.

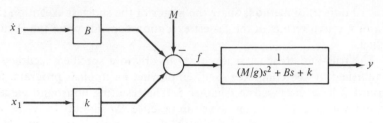

FIGURE 3-24

will be no nonlinear effects involved in the interconnections of the transfer blocks involved in the simplification process. In the Chapter 1 example this would mean being sure that the spring rate k and the damping effects B were truly linear and that no discontinuous effects, such as the engagement of limit stops (discussed in Chapter 6), would occur.

The particular block shown in Figure 3-24 that relates y and f will be described as a *quadratic* lag. Digital procedures will be shown that handle this type of transfer operation as one module rather than by successive integration operations. In some instances this can result in a substantial increase in the speed of execution of the simulation program.

Such digital procedures are based, fundamentally, on the principle of rectangular integration. They can be extended, however, to multipass methods, such as Runge–Kutta. They are described most easily by a transient-response analysis carried out in the time domain and based upon the assumption that the input to the block (e.g., f in Figure 3-24) either remains constant or varies linearly with time during the iteration interval. As an example, let the case of simple integration be considered where the transfer function relating input and output is, in operational form,

$$\frac{y}{x} = \frac{1}{s} \tag{3-45}$$

If $x(t)$ is considered as constant and equal to $x(n)$ at the start of a given (nth) interval, then the time solution for the response will be

$$y(t) = y(n) + x(n)\,\Delta t$$

where t is measured from the *beginning* of the interval and therefore equals Δt at its end. Therefore,

$$y(n+1) = y(n) + x(n)\,\Delta t \tag{3-46}$$

This relation is identical to (3-5), the basis of rectangular integration.

The handling of the quadratic relationship, such as of y versus f in Figure 3-24, is somewhat more complicated. It will be discussed here on a more general basis where the input to the block will generally be described as x (not to be confused with the x of the Chapter 1 problem) and the output as y. The general form of this quadratic relationship would then appear as

$$\frac{y}{x} = \frac{D}{As^2 + Bs + C} \tag{3-47}$$

(In the Chapter 1 example, $A = M/g$, $B =$ the B of the example, $C = k$, and $D = 1$.) For the underdamped case, this transfer relation can also be expressed as

$$\frac{y}{x} = \frac{(\text{GAIN})\omega_n^2}{s^2 + 2\zeta\omega_n s + \omega_n^2} \tag{3-48}$$

where

$$(\text{GAIN}) = \frac{D}{C} \tag{3-49a}$$

$$\omega_n = \sqrt{\frac{C}{A}} \tag{3-49b}$$

$$\zeta = \frac{B}{2\sqrt{AC}} = \frac{B}{2A\omega_n} \tag{3-49c}$$

ω_n is the *undamped natural frequency* and ζ the *damping ratio*. These terms are applicable when ζ is less then unity (i.e., the oscillatory case). The more general case (where ζ may be unity or greater than unity) will be treated later. If it were assumed that $x(t)$ varied linearly with time over the interval, with an initial value $x(n)$ and constant slope $\dot{x}(n)$, the transient solution to relation (3-49) is

$$\dot{y}(t) = k_1 y(n) + k_2 \dot{y}(n) + k_3 x(n) + k_4 \dot{x}(n)$$
$$y(t) = k_5 y(n) + k_6 \dot{y}(n) + k_4 x(n) + k_8 \dot{x}(n)$$

where

$$k_1 = -\exp(-\zeta\omega_n t)\frac{\omega_n}{\sqrt{1-\zeta^2}}\sin(\omega_n t\sqrt{1-\zeta^2})$$

$$k_2 = \exp(-\zeta\omega_n t)\left[\cos(\omega_n t\sqrt{1-\zeta^2}) - \frac{\zeta}{\sqrt{1-\zeta^2}}\sin(\omega_n t\sqrt{1-\zeta^2})\right]$$

$$k_3 = -k_1(\text{GAIN})$$

$$k_4 = (1 - k_5)(\text{GAIN})$$

$$k_5 = \exp(-\zeta\omega_n t)\left[\cos(\omega_n t\sqrt{1-\zeta^2}) - \frac{\zeta}{\sqrt{1-\zeta^2}}\sin(\omega_n t\sqrt{1-\zeta^2})\right]$$

$$k_6 = -\frac{1}{\omega_n^2}k_1$$

$$k_8 = \left\{t - \frac{2\zeta}{\omega_n} + \frac{\exp(-\zeta\omega_n t)}{\omega_n}\left[2\zeta\cos(\omega_n t\sqrt{1-\zeta^2})\right.\right.$$
$$\left.\left. + \frac{2\zeta^2 - 1}{\sqrt{1-\zeta^2}}\sin(\omega_n t\sqrt{1-\zeta^2})\right]\right\}(\text{GAIN})$$

and t is measured from the beginning of the interval.

As interest is specifically in the response at the end of the interval when $t = \Delta t$,

$$\dot{y}(n+1) = c_1 y(n) + c_2 \dot{y}(n) + c_3 x(n) + c_4 \dot{x}(n) \tag{3-50a}$$

$$y(n+1) = c_5 y(n) + c_6 \dot{y}(n) + c_4 x(n) + c_8 \dot{x}(n) \tag{3-50b}$$

where, in general, $c_i = k_i(\Delta t)$ and, therefore,

$$c_1 = -\exp(-\zeta\omega_n \Delta t)\frac{\omega_n}{\sqrt{1-\zeta^2}} \sin(\omega_n \Delta t \sqrt{1-\zeta^2}) \tag{3-51a}$$

$$c_2 = \exp(-\zeta\omega_n \Delta t)\left[\cos(\omega_n \Delta t \sqrt{1-\zeta^2})\right.$$
$$\left. -\frac{\zeta}{\sqrt{1-\zeta^2}} \sin(\omega_n \Delta t \sqrt{1-\zeta^2})\right] \tag{3-51b}$$

$$c_3 = -c_1(\text{GAIN}) \tag{3-51c}$$

$$c_4 = (1 - c_5)(\text{GAIN}) \tag{3-51d}$$

$$c_5 = \exp(-\zeta\omega_n \Delta t)\left[\cos(\omega_n \Delta t \sqrt{1-\zeta^2})\right.$$
$$\left. +\frac{\zeta}{\sqrt{1-\zeta^2}} \sin(\omega_n \Delta t \sqrt{1-\zeta^2})\right] \tag{3-51e}$$

$$c_6 = -\frac{c_1}{\omega_n^2} \tag{3-51f}$$

$$c_8 = \left\{\Delta t - \frac{2\zeta}{\omega_n} + \exp(-\zeta\omega_n \Delta t)\left[2\zeta \cos(\omega_n \Delta t \sqrt{1-\zeta^2})\right.\right.$$
$$\left.\left. +\frac{2\zeta^2 - 1}{\sqrt{1-\zeta^2}} \sin(\omega_n \Delta t \sqrt{1-\zeta^2})\right]\Big/\omega_n\right\}(\text{GAIN}) \tag{3-51g}$$

(There is no c_7; it would be identical to c_4.)

Although the expressions for the c's are relatively complicated, they need be computed only once, at the start of the iteration. Thereafter they will remain unchanged as long as Δt is unchanged and only relations (3-50a) and (3-50b) need be executed during every iteration.

The rectangular version of the above relations is based upon the premise that, for lack of better information, the value of $\dot{x}(n)$ is considered to be zero; this will be applicable in a number of programs where a direct indication of $\dot{x}$ is not available. The relations then iteratively handled by the quadratic module will be

$$\dot{y}(n-1) = c_1 y(n) + c_2 \dot{y}(n) + c_3 x(n) \tag{3-52a}$$

$$y(n-1) = c_5 y(n) + c_6 \dot{y}(n) + c_4 x(n) \tag{3-52b}$$

The use of such a quadratic module on this basis will be referred to as method Q1a-1, because of its similarity to rectangular integration, method 1a-1. Figure 3-25 is a flow diagram showing the manner of executing this

SUBROUTINE Q1a-1(QUADS, ITERATIONS, A, B, C, D, t, Δt, y, ẏ, x)

INTEGER QUADS

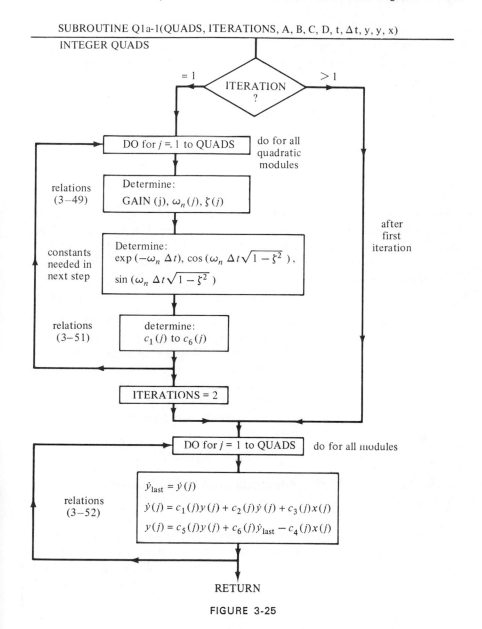

FIGURE 3-25

procedure. It is adapted for handling any number (QUADS) of such quadratic transfer functions, each being identified by its (jth) subscript.

Such a quadratic subroutine would be called by the main program in essentially the same manner that the integration subroutines are called, shown in Figure 3-22. Such a subroutine would have, however, two outputs,

y and $\dot{y}$. For the Chapter 1 example, the number of states handled by the integration subroutines was two to obtain y and $\dot{y}$. With the quadratic module only one module is necessary, y and $\dot{y}$ being obtained in one operation.

3-18   Modification of the Quadratic Module When Input Time Derivatives Are Available

In many instances, as in the example of Chapter 1, not only will an indication of the input to the quadratic transfer function [i.e., $x(n)$] be available, but also its time derivative, $\dot{x}(n)$. In such instances, all the terms of relation (3-50) may be employed. The operation is then based on the approximation that x varies linearly with time. [Therefore, when $x(t)$ is a ramp function, this method is no longer approximate but exact.] In the Chapter 1 example, the term corresponding to $\dot{x}(n)$ in relation (3-50) would be $\dot{f}$. From Figure 3-24 this would be

$$\dot{f} = k\dot{x}_1 + B\ddot{x}_1 \tag{3-53}$$

While an indication of $\ddot{x}_1$ is not available in this example, an indication of $\dot{x}_1$ is; this could be used as an approximate indication of $\dot{f}$ by employing only the first term in the above relation. The flow diagram of Figure 3-25 would then be modified in the sense that the c_8 term would also be computed during the first iteration and that the computation of $\dot{y}(n + 1)$ and $y(n + 1)$, made every iteration, is now based on relation (3-48) where the indication of $\dot{x}(n)$ is employed. This modified form of quadratic module is called here, for purpose of reference, method Q1a-2.

3-19   Use of Multipass Methods with the Quadratic Module

Just as much of the error inherent with rectangular integration may be substantially reduced by multipass methods, such as Runge–Kutta, multipass procedures may be used to advantage with more complicated methods, such as with the quadratic module. A Runge–Kutta adaptation to a quadratic module will be described here.

The Runge–Kutta type of relations would be as follows when the time derivative of the input, $\dot{x}(n)$, is not available:

$$\dot{y}_{p1}(n + \tfrac{1}{2}) = c_{1_h}y(n) + c_{2_h}\dot{y}(n) + c_{3_h}x(n) \tag{3-54a}$$

$$y_{p1}(n + \tfrac{1}{2}) = c_{5_h}y(n) + c_{6_h}\dot{y}(n) + c_{4_h}x(n) \tag{3-54b}$$

$$x_{p1}(n + \tfrac{1}{2}) = f[y_{p1}(n + \tfrac{1}{2}), \dot{y}_{p1}(n + \tfrac{1}{2}), t(n + \tfrac{1}{2})] \tag{3-54c}$$

$$\dot{y}_{p2}(n + \tfrac{1}{2}) = c_{1_h}y(n) + c_{2_h}\dot{y}(n) + c_{3_h}x_{p1}(n + \tfrac{1}{2}) \tag{3-54d}$$

$$y_{p2}(n + \tfrac{1}{2}) = c_{5_h} y(n) + c_{6_h} \dot{y}(n) + c_{4_h} x_{p1}(n + \tfrac{1}{2}) \tag{3-54e}$$

$$x_{p2}(n + \tfrac{1}{2}) = f[y_{p2}(n + \tfrac{1}{2}), \dot{y}_{p3}(n + \tfrac{1}{2}), t(n + \tfrac{1}{2})] \tag{3-54f}$$

$$\dot{y}_p(n + 1) = c_1 y(n) + c_2 \dot{y}(n) + c_3 x_{p2}(n + \tfrac{1}{2}) \tag{3-54g}$$

$$y_p(n + 1) = c_5 y(n) + c_6 \dot{y}(n) + c_4 x_{p2}(n + \tfrac{1}{2}) \tag{3-54h}$$

$$x_p(n + 1) = f[y_p(n + 1), \dot{y}_p(n + 1), t(n + 1)] \tag{3-54i}$$

$$\dot{y}(n + 1) = c_1 y(n) + c_2 \dot{y}(n) + \frac{c_3}{6}[x(n) + 2x_{p1}(n + \tfrac{1}{2})$$
$$+ 2x_{p2}(n + \tfrac{1}{2}) + x_p(n + 1)] \tag{3-54j}$$

$$y(n + 1) = c_5 y(n) + c_6 \dot{y}(n) + \frac{c_4}{6}[x(n) + 2x_{p1}(n + \tfrac{1}{2})$$
$$+ 2x_{p2}(n + \tfrac{1}{2}) + x_p(n + 1)] \tag{3-54k}$$

$$x(n + 1) = f[y(n + 1), \dot{y}(n + 1), t(n + 1)] \tag{3-54l}$$

A comparison of the above with relations (3-13) (applying to the Runge–Kutta four-pass method of numerical integration) would show that essentially the same principles are followed here. The c coefficients designated with h subscripts are based on the half-interval (i.e., on $\Delta t/2$) when relation (3-51) is applied [i.e., $\Delta t/2$ should be substituted for Δt when employing relations (3-51)]. These half-interval coefficients also need be computed only during the first iteration.

A flow diagram for this method, designated as Q4a-1 (the 4 referring to the four passes, the "a" to the fact that no interpolation is involved) would be based on the same transfer operations as in Figure 3-23. However, during the first pass of the first iteration, the c and c_h coefficients would be established. Then, during each of the four passes, computations based on relations (3-54) are performed in the place of relations (3-13) used with the conventional Runge–Kutta technique.

Similar Runge–Kutta type of multipass method could be employed with the quadratic module when an indication of $\dot{x}(n)$ is available. Relations (3-54) would then be modified as follows:

$$y_{p1}(n + \tfrac{1}{2}) = c_{1_h} y(n) + c_{2_h} \dot{y}(n) + c_{3_h} x(n) + c_{4_h} \dot{x}(n) \tag{3-55a}$$

$$y_{p1}(n + \tfrac{1}{2}) = c_{5_h} y(n) + c_{6_h} \dot{y}(n) + c_{4_h} x(n) + c_{8_h} \dot{x}(n) \tag{3-55b}$$

$$\dot{x}_{p1}(n + \tfrac{1}{2}) = \dot{f}[y_{p1}(n + \tfrac{1}{2}), \dot{y}_{p1}(n + \tfrac{1}{2}), t(n + \tfrac{1}{2})] \tag{3-55c}$$

$$\dot{y}_{p2}(n + \tfrac{1}{2}) = c_{1_h} y(n) + c_{2_h} \dot{y}(n) + c_{3_h} x(n) + c_{4_h} \dot{x}_{p1}(n + \tfrac{1}{2}) \tag{3-55d}$$

$$y_{p2}(n + \tfrac{1}{2}) = c_{5_h} y(n) + c_{6_h} \dot{y}(n) + c_{4_h} x(n) + c_{8_h} \dot{x}_{p1}(n + \tfrac{1}{2}) \tag{3-55e}$$

$$\dot{x}_{p2}(n + \tfrac{1}{2}) = \dot{f}[y_{p2}(n + \tfrac{1}{2}), \dot{y}_{p2}(n + \tfrac{1}{2}), t(n + \tfrac{1}{2})] \tag{3-55f}$$

$$\dot{y}_p(n + 1) = c_1 y(n) + c_2 \dot{y}(n) + c_3 x(n) + c_4 \dot{x}_{p2}(n + \tfrac{1}{2}) \tag{3-55g}$$

$$y_p(n + 1) = c_5 y(n) + c_6 \dot{y}(n) + c_4 x(n) + c_8 \dot{x}_{p2}(n + \tfrac{1}{2}) \tag{3-55h}$$

$$\dot{x}_p(n + 1) = \dot{f}[y_p(n + 1), \dot{y}_p(n + 1), t(n + 1)] \tag{3-55i}$$

$$\dot{y}(n + 1) = c_1 y(n) + c_2 \dot{y}(n) + c_3 x(n)$$
$$+ \frac{c_4}{6}[\dot{x}(n) + 2\dot{x}_{p1}(n + \tfrac{1}{2}) + 2\dot{x}_{p2}(n + \tfrac{1}{2}) + \dot{x}_p(n + 1)] \quad (3\text{-}55\text{j})$$

$$y(n + 1) = c_5 y(n) + c_6 \dot{y}(n) + c_4 x(n)$$
$$+ \frac{c_8}{6}[\dot{x}(n) + 2\dot{x}_{p1}(n + \tfrac{1}{2}) + 2\dot{x}_{p2}(n + \tfrac{1}{2}) + \dot{x}_p(n + 1)] \quad (3\text{-}55\text{k})$$

$$\dot{x}(n + 1) = \dot{f}[y(n + 1), \dot{y}(n + 1), t(n + 1)] \qquad\qquad (3\text{-}55\text{l})$$
$$x(n + 1) = f[y(n + 1), \dot{y}(n + 1), t(n + 1)] \qquad\qquad (3\text{-}55\text{m})$$

This technique will be described as Q4a-2. As with Q4a-1, it is based upon the weighted average of the varying part of the integrand, in this case $\dot{x}(t)$, over the interval. With input functions $x(t)$ that vary linearly with time, zero approximation error would result.

3-20   Comparison of the Execution Times with Quadratic Modules

The test case, applying to the Chapter 1 example, with the input $x_1(t)$, a ramp function of time, that was used as the basis of comparison leading to Tables 3-3 and 3-4, was also applied to the quadratic modules. A fair comparison can be made with this example only for those methods just described as Q1a-1 and Q4a-1. For an rms error of 0.01 per cent (corresponding to the last two columns of Table 3-4), the observations in Table 3-4a were made. Neither of these quadratic methods, based upon a lack of knowledge of the $\dot{x}(t)$ function, appear to have any advantage over the simpler integration

TABLE 3-4a

	rms Error of 0.01%	
Quadratic Method	Required Δt, sec	Exec. Time, min
Single pass (Q1a-1)	0.000018	1.90
Multipass (Q4a-1)	0.000070	1.58

procedures listed in Table 3-4, except for the rudimentary rectangular-integration method, 1a-1.

Such a comparison, unfavorable to the quadratic-module method, no longer would apply when there is a knowledge of $\dot{x}(n)$, so method Q1a-2 or Q4a-2 could be employed. Because the case used for purposes of comparison involved a simple ramp-type disturbance, negligible error exists with either of these methods. The iteration interval can be made as large as desired; when it was set equal to the desired printout interval of 0.002

sec (corresponding to 50 iterations to cover the total simulated time duration of 0.100 sec), execution times were 0.09 and 0.26 sec, respectively, for methods Q1a-2 and Q4a-2. As discussed before, the choice of optimum method, and the matter of whether the use of such a quadratic module presents any advantage, depends very much on the system being simulated and the type of disturbances to which it is subject.

3-21 Commonly Encountered Linear Modules

The example of a quadratic module just described applied only to those instances involving an underdamped response ($\zeta < 1$). It was only one

TABLE 3-5

Transfer Function in s Domain	Numerical Relationship	Pertinent Coefficients
1. Simple lag $$\frac{y(s)}{x(s)} = \frac{G}{1 + \tau s}$$	$y(n + 1) = c_1 y(n) + c_2 x(n)$	$c_1 = \exp(-\Delta t/\tau)$ $c_2 = G(1 - c_1)$
2. Lead–lag $\dot{x}(t)$ available $$\frac{y(s)}{x(s)} = G\frac{1 + \tau_n s}{1 + \tau_d s}$$	$y(n + 1) = c_1 y(n) + c_2 x(n)$ $\qquad + c_3 \dot{x}(n)$	$c_1 = \exp(-\Delta t/\tau)$ $c_2 = G(1 - c_1)$ $c_3 = G\,\Delta t - c_2(\tau_n - \tau_d)$
3. Lead–lag $\dot{x}(t)$ not available $$\frac{y(s)}{x(s)} = G\frac{1 + \tau_n s}{1 + \tau_d s}$$	$y(n + 1) = c_1 y(n) + c_2 x(n)$ $\qquad + c_3 x(n - 1)$	$c_1 = \exp(-\Delta t/\tau)$ $c_2 = G\tau_n/\tau_n$ $c_3 = G(1 - c_1) - c_2$
4. Double integral $$\frac{y(s)}{x(s)} = \frac{G}{s^2}$$	$\dot{y}(n + 1) = \dot{y}(n) + c_1 x(n)$ $y(n + 1) = y(n) + c_2 \dot{y}(n)$ $\qquad + c_3 x(n)$	$c_1 = G\,\Delta t$ $c_2 = \Delta t$ $c_3 = G(\Delta t)^2/2$
5. Integral with lag $$\frac{y(s)}{x(s)} = \frac{G}{s(1 + \tau s)}$$	$\dot{y}(n + 1) = c_1 \dot{y}(n) + c_2 x(n)$ $\qquad + c_3 \dot{x}(n)$ $y(n + 1) = y(n) + c_4 \dot{y}(n)$ $\qquad + c_3 x(n) + c_5 \dot{x}(n)$ $\dot{x}(n)$ terms omitted when not available	$c_1 = \exp(-\Delta t/\tau)$ $c_2 = G(1 - c_1)$ $c_3 = G\,\Delta t - \tau c_2$ $c_4 = \tau(1 - c_1)$ $c_5 = G(\Delta t)^2/2 - \tau c_3$
6. Quadratic lag $$\frac{y(s)}{x(s)} = \frac{D}{As^2 + Bs + C}$$ relation (3-45)	$\dot{y}(n + 1) = c_1 y(n) + c_2 \dot{y}(n)$ $\qquad + c_3 x(n) + c_4 \dot{x}(n)$ $y(n + 1) = c_5 y(n) + c_6 \dot{y}(n)$ $\qquad + c_4 x(n) + c_8 \dot{x}(n)$	See Table 3-5a for values of c's.
7. Triple integral $$\frac{y(s)}{x(s)} = \frac{G}{s^3}$$	$\ddot{y}(n + 1) = \ddot{y}(n) + c_1 x(n)$ $\dot{y}(n + 1) = \dot{y}(n) + c_2 \ddot{y}(n)$ $\qquad + c_3 x(n)$ $y(n + 1) = y(n) + c_2 \dot{y}(n)$ $\qquad + c_4 \ddot{y}(n) + c_5 x(n)$	$c_1 = G\,\Delta t$ $c_2 = \Delta t$ $c_3 = Gc_4$ $c_4 = (\Delta t)^2/2$ $c_5 = G(\Delta t)^3/6$

example of useful module forms for the simulation of linear operations. For the general case of the quadratic response, described by relation (3-47), the relations for the c coefficients [listed in (3-51) for $\zeta < 1$] would be modified when $\zeta = 1$ or $\zeta > 1$. The general form of quadratic module could still be employed; the computation would simply transfer during the first iteration only, while the c coefficients are being determined, to a different procedure for the computation of these coefficients.

In addition to the quadratic-transfer function, there are other commonly encountered forms where the module approach might be employed effectively. Some examples are listed in Table 3-5, along with the time relations and associated coefficients used for progressing from one iteration interval to the next. Either a single-pass procedure, such as Q1a-1 or Q1a-2, or a multipass procedure, such as Q4a-1 or Q4a-2, might be employed in connection with the modules that are listed in Table 3-5.

TABLE 3-5a

---

6. Details of the quadratic-lag module:

$$\frac{y(s)}{x(s)} = \frac{D}{As^2 + Bs + C}$$

Extablish $G = D/C$

$$\omega_n = \sqrt{C/A}$$
$$\zeta = B/2A\omega_n$$

a. The oscillatory case   Determine $\sqrt{1 - \zeta^2}$
   $\zeta < 1$

$$\sigma = -\zeta\omega_n$$
$$\omega = \omega_n\sqrt{1 - \zeta^2}$$

Then employ relations (3-51).

b. The critically damped case
   $\zeta = 1$

$$c_1 = -\omega_n^2 \Delta t \exp(-\omega_n \Delta t)$$
$$c_2 = \exp(-\omega_n \Delta t)(1 - \omega_n \Delta t)$$
$$c_3 = -c_1 G$$
$$c_4 = G(1 - c_5)$$
$$c_5 = \exp(-\omega_n \Delta t)(1 + \omega_n \Delta t)$$
$$c_6 = \exp(-\omega_n \Delta t) \Delta t$$
$$c_8 = [\Delta t - 2/\omega_n + \exp(-\omega_n \Delta t)(2/\omega_n + \Delta t)]G$$

c. The overdamped case   Establish $\tau_1 = (\zeta + \sqrt{\zeta^2 - 1})/\omega_n$
   $\zeta > 1$ $\tau_2 = (\zeta - \sqrt{\zeta^2 - 1})/\omega_n$

Then

$$c_1 = [\exp(-\Delta t/\tau_2) - \exp(-\Delta t/\tau_2)]/(\tau_1 - \tau_2)$$
$$c_2 = [\tau_1 \exp(-\Delta t/\tau_2) - \tau_2 \exp(-\Delta t/\tau_1)]/(\tau_1 - \tau_2)$$
$$c_3 = -Gc_1$$
$$c_4 = G(1 - c_5)$$
$$c_5 = [\tau_1 \exp(-\Delta t/\tau_1) - \tau_2 \exp(-\Delta t/\tau_2)]/(\tau_1 - \tau_2)$$
$$c_6 = -\tau_1\tau_2 c_1$$
$$c_8 = G\{\Delta t - \tau_1 - \tau_2 + [\tau_1^2 \exp(-\Delta t/\tau_1)$$
$$- \tau_2^2 \exp(-\Delta t/\tau_2)]/(\tau_1 - \tau_2)\}$$

3-22   Use of the Module Approach to Handle Short Time Lags

Let the situation illustrated by the block diagram of Figure 3-26 be considered. If the ordinary procedures of numerical integration are employed, the size of the iteration interval Δt would be dictated by the shortest time constant of 0.01 sec; in general, Δt would have to be considerably shorter than this value even with one of the more sophisticated methods, such as Runge–Kutta. On the other hand, the long time constant of 10 sec, also appearing in the dynamics of the problem, would result in a long settling time, and hence there would be interest in the response for an interval that was considerably longer than this latter value (e.g., 100 sec). The net result would be that many iterations would be required; the execution time of what should be a simple problem would be long and the cost high.

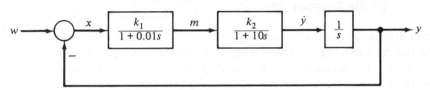

FIGURE 3-26

The module approach just described could reduce the execution time for handling such a simulation problem while permitting some specified accuracy of computation of all variables of interest including that which varies most rapidly (m). Different module approaches could be employed. One technique would be to represent the first block by the single time-lag module, item 1 of Table 3-5. Another would be to combine the first two blocks into a quadratic transfer function. Then situation 6 of Table 3-5 would apply. Referring to the extension of this table, Table 3-5a, the overdamped case would be the one applicable. The gain G would be simply $k_1 k_2$; τ_1 would be 10 sec and τ_2 would be 0.01 sec. By employing either module technique, much larger iteration intervals would be permissible than if ordinary numerical integration were used; the reduction of required execution time would be substantial.

Still other module techniques could be used, of course, to handle the type of simulation problem illustrated by Figure 3-26. All the blocks could be combined into a single module, eliminating the necessity of a separate integration. This would require a third-order module beyond the scope of the methods listed in Table 3-5. Its construction should be obvious, however, in view of the techniques already described.

The ultimate limit of the module approach is a single module representing the analytically determined response of the entire system. When feasible, this is, of course, the practical thing to do. When the simulation procedure is carried out to this extreme, the model apprach no longer is employed. Most systems requiring simulation will be too complicated or will involve nonlinear elements, so this analytic approach will not be possible. Furthermore, after a simulation model has been established for a given system, it will often be necessary to add nonlinear effects as afterthoughts. Too-extensive use of the module approach (which is based on linear relationships between the elements involved) "freezes out" such a possibility. In summary, *when* the module approach is practical, as in the example illustrated by Figure 3-26, it will permit a substantial reduction of execution time and computation expense.

3-23   Establishing the Necessary Size of the Iteration Interval

It is difficult to predict in advance the size of the iteration interval that will be required to achieve a given degree of accuracy in a simulation problem. In theory, the necessary size of the interval could be determined for linear problems by an analysis in the z-transform domain; in practice such a procedure would be exceedingly cumbersome for all except the most trivially simple problems. In practice, trial-and-error methods are necessary. These preferably are conducted during short but typical runs.

With some of the standardized module techniques, such as IBM 360 CSMP, optional means are often provided for having the interval Δt adjusted automatically, iteration by iteration, so that given accuracy requirements will be met. This is often done by employing two different integration techniques that will tend to produce complementary errors and then using the difference between the results produced as a measure of the computation error; the interval is reduced (but always to some integer submultiple of the printout interval) until the error specification is met.

One practical method for selecting Δt to meet given error specifications is based upon the assumption that the error caused by the use of finite intervals will converge to zero as the interval itself is reduced to zero. It should be noted, however, that the error itself cannot be measured directly because of a lack of knowledge of what the correct results should be (Only in the most trivially simple simulation problems is a computation of the correct results practical.)

It first is necessary to establish the criterion by which error is to be described. One of the most convenient, and also most realistic, is the rms error. If the value of the variable of interest, say y, is designated as y_i when it is computed at the ith iterative interval, as contrasted with the correct value y_{c_i}, the error at the ith iteration is then

$$e_i = y_{c_i} - y_i \qquad (3\text{-}56)$$

The rms error, for a total of n iterations over the trial run, would then be

$$e_{\text{rms}} = \sqrt{\frac{\sum_{i=1}^{n} e_i^2}{n}} \qquad (3\text{-}57)$$

Such an rms-error criterion places particularly heavy penalties on large transient errors.

It is not possible to employ relation (3-56) and (3-57) directly because of the lack of knowledge of what the correct value y_c is. It is, however, possible to complete the test simulation run more than once, first with $\Delta t = t_1$ and then with $\Delta t = t_2$. The computed values of the variables of interest resulting from each of these computations are designated as y_1 and y_2, respectively. If Δt_1 and Δt_2 are related in such a way that some of the iteration intervals occur at the same value of t, the values of y_1 and y_2 may then be compared.

For example, if $\Delta t_2 = \frac{1}{2}\Delta t_1$, then y_1 and y_2 may be compared during every Δt_1 iteration (every other Δt_2 iteration). The differences between the computed values for each ith Δt_1 iteration are then observed; i.e.,

$$\Delta y_i = y_{1_i} - y_{2_i} \qquad (3\text{-}58)$$

Then the rms value of y_i is computed; i.e.,

$$\Delta y_{\text{rms}} = \sqrt{\frac{\sum_{i=1}^{n} (\Delta y_i)^2}{n}} \qquad (3\text{-}59)$$

The *basic* assumption is then made that

$$e_{1_{\text{rms}}} < \Delta y_{\text{rms}} \qquad (3\text{-}60)$$

where $e_{1_{\text{rms}}}$ is the rms error that would result if the larger interval, Δt_1, were employed.

The above assumption can be established by a statistical analysis that will not be described here. This analysis is, in turn, however, dependent on a number of additional assumptions concerning the absence of cross-correlation between the computation errors caused by successive trial runs. The best justification for the assumption stated by relation (3-60) is that it has applied for all test cases when it was tried (test cases where it was possible to determine y_c exactly).

If the *specified* rms error is designated as e_{sp}, the required condition that

$$e_{\text{rms}} \leq e_{\text{sp}} \qquad (3\text{-}61)$$

will be met provided that

$$y_{\text{rms}} \leq e_{\text{sp}} \qquad (3\text{-}62)$$

and the larger iteration interval that was employed, Δt_1, can be used in the simulation runs with the accuracy requirements being met.

The size of the iteration interval Δt is also restricted in the sense that it must be equal to $\Delta t_{pt}/k$, where Δt_{pt} is the required printout interval at which results will be recorded or stored and k is any integer. The most effective procedure for establishing the minimum permissible value of k that will meet the error criterion of relation (3-60) consists of trying, progressively, values of k equal to 1, 2, 4, 8, etc. (i.e., values of k equal to 2^n, where n is the number of trial-simulation runs made after the first, where Δt was set equal to Δt_{pt}). If the criterion should be met on the nth trial, it will then be known that the minimum permissible value of the divisor k will lie between 2^{n-2} and 2^{n-1}. The range of integers lying between these values might be subdivided into, say, 10 equal parts to establish the next range of trial values.

Suppose, for example, that 10 trials were made following the first (where $k = 1$) before the error criterion is met. The last value of k employed would then be 2^{10} or 1024 (i.e., Δt was $\Delta t_{pt}/1024$). The minimum permissible value of k lies between 2^8 and 2^9, or between 256 and 512. This range would then be divided into roughly 10 equal parts of integer size (i.e., Δk is 256/10 rounded off, or $\Delta k = 26$). Hence the effects of values of k equal to 282, 308, 334, 360, etc., would be investigated.

Suppose, in the above example, that it is found that the error criterion is met again when y_1 is based on $\Delta t = \Delta t_{pt}/334$ and y_2 on $\Delta t = \Delta t_{pt}/360$. The value of k equal to 334 would then be considered adequate and Δt would be so selected, as $\Delta t_{pt}/334$. The minimum permissible value of k could be determined still more closely to exactly the lowest permissible integer, but normally there would be little point in continuing the search that far.

In some instances it fortunately may be found that the error criterion of relation (3-62) is met the first time it is tested (when $k = 1$). Under these circumstances, Δt would be set equal to the printout interval Δt_{pt}.

Suggested Problems

3-1. A system to be simulated is described in block-diagram form in Figure P3-1. Draw block diagrams expressed in terms of the $\mathfrak{z}$ operator to show the computation processes that would take place when each of the methods listed in Section 3-3 is employed in the simulation process.

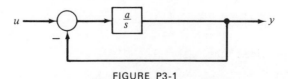

FIGURE P3-1

3-2. Assume that method 1a-1 is to be employed for simulating the system described by Problem 3-1. u is constant and nonzero; y initially is zero. Use the z transform to obtain an expression for $y(n)$ and then for $y(t)$ (valid, of course, only when $t = n \, \Delta t$) that would result with this method for any given choice of iteration interval Δt. Compare this with the correct result, $y_i(t)$, and comment on the relationship of the computation error to the size of the interval Δt.

3-3. It has already been stated that method 1a-2 will result in an unstable computation response when applied to many simulation problems involving feedback. Show that this will be the case when this method is applied to Problem 3-1, using either the $\mathfrak{z}$ operator or the z transform.

3-4. Repeat Problem 3-3, this time with integration method 1b-2.

3-5. Repeat Problem 3-2, this time with integration method 2a-1.

3-6.

(a) The system represented in Figure P3-6a is a positional-control system. It is to be simulated by digital means. Prepare a program for this purpose which can employ any of the following numerical methods of integration by calling the appropriate subroutine: (1) method 1a-1, (2) method 1b-1, (3) method 2a-1, (4) method 4a-1.

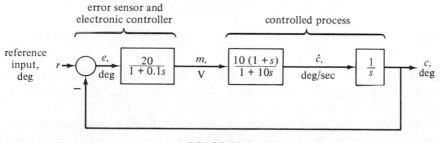

FIGURE P3-6a

(b) The reference input in this problem, r, is assumed to follow the time relationship illustrated in Figure P3-6b. The response is of interest for

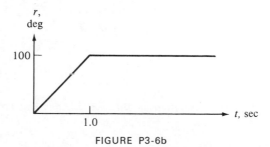

FIGURE P3-6b

$t = 1$ to $t = 20$ sec. Assume initial conditions of rest. A printout of response is desired every second.

Execute the program of part (a) on this basis. (This assumes that sub-programs for the various methods of numerical integration have been pre-pared.) First use method 4a-1 with $\Delta t = 0.01$ sec. The results thus obtained may be considered as substantially correct and can be used as the basis of comparison (as y_c) with the runs to follow. Then determine for each of the methods of integration proposed the required Δt and execution time to achieve an accuracy of roughly 1 per cent in the determination of c. (1 per cent accuracy means 1 per cent of the 100 deg change, or ± 1.0 deg.)

3-7. Repeat Problem 3-6, now using the simple lag module, item 1 of Table 3-5, to represent the transfer function

$$\frac{20}{1 + 0.1s}$$

Compare the required Δt and execution time with those observed in Problem 3-6.

3-8. Design a single module (i.e., add to Table 3-5) that could represent the combination of the first two transfer blocks in the block diagram of Problem 3-6, i.e.,

$$\frac{200(1 + s)}{(1 + 0.1s)(1 + 10s)}$$

3-9. Repeat Problem 3-6, now using the module just designed in the preceding problem.

3-10. As a later study concerning the system of Problem 3-6, the limiting of the signal designated as m to some maximum value will have to be considered. This can be represented in the block diagram by inserting Figure P3-10 in the signal path involving m. We are not being asked to simulate this now. However, with this future problem kept in mind, what restrictions are placed on the module approaches suggested in Problems 3-7 and 3-9?

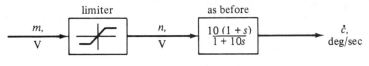

FIGURE P3-10

References

1. W. E. Milne, *Numerical Solution of Differential Equations* (New York: John Wiley & Sons, Inc., 1953).

2. R. W. Hamming, *Numerical Methods for Scientists and Engineers* (New York: McGraw-Hill, Inc., 1966).

3. H. R. Martens, A Comparative Study of Digital Integration Methods *Simulation*, Vol. VII (Feb. 1969), 87–96.

4. M. L. James, G. M. Smith, J. C. Wolford, *Applied Numerical Methods for Digital Computation with Fortran* (Scranton, Penn.: International Textbook Co., 1967).

5. J. R. Ragazzini and L. A. Zadeh, The Analysis of Sampled-Data Systems *Transactions of the AIEE*, Vol. LXXI, Part II (Applications and Industry), (1952), 225–232.

Appendix 3A:
Introduction to the z Transform

When dealing with continuous linear functions of time, it is frequently convenient to work in terms of the Laplace transform of the time function rather than with an operational form based on the operator, $p = d/dt$. $F(s)$ will be described as the Laplace transform of the function $f(t)$ (i.e., $F(s) = \mathcal{L}[f(t)]$) when

$$F(s) = \int_0^\infty f(t)e^{-st}\,dt \qquad (3A\text{-}1)$$

with appropriate restrictions placed on $f(t)$ and the range of s to guarantee convergence of this complex integral).

It then is found that when a differential equation in t is expressed in terms of its Laplace transform, the variable s appears in the transformed equation in the same manner as the operator p would have appeared with the operational approach, except that *additional* terms also appear to account, automatically, for the initial condition. For example, consider the differential equation

$$a\frac{d^2y}{dt^2} + b\frac{dy}{dt} + cy = 0 \qquad \text{with } y(0) \text{ and } \dot{y}(0) \text{ given}$$

The operational version of this equation is

$$(ap^2 + bp + c)y = 0$$

Solutions for $y = y(t)$ based on the operational approach yield terms with

142

unknown coefficients; it is necessary to insert these initial conditions into the problem to solve for these coefficients. On the other hand, the Laplace transform of the equation is

$$(as^2 + bs + c)Y(s) = (as + b)y(0) + a\dot{y}(0)$$

The effects of the initial conditions are now included. The characteristic equation is, however, the same with either method and is

$$(ap^2 + bp + c) = 0 \quad \text{or} \quad (as^2 + bs + c) = 0$$

In either event, the roots (poles of the y response function) are the same.

When a continuous function $f(t)$ is changed to a discrete form, where it is evaluated at only discrete sampling instants spaced by a constant interval Δt, it will be described as $f^*(t)$. It has significance only when $t = n\,\Delta t$, where n is an integer (i.e., only values of $f(n) = f(n\,\Delta t)$ are known). This *sampled* version of $f(t)$, or $f^*(t)$ is considered most conveniently as a train of impulses (Dirac functions). That is,

$$f^*(t) = f(0)\delta(t) + f(1)\delta(t - \Delta t) + f(2)\delta(t - 2\,\Delta t) + \cdots$$
$$+ f(n)\delta(t - n\,\Delta t)$$

or

$$f^*(t) = \sum_{n=0}^{\infty} f(n)\delta(t - n\,\Delta t) \tag{3A-2}$$

The Laplace transform of $f^*(t)$ then is

$$F^*(s) = \mathcal{L}f^*(t) = \mathcal{L} \sum_{n=0}^{\infty} f(n)\delta(t - n\,\Delta t)$$

$$= \sum_{n=0}^{\infty} f(n)\mathcal{L}[\delta(t - n\,\Delta t)]$$

or

$$F^*(s) = \sum_{n=0}^{\infty} f(n)e^{-n\Delta ts} \tag{3A-3}$$

The variable s appears in such a transform only within the exponent $(-n\,\Delta ts)$. It, therefore, is convenient to make the substitution

$$z = e^{\Delta ts} \tag{3A-4}$$

and $F^*(s)$ now becomes a new function of z, called simply $F(z)$, and equal to

$$F(z) = \sum_{n=0}^{\infty} f(n)z^{-n} \tag{3A-5}$$

This is called the z *transform* of $f(n)$. In reiteration, it is simply the Laplace transform of the sampled version of $f(t)$ [i.e., $f^*(t)$, with the substitution made that is expressed in relation (3A-4)].

Construction of a table of z transforms is often quite simple. Suppose, for example, that $f(t) = K = $ constant. Then

$$F(z) = \sum_{n=0}^{\infty} Kz^{-n} = K\left(1 + \frac{1}{z} + \frac{1}{z^2} + \frac{1}{z^3} + \cdots\right) = K\frac{z}{z-1} \qquad (3A\text{-}6)$$

The conversion to a closed form is not always as simple as in the above example. Another very useful case is when $f(n) = Ke^{an}$. Then, from relation (3a-5),

$$F(z) = \sum_{n=0}^{\infty} Ke^{an}z^{-n} = K\sum_{n=0}^{\infty} \frac{1}{(ze^{-a})^n}$$

$$= K\left[\frac{1}{ze^{-a}} + \frac{1}{(ze^{-a})^2} + \frac{1}{(ze^{-a})^3} + \cdots\right]$$

$$= K\frac{ze^{-a}}{ze^{-a} - 1}$$

or

$$F(z) = K\frac{z}{z - e^a} \qquad (3A\text{-}7)$$

It should be noted that when $f(n) = Ke^{an}$, as in the above example, then, since $n = t/\Delta t$,

$$f(t) \times Ke^{(a/\Delta t)t} = Ke^{bt} \qquad \text{where } b = a/\Delta t \qquad (3A\text{-}8)$$

A table of transforms may be built up in this manner. Transforms of sinusoidal functions can be established from relation (3A-7) with a becoming imaginary. Such a resulting tables of transforms is shown as Table 3A-1. More complete tables are available in textbooks that treat this subject in more detail, but the list given here should be adequate for the types of problems that are discussed in this chapter.

   Just as with the Laplace transform, there is a corresponding inversion relationship for the z transform that permits the obtaining of $f(n)$ directly from $F(z)$. However, as with the Laplace transform, this relationship involves integration in the complex plane. Hence this procedure generally is avoided; instead, implicit methods are used based on partial fraction expansions. Use may then be made of the transform table, particularly transform pairs (1), (2), (5), (6), and (7).

   When direct use of the table is not possible, to obtain the inverse transform of more complicated expressions involving the ratio of polynomials of z, use may be made of partial fraction expansions, just as is done to find inverse Laplace transforms. As an example of this, let it be supposed that transform pair (10) of Table 3A-1 was not furnished, and it was desired to find the inverse transform of

$$F(z) = \frac{z}{(z - f)(z - g)}$$

TABLE 3A-1   Table of z Transforms

$f(n)$	$f(t)$	$F(z)$
(1) 1 or $u(n)$	1 or $u(t)$	$\dfrac{z}{z-1}$
(2) e^{an}	e^{bt}, where $b = \dfrac{a}{\Delta t}$	$\dfrac{z}{z-e^a}$
(3) $\cos \beta n$	$\cos \omega t$, where $\omega = \dfrac{\beta}{\Delta t}$	$\dfrac{z(z-\cos \beta)}{z^2 - 2z \cos \beta + 1}$
(4) $\sin \beta n$	$\sin \omega t$, where $\omega = \dfrac{\beta}{\Delta t}$	$\dfrac{z \sin \beta}{z^2 - 2z \cos \beta + 1}$
(5) n or $nu(n)$	ct or $ctu(t)$, where $c = \dfrac{1}{\Delta t}$	$\dfrac{z}{(z-1)^2}$
(6) n^2 or $n^2 u(n)$	ct^2 or $ct^2 u(t)$, where $c = \dfrac{1}{(\Delta t)^2}$	$\dfrac{z(z+1)}{(z-1)^3}$
(7) ne^{an}	cte^{bt}, where $c = \dfrac{1}{\Delta t}$, $b = \dfrac{a}{\Delta t}$	$\dfrac{e^a z}{(z-e^a)^2}$
(8) $e^{an} \sin \beta n$	$e^{bt} \cos \omega t$, where $b = \dfrac{a}{\Delta t}$, $\omega = \dfrac{\beta}{\Delta t}$	$\dfrac{z e^a \sin \beta}{z^2 - 2z e^a \cos \beta + 1}$
(9) $e^{an} \cos \beta n$	$e^{bt} \sin \omega t$, where $b = \dfrac{a}{\Delta t}$, $\omega = \dfrac{\beta}{\Delta t}$	$\dfrac{z(z - e^a \cos \beta)}{z^2 - 2z e^a \cos \beta + 1}$
(10) $\dfrac{e^{a_1 n} - e^{a_2 n}}{e^{a_1} - e^{a_2}}$	$\dfrac{e^{b_1 t} - e^{b_2 t}}{e^{a_1} - e^{a_2}}$, where $b_1 = \dfrac{a_1}{\Delta t}$, $b_2 = \dfrac{a_2}{\Delta t}$	$\dfrac{z}{(z - e^{a_1})(z - e^{a_2})}$

The partial fraction expansion of this expression would be

$$F(z) = k_f \frac{z}{z-f} + k_g \frac{z}{z-g}$$

If k_f and k_g are evaluated, use can then be made of transform pair (2) of the table to find the inverse transform $f(n)$. The coefficients of the partial fraction expansion, k_f and k_g, may be found in a manner somewhat similar to that used for Laplace transforms:

$$k_f = \left[\frac{z-f}{z} F(z) \right]_{z \to f} = \left[\frac{1}{z-g} \right]_{z \to f} = \frac{1}{f-g}$$

$$k_g = \left[\frac{z-g}{z} F(z) \right]_{z \to g} = \left[\frac{1}{z-f} \right]_{z \to g} = -\frac{1}{f-g}$$

From transform pair (2), the term $z/(z-f)$ corresponds to the transform $z/(z - e^a)$, if e^a is considered equivalent to f. Hence, for this term alone, $f(n)$ would be $k_f f^n$. Similarly, for the second term in the expression for $F(z)$, $f(n)$ would be $k_g g^n$. If the values of the coefficients k_f and k_g, as just determined, are then substituted, the complete inverse transform is

$$f(n) = \frac{f^n - g^n}{f - g}$$

Naturally, since transform pair (10) was available in the table, this inverse transform could have been evaluated without such a partial fraction expansion.

The significance of the pole locations of a z transform is also of interest. This has already been discussed to some extent in Section 3-12. The general considerations concerning this may be summarized by comparing the corresponding s and z planes with the connecting relation (3A-4) kept in mind.

Complex pole locations in the s plane are described most conveniently in terms of the undamped natural frequency ω_n and damping ratio ζ. The conjugate pair of poles will then be located at

$$s = -\zeta\omega_n \pm j\omega_n\sqrt{1 - \zeta^2} \tag{3A-9}$$

This is shown in Figure 3A-1a. From relation (3A-4), the corresponding z-plane locations of these poles are

$$z = e^{s\,\Delta t}$$
$$= \exp\left(-\zeta\omega_n\,\Delta t\right)\exp\left(\pm j\omega_n\,\Delta t\,\sqrt{1 - \zeta^2}\right) \tag{3A-10}$$

In other words, these poles will be located at a radius from the origin

$$|z| = \exp\left(-\zeta\omega_n\,\Delta t\right) \tag{3A-11}$$

and will be on the unit circle for zero damping, within it for positive damping, and outside it for negative damping (a divergent process). The poles will lie on radial lines forming the angles $\pm v$ with the positive real axis, where

$$v = \omega_n\,\Delta t\,\sqrt{1 - \zeta^2} \tag{3A-12}$$

This is shown in Figure 3A-1b. The discussion of Section 3-12 illustrates how this interpretation may be used to determine the frequency of any oscillatory computation response that might result and the extent to which it is damped (is convergent).

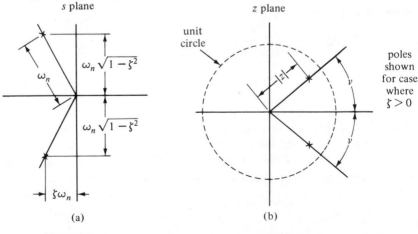

(a)   (b)

FIGURE 3A-1a   FIGURE 3A-1b

To apply the z transform to the difference equations that describe the effects of iterative computation procedures, use is made of the shifting theorem. If Z is used to represent the process of z transformation, [i.e., if $Z[f(n)] = F(z)$, then

$$Z[f(n + 1)] = zF(z) - zf(0) \qquad (3A\text{-}13)$$

and

$$Z[f(n + 2)] = z^2F(z) - z^2f(0) - zf(1) \qquad (3A\text{-}14)$$

etc. The above relations were presented as relations (3-27). Their proof is fairly simple. Restating relation (3A-5),

$$F(z) = \sum_{n=0}^{\infty} f(n)z^{-n}$$

If a new integer variable, $k = n - 1$, is now substituted, this becomes

$$
\begin{aligned}
F(z) &= \sum_{k=-1}^{\infty} f(k + 1)z^{-(k+1)} \\
&= [f(k + 1)z^{-(k+1)}]_{k=-1} + z^{-1} \sum_{k=0}^{\infty} f(k + 1)z^{-k} \\
&= f(0) + z^{-1} \sum_{k=0}^{\infty} f(k + 1)z^{-k}
\end{aligned}
$$

Multiplying all terms by z and rearranging yield the result

$$\sum_{k=0}^{\infty} f(k + 1)z^{-k} = zF(z) - zf(0)$$

The symbol n may now be substituted for k in the above without changing the validity of that statement. Then

$$\sum_{n=0}^{\infty} f(n + 1)z^{-n} = zF(z) - zf(0)$$

However, from (3A-4),

$$Z[f(n + 1)] = \sum_{n=0}^{\infty} f(n + 1)z^{-n}$$

If the above relation and that preceding are combined, relation (3A-9) is proved. Relation (3A-10) may also be proved by an extension of the above procedure.

Nonlinear Operations with Analog Computers 4

4-1 General Comments

The analog-computer elements that have been described thus far included summer, integrator, and inverter types of amplifiers, potentiometers, and various forms of auxiliary output equipment. As a result, the situations that could be simulated with that equipment have been limited to those describable by linear differential equations (i.e., those where analytic solutions are always possible). The range of application of analog-computer simulation is enhanced greatly by the addition of elements that allow various types of nonlinear operations to be performed. The most basic of these elements will be described in this chapter.

4-2 Diodes

In an analog computer-program diagram, the conventional circuit symbol shown in Figure 4-1 is used to represent a diode element. An *ideal diode* is one that possesses zero resistance to current flowing from the anode to the cathode and infinite resistance to inverse current flowing in the opposite direction. Therefore, it would have a volt–ampere characteristic that appears as shown in Figure 4-2. Actual diodes used in analog computers normally

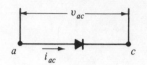

a represents anode
c represents cathode

FIGURE 4-1

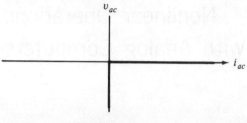

FIGURE 4-2

are of the high-vacuum (becoming obsolete) or the semiconductor type. (Zener diodes represent a special case to be considered separately.) They are never ideal but approach being so as their quality (and cost) increases. Their volt–ampere characteristics might appear as shown in Figure 4-3. Actual diodes, therefore, do at least tend to favor strongly the flow of current in one direction and to oppose it in the other.

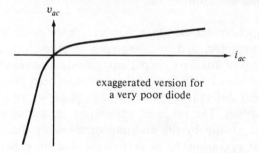

exaggerated version for
a very poor diode

FIGURE 4-3

Separate individual diodes are often available in analog computers, either built in with the terminals brought out for connection as desired to other elements, or as loose elements attached to leads for direct insertion into the patchboard. Such individual diodes are used to construct a number of special-purpose circuits and to simulate various nonlinear situations. These applications include the generation of various nonlinear continuous functions, to be discussed in this chapter, and also the simulation of various discontinuous effects, to be discussed in Chapter 6.

Circuits that employ diodes to produce nonlinear but continuous functions of one variable are called *diode function generators*. These may be subdivided into three categories:

1. Special function-generator circuits patched up by the person establishing the program.
2. Special-purpose function generators used to develop some specific commonly used functions. These are prefabricated.
3. Adjustable general-purpose diode function generators, also prefabricated.

4-3 Diode Limitations—The Ideal Diode Circuit

Figure 4-3 showed (in exaggerated form) the volt–ampere characteristics of an actual, and hence imperfect, diode. These imperfections are caused by the fact that even a high-quality diode is not a perfect conductor in its forward direction nor a perfect nonconductor in its backward or inverse direction.

These imperfections may be reduced markedly by the ideal diode circuit shown in Figure 4-4. The circuit employs two actual diodes in con-

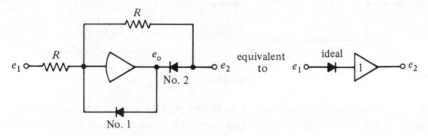

FIGURE 4-4

nection with the components of a normal inverter circuit. When input voltage e_1 is negative, diode 1 conducts, resulting in such effective negative feedback about the operational amplifier that negligible output voltage e_o results. Diode 2, therefore, is cut off and e_2 is zero. As a result of this reinforcing action of the two diodes employed in the circuit, a very sharp cutoff characteristic is achieved whenever e_o is negative.

On the other hand, whenever e_1 is positive, diode 1 is cut off and 2 conducts, resulting in e_o being an almost perfect version of $-e_1$. The result is a characteristic that approaches much more closely the ideal characteristics shown in Figure 4-2. The term ideal diode circuit is, of course, somewhat of a misnomer; the diode performance resulting is not completely ideal, but it is far closer to being ideal than would be possible with a single diode alone, even one of high quality. This convenient and useful technique presents one example of why the astute analog programmer should have some rudimentary knowledge of the electronic principles involved. Occasions may well arise when such a circuit is necessary but, in many modern computers, will not be available in an already packaged form. It must be arranged by the programmer.

4-4   Example of a Simple Diode Function Generator—Absolute-Value Circuits

The simplest nonlinear function to be generated is the absolute-value function $y = |x|$; the simplicity of the arrangement generally used for accomplishing this is such that the circuit scarcely rates the complexity implied in the term diode function generator. Such a circuit is shown in Figure 4-5; its method

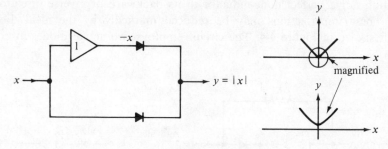

FIGURE 4-5

of operation is self-explanatory. The lower plot of y versus x illustrates the effect of the diode's deviation from being truly ideal. Such absolute-value circuits are generally constructed directly on the patchboard.

The imperfections shown in the y versus x plot of Figure 4-5 can be reduced significantly by substituting an ideal diode circuit for the simple diode circuit shown in that diagram. After some modifications to reduce the number of elements required, this circuit appears as in Figure 4-6. In the circuit of Figure 4-6, when $x < 0$, the ideal diode circuit is cut off and the only signal transmitted is through the upper input connection to the summer;

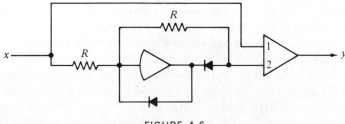

FIGURE 4-6

the summer then serves as a simple inverter and $y = -x$, or $|x|$. When $x > 0$, the ideal diode conducts, applying $-x$ to the summer with a gain of two. Hence the output is $-x - 2(-x) = x = |x|$. In any event, the output always is $|x|$ and an absolute-value circuit has been implemented that is capable of more precise operation than is the simpler circuit of Figure 4-5.

4-5   Generation of Continuous Functions

The preceding example represented a function that was in itself continuous, but which was discontinuous in its slope. (Functions that are in themselves discontinuous, involving abrupt jumps in value, are developed by methods discussed in Chapter 6.) Even analytic functions (i.e., those involving no discontinuities in the function itself or in its derivatives) are developed by techniques generally similar to that shown in Figure 4-5 (i.e., the function is divided into approximate *straight-line segments*). The intersection points at the junctions of these segments are referred to as *breakpoints*. The function is then represented in a *piecewise linear* fashion. In other words, the analog procedure used is equivalent to the digital procedure of table "look-up" with subsequent linear interpolation.

Figure 4-7 shows an example of a crude straight-line approximation of the cosine relationship over the range of x from $-\pi$ to $+\pi$ radians. In terms of machine variables, the following scale factors are employed as an example (applicable to 100 V machines):

$$y = 0.01y_m \qquad \text{and} \qquad x = 0.01\pi x_m$$

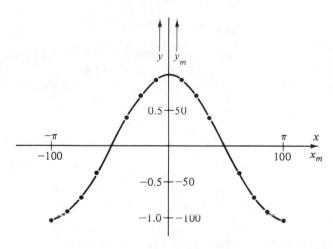

FIGURE 4-7

Hence the relationship becomes $y_m = 100 \cos (\pi x_m/100)$. A tabulation is prepared corresponding to the breakpoints in Figure 4-7, which is shown here as Table 4-1. (It should be realized that Figure 4-7 is not intended to represent a good approximation; in practice more segments would be required. The example is simply for the purpose of illustrating the principle of the diode function generator.)

In Table 4-1 it may be noted that first the range of positive x_m is covered,

TABLE 4-1

Breakpoints x_m	Correct y_m	Adjusted[1] y_m	Δx_m	Δy_m	$\dfrac{\Delta y_m}{\Delta x_m}$	$\Delta\left(\dfrac{\Delta y_m}{\Delta x_m}\right)$	Comment
0	100.0	100.0				−0.608	100 V parallax
			12.5	−7.6	−0.608		Constant negative slope
12.5	92.4	92.4				−1.128	Fourth quadrant
			12.5	−21.7	−1.736		
25.0	70.7	70.7				−0.856	Fourth quadrant
			12.5	−32.4	−2.592		
37.5	38.3	38.3				−0.472	Fourth quadrant
			25.0	−76.6	−3.064		
62.5	−38.3	−38.3				0.472	First quadrant
			12.5	−32.4	−2.592		
75.0	−70.7	−70.7				0.856	First quadrant
			12.5	−21.7	−1.736		
87.5	−92.4	−92.4				1.128	First quadrant
			12.5	−7.6	−0.608		
100.0	−100.0	−100.0					
						−0.608	
0	100.0	100.0				1.212	Third quadrant
			−12.5	−7.6	0.608		
−12.5	92.4	92.4				1.128	Third quadrant
			−12.5	−21.7	1.736		
−25.0	70.7	70.7				0.856	Third quadrant
			−12.5	−32.4	2.592		
−37.5	38.3	38.3				0.472	Third quadrant
			−25.0	−76.6	3.064		
−62.5	−38.3	−38.3				−0.472	Second quadrant
			−12.5	−32.4	2.592		
−75.0	−70.7	−70.7				−0.856	Second quadrant
			−12.5	−21.7	1.736		
−87.5	−92.4	−92.4				−1.128	Second quadrant
			−12.5	−7.6	0.608		
−100.0	−100.0	−100.0					

[1] In this example the correct values of the function and the adjusted values at the breakpoints happen to be the same; hence the two columns are alike. In general, better curve fitting results when this is not the case.

starting from $x_m = 0$. The results from this part of the table indicate that the following procedure should be employed. The steps described are illustrated in Figure 4-8.

(a)   A constant output voltage corresponding to the value of y_m at $x_m = 0$ should be established. This is 100 V and is called the *parallax*.

(b)   A constant slope of -0.608 is then to be added (i.e., $y_m = -0.608x_m$).

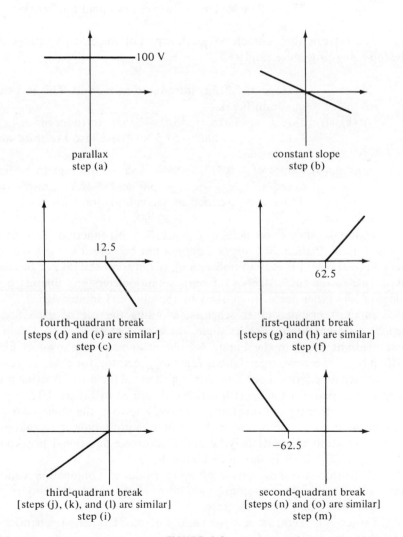

FIGURE 4-8

(c)	A slope of -1.128 is to be added, starting at the $x_m = 12.5$ V breakpoint. The diagram for step (c) shows why this is described as a fourth-quadrant break.
(d), (e)	Slopes of -0.856 and -0.472 are to be introduced at $x_m = 25.0$ and 37.5 V breakpoints, respectively. These also are fourth-quadrant breaks.
(f)	A slope of 0.472 is to be introduced at $x_m = 62.5$ V. This is called a first-quadrant break.
(g), (h)	Slopes of 0.856 and 1.128 are to be introduced at $x_m = 75$ and 87.5 V. These also are first-quadrant breaks.

The table is then completed as shown. For the negative range of x the following procedure results:

(i)	A slope of 1.212 is introduced at $x_m = 0$. This is a third-quadrant break.
(j), (k), (l)	Slopes of $1.128, 0.856, 0.472$ are introduced at $x_m = -12.5, -25.0$, and -37.5 V. These also are third-quadrant breaks.
(m), (n), (o)	Slopes of $-0.472, -0.856$, and -1.128 are to be introduced at $x_m = -62.5, -75.0$, and -87.5 V, respectively. These are described as second-quadrant breaks.

Figure 4-9 shows one method of generating this function. This method is based upon floating *bias supplies*, chosen not because it is the most practical, but because it is easy to understand. (Confusion should not be caused by the use of the circle symbol for both potentiometers and floating power supplies; the latter are distinguished by the plus and minus signs.)

In most practice other schemes, avoiding the use of such floating supplies, are employed. For example, the arrangement used to obtain the first-quadrant break in the Figure 4-9 circuit appears as shown in Figure 4-10; it is called a *series type* of diode function generator, for obvious reasons.

Alternative series-diode methods, which avoid the use of floating power supplies but perform the same function, are shown in Figure 4-11.

Still another type of function generator, known as the *shunt-diode type*, may be used to establish any of the four quadrant type of breakpoints. Additional shunt elements may be added to create additional breakpoints in any quadrant. This is shown in Figure 4-12.

Still other methods consist of using diodes in conjunction with the feedback elements of a summing amplifier. Here, again, the diodes may be used in the shunt or series sense.

In general, there are a large variety of diode function-generator circuits that may be invented to solve specific problems. Usually such circuits

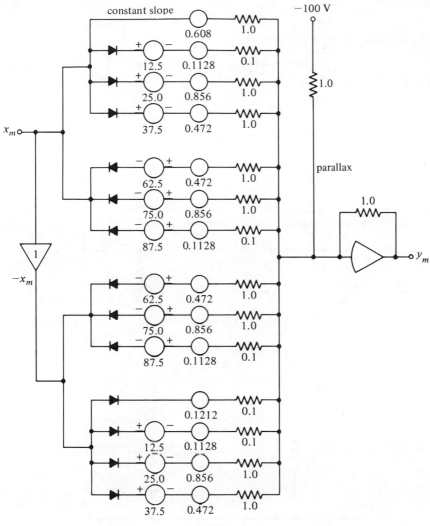

FIGURE 4-9

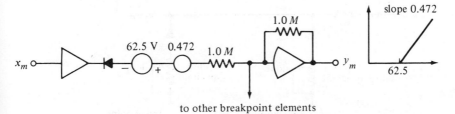

FIGURE 4-10

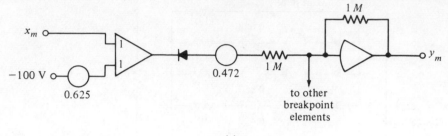

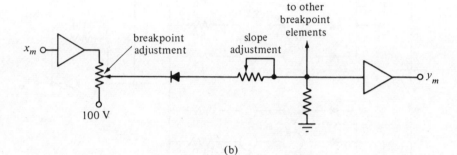

(b)

FIGURE 4-11

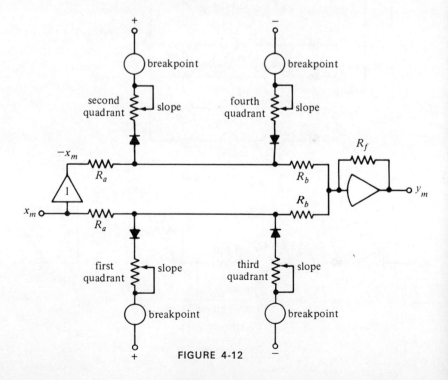

FIGURE 4-12

are planned by the person doing the programming when only a few break-points are needed. For a situation involving many breakpoints, it is far easier to use a prefabricated function generator. These are either special-purpose units to produce specific commonly required functions as shown in Figure 4-13, or general-purpose units where the adjustments must be established manually in order to meet a given relationship.

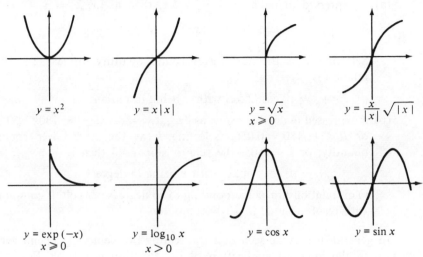

$$y = x^2 \qquad y = x|x| \qquad \begin{array}{c} y = \sqrt{x} \\ x \geqslant 0 \end{array} \qquad y = \frac{x}{|x|}\sqrt{|x|}$$

$$\begin{array}{c} y = \exp(-x) \\ x \geqslant 0 \end{array} \qquad \begin{array}{c} y = \log_{10} x \\ x > 0 \end{array} \qquad y = \cos x \qquad y = \sin x$$

FIGURE 4-13

4-6 Scaling of Function Generators

When generating a desired functional relationship, the same general considerations regarding scaling apply as were considered in Chapter 2. Several examples are given here, as they would be applied to a 10 V computer (V_r = 10 V).

EXAMPLE 1 $y_m = k x_m^2$ with x_m having a voltage range of $\pm V_r$:

$$|y_{m_{max}}| = k(V_r)^2 \leq V_r \qquad \text{or} \qquad k \leq \frac{1}{V_r} = 0.1$$

With k then selected as 0.1, the relationship used is

$$y_m = 0.1 x_m^2$$

EXAMPLE 2 $y_m = k\sqrt{x_m}$ with x_m having a voltage range $0 < x_m < V_r$:

$$|y_{m_{max}}| = k\sqrt{x_{m_{max}}} = k\sqrt{V_r} \leq V_r \qquad \text{or} \qquad k \leq \sqrt{V_r} = 3.16$$

Selecting the next lowest round factor, $k = 2.50$ and

$$y_m = 2.50\sqrt{x_m}$$

EXAMPLE 3 $y = \cos x$ with x ranging from $-\pi$ to $+\pi$ radians. As the maximum magnitude of y will be unity, logical scaling for y is

$$y_m = V_r y = 10y \qquad \text{V}$$

Scaling for x depends upon whether the angle x is being expressed in radians or degrees.

(a) x expressed in radians: if $x_m = kx$, then as $|x_{\max}| = \pi$,

$$|x_{m_{\max}}| = k\pi \leq V_r \qquad \text{or} \qquad k \leq \frac{V_r}{\pi} = 3.18$$

Selecting k as the next lower round quantity, or $k = 2.5$, the relation is

$$y_m = 10 \cos (2.5x) \text{ with } x \text{ being in radians}$$

(b) x expressed in degrees: now, as $|x_{\max}| = 180$, $|x_{m_{\max}}| = 180k \leq V_r$, or $k \leq V_r/180 = 0.056$. Selecting k as the next lower round quantity, or $k = 0.05$, the relationship used then is

$$y_m = 10 \cos (0.05x) \text{ with } x \text{ being in degrees}$$

(This relationship, corresponding to 20 degrees per volt, is common with resolvers used in 10 V computers.)

In general, it may be seen that the scaling problem will depend very much upon the intended application of the function generator. For this reason, there are a limited number of specific functions for which it is practical to provide special purpose fixed function generators. Often it is more convenient to employ an adjustable general purpose unit instead of one that is scaled to meet the specific requirements of the problem being simulated.

4-7   General Purpose Function Generators—Adjustment Procedures

Most modern general purpose computers will be equipped with a sufficient number of general purpose function generators, so that the programmer need never be concerned with constructing arrangements of the type shown in Figures 4-9 to 4-12. He need, instead, merely prepare a listing of slopes and breakpoints, as in Table 4-1, and proceed from there in adjusting a commercial form of general purpose function generator in accordance with the instructions furnished by the manufacturer of that particular unit. Such function generators are designed on the basis of the principles described in Section 4-5. However, an understanding of their principles isn't necessary for their successful use. Nevertheless, such principles will be important later, when the subject of simulating discontinuous functions is discussed in Chapter 6. Hence they were described here. These principles will also be of interest to those concerned with the design of special purpose analog simulators for "permanent" programs, where the use of general purpose units would be unnecessary and wasteful.

Manual adjustment of even the most modern general purpose function generator is a somewhat tedious process, particularly if a high degree of precision is required. More elaborate hybrid installations can avoid this tedium by providing means by which breakpoints and slopes are established automatically from instructions fed to the digital portion of the computer. This may even be combined with a program that establishes optimum slopes and breakpoint locations on the basis of some curve fitting technique, such as that involving the least-mean-square error.

When such elaborate hybrid facilities are not available and manual adjustment of function generators is necessary, a rapid and convenient method exists that is adequate when the accuracy requirements are moderate. (In many simulation problems, the function to be simulated is not known more closely than, say, $\pm 5\%$.) This method is illustrated in Figure 4-14 and involves the use of a cathode-ray oscilloscope. The independent variable x is produced by a *sweep circuit* [i.e., merely an integrator developing the relation $x = kt$ that is operated in the high-speed-repetitive (HRO) mode]. This sweep voltage is applied to both the horizontal plates of the oscilloscope and also to the input terminals of the function generator, where it serves as the test input voltage. The output of the function generator is connected to the vertical plates so that the function being produced may be observed

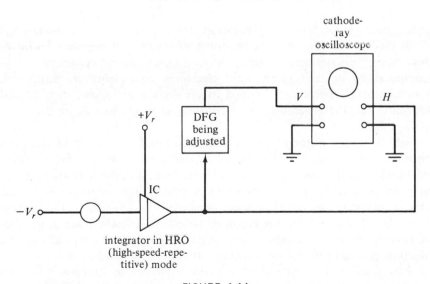

FIGURE 4-14

during the course of its adjustment. This function, so plotted on the oscilloscope screen, is matched against either a template or a pattern drawn on the screen representing the actual function desired. In this manner, adjustment of the function generator's breakpoints and slopes is greatly facilitated. The accuracy of such a procedure depends to a large extent on the size of the oscilloscope screen; one about 20 in. in diameter is most desirable.

The theory of function generators employing diodes is based upon straight-line segments and hence upon linear interpolation. This introduces sharp discontinuities in the functions generated that could, in some instances, cause various extraneous effects in the simulated response of the system being studied. The very imperfections, however, of the actual diodes used prevent such sharp discontinuities from occurring and introduce some curvature at each breakpoint. In other words, the diode imperfections actually constitute an advantage in this respect.

In instances when the curvature thus afforded by diode imperfections is not adequate, additional curvature may be introduced by adding a very high frequency (well beyond the frequency range of interest of the problem being simulated and beyond the frequency range of the output equipment) sinusoidal voltage to the voltage that establishes the segment's breakpoints. This signal is generally introduced into the circuit by means of a transformer and may be used to introduce considerable curvature at the breakpoint when this is desired.

4-8   Other Types of Function Generators

Other methods of function generation are also employed, although the diode method has proved to be the most successful and popular. To introduce sharp discontinuities, or sudden jumps, electromechanical relays (comparators) or their more rapid electronic equivalents are employed. Such comparators will be described in the section to follow; their special application to the generation of discontinuous functions will be discussed in Chapter 6.

Still another method that might be mentioned for reasons of primarily historical interest involves the use of tapped potentiometers. Here, servomechanisms of the type used with electromechanical multipliers are required to position a linear potentiometer to a setting that corresponds to the abscissa value of the function being generated. In addition to the normal movable tap available on an ordinary potentiometer, there are a number of equally spaced fixed taps. These correspond to the breakpoints of the function generator (hence the breakpoints cannot be selected at will). Each of these fixed taps is supplied an adjustable voltage by its own individual potentiometer; this voltage corresponds to the ordinate value desired at each breakpoint. As with diode function generators, a linear interpolation effect occurs within breakpoints. Although this method sounds straightforward and convenient, it is subject to the following disadvantages:

1. The breakpoints are established in the construction and cannot be changed to suit the function being simulated, as they can with diode units.
2. There is a maximum slope limitation because of the limits imposed on the voltage difference permitted between any two adjacent taps.
3. It has the disadvantage of all servomechanism-driven elements in its relatively slow response to changing values of the abscissa.

Another method of function generation involves the use of an XY plotter, employed in other than its usual sense as an output element. Many such units have a curve-following attachment for this purpose. The pen is replaced by a sensing unit, either a pickup coil or a photoelectric scanner. The curve representing the function to be generated may be drawn in various ways, depending on the sensing mechanism used. In some instances a conducting wire or ferromagnetic wire is mounted on the paper following a curve corresponding to the function's relationship; in others the curve is painted on with a conducting paint; in still others, employing photocell scanning methods, a simple India-ink curve is drawn. In all instances the independent variable is used to position the X axis, and the Y position, established by the servomechanism following the curve, is also indicated electrically, this indication serving as the function generator's output. This method of function generation shares with the tapped-potentiometer method the response-speed limitations inherent in all servomechanism-driven devices; as a matter of fact, the servomechanisms used with XY plotters generally tend to be slower (because of the larger masses to be positioned) than those used to position potentiometers.

Still another method of function generation that is especially convenient when the accuracy requirements are moderate (within 2 per cent) are *photoformers*. This is the cathode-ray oscilloscope counterpart of the XY-plotter function-generation technique described above; its application is shown in Figure 4-15. The functional relationship desired is plotted and used as the basis of an opaque mask placed against the screen of a conventional cathode-ray oscilloscope. All areas of the oscilloscope screen above the curve are kept clear while all below are masked. The oscilloscope screen is then covered by a light-tight shield containing a photocell. The photocell output is then connected, as shown in Figure 4-15, through an amplifier to the vertical input terminals of the oscilloscope.

The small bias voltage shown is sufficient to drive the oscilloscope beam to the top of the screen, but, as the mask is uncovered, the photocell

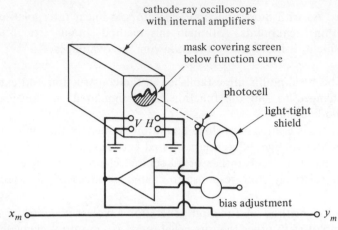

FIGURE 4-15

voltage will tend to drive the beam downward, below the mask. The result is that the beam tends to ride the edge of the mask and follow the curve as the oscilloscope is scanned horizontally by the x_m input voltage. Therefore, the voltage that is applied to the vertical input terminals of the oscilloscope is an indication of y_m.

It may be seen that this method is basically similar to the use of an *XY* plotter as a function generator, just described. It does not, however, have the response-speed limitations of the *XY* plotter because of the negligible inertia of the beam and the other negligible response lags involved. The method is simple and, although specially made photoformers may be purchased, any reasonably high-quality cathode-ray oscilloscope can be converted to a photoformer in any well-equipped electronics laboratory by the addition of a few additional components.

When hybrid (digital–analog) combinations are being employed, the function-generation feature may be assigned to the digital computer. This is especially convenient when the function can be expressed in closed algebraic form. When the function is an empirical one, both analog and digital procedures depend upon a tabulation (segmentation) of the function with suitable interpolation techniques added. When only a small number of segments are required (e.g., less than, typically, 24), the analog-diode function generator may prove to be the most convenient method; on the other hand, for the equivalent of many segments, the digital computer would be preferred.

No mention has been made here of the generation of functions of a random variable. This will be handled as a separate subject when the various problems associated with such variables and the techniques for their various statistical measurements are discussed.

The discussion of function generators, to this point, has been confined to functions of only one variable. Analog methods for generating functions of two variables have been developed, but none of these can claim to be simple. XY plotters have been used for this purpose to produce $z(x, y)$, where z is represented by the height of the surface (generally made of plaster of paris or a similar material) representing the function. Obviously, some sensing method for determining this height is required. Mechanical three-dimensional cams have been used for establishing functions that are not subject to adjustment changes; as a matter of fact, this technique was used in antiaircraft gun directors during World War II long before electronic analog computers were in general use. Similar to the XY-plotter method, the photoformer can be used by employing a variable density mask so that the transmission of the beam, measured in terms of its intensity at the photocell, is an indication of $z(x, y)$. In general, the problem can be simplified if a suitable valid approximation can be made so that

$$z_1 = z_1(x)$$
$$z_2 = z_2(y) \tag{4-1}$$
$$z = k_1 z_1 + k_2 z_2 + k_3 z_1 z_2$$

The last term in the third relation represents the multiplication of machine variables, a process to be discussed later. With such a multiplier, summers, and a combination of ordinary function generators (handling functions of only one variable), a number of functions of two variables can be satisfactorily simulated.

4-9 Comparators

A comparator is a device that may be used for various logical operations; its operation is based upon the algebraic sum of two applied voltages. The simplest (but not necessarily the most satisfactory) type of comparator consists of a conventional electromagnetic relay actuated by summing amplifiers. This is illustrated in Figure 4-16. Because of the diode shown

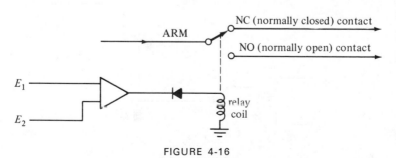

FIGURE 4-16

there, the relay coil is acutated only when $(E_1 + E_2) > 0$. If one of these signals, E_1 or E_2, had previously been inverted, a *comparison* would have been made, establishing which of the signals was algebraically the greater, hence the term *comparator*. Figure 4-16 represents a single-pole relay comparator. In practice a number of poles could be employed, all actuated by the same relay coil.

More modern equipment is apt to employ semiconductor comparators that involve no moving parts and hence are capable of much faster operation. The conventional signal for the comparator is shown in Figure 4-17.

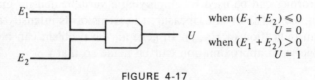

$$E_1$$
$$U$$
when $(E_1 + E_2) \leqslant 0$
$$U = 0$$
when $(E_1 + E_2) > 0$
$$U = 1$$
$$E_2$$

FIGURE 4-17

Here the output U is a logical variable, either one or zero (true or false). U may possess a number of physical forms; for example, it may be some positive voltage for $U = 1$ and some negative voltage for $U = 0$. In Figure 4-16, U would have represented actuation of the relay coil. ($U = 1$ means the coil is actuated and normally open contacts are closed.) The comparator is not necessarily connected to a relay or switch. Its binary output might instead be fed to various binary logic circuits. When it is so connected to a relay, the combination is variously referred to as a relay *comparator* or a *comparator switch*. The general diagram for such a combination is shown in Figure 4-18. The arrangement shown schematically in Figure 4-18 performs the same function as that of Figure 4-16, except that it switches two channels, labeled *a* and *b*, and hence is a two-pole relay comparator.

The numerical designation (13 in the example) is used when a number

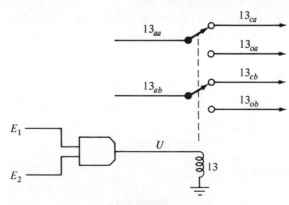

FIGURE 4-18

of such relay comparators are employed in a program and must be separately identified. The subscripts shown are necessary when the comparator and the relay contacts do not appear adjacent in the diagram of the program. The first subscript will be an *a, c,* or *o,* referring respectively to the arm, normally closed, and normally open terminal of the switch. The second sub-

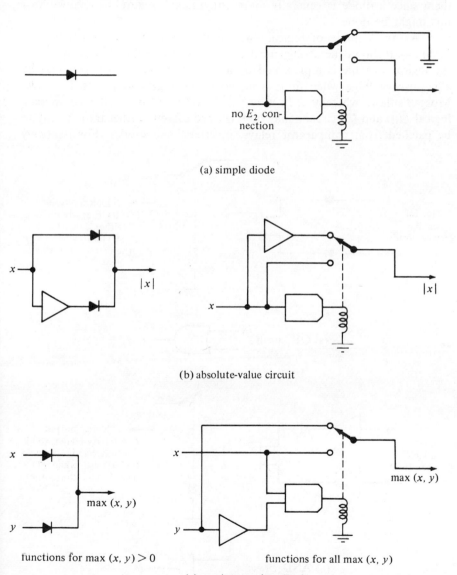

(a) simple diode

(b) absolute-value circuit

(c) maximum-value circuit

FIGURE 4-19

script is used only with a multipole relay and identifies the switching channel involved. This subscript designation is somewhat arbitrary but it has been proposed as the standard convention.

Such comparators have many applications. As mentioned before, they can replace diodes (although there rarely is a reason for so employing them since a diode is generally more convenient). Figure 4-19 shows how this might be done.

As an example of logical operations performed with comparators, Figure 4-20 shows the arrangement for simple AND and OR circuits. Here the logical variable is represented by a positive voltage when *true* and by a negative voltage when *false*. The second arrangement is based on De-Morgan's law, whereby $x \cap y = \overline{x} \cup \overline{y}$. With many analog computers, logical AND and OR circuits may be furnished directly rather than having to be patched from comparator relays, inverters, and diodes. For relatively

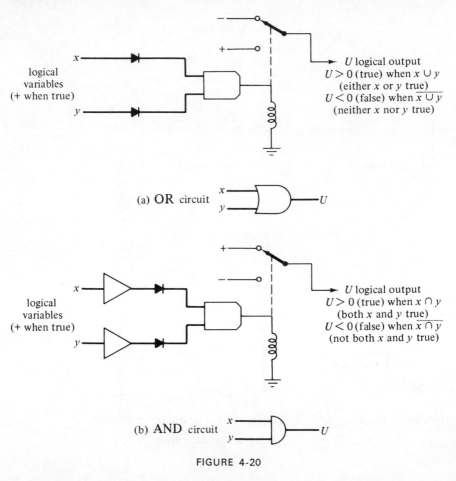

(a) OR circuit

(b) AND circuit

FIGURE 4-20

complicated logical arrangements, a knowledge of switching theory employing Boolean algebra is a definite aid to program planning.

4-10   Multivibrator Circuit Employing Comparators

In some applications to follow it will be necessary to develop a periodic wave to serve as a synchronizing clock for various discrete operations. Provisions for this are sometimes included in the computer, certainly in all hybrid computers. However, such a clock circuit is easy to synthesize from standard analog elements. Two useful types of such waves are of the square-wave form and the triangular-wave form. From these forms other forms may be obtained by *shaping circuits*. A variety of circuits exists for such *multivibrators*. Some of these depend upon feedback circuits involving discontinuous functions, as discussed in Chapter 6. One simple multivibrator circuit that uses only the simplest analog-computer components plus one comparator is shown in Figure 4-21.

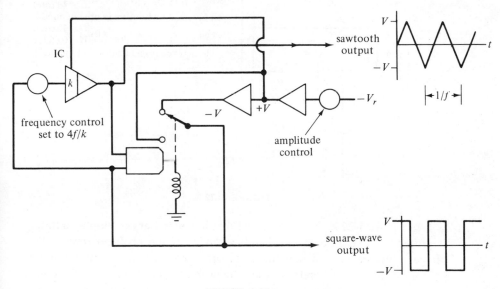

FIGURE 4-21

4-11   Comparator Control of Integration Time

One very useful application of a comparator is in stopping the program or part of a program (throwing one or more integrators into hold) when a specified terminal result has been achieved. Suppose, for example, that the simulation program develops a variable of interest, $y(t)$, in response to disturbances, $x(t)$, and the item of interest is specifically $y(t_1)$. By stopping the simulation at what corresponds to problem time t_1, $y(t_1)$ may be easily and accurately read by a digital voltmeter. The general procedure for handling such operation is shown in Figure 4-22.

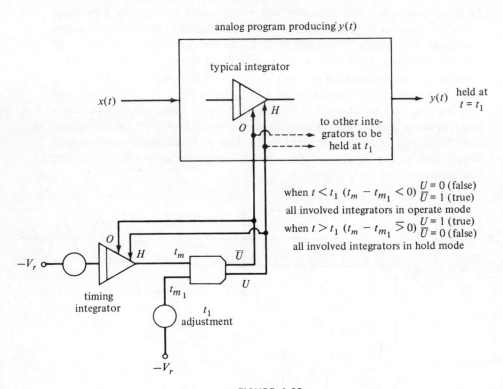

FIGURE 4-22

In Figure 4-22 it should be noted that it is necessary to employ a timing integrator to develop a machine indication t_m of the problem time t. This voltage, representing elapsed time, is compared with one representing t_1 (i.e., the voltage t_{m_1}). Therefore, when the problem time t reaches the assigned value t_1, the comparator causes all integrators of the program (including the timing integrator) to be thrown from the operate to the hold mode. Figure 4-22 is a logical diagram of this operation. It means that when $\bar{U}$ (not U) is true, the integrators are in the operate mode; when U is true, in the hold mode. The actual mechanization of this operation depends upon the computer equipment that is available. One method consists of using the comparator in connection with a relay that will open the summing junction whenever the comparator becomes actuated (U is true).

It need not be elapsed time that causes a program to terminate by throwing the computer (or portions of it) in the hold mode. This termination decision may be affected by any problem variable.

EXAMPLE Let the traditional trajectory problem be considered, as illustrated in Figure 4-23. The details of the actual simulation program need

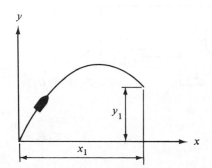

FIGURE 4-23

not be discussed here. It will suffice to say that the program will develop machine indications of the horizontal and vertical coordinates, x and y, and of their time derivatives, $\dot{x}$ and $\dot{y}$.

Let it be considered that the question of interest relates to the horizontal range x_1 attained when the missile reaches some vertical coordinate y_1 *on the way downward*. This may be determined by stopping the program when the event $\{(y \leq y_1) \cap (\dot{y} < 0)\} = \overline{\{(y > y_1) \cup (\dot{y} > 0)\}}$ occurs. The program for accomplishing this is shown in Figure 4-24.

4-12 Track-and-Hold Circuits

There are a number of applications when an amplifier is to follow or track various program variables during what is called the *tracking period* but is to hold them at their last tracked value during other intervals, known as the *holding period*. There are a variety of circuits employing comparators for accomplishing this; one example employing a relay comparator is shown in Figure 4-25.

With this circuit, when the comparator is not actuated ($E_1 + E_2 \leq 0$ and $U = 0$), the operational amplifier serves as a simple inverter and $y_m = -x_m$. The capacitor C connected to the output (through a small resistance R_c used to limit the flow through the relay contacts) has its other end grounded and hence is charged to y_m volts. (The time delay associated with this charging should be negligible if the total charging resistance, i.e., the

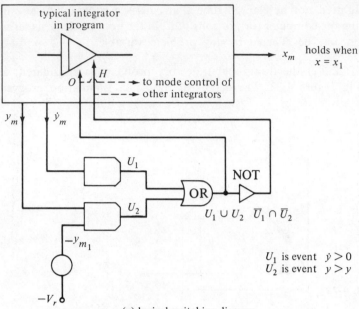

x_m holds when
$x = x_1$

$U_1 \cup U_2$ $\overline{U}_1 \cap \overline{U}_2$

U_1 is event $\dot{y} > 0$
U_2 is event $y > y$

(a) logical switching diagram

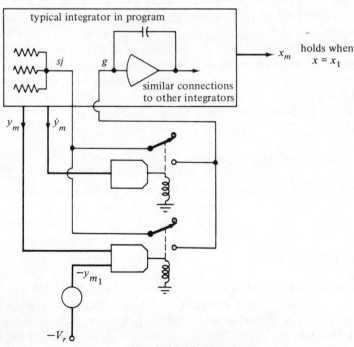

x_m holds when
$x = x_1$

(b) typical implementation

FIGURE 4-24

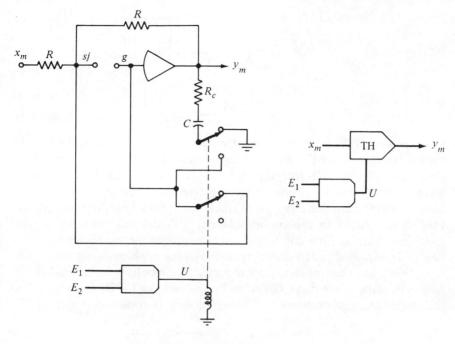

FIGURE 4-25

source resistance presented by the amplifier's output plus R_c, is not too large.)

When the comparator is actuated ($E_1 + E_2 > 0$ and $U = 1$), the summing junction is disconnected from the grid and, simultaneously, the formerly grounded end of the capacitor C is connected to the grid. The amplifier then acts as would an integrator when in the hold mode; the value of y_m is maintained constant (i.e., stored) at the value that it had at the instant of comparator actuation.

It should also be noted that by using more than one input resistor, inputs may be added and their sum then tracked; hence the simplified symbolism shown in Figure 4-25 may show more than one input signal applied. Furthermore, the input and feedback resistors need not be of the same value, so multiplication by a gain factor is also possible. This more general case is shown by the symbolism of Figure 4-26. In the simplified symbolism suggested here, the sequence of the letters TH has significance. They mean that the amplifier normally tracks (when the comparator is not actuated); when the comparator is actuated, holding takes place. It should also be noted that the same comparator may be used to control more than one track–hold amplifier.

The particular implementation of Figure 4-25 represents but one technique. One other very common method is based on the principle that if a signal is applied to the *initial condition* terminal of an ordinary integrator,

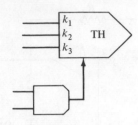

FIGURE 4-26

the integrator will act as a simple inverter, possessing, however, some response lag because of the *RC* time lag associated with the initial condition circuit (see Figure 2-24). Integrators, so utilized, become tracking amplifiers when in the IC mode and hold, of course, when switched to the hold mode. Integrators intended for this type of track–hold operation (they also may be used as integrators in the ordinary sense) are designed with the initial-condition charging-time constant short enough that the tracking lag will be negligible in consideration of the dynamics of the problem being simulated.

What has been proposed as the official symbolism for a track–hold amplifier, rather than those shown in Figures 4-25 and 4-26, is based upon this particular implementation. This symbolism is shown in Figure 4-27;

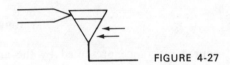

FIGURE 4-27

it is simply that of an ordinary integrator, given, however, a vertical orientation. Inputs are shown as applied to the IC rather than normal input terminals. Mode-control inputs are shown as arrows; these might be O (operate), H (hold), IC (initial condition), and/or T (track), depending upon the particular equipment. The association of these mode control signals with the actual operating function of the amplifier is then shown by a truth table. This suggested symbolism is *not* employed in this book because this manner of showing mode controls is somewhat awkward and, although unambiguous, is hard to follow. Furthermore, this symbolism is somewhat "equipment peculiar" in that it refers to one specific method for implementing track–hold operation—that of applying the signal to be tracked to the initial-condition terminals of an integrator.

One example of the use of a track–hold circuit is the storage of machine variables of interest as they are developed at specific instants of problem time. With such circuits this storage may be accomplished without interrupting the continued simulation of the problem for future time. Suppose, for example, that $y(t)$ is being generated by some program and the values of y at time instants $t_1, t_2, \ldots$ are to be stored. Figure 4-28 shows an arrangement for accomplishing this.

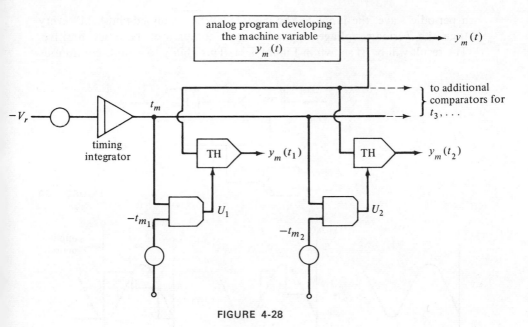

FIGURE 4-28

4-13   Ratchet Circuits (Memory Pairs)

The function of the track–hold circuit may always be reversed (i.e., it may be converted to a *hold–track* circuit by reversing the controlling function of the associated comparator). When relay comparators are used, this would mean simply interchanging the connections to normally open and normally closed relay contacts. This complementary arrangement of a hold–track circuit is represented symbolically in Figure 4-29. Now the amplifier will hold when $E_1 + E_2 \leq 0$, and track when $E_1 + E_2 > 0$.

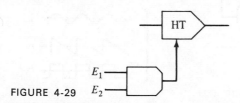

FIGURE 4-29

The cascade combination of track–hold circuit and a hold–track circuit is an especially useful combination, known as a *ratchet circuit*, or *memory pair*. The symbolic diagram to be used here for such a circuit is shown in Figure 4-30. By means of a ratchet circuit, discrete sampling of continuous functions becomes possible. For example, if the comparator is actuated by a periodic wave, the input to the circuit will be "sampled-and-held" every time the periodic voltage applied to the comparator becomes positive. The result will be as shown in Figure 4-31. This ability to sample continuous

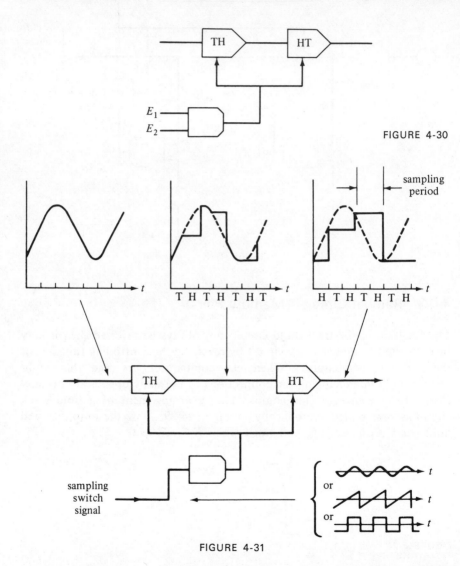

FIGURE 4-30

FIGURE 4-31

data (specifically, in this example, in a manner known as sampling with *zero-order hold*) is particularly useful in the simulation of digitally controlled systems, where precisely such a sampling effect does take place.

Another use of the ratchet circuit is as a pulse counter. This circuit, employing positive feedback around the ratchet circuit, is shown in Figure

4-32. The circuit of Figure 4-32 is an example of the employment of a hold–

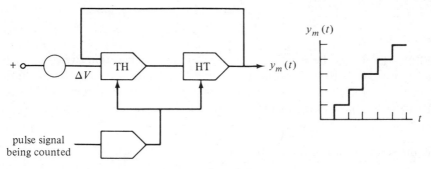

FIGURE 4-32

track amplifier also used in a summing capacity. It should also be noted that if a time-varying voltage $x(t)$ should be substituted for the constant bias voltage ΔV and if the pulse signal should be periodic, this circuit would simulate the process of numerical integration by the rectangular method, method 1a-1 (see Chapter 3).

The most useful applications of ratchet circuits are for the purpose of dynamic storage. For such applications it is necessary to operate the ratchet circuit and other associated portions of the program in a high-speed-repetitive mode. Ordinary electromechanical-relay comparators are usually not fast enough for this purpose and normally high-speed-electronic (solid-state) comparator units are employed.

4-14   Dynamic Storage

In brief, dynamic storage [1, 2] of a problem variable does not mean that it is stored in the sense used with digital computation, such as core storage, but rather that it is computed repeatedly and its value stored by means of a holding capacitor between cycles of the computation. This implies, correctly, that the computation should be conducted in a high-speed-repetitive mode. Normally, when dynamic-storage techniques are employed, some of the computer's integrators will be operating in the normal time mode and others in this high-speed (HRO) mode. This will require localized mode controls so that only selected integrators will have such HRO operation. In the program diagrams to be used here, those integrators that are to be operated in the HRO mode will be identified as shown in Figure 4-33. One of the applications of dynamic storage is in function generation. *Dynamic-storage techniques permit any function that can be generated as a function of machine time to be generated as a function of any other machine variable.*

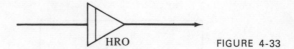

HRO   FIGURE 4-33

EXAMPLE 1 Let the function $y_m = 0.1x_m^2$ require generation over the range of x_m from 0 to 10 V. This function could be produced by a diode function generator. Still another convenient way is the dynamic-storage method to be described now. This method is possible because the relation

$$z_m = kt_m^2$$

is the solution of the differential equation

$$\frac{d^2 z_m}{dt_m^2} = 2k \qquad \text{with } z_m(0) = 0 \text{ and } \dot{z}_m(0) = 0$$

The computer program for this is shown in Figure 4-34. So far, the program shown in Figure 4-34 simply generates a voltage following a parabolic time

$$\frac{2k}{k_1 k_2} \text{ V} \xrightarrow{\hspace{2cm}} \boxed{k_1} \xrightarrow{\frac{-2k}{k_2} t_m} \boxed{k_2} \xrightarrow{\hspace{1cm}} z_m = kt_m^2$$

FIGURE 4-34

relationship that eventually would exceed the voltage range of the computer and cause an overload if the computation were not interrupted. However, this function is to be generated in the HRO mode and k will be such that z_m never exceeds the rated voltage range of the computer before computation is interrupted and reset for another cycle. Suppose that the period of computation is to be 20 msec and the computer has a nominal range of 10 V. The desired value of k would then be $10/(0.020)^2 = 25,000$, so this 10 V limit will be reached in 0.020 sec. If integrator gains of 100 are employed ($k_1 = k_2 = 100$), the required voltage to be applied to the first integrator will be $(2)(25,000)/(100)(100) = 5$ V. The Figure 4-34 program then appears as shown in Figure 4-35. What is desired is the value of $y_m = 0.1x_m^2$; this is identical to z_m when

$$0.1x_m^2 = 25,000t_m^2$$

or when $500t_m = x_m$.

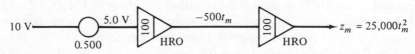

FIGURE 4-35

It therefore is necessary to generate, as well, the voltage corresponding to $500t_m$. This is done by means of a third integrator, also operated in the HRO mode, as shown in Figure 4-36.

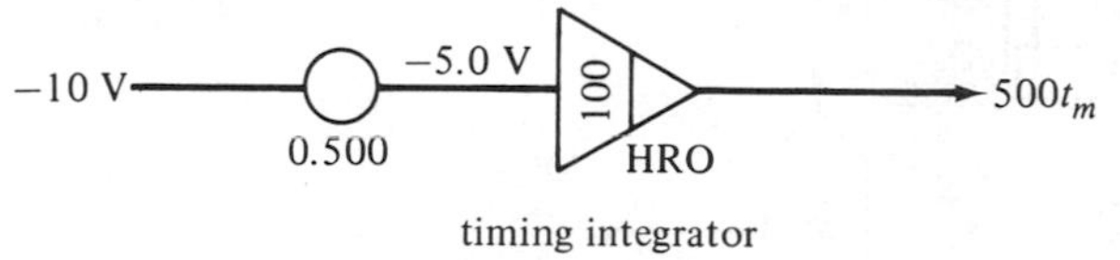

timing integrator

FIGURE 4-36

If a ratchet circuit is added so that the result of the z_m computation is sampled at every iteration of the instant when $500t_m = x_m$, the result will be the correct computation of y_m as it applies at that time. The computer program for this is shown in Figure 4-37.

The asterisk attached to the output y_m should be noted. This is to serve as a reminder that y_m is *sampled* every repetition period (in this example, about every 25 msec) and that a continuous computation of y_m is not being obtained. However, if the sampling frequency is beyond the significant frequency range of the system being studied, no significant sampling error would result. (Here the sampling frequency is about 40 Hz, considering the 20 msec computation time per repetition and estimating about 5 msec for the reset time; this method, therefore, would be adequate with this repetition rate if the system being simulated had no significant response, in terms of machine time, at that frequency.) For some applications a higher rate of HRO repetition would be required than in the example here.

In the particular example shown, it happens that one less integrator could be used since the required timing signal, $500t_m$, happens to be produced, in the inverted sense, in the function generation itself. This modified circuit would appear as in Figure 4-38.

In the circuit of Figure 4-38, as the two signals are applied to the comparator in the sense opposite to that of Figure 4-37, it is necessary to reverse the ratchet circuit by making the first amplifier a hold–track unit and the second a track–hold unit.

EXAMPLE 2 This example is the same as 1 except that x_m now varies between -10 and $+10$ V. Ordinarily, this would require a major modification of the program (as the next example will show) as t_m necessarily starts at zero. However, in this instance advantage may be taken of the fact that the function to be generated, $y_m = 0.1x_m^2$, is an even function of x_m. An absolute-value circuit (Figure 4-19b) can be used and the signal $-x_m$ applied to the comparator instead.

EXAMPLE 3 Here $y_m = \exp(0.2x_m)$, where $-10 < x_m < 10$ V.

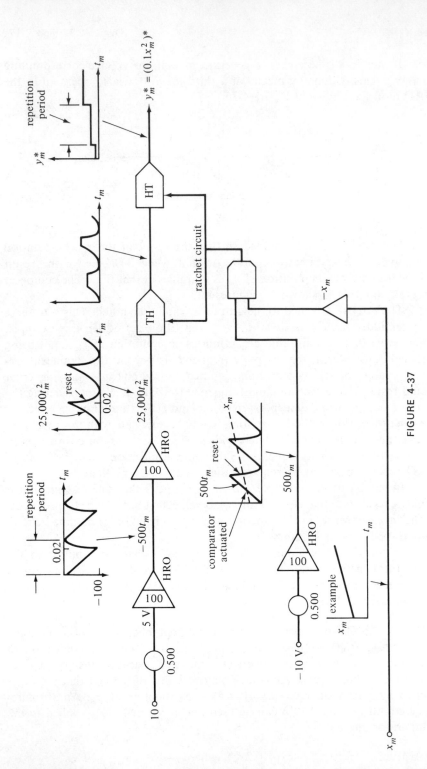

FIGURE 4-37

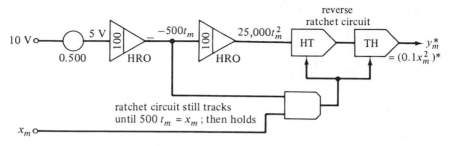

FIGURE 4-38

The function $z_m = k_1 \exp(k_2 t_m)$ can easily be generated as it is the solution of the differential equation

$$\frac{dz_m}{dt_m} = k_2 z_m \qquad \text{with } z_m(0) = k_1$$

Let it again be supposed that the computation time per repetition is selected as 0.020 sec. Then $t_m = 0$ should represent the lower end of the range of x_m, or $x_m = -10$ V, and $t_m = 0.020$, the upper end, or at $x_m = 10$ V; i.e.,

$$t_m = \frac{0.020}{10 - (-10)}(x_m + 10) = 1.0 \times 10^{-3}x_m + 0.010$$

Equating the y_m and z_m relationships,

$$\exp(0.2x_m) = k_1 \exp(10^{-3}k_2 x_m + 0.01k_2)$$
$$= k_1 \exp(0.01k_2) \exp(10^{-3}k_2 x_m) \qquad \text{for all } x_m$$

or

$$0.2x_m = 10^{-3}k_2 x_m \qquad \text{and} \qquad k_2 = \frac{0.2}{10^{-3}} = 200$$

and

$$1 = k_1 \exp(0.01k_2) = k_1 \exp(2) = 7.39k_1 \qquad \text{and} \qquad k_1 = 0.1354$$

The function z_m to be generated is, therefore,

$$z_m = 0.1354 \exp(200t_m)$$

It is to be sampled by the ratchet circuit when $t_m - 0.01 = 10^{-3}x_m$, or when $1000t_m - 10 = x_m$.

The program for accomplishing this is shown in Figure 4-39.

4-15   Multiplication by Dynamic Storage
(Time-Division Multiplier)

Up to now one of the basic arithmetic operations, multiplication, has been neglected in the discussion of analog computers because it is, admittedly, a more difficult operation using analog methods than digital. However,

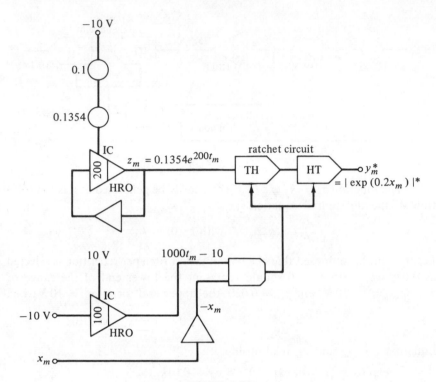

FIGURE 4-39

dynamic-storage techniques do permit this operation to be accomplished in a reasonably simple fashion.

(a) *Two-quadrant multiplication:*

$$z_m = \frac{x_m y_m}{V_r}$$

where

$$0 \leq x_m \leq V_r, \qquad -V_r \leq y_m \leq V_r$$

Here one of the factors, x_m, is always positive and values of x_m, y_m, and z_m can be accommodated within the voltage range, V_r, of the computer. A general program for accomplishing this type of multiplication is shown in Figure 4-40a; a specific program for the special case when $V_r = 10$ V and the computation interval in the HRO mode, t_c, is 20 msec is shown in Figure 4-40b.

The operation of this method is explained most easily in terms of Figure 4-40b. The upper integrator in that diagram produces, in reality, the final integral $50 \int_0^{t_m} y_m \, dt_m$ but, *if* the computation interval t_c is sufficiently short so that y_m essentially is constant during the interval, this is a valid

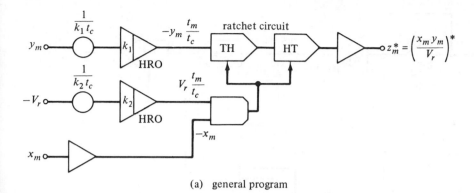

(a) general program

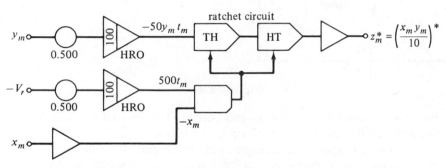

(b) program for computation period, $t_c = 0.020$ sec, $V_r = 10$ V

FIGURE 4-40

approximation of the quantity $50y_m t_m$. In the meantime, the lower timing integrator is producing a sawtooth wave of voltage indicative of the quantity $500t_m$. When this voltage becomes equal to the voltage $-x_m$, the ratchet circuit will sample and hold the output of the upper integrator. That is, when $500t_m = x_m$, or $t_m = x_m/500$, the voltage $-50y_m t_m$ will be sampled and held until the next repetition of the HRO mode. But this voltage is $-50y_m(x_m/500) = -x_m y_m/10$, the desired product (when inverted). Hence multiplication has been accomplished.

(b) *Four-quadrant multiplication:*

$$z_m = \frac{x_m y_m}{V_r}$$

where

$$-V_r \leq x_m \leq V_r \qquad -V_r \leq y_m \leq V_r$$

When both factors may appear in both the positive and negative ranges of voltage, the multiplication program must be modified to accomplish this.

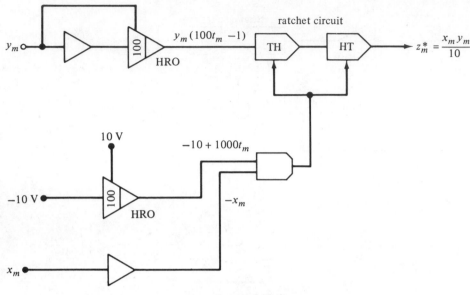

FIGURE 4-41

Figure 4-41 shows one type of program used to handle such a four-quadrant problem for the specific case where $t_c = 0.020$ sec and $V_r = 10$ V.

Other multiplication arrangements employing dynamic storage are also possible. As a matter of fact, this general principle of multiplication was known long before dynamic-storage techniques, in general, were developed. Units employing this method frequently are described as *time-division multipliers*. They are furnished as self-contained units by a number of manufacturers and employ a variety of electronic circuits; these may be used with computers that do not, in other respects, have dynamic-storage capability. However, when dynamic-storage capability is present, such multipliers can always be fabricated directly on the patchboard.

Static accuracy depends upon accuracy of switching but, in well-designed units, 0.1 per cent is obtainable. Dynamic accuracy depends on the ratio of the repetition rate to the significant response frequencies of the system being simulated and can always be improved by increasing the frequency of repetition. (Higher repetition frequencies may, on the other hand, aggravate the problem of accurate switching.)

4-16 Quarter-Square Multipliers

Another popular method of analog multiplication, which does not involve switching schemes as does dynamic storage, is the *quarter-square method*. This method employs only conventional amplifiers plus diodes.

Quarter-square multiplication is based upon the following algebraic identity:

$$xy = \frac{(x + y)^2 - (x - y)^2}{4} \qquad (4\text{-}2)$$

From this relationship, it is obvious that what is required in addition to conventional summers are two square-law diode function generators. As mentioned previously, these are often available as prefabricated units. The program utilizing relation (4-2) for four-quadrant multiplication would then appear as in Figure 4-42. Naturally, there are many variations of this program but the basic principles remain the same.

Such quarter-square multipliers are generally prefabricated units, sometimes complete in themselves and sometimes of the type that must

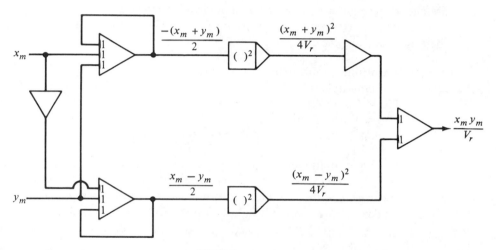

FIGURE 4-42

borrow operational amplifiers or inverters from the computer in which it is installed. (These are borrowed on the patchboard; the amplifiers are then available for other purposes when the multiplier is not in use.) However, the multiplication program may be fabricated directly on the patchboard.

Usually, because of the limitations on the accuracy of the square-law function generators, the *static* accuracy of these multipliers is not as good as with the time-division type mentioned previously. Typical would be 0.1 per cent meaning 0.1 per cent of the maximum voltage range V_r. For a 10 V computer this would mean that the product would be obtained correctly within 0.01 V. But, for example, if $x_m = 1.0$ V and $y_m = 1.0$ V, the correct product would be $x_m y_m / 10$, or 0.1 V and a 0.01 V error would mean an actual error of 10 per cent. Somewhat better static accuracy is possible with a well-designed time-division multiplier. On the other hand, the time-division type has the upper-frequency limitations mentioned previously because of its sampling nature. The upper-frequency limitations of the quarter-square type of multiplier are, on the other hand, usually the frequency-response limitations of the operational amplifiers involved. Hence the *dynamic* accuracy of the quarter-square type might well be superior. Which of these two types of multipliers should be employed depends on the problem to be simulated and on the time scaling chosen.

4-17   Other Types of Multipliers—General Program Diagram for a Multiplier

Other methods of multiplication have been, and sometimes still are, used with analog computers. Because they are encountered much less often than are either the quarter-square or the time-division methods, detailed discussions of them have been postponed until Appendices 4A to 4C. Among these methods are the following:

1. Logarithmic multipliers.
2. Servomultipliers.
3. Hall-effect multipliers.
4. Crossed-field multipliers.
5. Digital multiplication with hybrid computers.

Logarithmic multipliers employ diode function generators capable of developing logarithmic functions; their application to multiplication is obvious. They possess the advantage that they can multiply when the factors involved appear to any power [i.e., they can perform the operation

$$z_m = k(x_m)^a(y_m)^b$$

where a and b need not be integers]. On the other hand, they possess obvious disadvantages. When either of the factors goes "through zero," difficulty is encountered because the logarithm of zero is minus infinity and the logarithm of a negative number is complex. This disadvantage can be overcome by various "trick" programs. Scaling difficulties also may occur; these are discussed in Appendix 4A.

Servomultipliers are based on the mechanical setting of potentiometers to positions that correspond to one of the factors of the multiplication process. At one time such multipliers represented the type most often found in analog installations. Such multipliers are capable of satisfactory *static* accuracy, but, because of the response-speed limitations of mechanical positioning devices (servos), their dynamic accuracy is severely limited. There are also obvious adjustment and maintenance problems associated with such electromechanical equipment. Nevertheless, servomultipliers still exist in a number of analog installations. They are particularly convenient when a number of products must be obtained that are all associated with one common factor.

Hall-effect and crossed-field multipliers are ingeneous schemes proposed during the earlier development of the analog-computer art. They are rarely if ever employed in modern equipment but are mentioned in Appendix 4C because of their historical interest. Digital multiplication is an obvious method with hybrid computers but is practical only in such installations where the necessary interface equipment is available.

The proposed standard symbol, to be applied to all multipliers regardless of the method employed, is shown in Figure 4-43. With this symbol, a $+$ or $-$ sign should be affixed to the symbol signifying the output to indicate whether or not inversion takes place. The divisor α usually, but not always, will be the reference voltage V_r.

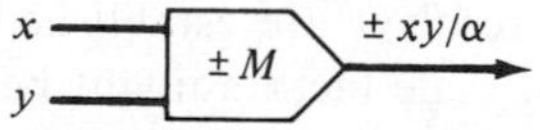

FIGURE 4-43

4-18 Resolvers

The name *resolver* is given to analog-computer elements that perform the operations

$$x = r \cos \theta$$

and/or

$$y = r \sin \theta$$

Usually a given resolver can perform both of these functions simultaneously, and there are frequent occasions when it is called on to do so.

These resolver operations, called *rectangular resolution* because they transform polar to rectangular coordinates, are really a combination of sine and cosine function generation with multiplication. Indeed, one metl for accomplishing such resolution is by means of ordinary diode function generators, adjusted to develop the sine and cosine relationships, in association with two multipliers. Ordinarily, however, in commercially furnished resolvers the operations of function generation and multiplication are handled together so that the programmer need not be concerned with these separate operations. The program diagram to be employed here to represent a resolver (polar to rectangular resolution) is shown in Figure 4-44.

At the start of the development of analog computers, resolvers were exclusively electromechanical. They were called *servo resolvers*, employing

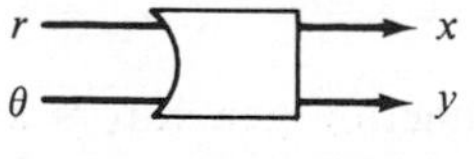

FIGURE 4-44 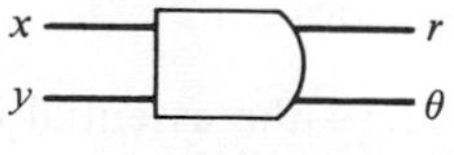   FIGURE 4-45

positioning servomechanisms, just as do servo multipliers. These are used to position nonlinear potentiometers specially wound so that the potentiometer's transfer factor β will be a sinusoidal (or cosinusoidal) function of its angular rotation. Such servo resolvers possess the same advantages and disadvantages as servo multipliers. Nevertheless, they are still used in many existing computer installations. As more details concerning their operation may be of interest to some readers, they are described more completely in Appendix 4D.

The modern trend has been toward purely electronic (solid-state) resolvers possessing no moving parts. These again are combinations of diode function generators and multipliers. Various arrangements are provided by component manufacturers. In some instances, both $\pm x$ and $\pm y$ are available at the output terminals; in others, any required inversion of the output must be external.

Scale factors associated with a resolver are established by the manufacturer. For a 10 V computer typical scale factors might be such that

$$x_m = r_m \cos (20\theta_m)^\circ$$
$$y_m = r_m \sin (20\theta_m)^\circ$$

In other words, in this example one degree of angle is represented by 0.05 V. A total angular range of $\pm 200°$, therefore, could be accommodated by the voltage range of the computer. Other scale factors are also provided to accommodate larger or smaller angular ranges. Resolvers are also available with the angular scale factor based on radians rather than degrees.

The inverse operation of *polar resolution* (i.e., of converting rectangular to polar coordinates) may also be handled by resolvers. Then the operation that effectively is performed is

$$r_m = \sqrt{x^2 + y^2}$$
$$\theta = \tan^{-1} \frac{y}{x}$$

Usually these mathematical operations are not performed directly. Instead implicit methods are used, to be described in Chapter 5.

The program diagram to be used to represent a resolver performing polar resolution is shown in Figure 4-45.

4-19 Summary

The basic tools that enable analog computers to handle nonlinear as well as linear operations are

1. Diodes—the essential element of function generators and of many of the techniques for simulating discontinuous operations that are treated later in Chapter 6.

2. Function generators.
3. Comparators—sometimes playing a role similar to diodes but also making possible such important operations as dynamic storage; they also may be used to perform logical operations and to change the program configuration.
4. Track-and-hold circuits—essential for use with dynamic storage methods; they will prove to be very important with hybrid installations.
5. Multipliers—a number of schemes have been used but time division (based on dynamic storage) and quarter-square remain the most successful and convenient methods.
6. Resolvers—for both polar to rectangular and rectangular to polar conversion.

Not all the tools have been described in this chapter. Others are available that depend upon implicit procedures, the subject of Chapter 5.

Suggested Problems

4-1. Design a function generator to develop the nonlinear function shown in Figure P4-1 that uses

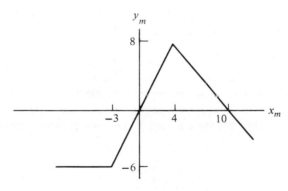

FIGURE P4-1

(a) An open computer with floating power supplies.
(b) A closed computer with diodes and both conventional grounded and floating potentiometers. No floating power supplies nor resistive or capacitive elements are to be used except for those directly associated with amplifiers.
(c) A closed computer, as in (b), but with comparators instead of diodes.

4-2. The following differential equation is to be represented:

$$\frac{dy}{dt} = +f(y, t) = 0$$

where

$$f(y, t) = f_1(y) \quad \text{when } f_1(y) \geq f_2(t) \text{ and } f_1(y) \geq 0$$
$$= f_1(t) \quad \text{when } f_1(y) < f_2(t) \text{ and } f_2(t) \geq 0$$
$$= 0 \quad \text{when } f_1(y) < 0 \text{ and } f_2(t) < 0$$

Assume that the functions f_1 and f_2 have already been defined and set up on diode function generators. Prepare a program (without regard to scaling) to handle the above problem

(a) Using diodes, but no comparators.

(b) Using comparators, but no diodes (except those internal to the function generators establishing f_1 and f_2).

4-3. Assuming a computer of voltage rating V_r, select the best scaling factor, k, to be used when the following functions are generated; then express K in a practical form for 100 and 10 V computers.

(a) $y_m = K \ln x_m$ \hfill $0.0001 V_r < x_m < V_r$

(b) $y_m = K \exp (ax_m)$ \hfill $0 < x_m < V_r$

(c) $y_m = K x_m^{3/2}$ \hfill $0 < x_m < V_r$

(d) $z_m = K x_m y_m^a$ \hfill $0 < x_m < V_r$ \hfill $0 < y_m < V_r$
\hfill $a > 1$

(e) $y_m = K x_m^{1/2}$ \hfill $0 < x_m < V_r$

(f) $z_m = K \sqrt{x_m^2 + y_m^2}$ \hfill $-V_r < x_m < V_r$ \hfill $-V_r < y_m < V_r$

(g) $p_m = K q_m |q_m|$ \hfill $-V_r < q_m < V_r$

4-4. When a linkage drives a second element having friction but negligible inertia through a coupling having backlash (free play), the relation between the input displacement x and the output displacement y is as shown in Figure P4-4. Develop a program using comparators for generating the functional relationship between x and y. Do not consider scaling.

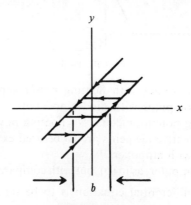

FIGURE P4-4

4-5. In Problem 1-1 when applying different trial interest rates, the only quantity of interest is that principal that applies at the end of 10 years. Arrange to stop the analog computation when that period of time has been reached.

4-6. A proprietary device called a NO–BACK is sometimes used to couple a driving source and load. The mechanical design of this device is too complicated to describe here, but its action may be described approximately as follows: Q_1 is the input torque and Q_2 the output torque; ω is the velocity.

1. When $|Q_2| > |Q_1|$ *and* $\omega = 0$, a braking torque, Q_b, is established by the device that will be just sufficient to prevent rotation.
2. When $|Q_2| < |Q_1|$ *or* $\omega \neq 0$, this braking torque is removed.

In this problem the driving source is a motor that will develop the torque Q_0 under steady-state conditions:

$$Q_0 = 4V - 20\omega \quad \text{kg-cm}$$

where V is the applied armature voltage, ranging from -100 to $+100$ V, and ω is in rad/sec. The motor and no-back input have a combined inertia of 5 kg-cm/(rad/sec^2). The no-back output and load have a combined inertia of the same amount. The load also consists of a variable torque Q_L that can range between -50 and $+50$ kg-cm.

Consider that the no-back has negligible friction (other than braking torque Q_b). Prepare an analog program that will show the response of the velocity ω to varying values of V and Q_L.

4-7. This relates to the example of Figure 4-23. Assume that the projectile (having no self-propulsive means) has an initial angle θ_1 adjustable from 0 to 30° and that it has an initial velocity of 300 yards/sec. All forces acting on it other than gravity are being neglected. The shape of the terrain is given by the following table:

x, yards	y, yards
0	0
500	50
1000	160
1500	360
1680	400 (peak)
2000	270
2500	250
3000	360
3350	500 (peak)
3500	480
4000	440
4500	400

Prepare a program that will simulate this situation and will plot, automatically, the range x at which contact with the ground occurs, versus the angle θ_0.

4-8. This is an extension of Problem 4-5. Modify the analog program to simulate the quarterly compounding of interest.

4-9. A continuous variable $x(t)$, ranging from -100 to $+100$ V, is to be quantized to the nearest volt. Develop an analog-computer program for accomplishing this.

4-10. Figure 4-40 shows a two-quadrant multiplier and Figure 4-41 a modification for the handling of four quadrants. Develop a different modification of Figure 4-40b, employing diodes and/or comparators, for handling four-quadrant multiplication.

4-11. Simulate the situation described by the following differential equation:

$$\frac{d^2y}{dt^2} + \frac{dy}{dt} + e^{-ay} = 0 \qquad \text{where } a > 0$$

Assume that dynamic-storage facilities are available.

4-12. Prepare a program for evaluating the double integral:

$$I = \int_0^w \left[\int_0^{f(x)} f_1(r)\, dr \right] dx$$

where $f_1(r)$ ranges from -10 to $+10$ V, $f(x)$ ranges from zero to $+10$ V, x ranges from zero to $+10$ V, and w ranges from zero to $+10$ V. $f(x)$ and $f_1(r)$ are particular functions already established on diode function generators. Use dynamic storage to develop the program.

4-13. Given independent variables x and y, produce the function

$$z = Kx^2y^3 \qquad \text{where } 0.1 < x < 10 \text{ V}, 0.1 < y < 10 \text{ V}$$

The only function generators assumed to be available are fixed-diode function generators capable of the operations $u = 10\log_{10}v$ or $v = (10)^{u/10}$. Assume that multipliers are not available. Prepare a program, taking scaling into account. (A suitable value of K must be chosen.)

4-14. What time function is generated by the program found in Figure P4-14?

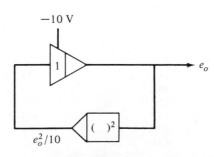

FIGURE P4-14

4-15. The assembly in Figure P4-15, which consists of a triangular plate supported by three vertically aligned springs connected to a horizontal supporting member, is completely submerged in sea water. The support is subjected to vertical motion only and the three points of support of the plate may also move only vertically. The support displacement from some designated neutral position is described as x ft. The plate displacement, measured from the normal steady-state position when $x = 0$, is described as y ft, with y_1, y_2, and y_3 being the specific values of y at the three spring contact points.

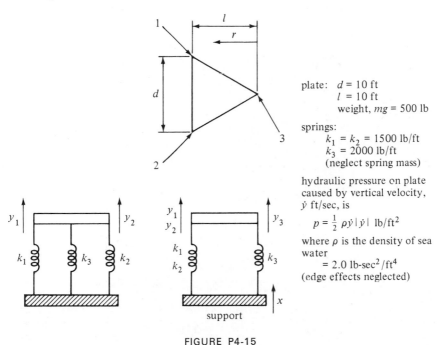

plate: $d = 10$ ft
$\quad\quad\quad l = 10$ ft
$\quad\quad\quad$ weight, $mg = 500$ lb

springs:
$\quad\quad k_1 = k_2 = 1500$ lb/ft
$\quad\quad k_3 = 2000$ lb/ft
$\quad\quad$ (neglect spring mass)

hydraulic pressure on plate caused by vertical velocity, $\dot{y}$ ft/sec, is

$$p = \tfrac{1}{2}\rho\dot{y}|\dot{y}| \ \text{lb/ft}^2$$

where ρ is the density of sea water
$\quad\quad = 2.0$ lb-sec^2/ft^4
(edge effects neglected)

FIGURE P4-15

Prepare a program to simulate the dynamics of this situation in response to imposed motions x. The range of $\ddot{x}$ is ± 200 ft/sec^2; of $\dot{x}$, ± 10 ft/sec; and of x, ± 10 ft.

References

1. W. Dhen, *Special Computer Units in the Darmstadt Repetitive Electronic Analog Computer*, *Proceedings of the IACM*, Brussels, 1956, pp. 46–48.

2. Rajko Tomovic and W. J. Karplus, *High-Speed Analog Computers* (New York: John Wiley & Sons, Inc., 1962).

Appendix 4A:
Logarithmic Multipliers

As described in the main body of this chapter, logarithmic multipliers are particularly convenient for performing operations of the form

$$z = x^a y^b \qquad \text{when } x > 0 \text{ and } y > 0$$

Scaling requirements are specially important and not obvious on the surface. In terms of machine variables the relationship would be

$$z_m = \frac{x_m^a y_m^b}{c}$$

where c is some constant that will provide proper scaling. Usually c is determined by $z_{m_{max}}$, which should not exceed V_r when both x_m and y_m are equal to V_r. That is,

$$z_{m_{max}} = \frac{V_r^a V_r^b}{c} \leq V_r \qquad \text{or } c \geq V_r^{(a+b-1)}$$

As a specific example, consider a 10 V computer ($V_r = 10$) where the multiplication operation is to be

$$z = x^{1.4} y^2$$

Then $c \geq 10^{2.4} = 250$ and c is chosen as 250 since this is sufficiently round. The machine relation will be

$$z_m = \frac{x_m^{1.4} y_m^2}{250} \qquad \text{volts} \tag{4A-1}$$

Now let it be supposed that the logarithmic function generators used are of the type that will cover a logarithmic range of four decades, i.e., from 0.001 to 10 V. Their relationship (with u_m and w_m being simply any general machine variables) will be

$$u_m = 5 \log_{10} (10w_m) \qquad \text{volts} \qquad (4\text{A-2})$$

The inverse, antilog function generator would be of the form

$$w_m = 0.1(10)^{u_m/5} \qquad \text{volts} \qquad (4\text{A-3})$$

Relation (4A-1) may be converted to a form compatible with the logarithmic function generator [i.e., with relation (4A-2)]. Then

$$10x_m = \frac{(10x_m)^{1.4}(10y_m)^2}{250(10)^{2.4}} = \frac{(10x_m)^{1.4}(10y_m)^2}{62,500}$$

or

$$\log_{10} (10z_m) = 1.4 \log_{10} (10x_m) + 2.0 \log_{10} (10y_m) - 4.796$$

The actual computer operation, therefore, would consist first of the intermediate step involving a variable designated as u_m.

$$u_m = 5 \log_{10} (10z_m) = y \log_{10} (10x_m) + 10 \log_{10} (10y_m)$$
$$\qquad - 2.398 \qquad \text{volts} \qquad (4\text{A-4})$$

The second step would consist simply of the antilog operation

$$z_m = 0.1(10)^{u_m/5} \qquad \text{volts} \qquad (4\text{A-5})$$

The value of z_m that would result would then be in accord with relation (4A-1). Figure 4A-1 shows a program that might be used for accomplishing this.

In this program it should be noted that care is taken that not only the final output z_m will not overload, but also that the intermediate amplifiers will not overload nor underload. This type of multiplier is limited to operation in the first quadrant; it is also limited to values of x_m and y_m that are not

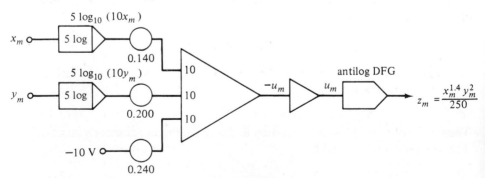

FIGURE 4A-1

less than 0.001 V (so that the logarithmic DFG's do not underload). These limits on the range of operation are shown in Figure 4A-2.

The lower limits could have been extended by employing logarithmic function generators that covered a wider range of signal, more than the four logarithmic decades covered by the type that develops the function $5 \log_{10}(10w_m)$. However, accuracy is then impaired as the number of decades covered is increased.

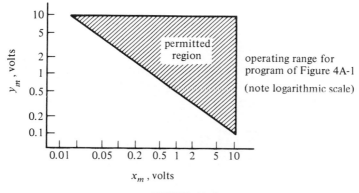

FIGURE 4A-2

Similar scaling problems are encountered with digital computers when multiplying variables that are raised to noninteger powers since then, also, logarithmic methods are employed in the actual machine program. However, with digital computers the range latitude is far greater.

In Chapter 5, implicit methods will be mentioned, including techniques by which the antilog function generator shown in Figure 4A-1 may be eliminated and replaced with a third logarithmic function generator.

Ordinary multiplication over four quadrants can also be accomplished by logarithmic methods. Use is made of the relation

$$z_m = \frac{x_m y_m}{V_r} = 4\left[\frac{\left(\dfrac{x_m + V_r}{2}\right)\left(\dfrac{y_m + V_r}{2}\right)}{V_r} - \frac{x_m}{4} - \frac{y_m}{4} - \frac{V_r}{4}\right] \quad (4A\text{-}6)$$

The multiplication

$$\left(\frac{x_m + V_r}{4}\right)\left(\frac{y_m + V_r}{4}\right)$$

always involves positive factors; this multiplication may be done logarithmically without any possibility of underload. To prevent overload, the final multiplication by 4 must be done after the other terms are subtracted.

Appendix 4B:
Servo Multipliers

The servomechanism type of multiplier was the first to be used to any extent with electronic analog computers. It still enjoys wide popularity, although this is decreasing with the modern tendency to avoid mechanical parts. It has the advantages of a high degree of static accuracy and the ability to multiply conveniently a number of variables by the same common factor. Its disadvantages are the additional maintenance required of electromechanical elements and its relatively slow response (and hence poor dynamic accuracy).

In order to multiply one or more variables, say $y_{m_1}, y_{m_2}, \ldots, y_{m_k}$, by a common factor x_m, and to obtain the results

$$z_{m_1} = \frac{x_m y_{m_1}}{V_r}, \qquad z_{m_2} = \frac{x_m y_{m_2}}{V_r}, \ldots, \qquad z_{m_k} = \frac{x_m y_{m_k}}{V_r}$$

$(k + 1)$ precision potentiometers, mechanically coupled to each other to maintain the same setting (ganged), are positioned accurately to a *factor* (not *setting*; note the distinction made in Section 2-17) corresponding to the common factor x_m. Normally, for x_m positive this setting would be simply

$$\beta = \frac{x_m}{V_r} \tag{4B-1}$$

i.e., an x_m of 10 V would correspond to full potentiometer rotation in a

10 V computer. Each of the y_m signals is applied to one of these potentiometers. Since the output voltage is β times the input voltage applied to each potentiometer, the appropriate multiplication will take place.

The $(k + 1)$th potentiometer is used as the *feedback* potentiometer and provides a signal to the servo amplifier telling it what the actual output setting β is so that it may be compared with the setting desired. The voltage V_r is applied to this potentiometer; hence, if it is set correctly, the output voltage will agree with x_m. Any deviation between the two (as will occur when x_m is varying rapidly in consideration of the servomechanism response) will call for a correction of β until the indicated and desired x_m's agree.

To explain this in terms of the servomechanism operation, relation (4B-1) should be rewritten as

$$\beta = \frac{x_{m0}}{V_r} \tag{4B-2}$$

where x_{m0} is the value of x_m indicated by the potentiometer's *actual* setting, as contrasted with the x_m desired. The servomechanism operation may then be explained by means of the block diagram of Figure 4B-1, where x_{me}

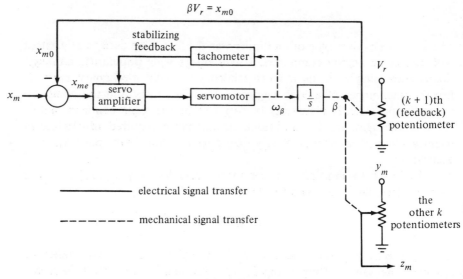

FIGURE 4B-1

represents the error or difference between the value of x_m called for and that corresponding to the potentiometer setting that has been established. Any such error operates to reduce itself to zero through the action of the electronic servo amplifier and then, in turn, the servomotor that positions the potentiometer. As the existence of any error will result in a corrective velocity ω_β, it follows that a steady-state error cannot exist whenever x_m is constant (except for errors in the potentiometer itself and null errors in the servo amplifier). Under dynamic conditions (x_m varying), some error can exist, but this is maintained small unless the frequencies associated with the x_m variation exceed the frequency range of the servo system.

There are many problems involved in obtaining a satisfactory design of a servomechanism for this purpose; these are handled by various specialized techniques that are not within the range of subjects to be discussed here. It should be noted, however, that a tachometer almost always is employed for auxiliary feedback purposes to improve the dynamic response of the system.

The arrangement of Figure 4B-1 will handle only positive values of x_m. With that arrangement, if x_m was to become negative, the servomechanism would attempt to make the potentiometer setting negative; this is not possible and the setting would simply be zero at the extreme end of travel. In other words, the arrangement shown there represents a *two-quadrant* multiplier.

To handle the possibility of negative as well as positive x_m's and hence achieve four-quadrant multiplication, a modification of Figure 4B-1 is necessary. All potentiometers are of the floating type and the lower end of the feedback, $(k + 1)$th, potentiometer, is not connected to the ground but to the negative reference voltage $-V_r$.

The potentiometer setting β must now be redefined in the sense that $\beta = 1$ represents the extreme top of the potentiometer; $\beta = 0$, the center; and $\beta = -1$, the bottom. Furthermore, it will be necessary to connect the *inverted* versions of the y_m signals to the bottom of their respective potentiometers. Four-quadrant multiplication is thus achieved.

All of the potentiometers of a multiplier are ganged mechanically; that is, their mechanical settings (or α's) are the same. This is no guarantee that their actual multiplication factors, or β's, will also be the same unless all potentiometers, including the feedback potentiometer, are *identically* loaded. This is an important precaution if accurate multiplication is to be realized.

There are many details to be followed and precautions to be taken when servo multipliers are used. These will vary with the particular units employed and the best instruction that can be given here is that the manufacturer's advice be followed carefully. Rules for connecting such multipliers on a patchboard can be slightly complicated; these will vary depending on the equipment employed.

A detailed program diagram naturally should be kept as a record of the patchboard connections when using a servo multiplier. The nature of such a diagram will depend upon the particular unit employed. Such details, however, would complicate the overall diagram describing the entire simulation program and, therefore, in the macroscopic program diagram the general symbol for a multiplier shown in Figure 4-43 is recommended.

Appendix 4C:
Other Types of Multipliers

Other types of analog-computer multipliers have been employed. One type that depends upon the multiplication of quantities describing physical phenomena is the Hall-effect multiplier.[1] This depends upon the fact that the Hall-effect voltage generated across a thin slab (of thickness t) of an appropriate semiconductor material is given by

$$v = \frac{R_h i B}{t}$$

where R_h is the Hall-effect factor, i the transverse current, and B the density of the magnetic flux component that is mutually transverse to both the v and i vectors. Obviously, if i is made proportional to one of the factors and B to the other, an analog multiplication will take place.

Another type is the crossed-fields type, proposed first by MacNee.[2] It makes use of the fact that the force deflecting an electron beam is given by

$$f = e(v \times B)$$

where e is the charge on the electron and v and B are, respectively, the beam-velocity and magnetic-flux-density vectors.

[1]L. Lofgren, Analog Multiplier Based on the Hall Effect, *Journal of Applied Physics*, Vol. XXIX (1958), 158–66.
[2]A. B. MacNee, An Electronic Differential Analyzer, *Proceedings of the IRE* (Nov. 1949), 1315–1324.

Both of the above types of multipliers introduce design problems, so accuracies better than 1 per cent are difficult to realize. Neither have any inherent limits in regard to frequency response, but, in practice, limitations are imposed by the design of the coil that establishes the magnetic flux B.

Appendix 4D:
Servo Resolvers

Servo resolvers are basically similar to servo multipliers and, as a matter of fact, combined units (i.e., multiplier–resolvers) are quite common. Figure 4B-1 still applies in the general sense. A required angular setting of the potentiometers corresponding to the argument, θ, is established. This would correspond to the angle described as β in Figure 4B-1, except that it is expressed directly in terms of angle while β usually is described in terms of the fraction of the potentiometer's travel. A linear (conventional) feedback potentiometer is employed to indicate this angle, just as is done in Figure 4B-1; this indication is fed back to the servo amplifier. The feedback potentiometer must be of the floating type and have its ends connected to $\pm V_r$ if both positive and negative angles are to be accommodated.

The other resolving potentiometers are of a nonlinear type requiring the voltages $\pm r_m$ to be connected to their end terminals if they are to generate the products $r_m \cos \theta$ and $r_m \sin \theta$. These potentiometers normally have two outputs, one for the sine and one for the cosine.

As with multipliers (and possibly more so), there are a number of precautions to be taken with servo resolvers if correct resolution is to take place. Rules regarding potentiometer loading particularly must be followed carefully. Again, because of the variety of designs, these precautions are described best by the manufacturer of the particular units used.

Appendix 4D
Servo Resolvers

Implicit Methods
of Function Generation

5

5-1 Introduction

Analog-computer methods for generating various commonly used functions by means of function generators of various types were described in Chapter 4. There will be a number of instances when these techniques will not be necessary and when it will be possible to generate the desired function by *implicit methods*. These methods will often be convenient for digital as well as analog-computer simulation in instances where they can prevent difficulties caused by redundant operation or can be used to shorten the execution time.

5-2 Methods Based on the Time Derivative
of the Independent Variable

When a function $y = f(x)$ is to be produced and the time derivative dx/dt is available, implicit methods can often be used. By taking the time derivative of both sides of this relation, the result is obtained:

$$\frac{dy}{dt} = f'(x)\frac{dx}{dt} \tag{5-1}$$

If $f'(x)$ can be expressed as a function of x and $f(x)$ that can be represented by the computer, i.e., if

$$f'(x) = g[x, f(x)] \tag{5-2}$$

then the operation to be performed is as shown in Figure 5-1.

EXAMPLE The function $y = e^{ax}$ is to be generated. Taking the time derivative of both sides yields

$$\frac{dy}{dt} = ae^{ax}\frac{dx}{dt}$$

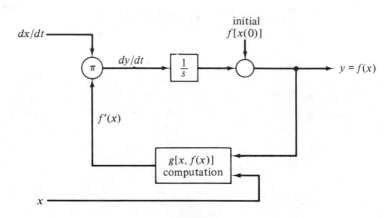

FIGURE 5-1

[i.e., $f(x) = e^{ax}$ and $f'(x) = ae^{ax}$]; hence $f'(x) = af(x) = g[f(x)]$. In this instance the general feedback function $g[x, f(x)]$ happens to be independent of x itself and may be obtained simply by multiplying $f(x)$ by the constant a. The resulting block diagram is an shown in Figure 5-2. The analog-computer program might appear as in Figure 5-3.

A slightly more complex version of this method might be employed to generate the trigonometric functions, as shown in the following example.

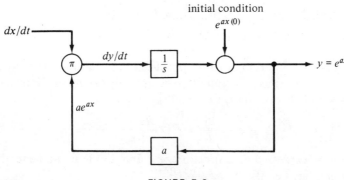

FIGURE 5-2

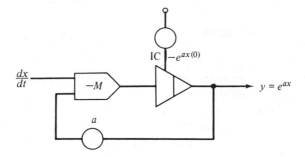

FIGURE 5-3

EXAMPLE The function $y = \cos ax$ is to be generated. Defining $z = \sin ax$, it can then be established that

$$\frac{dy}{dt} = -a \sin ax \frac{dx}{dt} = -az \frac{dx}{dt}$$

and

$$\frac{dz}{dt} = a \cos ax \frac{dx}{dt} = ay \frac{dx}{dt}$$

The block diagram of Figure 5-4 illustrates the program. From Figure 5-4

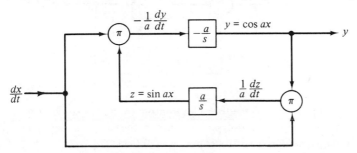

FIGURE 5-4

it may be seen that two integrators and two multipliers are needed. However, if a servo multiplier is available (and can be used in consideration of the speed of computation requirements), only one such multiplier would be needed since dx/dt is a common factor and may be used to position two ganged potentiometers, one to produce dy/dt and the other to produce dz/dt.

It may also be seen that with this method the function $\sin ax$ is also generated. In many applications this function would also be required.

---

[1]Note the symbol $\prod$ used within a circle in the block diagram to represent multiplication. If division is intended instead, the conventional arithmetic symbol ($\div$) is affixed outside of the circle where the input arrow representing the divisor enters; in the absence of such a $\div$ symbol, multiplication is implied.

5-3   General Philosophy of Implicit Methods

The implicit method of function generation is possible when there exists some mathematical conversion of the function to be generated that permits the use of simpler programs or equipment than would be required if the function desired was to be generated directly (i.e., explicitly). These mathematical relationships are not always clearly indicated, and finding them depends upon the ingenuity of the person establishing the program. One general example of this approach is the quarter-square multiplier described in Chapter 4.

5-4   Implicit Methods Based upon Feedback About Infinite-Gain Amplifiers

Functions that might be difficult to generate directly can often be produced if their inverse form is readily generated. For computers in general, the block diagram illustrating this method is shown in Figure 5-5. The algebraic

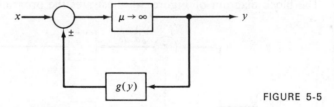

FIGURE 5-5

sign associated with the feedback summing point must be negative if the slope of $g(y)$ is positive, and positive when the slope is negative. Then the output y will be related to the input x as follows:

$$y = \mu[x - g(y)] \tag{5-3}$$

or

$$y + \mu g(y) = \mu x$$

However, as $\mu \longrightarrow \infty$, $g(y) \longrightarrow x$ and

$$y \longrightarrow g^{-1}(x) \qquad \text{as } \mu \longrightarrow \infty \tag{5-4}$$

In other words, the inverse of the $g(y)$ function has been generated.

The *infinite-gain element* actually employed in analog computers is an operational amplifier without feedback. The gain then is actually μ, the operational amplifier gain; ordinarily, however, this gain may be considered as equivalent to infinite on the basis of the same considerations as in Section 2-2.

For example, the circuit of Figure 5-6, or variations of it, is often

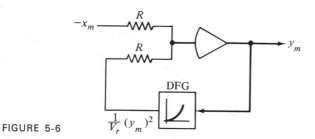

FIGURE 5-6

employed. Here $g(y_m) = (1/V_r)(y_m)^2$, where V_r is the voltage rating of the computer. Hence $g^{-1}(x_m) = \sqrt{V_r}\,\sqrt{x_m}$ and the square-root function has been generated (incidently, with an appropriate scaling) using a square-law function generator. This function generator need be of only the one-quadrant type since it would accommodate only positive x_m's and y_m's.

It must also be pointed out that the net transmission in the feedback loop *must always be negative*. Positive feedback would simply drive the operational amplifier to another operating point or to overload. This condition of negative feedback is satisfied in the Figure 5-6 arrangement.

In view of the above, the functions $g(y)$ and $g^{-1}(x)$ both must be monotonic. (In other words, in the strict mathematical sense, both must be true functions, not what are loosely called multivalued functions.) The difficulty that could be encountered otherwise is illustrated in Figure 5-7. In this arrangement, operation would be normal as long as x did not exceed x_1. As soon as it did, the then-negative slope of the curve would result in a positive-feedback effect driving y finally to y_4, where equilibrium would take place. A similar jump effect would occur during the reversal of this process; as x was decreased again to less than x_1, y would jump from y_2 to y_3. The pattern of the y versus x response, therefore, would appear as in Figure 5-8.

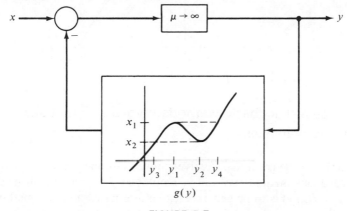

FIGURE 5-7

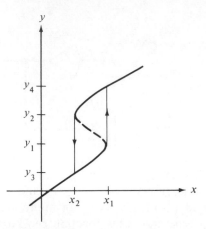

FIGURE 5-8

This type of nonreversible pattern will prove useful for the generation of various discontinuous functions, as discussed in Chapter 6. However, it will not produce the inverse of $g(y)$.

If, unlike the situation of Figure 5-7, $g(y)$ had been a function that did not again recover its positive slope, the positive-feedback action would have driven the operational amplifier to overload. An example of a $g(y)$ function that would cause this is shown in Figure 5-9. Here if x were to exceed x_1, y would continue to increase until limited by the overload conditions on the amplifier.

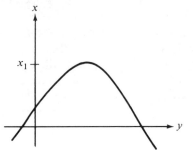

FIGURE 5-9

5-5   Negative-Feedback Methods Involving Functions of Two Variables

If the function to be generated involves more than one variable, the implicit negative-feedback method may still be employed. For example, if the desired function $z = f(x, y)$ is to be generated, two alternative implicit methods are available, shown in Figure 5-10. Which of the alternatives is employed depends upon convenience. The next section shows an example.

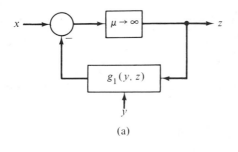

$g_1(y, z)$ = inverse of $f(x, y)$ with relationship of z and x inverted

(a)

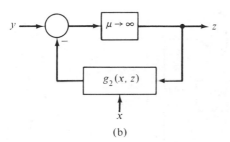

$g_2(x, z)$ = inverse of $f(x, y)$ with relationship of z and y inverted

(b)

FIGURE 5-10

5-6   Division by Implicit Methods

Suppose that the basic division operation is desired, $z = y/x$. Two alternative approaches are offered by Figure 5-10. $g_1(y, z)$ is the relation $x = y/z$ and offers no advantages since it merely converts one division problem to another. On the other hand, $g_2(x, z)$ is the relation $y = xz$ and is the one that would be employed if some form of multiplier (e.g., quarter square, time-division, servo) were available. The block diagram and analog-computer program would then appear as in Figure 5-11. It should be noted that negative feedback is maintained only if x_m is positive. If x_m is to be negative, a sign inversion should be incorporated in the multiplier to correct for this ($-M$ type). Furthermore, as x_m approaches zero too closely, the difficulty of division by zero, common to all types of computers, is encountered. In this case an overload of the operational amplifier will result. To analyze this the *worst* case should be considered, where $y_m = V_r$. Then

$$z_m = \frac{V_r^2}{kx_m} \le V_r$$

or

$$x_m \ge \frac{V_r}{k}$$

The attenuation factor k used to reduce the y_m signal should comply with

$$k \ge \frac{V_r}{x_{mmin}}$$

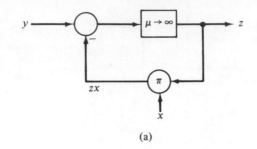

(a)

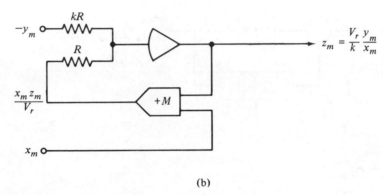

(b)

FIGURE 5-11

Suppose, for example, in a 10 V computer that $10 > x_m > 0.01$ V or $x_{m\,min}$ $= 0.01$. Then $k \geq 10/0.01 = 1000$ and the division operation would be

$$z_m = 0.01 \frac{y_m}{x_m}$$

z_m then has the maximum permitted value of 10 V when $y_m = 10$ V and x_m $= 0.01$ V.

In addition to the problem of overload when the divisor becomes too small, there is also the problem of decreasing accuracy of computation. To illustrate this let the circuit of Figure 5-11 be considered again with V_r $= 10$ and $k = 1000$, and with the gain of the operational amplifier considered as $-\mu$. Then actually

$$z_m = \mu \left(\frac{y_m}{1000} - \frac{z_m x_m}{10} \right)$$

or

$$z_m = \frac{\mu y_m}{1000 + 100 \mu x_m} = 0.01 \frac{y_m}{x_m + 10/\mu}$$

while the correct value of z_m would be

$$z_m = 0.01 \frac{y_m}{x_m}$$

The per-unit error, therefore, is approximately $10/\mu x_m$. As x_m has the minimum value of 0.01 V, μ must then be at least 100,000 to maintain an accuracy of 1 per cent. Furthermore, and possibly more important, *null errors* of only a small fraction of a volt can cause very significant errors in the quotient when the divisor becomes small.

The range limitation of analog computers is a significant handicap when division is executed that involves divisors with large variations in magnitude. Digital computers do not show this same degree of disadvantage, although there, as well, there is the possibility of an overflow occurring if the divisor becomes too small. Digital computers also have the disadvantage that division is a much slower operation than multiplication and that whenever a program calls for this arithmetic operation, considerable additional execution time is required.

In general, the relative desirability of a multiplication operation in preference to a division operation is similar to the preference for integration rather than differentiation. Whenever it is possible to do so by proper planning of a simulation model, multiplication is always the better choice.

5-7 Polar Resolution Involving Sine–Cosine Generators

Chapter 4 discussed resolvers (i.e., devices for obtaining the rectangular coordinates when the polar coordinates are given) performing the operations

$$x = r \cos \theta \tag{5-5}$$

$$y = r \sin \theta \tag{5-6}$$

This could be done in an analog computer by a combination of electronic sine and cosine function generators in conjunction with multipliers. It is also accomplished conveniently and precisely by means of servo resolvers, mentioned in Appendix 4D, provided the response-speed requirements of the problem are sufficiently slow.

The inverse operation, or *polar resolution*, normally consists of making use of the relations

$$\theta = \tan^{-1} \frac{y}{x} \tag{5-7}$$

$$r = \sqrt{x^2 + y^2} \tag{5-8}$$

Both of these are awkward functions to employ directly. An implicit technique is more convenient. From relations (5-5) and (5-6),

$$x \sin \theta - y \cos \theta = r(\sin \theta \cos \theta - \sin \theta \cos \theta) = 0 \tag{5-9}$$

This is a converted form of relation (5-7) obtained by means of trigonometric identities. The desired operation is then as shown in Figure 5-12.

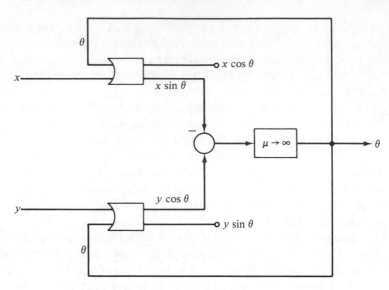

FIGURE 5-12

This polar resolution technique can handle angles, θ, within the range $-\pi < \theta < \pi$. If the range is greater than this, the $\tan^{-1}$ function is, of course, multivalued (not a true function). It is capable of handling both positive and negative rectangular components; note that, for example, $x = 2$ and $y = -2$ will give the correct result of $\theta = -\pi/4$, while $x = -2$ and $y = 2$ will give the correct result of $\theta = +3\pi/4$.

It is also important to observe that the *net* feedback will always be negative. To check this let the actual (as contrasted to the correct) value of θ be designated as θ_0. The *input* to the amplifier of gain μ is then

$$-x \sin \theta_0 + y \cos \theta_0 = r(-\sin \theta_0 \cos \theta + \cos \theta_0 \sin \theta)$$
$$= r \sin (\theta - \theta_0) \qquad (5\text{-}10)$$

As only angles between $-\pi$ and $+\pi$ radians are being dealt with:

1. When $\theta - \theta_0 > 0$ (i.e., θ_0 is less than the correct angle), a proper positive correction results.
2. When $\theta - \theta_0 < 0$ (i.e., θ_0 is greater than the correct angle), a proper negative correction results.

This implicit solution of relation (5-7) is only one half of the polar-resolution problem. The other is the determination of r. This second operation actually is now an explicit one, although relation (5-8) is not employed directly. Instead, use is made of the identity

$$x \cos \theta + y \sin \theta = r(\cos^2 \theta + \sin^2 \theta) = r \qquad (5\text{-}11)$$

This operation is combined with that of determining θ in Figure 5-13. The arrangement shown can produce difficulties when x and y become small, making r small as well. Relation (5-10) indicates that the input to the amplifier, of gain μ, is proportional to r for any given angular error. When r is too small, the feedback gain is reduced to the point where appreciable error could result.

This difficulty is overcome by using a very high gain μ beyond what normally would be required (or be compatible with stable operation) when r is large. An *automatic gain control* (AGC) feature is then added, as shown by the dashed lines in Figure 5-13. This reduces the gain when r is large but

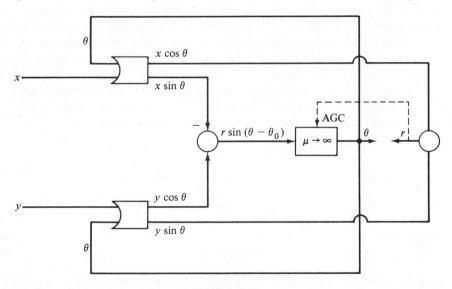

FIGURE 5-13

permits it to increase when r is small, thus maintaining what is essentially constant-feedback loop gain. Obviously, this process has its limitation; μ cannot be made actually infinite, and when r becomes excessively small, the loop gain will still fall off and errors will result. Nevertheless, the range of r that can be accommodated is adequate for most simulation problems.

Usually, the feedback connections required for this implicit method of polar resolution do not have to be planned by the programmer. Manufacturers of commercial resolvers, both of the servo and solid-state electronic type, generally provide this feature, including the AGC feature described above.

5-8   Substitution of Fast Integrators for the Infinite-Gain Amplifier

The methods of implicit function generation discussed up to now, involving infinite-gain amplifiers ($\mu \rightarrow \infty$), do not, of course, employ such hypothetical amplifiers in actuality. They employ, instead, operational amplifiers of very high gain. Under some conditions this gain is insufficient to establish a sufficiently high feedback-loop gain in the loop that establishes the function desired. Hence computation errors result. In other instances it is necessary to reduce the gain because inherent response lags, even though very short, that exist in all functional amplifiers result in the feedback loop becoming unstable. (An analysis of the conditions leading to such instability and the development of methods for avoiding such problems comes within the subject of feedback-amplifier design. It is an important consideration to those responsible for the design of analog-computer components but is not within the realm of this book.)

Often, one way of avoiding this problem is to substitute *fast integrators* for the infinite-gain amplifiers. The procedure for converting the amplifier is simple and is shown in Figure 5-14. Since what formerly was an operational

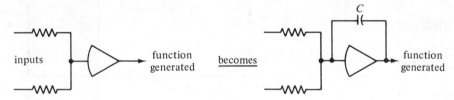

FIGURE 5-14

amplifier without feedback now becomes an integrator, infinite gain is achieved under *steady-state* conditions and it is theoretically possible for absolute static accuracy to be achieved; it is, of course, not completely possible in practice because of inevitable null errors. Perfect dynamic accuracy is still not achieved because of the response lag introduced by the integrator. However, if C is sufficiently small, this response lag will be negligible in consideration of the significant response times associated with the machine solution of the problem being simulated.

5-9   Avoiding Parasitic Oscillations in High-Gain Feedback Circuits

One of the chief reasons for substituting fast integrators for raw operational amplifiers with implicit function generation is, as just mentioned, the avoidance of *parasitic oscillations*. These are oscillations that occur because of the fact that all components involved do have some response lags (i.e., modifications of the amplitude response and phase shift with frequency). Therefore, the analog-computer program that might appear in theory to be perfectly stable may in practice be subject to such oscillations. These oscillations are almost always at high frequencies well beyond the range of the problem being simulated and therefore do not normally show up in output equipment, with the exception of cathode-ray oscilloscopes. Nevertheless, these oscillations are likely to cause periodic overloads of a particularly objectionable type, since the operator may not be aware of their existence. The moral of this is the advisability of always looking at the signals being produced by such high-gain amplifiers with a cathode-ray oscilloscope. The periodic overloads such oscillations cause can result in completely fallacious results.

When a problem such as the above is encountered, the substitution of fast integrators sometimes, but not always, provides the solution. There is another technique that usually is more effective and is based upon the principle of phase-lag networks used to permit high loop gains in feedback-control systems without jeopardizing stability. This consists of changing the operational amplifier to the circuit shown in Figure 5-15. In this circuit

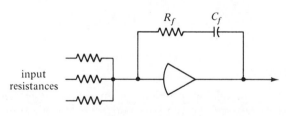

FIGURE 5-15

R_f should be about $\frac{1}{100}$ of the minimum input resistance employed. The capacitance C_f is then selected as follows: The parasitic oscillations that occur prior to this modification are observed on a cathode-ray oscilloscope and their frequency measured roughly (within 20 per cent) and translated to radians per second, ω_p. The recommended value of C_f is then given by the relation

$$C_f = \frac{10}{\omega_p R_f} \quad \mu\text{F}$$

with R_f being expressed in megohms.

This procedure will normally result in introducing response lags in the amplifier only at frequencies much higher than those significant in the simulation problem. The circuit functions by sharply reducing the gain of the amplifier at the higher frequencies, particularly those involved in the generation of the parasitic oscillations. In almost all cases encountered, the circuit of Figure 5-15 has proved successful in eliminating such oscillations.

5-10   Implicit Computations with Digital Computers

Many function-generation problems that require implicit techniques with analog computers may be handled directly with digital computers. This will be true when the function involved can be described in some arithmetic way, or when it can be obtained from a library subroutine.

There will, however, be instances when implicit techniques will be necessary with digital computation as well. Often a function $g(y)$ is available as an arithmetic operation or through an available subroutine, but its inverse, $y = f(x)$, is required. In such an event implicit techniques are necessary.

One example of this exists when $g(y)$ is available as tabulated data with interpolation included in the table look-up procedure. Another is in the solution of equations where the inverse solution is not analytically expressible, as in many transcendental functions. As one example, consider the simple relationship

$$x = g(y) = \frac{ay + be^{cy}}{dy + fe^{ky}} \tag{5-12}$$

x is given. How is y found? The inverse function, $y = f(x)$, cannot be expressed analytically.

If this were an analog problem, it might be suggested that it be approached by a program as in Figure 5-16. Such a program would converge to produce the correct value of y and, if k were sufficiently large, this convergence would be sufficiently rapid to meet the simulation needs. With digital computers the same basic program might be suggested with a rectangular-integration procedure substituted for the continuous procedure

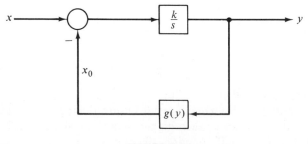

FIGURE 5-16

of Figure 5-16. The program would then appear as in Figure 5-17. There, α corresponds to $k \, \Delta t$. As $g(y)$ is almost always nonlinear, the stability (convergence capability) of such a program cannot be evaluated easily. However, for *small* perturbations about the correct value of y, it is possible to analyze this in terms of small increments of y and x_0 from their correct

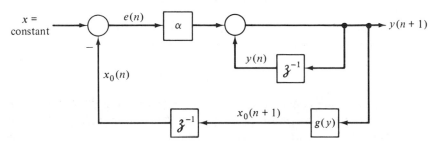

FIGURE 5-17

values. This is shown in Figure 5-18 with Δ used to denote that such incre-ments are being considered.

In Figure 5-18, h is strictly $[x_0(n + 1) - x_0(n)]/[y(n + 1) - y(n)]$, but may be considered approximately as the slope of the $g(y)$ relationship, or $g(y)$, at the point $y(n)$. An analysis of this situation by means of z transforms would show that

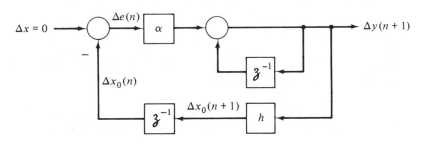

FIGURE 5-18

1. If $\alpha h < 1$, the solution would converge in a nonoscillatory fashion, approaching the correct solution. The lower αh is, the slower the convergence.
2. If $\alpha h = 1$, the solution would arrive directly at the correct result.
3. If $1 < \alpha h < 2$, the solution will converge in an oscillatory fashion upon the correct result. The higher αh is, the "wilder" will be the oscillations and the slower the convergence.
4. If $\alpha h > 2$, the solution will diverge in an oscillatory fashion.

From the above results it may be seen that the margin of adjustment of the integrator gain α is critical, since anything more than twice the optimum gain ($\alpha = 1/h$) results in divergence. Apparently, this gain must be adjusted to be the inverse of $g'(y)$ [i.e., what is estimated as the slope[2] of the $g(y)$ relationship, or the constant h]. Two recommendations, therefore, can be made about a program that would implement this procedure:

1. An automatic gain control feature is necessary so that α is adjusted to be the reciprocal of h, i.e., to the value

$$\frac{y(n) - y(n-1)}{x_0(n) - x_0(n-1)}$$

2. As complete convergence cannot be expected in a finite number of iterations, there must be a specified maximum permissible error (called e_{sp}); when the actual error ($e = x - x_0$) is within this magnitude range, the computation should terminate.

The fundamental portion of the digital program that would accomplish this is shown in Figure 5-19. The flow diagram of Figure 5-19 conforms to the block diagram of Figure 5-17 except for the addition of the following features:

1. A provision has been added for testing the error and accepting the value of y produced when error specifications are met.
2. The integration factor α is adjusted to be the reciprocal of what amount to the best guess of the value of $h = g'(y)$, based on the last two computations. That is, AGC has been added.

Four more features must be added to make the computation procedure of Figure 5-19 a workable subroutine.

1. There may be situations in which the computation will fail to converge and there must be a provision to stop the computation when this is observed.
2. There will be situations when convergence exists but is too slow in consideration of the time limitations of the program. When a specified maximum number of iterations have been performed

---

[2]If $g(y)$ is known as an analytically defined function, $g'(y)$ may, of course, be computed exactly. α would then, of course, be made equal to $1/g'(y)$. This procedure, known as *Newton's method*, would lead to a more rapid convergence. Unfortunately, with most simulation problems $g'(y)$ is not expressible as an analytic function and α must be determined on the basis of finite increments, as is done here. This latter procedure, described here and the basis of the subprogram described in the next section, is essentially a version of the well-known *Newton–Raphson method*.

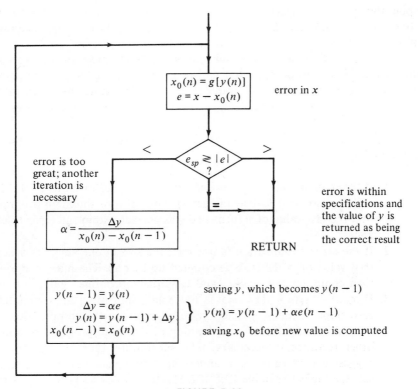

FIGURE 5-19

without reducing the error to within specifications, the computation is terminated.

3. There must be some first guess of α to provide a starting value for the first iteration since α cannot be computed, as there will be no $x_0(n-1)$ or $y(n-1)$. If the subroutine has been called previously, the last value of α that was employed may be a logical starting value.

4. There must be a first guess regarding the starting value of y. Again, if the program has been called previously, the last value of y determined may be the best first guess.

5-11 An Implicit Subprogram

It is convenient to employ a general subprogram that may be used regardless of the nature of the $g(y)$ function and the nature of the problem to which it is applied. Such a subprogram will be called here SUBROUTINE IMPLICIT. (The name of the procedure, for calling purposes, would depend upon the computer language employed; IMPLICIT would have to be abbreviated to, say, IMPLCT, for Fortran.) Figure 5-20 is a flow diagram of such a program.

Before the first call on this subroutine, the main program will specify the trial value of y to be used first and then compute the corresponding $x_0 = g(y)$. At the first call it will transmit to the subroutine the permissible error in x, or e_{sp}, the starting value of α, and will establish the number of tries (NTRIES) as 1.

When the subroutine returns to the main program, it will do one of the following:

1. If the error specification has been met, the logical variable, FINISH, will be made true (or the integer 1). This informs the main program that the last value of y furnished was correct within the error tolerance.
2. If the error specification is not met, the subroutine suggests a new trial value of y. NTRIES is counted up by one. The main program then computes the new x_0 and calls the subroutine again.
3. If $x_0(n) - x_0(n - 1) = \Delta x$ is too small, indicating approximately zero slope in the $g(y)$ function, an overflow in the computation of α would result. Either a replanning of the main program or some other recourse is necessary. The subroutine, therefore, does not suggest a new value of y under these circumstances but, instead, sets the logical variable ZEROSLOPE to true (or to 1) to so inform the main program.

The responsibility of setting initial trial values of α and y and of determining when the number of tries (NTRIES) has become excessive is assigned to the main program.

One implicit subroutine of this type could be used to handle a number of different implicit operations, either sequentially or in parallel. To accomplish this in parallel would, of course, require that the common arguments be listed as members of arrays.

Figure 5-21 shows how the main program would be arranged to make use of such an implicit subroutine. It should be noted that the program is permitted a maximum number of trials. Another test might be one of convergence; this test could be added easily to the implicit subroutine. Reference is made in Figure 5-21 to the prearranged corrective action to be taken whenever the zero-slope condition (discussed in more detail in the next section) is encountered or, because of slow or lack of convergence, an excessive number of trials is required. Usually such corrective action consists of changing the first trial values of y and α. How this is done depends upon the nature of the function being handled.

SUBROUTINE IMPLICIT($y, x, x_0, \alpha, e_{SP}$, NTRIES, FINISH, ZEROSLOPE)
LOGICAL FINISH, ZEROSLOPE

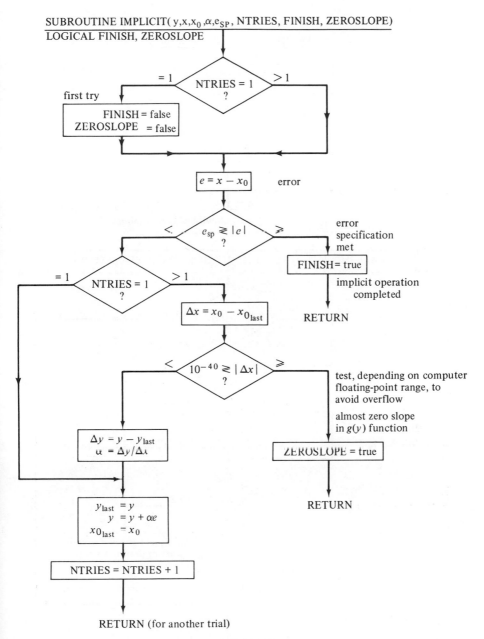

FIGURE 5-20

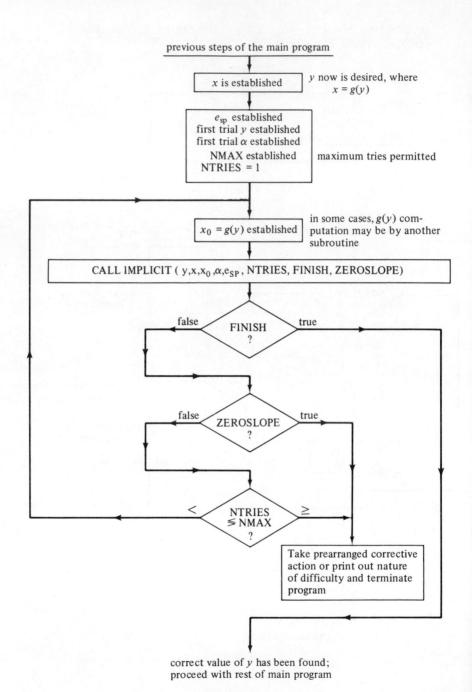

FIGURE 5-21

5-12　Graphical Description of the Implicit Procedure

Figure 5-22 illustrates what occurs when this implicit procedure is used. Point 1 represents the point corresponding to the first trial guess of y and the resulting computed value of x, or $x(1)$. The first error, $e(1)$, is the vertical distance between this point and the actual value of x. $\alpha(1)$ times this distance is the horizontal projection to the next value of y, or $y(2)$. [In this example

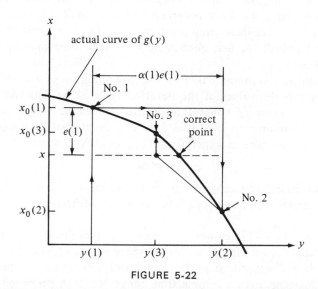

FIGURE 5-22

it may be seen that $\alpha(1)$ was too large and the next point, point 2, is about as far in the other direction from the correct point as was point 1.] Point 2 is the point on the true curve corresponding to this $y(2)$ and the resulting computed $x(2)$. The third iteration, in effect, projects upward from point 2 back to point 1, and selects $y(3)$ where this projection intersects the horizontal line corresponding to the correct x, and then projecting upward from this intersection determines, on the true curve, point 3 at the coordinates, $[y(3), x_0(3)]$. It can be seen that a continuation of this procedure will bring the intersection points on the curve progressively closer to the correct point.

This procedure can be an effective one requiring relatively few trial iterations (typically two to five) *if* the first guesses of $y(1)$ and $\alpha(1)$ are reasonable, and *if* the function $g(y)$ is monotonic (i.e., possesses a continuously positive or continuously negative slope).

Even with monotonic functions, difficulties can be experienced with this procedure if the values of $y(1)$ and $\alpha(1)$ are very far off. These difficulties may consist of (1) an excessive number of iterations being required, or (2) an underflow or overflow of numerical quantities as they range beyond the numerical capacity of the computer. This second difficulty is particularly apt to occur with functions having rapidly changing slopes.

Greater difficulties are encountered when the function $g(y)$ is not monotonic, as this means that its inverse $f(x)$ is not a true function and will have more than one solution. This was illustrated in Figure 5-8. In such an event, which solution will be found is a matter of chance and there is a strong possibility of an underflow or overflow occurring. Fortunately, in simulation problems such implicit programs will be employed during each time iteration and x will have progressed only a small increment from its previous value. Under these circumstances, once the first iteration has been successfully handled, the first guesses of y for later iterations of x will be rather good ones.

An implicit subroutine based on the flow diagram of Figure 5-20 was used to establish the values of the iteration interval Δt that will result in a specified rms error of computation; this procedure was used for the experimental development of Table 3-4. The functional relationship that has been described here in general terms as $g(y)$ then was

$$e_{rms} = g(\Delta t) \tag{5-13}$$

Here e_{rms} corresponds to x_0 in our general description. x now is the desired value of e_{rms} and is, of course, zero. y in our general description now becomes Δt.

Relationship (5-13) cannot be expressed practically as an analytic function (except for very trivial examples where a z transform analysis might lead to such a function). It is developed only by actually repeating the simulation problem over a sample time range for each proposed value of Δt. By means of the implicit subroutine it was possible to establish the value of Δt that would produce a specified rms error and thus provide a means for comparing different numerical methods, as was shown in Table 3-4.

5-13   Difficulties Encountered with Implicit Function Generation

As is discussed in Chapter 6, some functions arising in simulation problems will invove discontinuities. A memoryless discontinuity is shown in Figure 5-23. In such instances, difficulty will be encountered in meeting the error tolerance whenever x is specified in the discontinuous region. The implicit program just described will converge on $y = y_d$, but the value of x_0 will fluctuate from one side of this discontinuity to the other during each successive trial computation; naturally, the error specification e_{sp} will never be met.

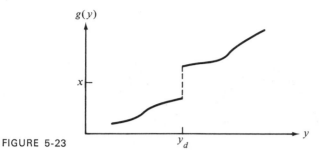

FIGURE 5-23

The recourse under such circumstances depends upon the context of this effect as it relates to the situation being simulated. In some instances it represents an error in constructing the program (x never should have been assigned a value in this range) and the program should terminate with a description of the difficulty. In other instances it may mean that $y = y_d$ *is* the correct result and the implicit computation should be considered as completed successfully with this as the result. In such latter instances it is necessary to add an algorithm to the implicit program to recognize that this is the case. Such an algorithm is based on recognizing that an oscillation of finite magnitude exists between two essentially constant values of x_0, with accompanying minute changes in the corresponding value of y. The mean value of y observed under such circumstances would be considered as the correct value.

Even when $g(y)$ is a continuous function, difficulties naturally would be encountered if a value of x should be specified that does not correspond to a real solution for y [e.g., $x = g(y) = \sin y$ when $x = 2$]. As this would indicate an error in planning the program or in the analysis leading to the program, the computations should then be terminated and would be terminated by the ZEROSLOPE condition.

A more common difficulty is encountered when $g(y)$ is not a monotonic function and, for some specified values of x, more than one solution for y exists. Which solution is reached by the implicit program will depend upon the trial starting values. On the other hand, which solution is the correct one will depend upon the nature of the problem. Figure 5-24 pictures such a situation. For values of x between the maximum and minimum (i.e., $x_1 < x < x_2$), three solutions, y_a, y_b, and y_c, would all be correct mathematically; only one of these could be correct in terms of the context of the actual problem being simulated. If the first two trial values of y lie between y_2 and y_1 (the y locations of the maximum and minimum), the implicit solution would always converge on y_b. If both trial values are less than y_2, the solution would always converge on y_a; if both are greater than y_1, on y_c. Other combinations of starting trial values lead to somewhat unpredictable solutions that would have to be traced out (following the procedure of

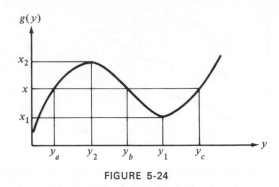

FIGURE 5-24

Figure 5-22) in each specific case. In other words, if the context of the problem calls specifically for one of these solutions as being the correct one,
then it is important that the trials be started in the vicinity of the correct
solution.

    In many instances involving multivalued solutions, the results that are
obtained will depend upon memory (i.e., upon past history). The correct
solution to the problem pictured in Figure 5-24 may be as shown in Figure
5-25. In other words, if *previous* solutions for y have been less than y_2, then

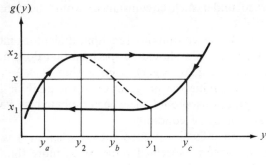

FIGURE 5-25

the correct solution for y, when x is as shown, would be y_a. However, when
x becomes greater than x_2, the solution for y will jump (as shown by the
arrow directed to the right) to the higher values of y. Then only when x
subsequently is reduced to a value less than x_1 will the solution jump again
(as shown by the arrow directed toward the left) to the lower range of y.
In other words, the correct solution, when in the multivalued range, will
depend upon past history. Under no circumstances would the correct solution be y_b. This type of jump and memory phenomena is discussed in more
detail in Chapter 6.

5-14   Implicit Solution of Simultaneous Relationships

Both analog and digital methods exist for the implicit solution of simultaneous relationships[3] of both linear and nonlinear form. The analog methods are, however, somewhat awkward to employ and can introduce stability problems, particularly when the number of simultaneous relations is large. Such analog techniques are described in the literature [1]. Digital techniques are generally better adapted for this purpose.

The digital solution of *linear* simultaneous equations is, of course, straightforward and well known. The methods are generally based on matrix-manipulation techniques. A procedure will be described here, related to the well-known Newton–Raphson method, that will handle *nonlinear* simultaneous relationships as well. It will be employed in Chapter 7 for the handling of boundary-value problems. The method is essentially an extension of the implicit subprogram described in Section 5-11.

This digital method will handle simultaneous relations of the form

$$[y] = f([x]) \qquad (5\text{-}14)$$

where $[y]$ and $[x]$ are vectors (arrays). In other words, for n equations,

$$y(1) = f_1[x(1), x(2), \ldots, x(n)]$$
$$y(2) = f_2[x(1), x(2), \ldots, x(n)]$$
$$\cdot$$
$$\cdot$$
$$\cdot$$
$$y(n) = f_n[x(1), x(2), \ldots, x(n)]$$

Given the desired values of the y's (i.e., the y_{sp}'s), the values of the x's are found by means of the following steps:

1. Starting values of the trial x's (i.e., the x_0's) are assumed, established by the main program. The main program then establishes the corresponding y's from the simultaneous relationships.
2. The subroutine computes the errors in the y's (i.e., their difference from the specified values) by the equation $y_e(i) = y_{sp}(i) - y(i)$.
3. A check is made of whether all these errors fall within the tolerance region. If they do, the original starting x's were correct, the job is done, FINISH is made true, and the operation is returned to the main program. Normally this does not happen on the first trial.

---

[3]The term "relationship" is preferred here rather than "equation" to indicate that the methods discussed are applicable to relationships established by computer simulation programs as well as those expressible algebraically.

4. If the errors do not all fall within the tolerance region, a check is made as to whether the maximum number of trials has been employed. (This would naturally not be the case on the first trial.) If so, the subroutine prints out this information and terminates the program.

5. Unless this is the first trial, the values of the perturbation increments, the Δx's, are all divided by 2.

6. The values of the errors in y, or the y_e's, are saved as the B vector prior to perturbating the values of x and getting new y's.

7. The subscript of the x to be perturbated, (j), is first established as 1.

8. PERTURBATING, a logical variable, previously established as false in the main program, is now made true.

9. The particular x to be perturbated is saved as x_{save}.

10. The reciprocal of the perturbation increment, $\Delta x(j)$, is found to avoid repeated division.

11. The value of $x_0(j)$ is now perturbated by the specified amount $\Delta x(j)$.

12. Operation is then returned to the main program for a computation of the y's based on the perturbated x.

13. After computing the new y's, operation is returned to subroutine SIMULTANEOUS. The new values of the errors in y, the y_e's, are again computed (the values prior to perturbation having been saved in the B vector).

14. Since PERTURBATING is true, operation is directed to step 15. Were it not, operation would have been transferred to step 3 for one more trial.

15. The ratio of the change in the y_e's resulting from the perturbating of $x(j)$ to the magnitude of $x(j)$ is computed as the jth column of the A matrix.

16. The value of the x_0 just perturbated is restored to its value prior to perturbation.

17. If all the x's have been perturbated (i.e., $j = n$) the operation continues with step 19. Otherwise it goes on to 18.

18. j is "upcounted" by one and operation goes back to step 9 to start the perturbation of one more x.

19. Here all x's have received the test perturbations. The complete A matrix relating the changes in the y's to the test-perturbation changes in the x's has been established. From this and the B vector that has stored the errors in y resulting from this trial, it would be possible to establish the changes of x, or the Δx_0's, that would reduce the errors in y to exactly zero *if* the relations

were linear. Since they usually will not be linear when this technique is employed, the resultant changes in x will simply bring their values closer to the correct answer. What is done is to solve the simultaneous relationships expressed in matrix form as

$$[A][\Delta x_0] = [B]$$

This is done by calling a standard form of subroutine, called SIMQ, which solves *linear* simultaneous equations. This subroutine is often a standard library program in larger scientific computer installations. It is, however, described in Appendix 5A for the benefit of those wishing to arrange their own subroutine. This subroutine finds the array of Δx_0's that would, if used to increment the previously used x_0's, bring them to exactly their prescribed values *if* the relations were linear. It converts the B vector to a vector containing these Δx_0's.

20. The values of x_0 are now incremented by the amounts of Δx_0 prescribed by the preceding step. PERTURBATING is made false and operation is returned to the main program for a computation of the values of y resulting from these new recommended x_0's.

21. When the subroutine is called again, since PERTURBATING is false, steps 2 and 3 are repeated and a new trial is conducted.

The result of the above procedure is the establishment of values of x_0's that are closer and closer to the correct values (i.e., the values that will make the computed y's equal to y_{sp}). The procedures just described are shown in flow-diagram form in Figure 5-26. The steps in that diagram are numbered to correspond with those described above.

There will be circumstances when the process described will not converge on a solution in a reasonable number of trials and may, in fact, diverge. The considerations governing this are similar to those discussed in Section 5-13 for the implicit subprogram. Convergence can always be obtained in a reasonable number of trials for appropriate selection of initial x_0's and Δx's; however, such a selection is not always easy to realize. Therefore, some maximum number of trials should be specified and the program stopped as unsuccessful after this number of trials has been made without the error tolerances having been met.

The implicit subprogram for function generation discussed previously in this chapter is but a special case of the procedure described here for $n = 1$. Figure 5-27 is an example of how such a subroutine might be employed. It should be noted that this subprogram constitutes a general-purpose module; it may be used for any set of simultaneous relationships provided the array dimensions are made adequate.

(1)

SUBROUTINE SIMULTANEOUS(n, x_0, y_{sp}, y_{tol}, y, Δx, FINISH, TRIALS, TRIALS$_{max}$, PERTURBATING)

LOGICAL: FINISH indicates operation completed; tolerances have been met; PERTURBATING means that a perturbation test is being made

n is number of simultaneous relations; x_0, Δx, y_{sp}, y_{tol}, y, y_e, and B are arrays of order n; initial x, n, y_{sp}, y_{tol}, TRIALS$_{max}$, and initial Δx are all furnished by the main program; on each call of this subroutine, the main program also furnishes the values of y resulting from the last suggested values of x

(2)

DO   for $i = 1$ to n

computation of errors in y

$y_e(i) = y_{sp}(i) - y(i)$

yes
(14)   PERTURBATING
                                 ?
                                                   no
                                                   (21)

a trial has just been made with given x's

(3)

DO for $i = 1$ to n

error tolerances not met; consider another trial

$<$ $y_{tol}(i) \lessgtr |y_e(i)|$ $>$
                      ?

$=$

continue

FIGURE 5-26

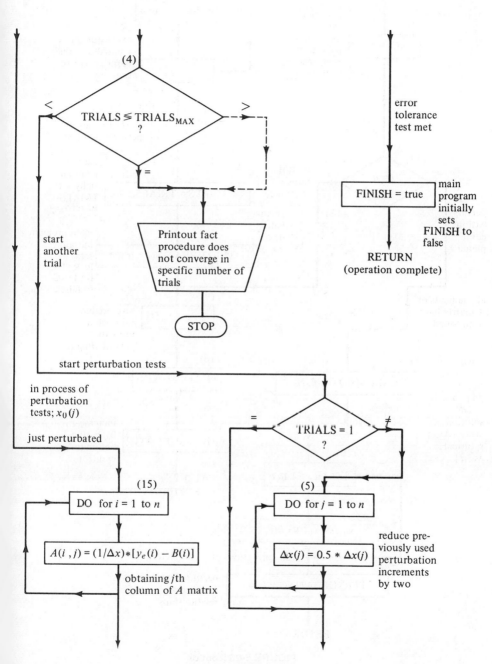

FIGURE 5-26 (cont'd)

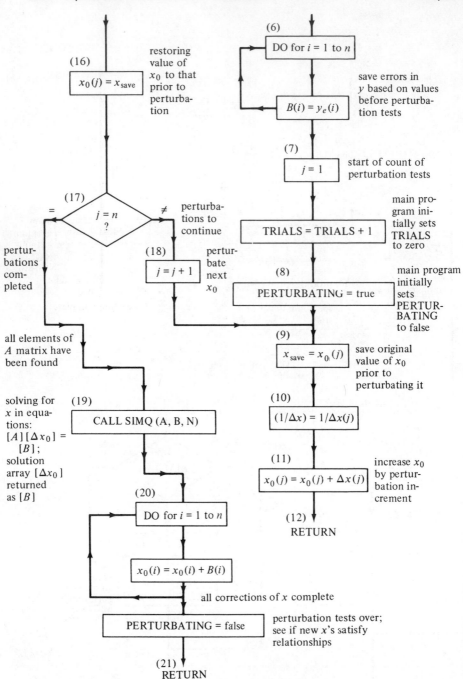

FIGURE 5-26 (cont'd)

Sample program for

$$y(1) = f_1[x(1), x(2), x(3)]$$
$$y(2) = f_2[x(1), x(2), x(3)]$$
$$y(3) = f_3[x(1), x(2), x(3)]$$

Given $y(1)$, $y(2)$, and $y(3)$ as $y_{sp}(1)$, $y_{sp}(2)$, and $y_{sp}(3)$, the values of $x(1)$, $x(2)$, and $x(3)$ are to be found.

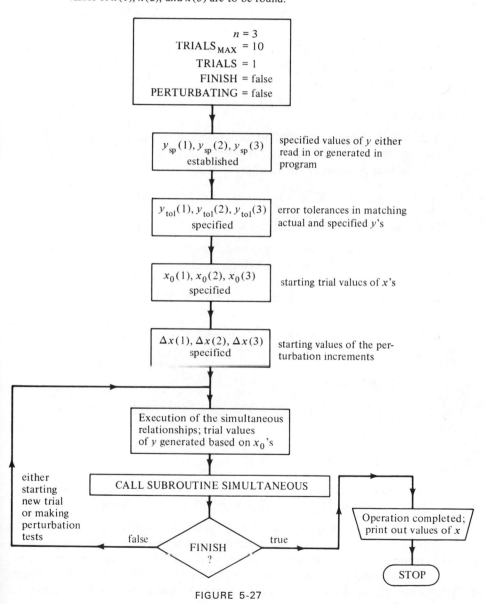

FIGURE 5-27

Suggested Problems

5-1. x is a time-varying signal that has been provided by an analog program already established. A related signal is to be generated, y, where

$$\frac{d^2y}{dt^2} + 2e^{-ay}\frac{dy}{dt} + y = x$$

No dynamic-storage facilities or function generators are available, only simple diodes that might, for example, be used in absolute-value circuits. Multipliers are, however, available. Develop the analog program required, disregarding scaling but showing the application of initial conditions to all integrators used.

5-2. Several nonlinear function generators are available capable of generating the function $50 \log_{10} x_m$. However, there are no multipliers available. It is desired to produce the function

$$z_m = 0.01\frac{x_m}{y_m} \text{ V} \qquad \text{where } 0.01 < x_m < 100, 0.01 < y_m < 100$$

Show how this function might be produced.

5-3. Figure 4A-1 shows a method for generating the function $z_m = 10^{-5}x_m^{1.4}y_m^2$. However, let it be assumed that the diode function generator producing the signal $10^{w/50}$ is not available, but additional fixed function generators of the type $50 \log_{10}$ are. Modify the program to handle this situation.

5-4. The functions described in Problem 4-3 are to be generated. However, only fixed-diode function generators of two types are available:

$$\text{(a) logarithmic:} \qquad y_m = 0.5V_r \log_{10}\left(\frac{100x_m}{V_r}\right)$$

$$\text{i.e., } y_m = 50 \log_{10} x_m \qquad \text{for a 100 V computer}$$

$$= 5 \log_{10}(10 x_m) \qquad \text{for a 10 V computer}$$

$$\text{(b) square law:} \qquad y_m = \frac{x_m^2}{V_r}$$

Develop these functions using only the function generators mentioned above. Diodes are not to be used, except in absolute-value circuits.

5-5. Develop a program that will produce the nonlinear function $y_m = k/(x_m + 1)$, where x_m is a given input signal within the range of $0 < x_m < V_r$ volts. A signal representing dx_m/dt is also available. Select for both 100- and 10-V computers the maximum round value of k that will avoid overload. Do not use diodes or relay comparators. A multiplier may be assumed to be available.

5-6. Take scaling into account in this problem. Using a sine–cosine resolver, generate the function

$$y_m = 0.1V_r \sec x$$

for $-84° < x < 84°$.

5-7. A function $g(y)$ is known as follows:

$$x = g(y) = e^y + e^{1.2y}$$

A digital program is desired that will provide the value of y when x is given within the range $0.005 < x < 200$. Prepare such a program. The value of y is to be found so that the corresponding value of x, or x_0, agrees within 0.1 per cent with the value specified. Test such a program (i.e., find y) when x is $0.005, 0.01, 0.02, 0.05, \ldots, 50, 100, 200$.

5-8. Refer to Problem 1-1(c), where for a given annual rate of interest, R, the value of a bond where for a given annual rate of interest, R, the value of a bond at maturity (after 10 years) was to be computed when interest is compounded quarterly. As stated in Chapter 1, it was required to find by trial and error the value of R that would result in a doubling of the value. Now apply the implicit procedure described in this present chapter for the purpose of performing this trial-and-error operation.

5-9. The input and output to a control system are related as follows:

$$\ddot{c} + 10\dot{c} + 100c = 100r$$

The input is given as the following time function:

$$r = 100 - 20e^{-5t}(\cos 3t + \cos 7t + \cos 17t + \cos 37t + \cos 73t)$$

$c(0)$ and $\dot{c}(0)$ are zero. The response is to be simulated over an interval of 2 sec.

Actually, this problem is simple enough to permit a ready analytic solution. The solution is

$$c = 100\left[1 - e^{-5t}\left(\cos 5\sqrt{3}\,t + \frac{\sqrt{3}}{3}\sin 5\sqrt{3}\,t\right)\right]$$
$$- 20e^{-5t}\left(\frac{\cos 3t - \cos 5\sqrt{3}\,t}{75 - 3^2} + \frac{\cos 7t - \cos 5\sqrt{3}\,t}{75 - 7^2}\right.$$
$$+ \frac{\cos 17t - \cos 5\sqrt{3}\,t}{75 - 17^2} + \frac{\cos 37t - \cos 5\sqrt{3}\,t}{75 - 37^2}$$
$$\left. + \frac{\cos 73t - \cos 5\sqrt{3}\,t}{75 - 73^2}\right)$$

Prepare a digital simulation program that can make use of any of the following methods of numerical integration: 1a-1, 2a-1, or 4a-1. With each of these methods find the value of Δt that will produce an rms error in the computation of c equal to 0.1 ± 0.005.

If facilities are available for measuring execution time with each of these methods (excluding any input or output time), compare the execution time required by each method when Δt is so selected.

5-10. Consider the following set of simultaneous equations:

$$y(1) = 3x(1)x(2) + x(3) = 12.50$$

$$y(2) = \sin x(1) + \exp [x(2)] = 3.317$$

$$y(3) = x(2) \ln x(3) = 1.609$$

Use the digital method of Section 5-14 to find $x(1)$, $x(2)$, and $x(3)$. Experiment with different starting values of the x's and Δx's and note the effect upon convergence of the solution.

References

1. A. S. Jackson, *Analog Computation* (New York: McGraw-Hill, Inc., 1960), specifically Chap. 9.

Appendix 5A:
Subprogram for the Solution of
Simultaneous Linear Equations

There are a number of approaches to the problem of solving simultaneous linear algebraic equations; the one described here is a modification of the Gauss–Jordan elimination method.[4] The procedure used is described below with a simple illustrative example given.

1. The n equations are presented in the form of an $n \times n$ matrix, A, and an $n \times 1$ vector, B. That is,

$$[A][x] = [B]$$

where $[x]$ also is a vector of order $n \times 1$, in other words, the array $x(1), x(2), \ldots, x(n)$. As an example, consider the equations

$$3x(1) - 2x(2) + x(3) = 4$$
$$2x(1) \qquad - x(3) = 0$$
$$x(1) + x(2) + x(3) = 9$$

$$[A] = \begin{bmatrix} 3 & -2 & 1 \\ 2 & 0 & -1 \\ 1 & 1 & 1 \end{bmatrix} \qquad [B] = \begin{bmatrix} 4 \\ 0 \\ 9 \end{bmatrix}$$

[4]Bruce Arden, *Introduction to Digital Computing* (Reading, Mass.: Addison-Wesley Publishing Company, Inc., 1963), Chap. 14.

241

2. First, column 1 of A is selected as the first *pivot column*. All rows of A are examined to determine which has the first-column element with the greatest absolute value. This is then made the first *pivot row*. It is made row 1; if it was not row 1 originally, the elements are interchanged with those of the present row 1 (including the row 1 element of the B vector). In effect, nothing has been changed except that now the equations may be listed in a different sequence. In the example given above, the original row 1 element, $A_{11} = 3$, would be chosen as the *pivot element* and no interchange would be necessary.

3. All elements in the pivot row (i.e., row 1) are divided by the pivot element. This included the B-matrix element in that row. In the example this would result in the A matrix and B vector becoming

$$[A] = \begin{bmatrix} 1 & -0.66\dot{6} & 0.33\dot{3} \\ 2 & 0 & -1 \\ 1 & 1 & 1 \end{bmatrix} \qquad [B] = \begin{bmatrix} 1.33\dot{3} \\ 0 \\ 9 \end{bmatrix}$$

4. Every element of row 1 is multiplied by the pivot-column element of row 2 (in the example, by $A_{21} = 2$), and the resulting element then subtracted from the elements below in row 2. This will make A_{21} zero.

5. Step 4 is repeated but now with respect to the next row; i.e., every row 1 element is multiplied by A_{31} and the resulting values subtracted from row 3. The process is continued until performed with all the rows below the pivot row (still row 1). For the example being used the A matrix and B vector will appear as follows when this step is completed:

$$[A] = \begin{bmatrix} 1 & -0.66\dot{6} & 0.33\dot{3} \\ 0 & 1.33\dot{3} & -1.66\dot{6} \\ 0 & 1.66\dot{6} & 0.66\dot{6} \end{bmatrix} \qquad [B] = \begin{bmatrix} 1.33\dot{3} \\ -2.66\dot{6} \\ 7.66\dot{6} \end{bmatrix}$$

6. Step 2 is repeated but now with column 2 as the pivot column. All rows from 2 below are searched to find the maximum pivot and, if this does not appear in row 2, an interchange is made. Row 2 (after such an interchange, if necessary) then becomes the pivot row. In the example being used the maximum pivot-column element appears in row 3, so an interchange *is* necessary. The A matrix and B vector will then appear as

$$[A] = \begin{bmatrix} 1 & -0.66\dot{6} & 0.33\dot{3} \\ 0 & 1.66\dot{6} & 0.66\dot{6} \\ 0 & 1.33\dot{3} & -1.66\dot{6} \end{bmatrix} \qquad [B] = \begin{bmatrix} 1.33\dot{3} \\ 7.66\dot{6} \\ -2.66\dot{6} \end{bmatrix}$$

Step 3 is repeated with row 2 as the pivot row, and then step 4, the subtraction operation now being performed on all rows below it. In the example the result as far as the A matrix and B vector are concerned would be

$$[A] = \begin{bmatrix} 1 & -0.66\dot{6} & 0.33\dot{3} \\ 0 & 1 & 0.400 \\ 0 & 0 & -2.200 \end{bmatrix} \quad [B] = \begin{bmatrix} 1.33\dot{3} \\ 4.600 \\ -8.800 \end{bmatrix}$$

7. Step 6 is performed again with all rows successively becoming the pivot row and corresponding columns becoming the pivot column until row $n - 1$ (row 2 in the simple example being used).

8. Element A_{nn} will be the last pivot. Only step 3 need be performed. For the example given the A matrix and B vector would appear as

$$[A] = \begin{bmatrix} 1 & -0.66\dot{6} & 0.33\dot{3} \\ 0 & 1 & 0.400 \\ 0 & 0 & 1 \end{bmatrix} \quad [B] = \begin{bmatrix} 1.33\dot{3} \\ 4.600 \\ 4.000 \end{bmatrix}$$

The equations for this example are now in the form

$$x_1 - 0.66\dot{6}x_2 + 0.33\dot{3}x_3 = 1.33\dot{3}$$
$$x_2 + 0.400x_3 = 4.600$$
$$x_3 = 4.000$$

Note the triangular form of the A matrix. The solution for $x(n)$ [$x(3)$ in the example] has already been found.

9. Now the *back solution* is performed, starting from the bottom row. This already holds (in the B matrix) the correct value of $x(n)$. If this is substituted in the equations above it, $x(n)$ will be eliminated and the correct value of $x(n - 1)$ will appear in the B vector. This in turn may be substituted until the values of all the x's appear as the vector B. The algorithm for this is shown in the flow diagram of Figure 5A-1. When all the back-substitution work has been completed, the B vector will appear as

$$[B] = \begin{bmatrix} 2.000 \\ 3.000 \\ 4.000 \end{bmatrix}$$

[i.e., $x(1) = 2$, $x(2) = 3$, $x(3) = 4$]. The flow diagram of Figure 5A-1 shows the entire process described here.

If ever a pivot element cannot be found that has an absolute value greater than the tolerance (set equal to 10^{-10} in this program), the matrix is singular and the equations have no solution. In this event (i_{max} remaining zero), the subprogram prints out this fact and then halts execution.

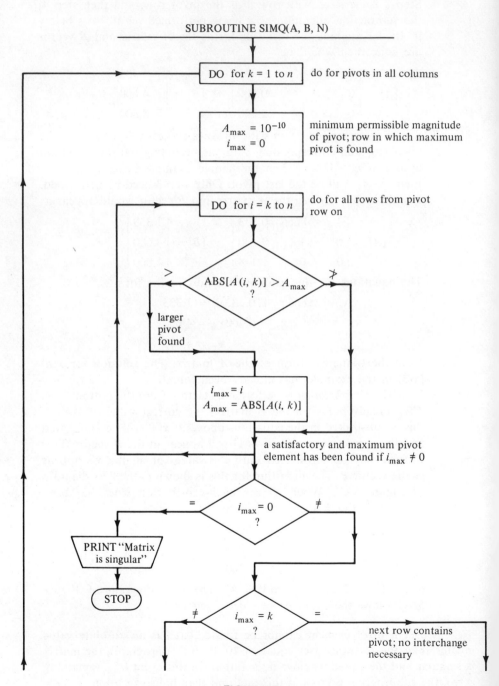

FIGURE 5A-1

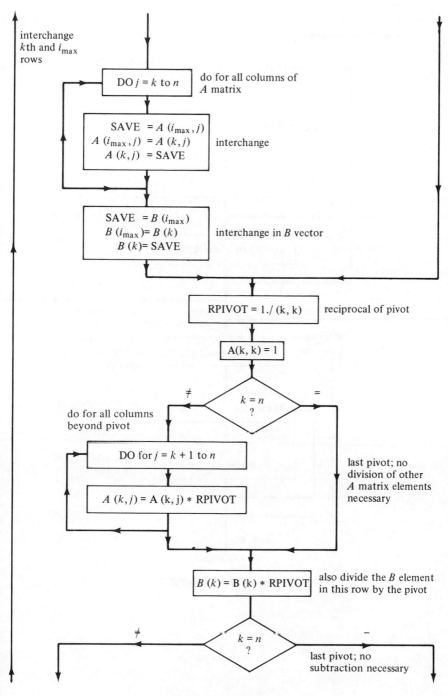

FIGURE 5A-1 (cont'd)

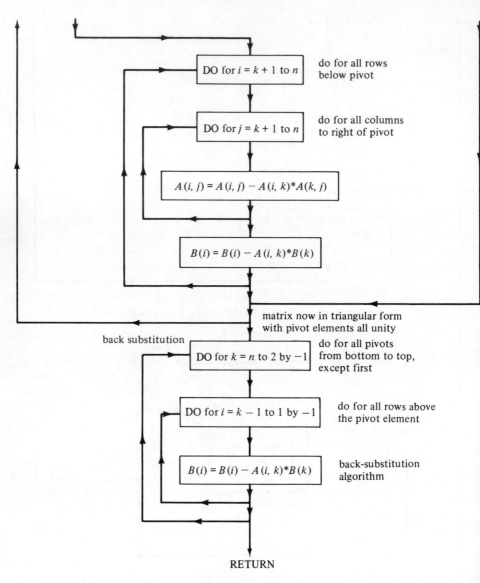

RETURN

FIGURE 5A-1 (cont'd)

Simulation of Discontinuous Relations   6

6-1   Instances Where Discontinuous Relations Occur

When the subject of discontinuous relations arises in regard to physical systems, first thought is normally given to such common phenomena as electrical-relay operation or mechanical limit stops. There are many more examples bound to arise in practical simulation problems. Other physical examples are limiting in the electrical sense, mechanical free play or backlash, Coloumb friction, stiction, and other effects. In linear programming (as applied to operations research as well as to physical simulation problems), the constraints that constitute a basic part of the problem are a form of limiting. The representation of such discontinuous effects on either an analog or digital computer is an important part of the general subject of simulation.

6-2   Limiting

Limiting may for example, occur as a saturation effect in an electrical amplifier, as in Figure 6 1. This is *soft limiting*; it does not represent a discontinuous relationship and generally is simulated by function-generator techniques treated in Chapter 4.

    Hard limiting is less likely to occur in electronic components, such as amplifiers, unless introduced purposely by some switching means, but occurs

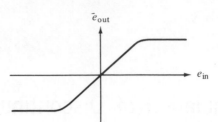

FIGURE 6-1

frequently in mechanical systems. It is shown by the relationships in Figure 6-2. It should be noted that the two abscissa values at which limiting occurs, $x_L(1)$ and $x_L(2)$, need not be of the opposite sign. The examples of Figure 6-2 represent bilateral limiting; unilateral limiting can also occur. Strictly speaking, these relationships are not discontinuous (although they are mathematically nonanalytic); they are discontinuous only in their slope. Nevertheless, it is convenient to include such a limiting phenomenon among the items discussed in this chapter.

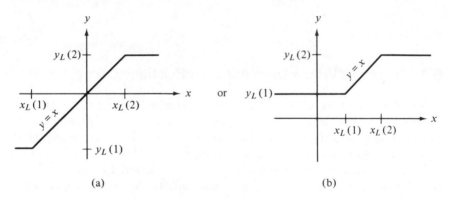

(a)   (b)

FIGURE 6-2

A variety of analog techniques is available for simulating such limiting. Two examples are shown in Figure 6-3. Both examples apply to the instance where $x_L(2)$ is positive and $x_L(1)$ is negative (as in Figure 6-2a). If either one of these quantities should be assigned the other algebraic sign, it would be necessary to apply the reference voltage of the sign opposite to that shown in the diagram (the diodes, however, maintain the direction shown).

In Figure 6-3a it should be noted that the bias voltages are not applied directly from the potentiometer that establishes them but rather through inverting amplifiers. The purpose of this is to provide the lowest possible source resistance associated with these bias voltages. Any significant bias-supply resistance results in imperfect limiting in that the slope of the y

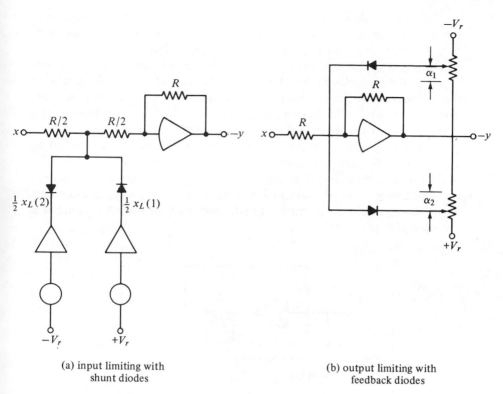

(a) input limiting with
shunt diodes

(b) output limiting with
feedback diodes

FIGURE 6-3

versus x relationship, as shown in Figure 6-2, would no longer be zero (horizontal) but would acquire some positive slope.

In Figure 6-3b this isolation of the potentiometers is not done; the
source resistance represented by the floating potentiometer adds to the
effective series resistance of the diode and causes the slope of the y versus
x relation to be finite rather than zero in the limited range of operation.
This effect might be avoided by the use of inverters operated from the outputs
of the floating potentiometers, but then a second inverter would also be
necessary in the feedback loop to maintain the negative sense of the feedback.

When applying the circuit in Figure 6-3b, the proper potentiometer
settings, α_1 and α_2, are given by the relation

$$\alpha_L = \frac{V_r}{y_L + V_i}$$

In most practice these settings are not established by this relation but rather
by a trial-and-error adjustment while the limited output is observed on a
voltmeter.

When absolutely sharp limiting is required, a circuit employing ideal diodes could be used. An example of such a circuit is shown in Figure 6-4.

In addition to those techniques employing diodes, comparators may be employed to simulate limiting. Figure 6-5 shows such an arrangement.

All the examples shown (Figures 6-1 to 6-5) relate to limiting when y is equal to x within the unlimited range. As a matter of fact, other operations may be combined with limiting. A gain factor could be introduced or the output amplifier could be employed as an integrator. In such instances there is a significant difference between *input*-limiting techniques, examplified by Figures 6-3a, 6-4, and 6-5, and *output* limiting, examplified by Figure 6-3b. In the former instance, x is limited; in the latter, y is. This is especially important when integrators are combined with limiting as then, with input limiting, it is the *integrand* that is being limited, whereas with output limiting it is the *integral* itself.

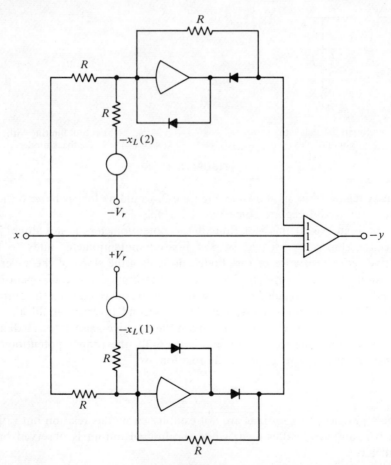

FIGURE 6-4

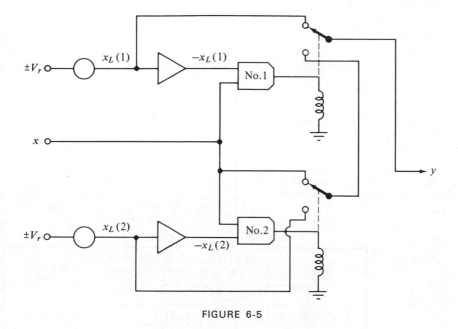

FIGURE 6-5

6-3   Digital-Comparator Module

Discontinuous effects may be simulated with digital equipment by using the digital equivalent of a comparator. For example, Figure 6-5 could be used as the basis of logic for simulating hard limiting by digital means.

A digital-computer version of a comparator is somewhat more complicated than it might appear at the outset. With digital simulation, the iteration intervals are specified on the basis of such considerations as required accuracy and required interval of printout. With methods such as Runge–Kutta this interval may be quite large. It is completely unlikely that a comparator will be actuated at exactly the end of any given iteration interval. However, it is important that the instant of time of comparator transition (actuation or deactuation) be established. This suggests a temporary variation of the iteration interval and a search for the transition instant.

Figure 6-6 is a flow diagram illustrating the operation of a general-purpose comparator module. It may be used to simulate any number (COMPS) of independent comparator units. The input signal to the comparator will be called here SIG, this is equivalent to the sum of the voltages applied to an analog comparator. When $\text{SIG} > 0$, the comparator is actuated ($\text{ACT} = $ true); otherwise, it is deactuated ($\text{ACT} = $ false).

At the first iteration of the simulation program ($\text{STATUS} = 1$), the actuation state (ACT) of each comparator is established. After each sub-

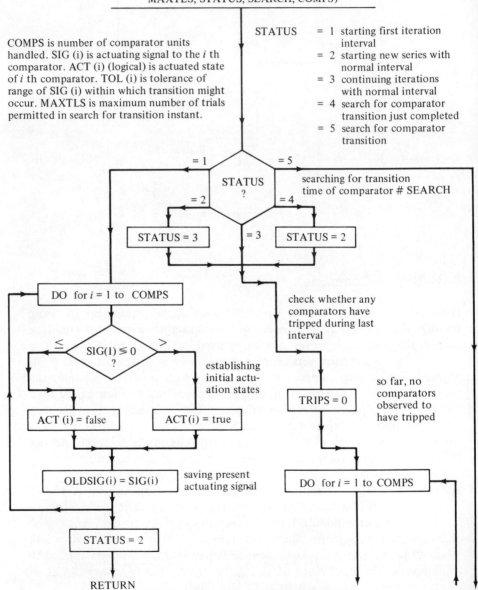

SUBROUTINE COMPAR(ACT, SIG, Δt , TOL,
MAXTLS, STATUS, SEARCH, COMPS)

COMPS is number of comparator units
handled. SIG (i) is actuating signal to the *i* th
comparator. ACT (i) (logical) is actuated state
of *i* th comparator. TOL (i) is tolerance of
range of SIG (i) within which transition might
occur. MAXTLS is maximum number of trials
permitted in search for transition instant.

STATUS = 1 starting first iteration
interval
= 2 starting new series with
normal interval
= 3 continuing iterations
with normal interval
= 4 search for comparator
transition just completed
= 5 search for comparator
transition

STATUS
?

= 1   = 5

searching for transition
time of comparator # SEARCH

= 2   = 4

STATUS = 3   = 3   STATUS = 2

DO for *i* = 1 to COMPS

check whether any
comparators have
tripped during last
interval

SIG(1) ≤ 0
?

≤   >

establishing
initial actu-
ation states

so far, no
comparators
observed to
have tripped

TRIPS = 0

ACT (i) = false   ACT(i) = true

OLDSIG(i) = SIG(i)   saving present
actuating signal

DO for *i* = 1 to COMPS

STATUS = 2

RETURN

FIGURE 6-6

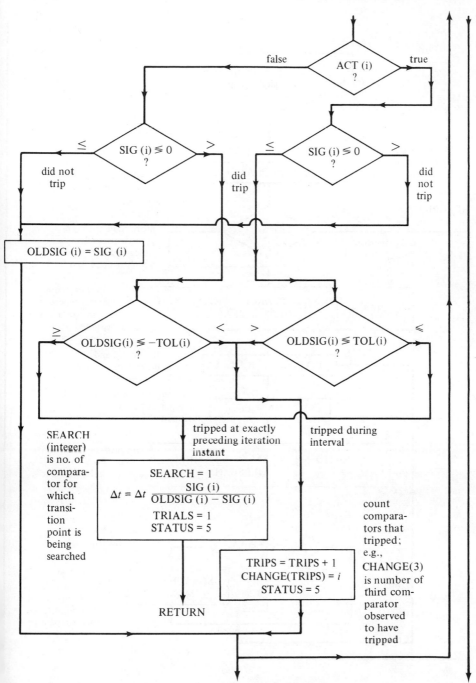

FIGURE 6-6 (cont'd)

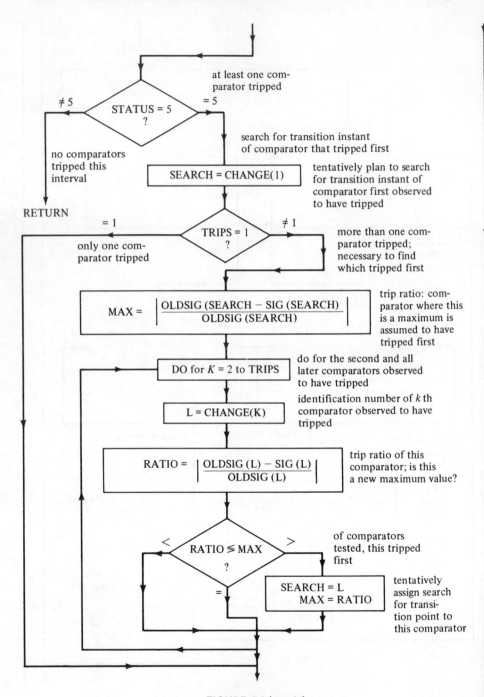

FIGURE 6-6 (cont'd)

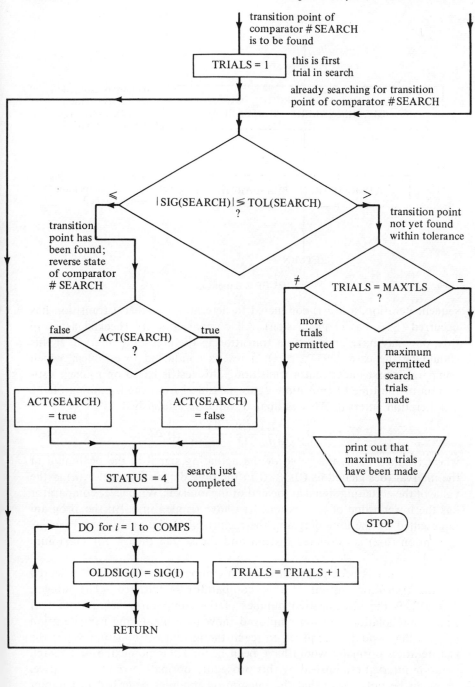

FIGURE 6-6 (cont'd)

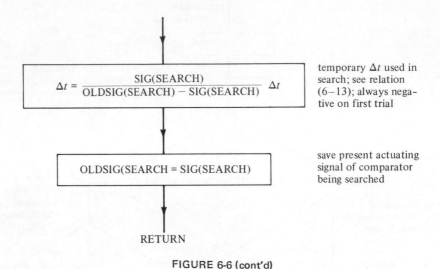

$$\Delta t = \frac{\text{SIG(SEARCH)}}{\text{OLDSIG(SEARCH)} - \text{SIG(SEARCH)}} \Delta t$$

temporary Δt used in search; see relation (6–13); always negative on first trial

OLDSIG(SEARCH = SIG(SEARCH)

save present actuating signal of comparator being searched

RETURN

FIGURE 6-6 (cont'd)

sequent iteration, a test is conducted to determine whether a transition has occurred (SIG has changed sign). All comparators are checked as more than one may have undergone a transition in the preceding interval. If this should be the case (TRIPS > 1), a test is conducted to establish which comparator first underwent a transition. This test is based on a linear estimation of the time of transition, t_t, as measured from the beginning of the last iteration interval. This estimated value is established as

$$t_t = \left\{ \left| \frac{\text{SIG}(n-1)}{\text{SIG}(n-1) - \text{SIG}(n)} \right| \right\} \Delta t \tag{6-2}$$

where $\text{SIG}(n-1)$ is the value of the actuating signal at the beginning of the interval (designated as OLDSIG in the flow diagram) and $\text{SIG}(n)$ is the value of the actuating signal at the end of the interval. Whichever comparator has the lower value of t_t is assumed to have tripped first. [In the program represented by the flow diagram, the reciprocal of the quantity in brackets in relation (6-2) is evaluated instead and the search then is for maximum value.]

Once it has been established which comparator tripped first, a search for the transition instant of that comparator is initiated. (The integer, SEARCH, is the identification number of the comparator being searched.) Linear intepolation is again employed, now to estimate the next iteration interval that would be required to reach the instant of transition. Since the last iteration normally would have been beyond this point, the first search iteration interval established by this procedure normally would be negative. (It might be noted here that the integration modules described in Chapter 3 operate as well for negative as for positive time iterations; it is possible to backtrack.) The relation used to establish the size of the search iteration interval is

$$\Delta t(n-1) = \frac{\mathrm{SIG}(n)}{\mathrm{SIG}(n) - \mathrm{SIG}(n-1)}\,\Delta t(n) \qquad (6\text{-}3)$$

The next to last operation shown in Figure 6-6 is the computer version of this relation. As the search procedure is based on linear interpolation, the first trial search normally will not be successful; further trials based on the same interpolation relation will be required. A successful search is one where the actuation will be required. A successful search is one where the actuation signal, SIG, is zero within specified tolerance limits (TOL in the flow diagram). A limit (MAXTLS) is imposed upon the number of search trials permitted; this is specified in the main program.

The comparator subprogram always disturbs the normal iteration pattern and it is desirable to return to this pattern after a transition point has been established and appropriate action taken. For this reason, an accompanying subprogram, SETDT, should always follow. The flow diagram of such a program is shown in Figure 6-7.

The SETDT routine has not been combined with the COMPAR subprogram because it sometimes is desirable to have the main program change the value of the normal iteration interval, DTSPEC; this may be determined by the comparator states. A later example will illustrate this.

Figure 6-8 shows how the main-program flow diagram would be modified in order to include such a combination of COMPAR and SETDT subprograms. The statements shown must be added to the initialization process. Then, following any last pass of the integration procedure, the comparator subroutine will be called. If any comparator states have changed, the program then establishes any new conditions (such as the engagement of a limit stop) that might have occurred and changes any relationships affecting the output-response variables that might result. It may also establish whether the specified value of Δt should be changed because of any comparator transitions and notes whether any special printout should be called for even though it is not the intended time for such a printout. (Printouts are generally desirable following any significant change in comparator states.) The SETDT subroutine is then called; this will play a role only following a comparator transition or when searching for the transition instant. The program then follows the general pattern of Figure 3-13 except for the added provision of an extra printout being possible when a comparator transition has occurred.

Because of the variable (and often negative) iteration intervals that occur during the search procedure, extrapolating types ("b" types) of numerical integration techniques generally are not suitable when the comparator module is employed. Furthermore, extrapolation methods are generally not desirable when gross discontinuities arise, as often is the case when

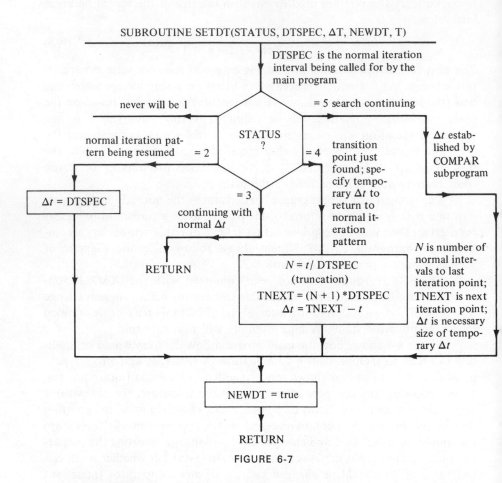

FIGURE 6-7

comparators are involved in the program. The methods of Chapter 3 described as 1a-1, 2a-1, 3a-1, and 4a-1 all function well with such a comparator module.

One example of the application of comparator modules is the establishment of instants when various dependent variables attain specified values. For example, Figure 1-34 represents a printout of the results of a simulation study relating to the Chapter 1 example. Suppose the instants that the variable y was equal to 1.000, 2.000, 3.000, etc., happened to be of interest. The output results listed in Figure 1-34 do not show these precise instants. However, by including a comparator module designed to be actuated whenever y achieves some integer value, these instants could easily be included in the printout. A printout would then be called for whenever a comparator transition was noted.

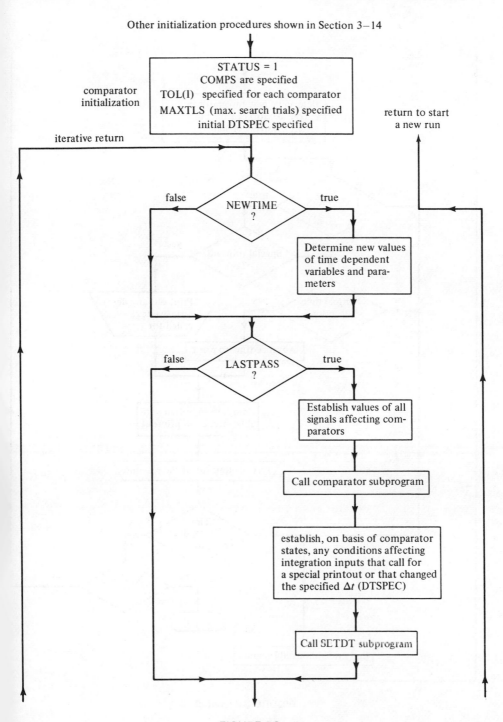

FIGURE 6-8

FIGURE 6-8 (cont'd)

6-4   Digital Simulation of Limiting

Figure 6-5 may be used to establish the method for simulating limiting by digital means once a comparator subroutine module is made available as described in the preceding section. The procedure should be obvious from this diagram. The limited output, called y in the example, is established *after* the comparator subroutine is called. Suppose, as shown in Figure 6-5, that comparator 1 establishes the lower limit [$x_L(1)$] and comparator 2 the higher limit [$x_L(2)$]. Then SIG(1) would be $x - x_L(1)$ and SIG(2) would be $x - x_L(2)$. Then

> if ACT(1) = false, then $y = x_L(1)$
>
> if ACT(1) = true, then
>
>> if ACT(2) = false, then $y = x$
>>
>> if ACT(2) = true, then $y = x_L(2)$

The appropriate expression relating y to x would continue to be used until the next time that the comparator module indicated a transition (STATUS = 4).

6-5   Inactive Zone

Many phenomena to be simulated involve what is variously called an *inactive zone*, a *dead zone*, an *inert zone*, etc. The significance of this effect is shown in Figure 6-9. This effect can arise from a number of reasons, including free play in mechanical couplings, linkage, and gearing. Figure 6-10 shows an analog program for simulating this effect based on the use of comparators. Figure 6-11 illustrates four techniques for simulating such an effect by means of diodes. Among them, method (a) is the simplest but can be employed only with computers that have floating power supplies available. Method (b) also is simple, but the potentiometers add to the effective diode

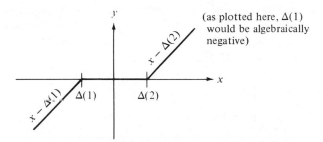

FIGURE 6-9

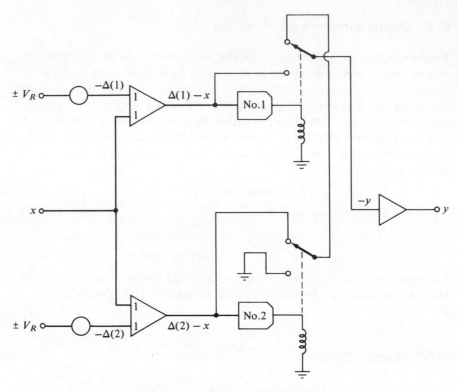

FIGURE 6-10

resistance and will cause some slight modifications of the slope when operating beyond the inactive-zone range. (The input resistance of the next ampilfier, therefore, should be large compared to the potentiometer resistance.) Method (c) avoids this difficulty but required three amplifiers. Methods (a) to (c) will all exhibit some rounding of the corners (referring to the plot of Figure 6-9) at the inactive-zone boundaries; this may be avoided by the use of ideal-diode circuits, illustrated by Figure 6-11d.

The digital simulation of the inactive zone is based on the same type of logic as represented by Figure 6-10, except that the inversions peculiar to analog-type amplifiers need not be considered. Say that the comparator module is employed with $\text{SIG}(1) = x - \Delta(1)$ and $\text{SIG}(2) = x - \Delta(2)$. Then

if $\text{ACT}(1) =$ false, then $y = x - \Delta(2)$

if $\text{ACT}(1) =$ true, then

  if $\text{ACT}(2) =$ false, then $y = 0$

  if $\text{ACT}(2) =$ true, then $y = x - \Delta(1)$

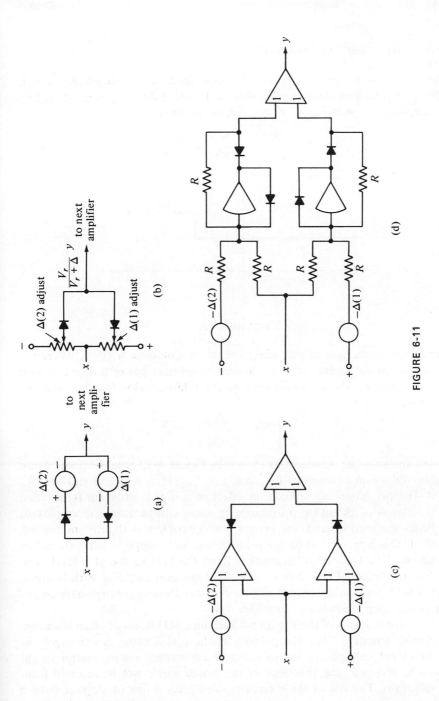

FIGURE 6-11

6-6   Two-Position Contactor

The *two-position-contactor effect*, also described as a "bang-bang" effect, occurs frequently in simulation problems. Its general nature is illustrated by Figure 6-12. Its mathematical description is obvious:

$$y = \begin{cases} y(1) & \text{when } x \leq x_c \\ y(2) & \text{when } x > x_c \end{cases} \tag{6-4}$$

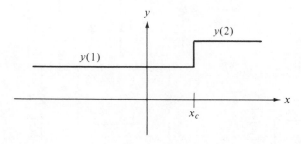

FIGURE 6-12

One frequent example of this effect relates to Coloumb friction, where the friction force (or torque) is of a constant magnitude but of a direction that depends only on the algebraic sign of the relative velocity v between the moving parts; i.e.,

$$f_f = \begin{cases} -f_c & \text{when } v < 0 \\ +f_c & \text{when } v > 0 \end{cases} \tag{6-5}$$

In this instance the relationship shown in Figure 6-12 would appear as an odd function with x corresponding to v, y to f_f, $y(1)$ to $-f_c$, and $y(2)$ to $+f_c$.

The programming of such an effect in a digital program is obvious. Also obvious is its analog programming when comparators are employed. If diodes are used instead, the programming problem is slightly more complicated. One approach is to use a finite, but high, slope in what should in Figure 6-12 be the vertical transition from the $y(1)$ to the $y(2)$ level. The analog simulation of this then combines a high-gain amplifier with limiting. Figure 6-13 shows schemes that may be employed where the high-gain amplifier is an open operational amplifier.

In applications of the Figure 6-13 circuits, $y(1)$ is, more often than not, a negative quantity. Then the polarity of the $y(1)$ floating power supply in (a) or of the voltage applied to the $y(1)$ adjustment potentiometer in (b) would be reversed; the directions of the diodes would not be reversed from those shown. The use of these circuits substitutes a line of slope μ (where μ is the gain of the operational amplifier) for the vertical transition from $y(1)$ to $y(2)$ in Figure 6-12.

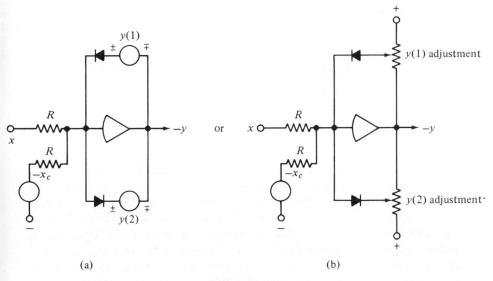

(a)   (b)

FIGURE 6-13

With some operational amplifiers, the use of the circuits shown in Figure 6-13 could lead to parasitic oscillations. For this reason the output should always be observed on a cathode-ray oscilloscope to ascertain that this is not the case. When this difficulty does arise, it can usually be cured by the methods discussed in Section 5-9. In some instances even this will not suffice and it is then necessary to reduce the effective gain of the operational amplifier by adding a small amount of negative feedback to the circuits of Figure 6-13 in the manner shown in Figure 6-14.

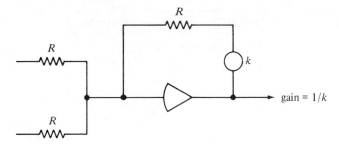

FIGURE 6-14

6-7 Three-Position Contactor

In general, multiposition-contactor effects (i.e., extensions of the relationships shown in Figure 6-12) can be simulated by the same basic procedures

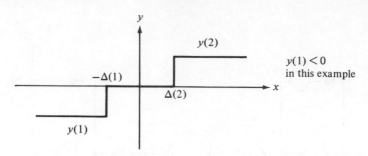

FIGURE 6-15

as have just been described. One special case occurs frequently, a three-position contactor with zero output for the midposition. This is shown in Figure 6-15. Often the operation is symmetrical [i.e., $y(1) = -y(2)$ and $\Delta(1) = \Delta(2)$]. This effect occurs in electrical-contactor equipment and in mechanical clutches; its equivalent appears in many other phenomena, including those of a nonphysical nature. The midrange between $-\Delta(1)$ and $\Delta(2)$ is referred to as the inactive zone. Although this zone may be inherent in the mechanism being simulated, it is often introduced purposely to provide a range within which the mechanism can rest.

The technique for simulating this effect in a digital program or by employing analog comparators is obvious and need not be described here. Analog simulation by means of diodes may be based on the viewpoint that the function being represented is a combination of a two-position contactor and an inactive zone. Figure 6-16 illustrates a general procedure that may be employed for the simulation of this effect.

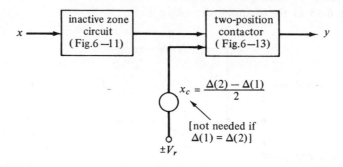

FIGURE 6-16

6-8   Attaining Infinite Slope in Contactor Simulations

In the preceding two sections relating to multiposition contactor simulation, those circuits that employed diodes had the disadvantage that the slope of the y versus x relationship was not truly infinite; unlike the digital scheme and schemes using comparators, an immediate transition from one output level to another was not obtainable. This might be a disadvantage in some simulation problems but can be overcome by making the amplifier one of the infinite-gain type by employing the unity positive-feedback principle shown in Figure 6-17.

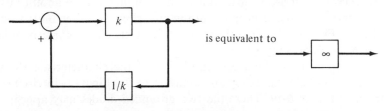

FIGURE 6-17

If this principle is combined with limiting, an *infinite slope* (i.e., an abrupt transition from one level to the other) will result in the transition region. This is shown in Figure 6-18 as applied to the two-position-contactor simulation problem represented by Figure 6-12. The circuit of Figure 6-18 happens to employ the shunt-diode input type of limiter of Figure 6-3a. Actually, any other type of limiting circuit could have been used as well. The reference-supply connection, $\pm V_r$, to the three potentiometers establishing x_c, $y(1)$, and $y(2)$ will be $+V_r$ or $-V_r$, depending upon the algebraic sign of those quantities.

A true vertical slope will be obtained (with reference to Figure 6-12) at the transition point only if the feedback gain is *exactly* unity. Obviously, this cannot be exactly the case. If less than unity, some finite slope will result;

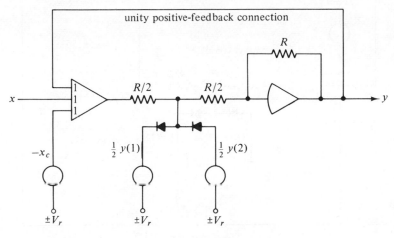

FIGURE 6-18

if more than unity, a *hysteresis* or detent action, to be discussed later, will result. The circuit of Figure 6-18, therefore, is sometimes modified by providing a vernier control of gain in the feedback connection so that a reasonably precise adjustment of unity feedback gain may be achieved.

This difficulty of obtaining precisely an infinite slope is not necessarily a disadvantage in simulation. Most physical effects being simulated do not possess this characteristic; their transition from one level to another usually occurs in terms of either a steep but not infinite slope (less than unity feedback gain in the Figure 6-18 circuit), or in a hysteresis effect (corresponding to slightly more than unity gain).

A three-position-contactor simulation of the characteristic shown in Figure 6-15 can be obtained by an extension of the Figure 6-18 circuit. This is shown in Figure 6-19. There the two grounded diodes may appear to be superfluous; actually, they guarantee that there will be no y output when

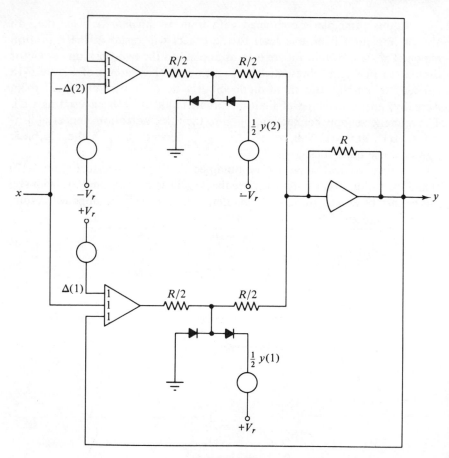

FIGURE 6-19

x is within the inactive-zone range [i.e., between $-\Delta(1)$ and $\Delta(2)$]. Again, while a shunt-diode input-type limiter is shown in Figure 6-19, other types of limiting circuits could be used instead.

6-9   Hysteresis in Discontinuous Circuits—The Acquiring of Memory

It has been stated that in a circuit of the type shown in Figure 6-18, had less than unity feedback gain been used, a finite rather than infinite slope would have resulted, and had more than unity gain been used, what has been referred to as a *hysteresis effect* would occur. This general effect of positive feedback can be explained by redrawing Figure 6-18 in a more general form, as in Figure 6-20. The implementation of that figure could employ any limiter with the characteristics shown. To understand its operation the steps of graphical analysis shown in Figure 6-21 should be considered. In (a), the

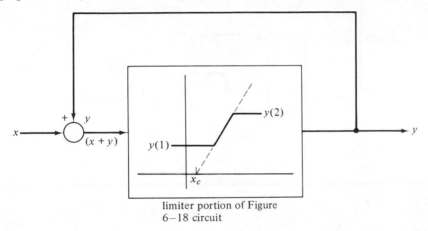

limiter portion of Figure
6–18 circuit

FIGURE 6-20

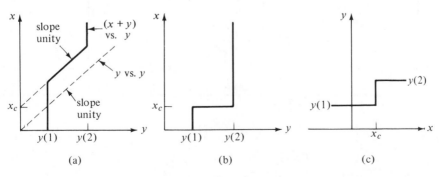

(a)   (b)   (c)

FIGURE 6-21

input to the limiter, $x + y$, is plotted versus the output, y. Superposed is a plot of y versus y itself, naturally a line of slope unity. The plot of y is then graphically subtracted from that of $x + y$ to obtain the plot of x versus y shown in (b). In (c) the inverse relation is shown, or of y versus x. This is the output–input relation of the complete circuit and it may be seen that a sudden transition does take place between the $y(1)$ and $y(2)$ levels.

Now let the general concept of Figure 6-20 be considered again, but this time with a feedback gain β, where β may be greater or less than unity. This is shown in Figure 6-22. Let the case where $\beta < 1$ be considered first. The graphical construction shown in Figure 6-21 would now be modified to that of Figure 6-23. As has been stated, a finite rather than infinite slope results as far as the output–input relationship is concerned; this slope is equal to $1/(1 - \beta)$.

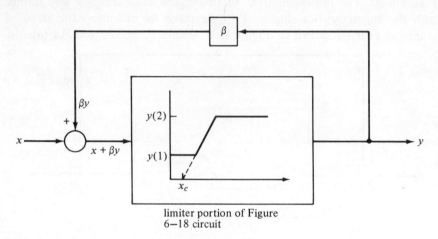

limiter portion of Figure
6–18 circuit

FIGURE 6-22

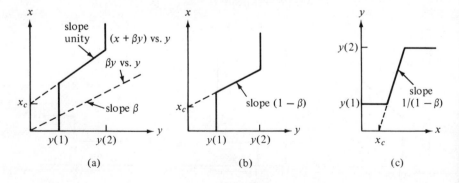

(a)   (b)   (c)

$\beta < 1$

FIGURE 6-23

Finally, let the case where $\beta > 1$ be considered. The graphical construction then becomes as shown in Figure 6-24.

Diagrams (a) and (b) of Figure 6-24 result from the same thought processes. Going to (c) requires some reflection. It should be recalled from Chapter 5 that the feedback effect results in an *implicit* solution for y [i.e.,

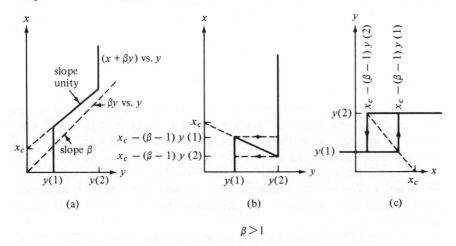

$$\beta > 1$$

FIGURE 6-24

y will automatically adjust itself to whatever value is required to match the input x in accordance with the relations plotted in (b)]. Say, for example, that x is increasing from some negative value. From (b) it may be seen that y will initially maintain its value at $y(1)$. This situation will continue as y is increased until x goes just beyond the value $x_c - (\beta - 1)y(1)$, or the first *trigger level*. At this point, y will jump to the point where it again attains a value sufficient to match the value of x [i.e., where $y = y(2)$]. Subsequent increases in x result in y remaining at the level $y(2)$.

If y should be decreased, the value of y required to satisfy the input x will, according to (b), remain $y(2)$ until x is decreased to a level below the previous trigger level [i.e., below $x_c - (\beta - 1)y(2)$]. Then y will jump immediately to the level $y(1)$. This is also shown in (c), where arrows have been added to the vertical lines representing the jump transitions to show the one-way path involved. The phenomenon described here is similar to that illustrated by Figures 5-7 and 5-8.

The circuit has now acquired *memory*, at least a one-bit memory. In the hysteresis region between $x_c - (\beta - 1)y(2)$ and $x_c - (\beta - 1)y(1)$, whether y is at the $y(1)$ or $y(2)$ level depends upon its past history.

There is nothing new about the hysteresis phenomenon. It is a form of flip-flop or trigger circuit. Of even longer standing is the mechanical use of hysteresis in the toggle shown in Figure 6-25. The lever shown in that figure

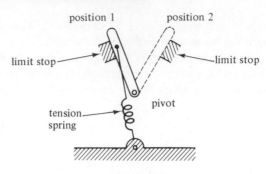

FIGURE 6-25

is unstable and is always forced from its vertical position (except at top dead center, where inertia is depended upon to carry it through). It must always lie against one of the limits. A definite amount of force is required to move it beyond the top dead-center position, beyond which it will drive itself to the other limit. This old principle is used frequently, in wall switches for example. The switch remembers where it was positioned last and maintains that position until sufficient effort is exerted to force it to the other position.

Electrical relays also have a certain inherent amount of hysteresis, unavoidable because of the change in the strength of the magnetic field as the armature position changes. In most relay applications, a certain amount of this is desirable so that the relay will exert sufficient contact force and will not be indecisive, possibly chattering, when the control voltage fluctuates slightly about the switching point. In such relays this effect is sometimes called *detent action*. An excessive amount of this effect, on the other hand, is undesirable and can introduce instability or limit cycling in the device the relay controls.

Relay comparators used in analog computers also possess a certain amount of this detent action, as shown in Figure 6-26. In good design this hysteresis is kept to a minimum and usually can be neglected. When hysteresis *is* to be simulated, it can be introduced by the method described in the following.

Figure 6-24c showed the simulation of a hysteresis effect by analog-computer means employing diodes. In summary, this produced an output–

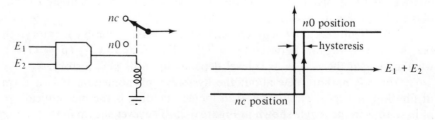

FIGURE 6-26

input relationship, as shown in Figure 6-27. This relationship could also have been produced by a circuit employing comparators rather than diodes, as shown in Figure 6-28. The lower contactor elements (as drawn in the diagram) provide the hysteresis action. Once the contactor has closed (comparator actuated), they reinforce its closure and require that additional. effort (additional change in y) be required to reverse their position again. (As a parenthetical note, but nevertheless useful, it may be observed that none of the voltages were applied directly from potentiometers to the con-

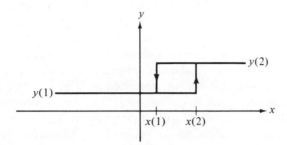

FIGURE 6-27

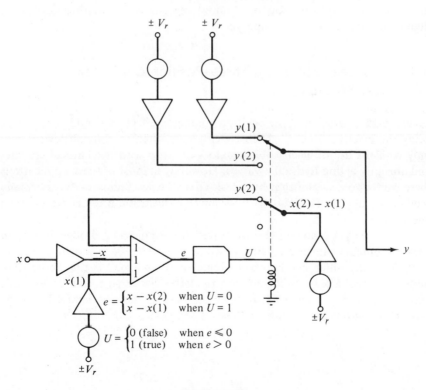

FIGURE 6-28

tactor terminals. In all cases isolating amplifiers were employed. This is done because the potentiometers can be adjusted, in consideration of their loading, only when connected to the proper output load. Had the potentiometers been connected directly, this would have meant assuring that each contactor was in the proper position to connect its potentiometer to the circuit during the potentiometer setting operation. To avoid this bother and easy source of adjustment error, it is far simpler to be somewhat wasteful of inverters and isolate the potentiometers in the fashion shown.)

Simulation of such a hysteresis effect in a digital program is a relatively simple procedure, following directly from the logic indicated by Figure 6-28. Only one comparator unit of the comparator-module subroutine described in Section 6-3 is required for this simulation. The signal designated as e in Figure 6-28 is equivalent to the actuation signal, called SIG, in the subprogram. The comparator output, described as U in Figure 6-28, is equivalent to the actuation state, described as ACT in the subprogram.

It should be noted that, since hysteresis involves a one-bit memory, another state has been added to the system being simulated. Hence, another initial condition must be given to start the program—the initial value of y (or the initial value of U, which provides equivalent information). This initial-condition information is required regardless of whether analog or digital simulation is being employed.

6-10 Representation of a Three-Position Contactor with Hysteresis

Figure 6-15 showed a three-position-contactor effect, the middle position being the inactive zone. Such an effect occurs often in control devices, not only with the use of electrical contactors but also with mechanical clutches and abruptly acting hydraulic valves. However, in most of these applications there will be some significant hysteresis effect. Hence Figure 6-15 is normally modified to appear as Figure 6-29. Again, the operation often is symmetrical and $y(1) = -y(2)$, $\Delta(1) = \Delta(2)$, and $h(1) = h(2)$.

A variety of analog-computer circuits employing diodes has been used to simulate this effect. One, based on Figure 6-19, is shown in Figure 6-30. The only difference between Figures 6-19 and 6-30 is that more than unity-gain feedback is employed with the latter circuit so that the hysteresis effect desired will be achieved. From Figure 6-24 it may be deduced that the proper potentiometer settings will be as follows:

$$P_{h_1} = \left(1 + \frac{2h(1)}{-y(1)}\right)/k \qquad P_{\Delta_1} = \frac{\Delta(1) + h(1)}{V_r}$$

$$P_{h_2} = \left(1 + \frac{2h(2)}{y(2)}\right)/k \qquad P_{\Delta_2} = \frac{\Delta(2) + h(2)}{V_r}$$

$$(6\text{-}6)$$

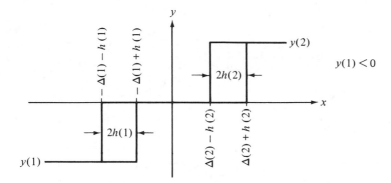

FIGURE 6-29

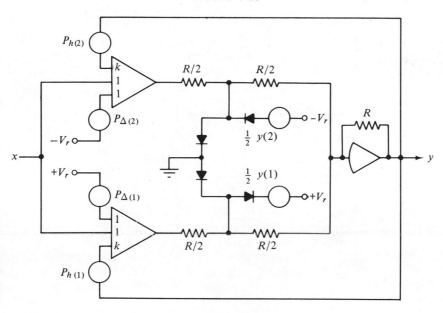

FIGURE 6-30

In the above, k is the gain of the summer input where the feedback signal is applied. Obviously this gain must be greater than unity.

Figure 6-28 has already indicated the general manner by which the characteristic of Figure 6-29 may be obtained by the use of comparators rather than diodes. The complete circuit is shown in Figure 6-31. The Program of that figure could be modified to reduce the number of inverters employed; however, it is shown there in a manner that makes the logic most clear.

Figure 6-31 may also be used as the basis of a digital-simulation program employing two comparator units. Again, regardless of whether

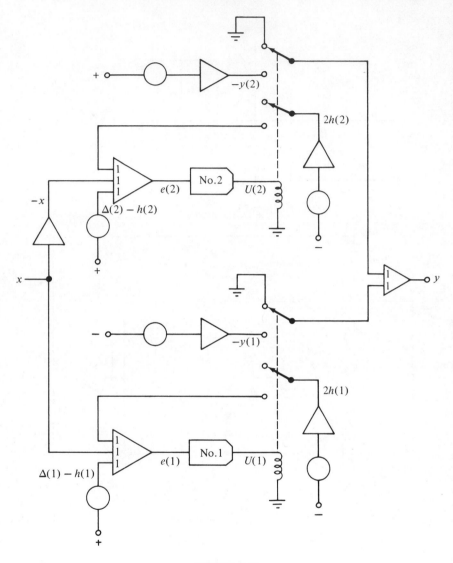

FIGURE 6-31

analog or digital simulation is involved, the initial value of y must be stated. This defines the initial actuation state of both comparators.

6-11 Multivibrator Based on the Hysteresis Effect

In Chapter 4 it was pointed out that some source of a periodic sawtooth or square wave is often required, especially for driving ratchet circuits in counting or digital-integrator applications. An example of such a circuit, employing relay comparators, was shown. If that circuit is examined further, it will be found that it is based on the principle illustrated in Figure 6-32. This two-

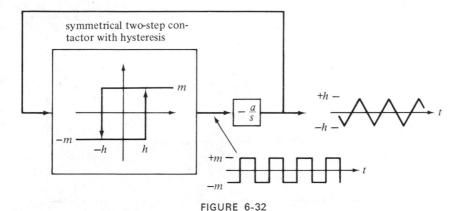

FIGURE 6-32

step contactor with hysteresis may be constructed by employing the arrangement shown in Figure 6-22 with the following adjustments:

$$y(1) = -m$$
$$y(2) = m$$
$$x_c = 0$$
$$\beta = 1 + \frac{h}{m}$$

The slope of the sawtooth wave generated will be $\pm am$ V/sec and the duration of one half period, $T/2$, will be the time required for that voltage to go between $-h$ and $+h$ V. Hence

$$\frac{T}{2} = \frac{2h}{am} \quad \text{or} \quad T = \frac{4h}{am} \quad \text{sec}$$

The multivibrator frequency will therefore be $f = am/4h$ Hz. The integrator gain should therefore be

$$a = \frac{4h}{m} f \quad \text{sec}^{-1}$$

One example of a multivibrator circuit employing this principle and using feedback limiting is shown in Figure 6-33.

6-12 Collision Processes—Mechanical Limit Stops

When simulating mechanical systems, the situation is often encountered when some moving member suddenly engages a second restricting member

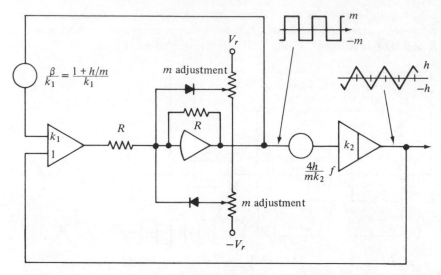

FIGURE 6-33

such as a limit stop. This cannot, in general, be represented by simple signal limiting as described in Section 6-2. Not only must the displacement limiting that results be considered; the force reactions that this process imposes on the involved members and other coupled members is also important.

It may appear simplest to consider such a collision process as involving the engagement of two nonresilient surfaces. Actually this is neither realistic nor convenient for purposes of simulation. Presumably both members involved will have some significant inertia; hence the sudden transfer of momentum assumed would correspond to infinite reaction forces being produced. In reality this does not occur, because of the inevitable resilience of the engaging members. In any event, such an assumption is difficult to handle with analog simulation because the infinite forces that would be computed at the moment of impact (actually, force impulses) would cause an overload. There are means for making such an assumption of zero resilience with digital simulation that will be discussed later.

Figure 6-34 is a general schematic diagram of a translational version of such a collision process. It would, of course, have its rotational counterpart. In Figure 6-34 the *driving* and *directly driven* members are coupled directly together and possess the same velocity, $u_2 = \dot{x}_2$. The forces f indicated on the diagram are considered as positive when the members involved are in compression. Part of the total force f_0 exerted by the driving member will be exerted on the directly driven member and is described as f_1.

There will also exist a *collision-engaged* member possessing a velocity $u_3 = \dot{x}_3$. When, as in (b), the surfaces are engaged, part of the force f_0 is applied as f_s exerted on this member. Hence $f_1 = f_0 - f_s$. If this collision-

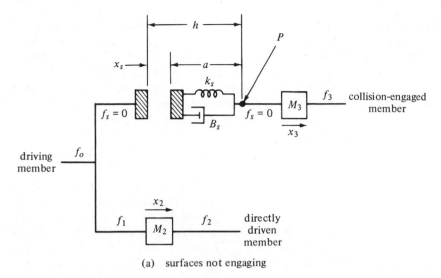

(a)   surfaces not engaging

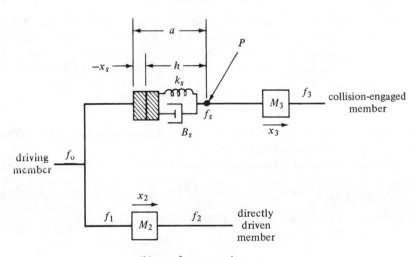

(b)   surfaces engaging

(forces shown are considered positive when
associated members are in compression)

FIGURE 6-34

engaged member happens to be a fixed limit stop, then u_3 would be zero.

Both of the engaging surfaces will possess inevitable continuously distributed resilience, internal friction, and inertia parameters. An exact analysis of the transmission of forces and velocities following collision involves a study of the traveling-wave phenomena involved and of the dynamics of elasticity. In most simulation problems this local effect need not be simulated in detail; only its effect on the general system (of which it usually is only a small part) is of interest. For such purposes it usually is an adequate approximation to show this effect as though it were attributed only to the collision-engaged member, and to show it as a combination of a lumped resilience (described in terms of the spring constant k_s) and viscous damping (described as B_s). The distributed mass is lumped with the total mass of the involved elements M_2 and M_3.

To discuss the relative displacement of the colliding surfaces, it is necessary to employ some reference point P in Figure 6-34 that is used as a measure of the displacement of the collision-engaged member; this point should be located far enough from the colliding surface so that it is not involved to any significant extent in the resilient distortion effect near the the surface when engagement occurs. The distance between this point P and the contacting surface of the driving member is described as h. Hence the rate of change of h will be

$$h = u_3 - u_1 \tag{6-7}$$

The distance between the reference point P and the *free* engaging surface of the collision-engaged member is described as a. By free surface is meant that surface location where, when there is no engagement and hence no compression of the effective spring k_s (no contact force), a, by its definition, remains constant. The *engagement distance*, x_s, is then defined as

$$x_s = h - a \tag{6-8}$$

This distance will be positive when there is no engagement; x_s then represents the actual spacing between surfaces.

When engagement occurs and the compression of k_s results, x_s becomes negative. Its negative value represents the amount of compression of the equivalent spring k_s. Hence

$$f_s = \begin{cases} -(k_s x_s + B_s \dot{x}_s) & \text{when } x_s < 0 \\ 0 & \text{when } x_s \geq 0 \end{cases} \tag{6-9}$$

A general block diagram of the effects just described is shown in Figure 6-35. That figure shows how the representation of the collision effect may be combined with other block diagrams that represent the dynamics of the driving element, of the directly driven members, and of the collision-engaged member. It is a somewhat unorthodox form of block diagram as it also includes the analog-computer symbol for a comparator. This is, however, the most effective way of describing relation (6-9) in block diagram form. The inclusion of the rectifier symbol in the diagram might also be noted; this represents the fact that the engaging surfaces can never exert tension on each other.

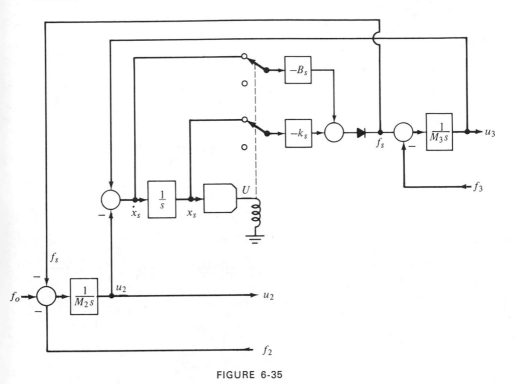

FIGURE 6-35

This discussion can be clarified by some simple examples.

EXAMPLE 1 The Bouncing-Ball Problem

Figure 6-36 is a schematic diagram of this situation. The ball is considered as though its contact surface were flat rather than spherical. (The latter consideration would result in extreme mathematical complications.) It is regarded as the directly driven member; hence $u = -dh/dt$. The collision-engaged member is the surface on which the "ball" bounces; as it is fixed, $u_3 = 0$. The resilience and damping effects are, of course, attributed partly to the ball and partly to the surfaces; however, they can be represented as though all of these were attributed to the surface alone, as Figure 6-36b indicates. The block diagram representing this situation would appear as shown in Figure 6-37. The arrangement of that figure is patterned after that of Figure 6-35. It may be noted that (because $u_3 = 0$) there is a redundant integration. This may be eliminated and Figure 6-37 simplified to the form shown in Figure 6-38.

The accuracy of algebraic signs may be checked by noting that with the comparator contacts in the normally closed position (indicating that the ball is in contact with the surface), there is a net negative feedback through both the loop involving k_s and that involving B_s.

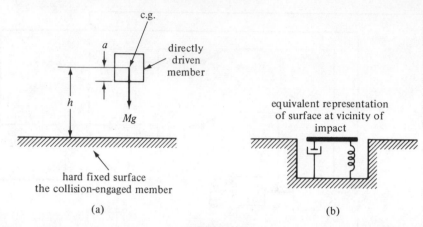

c.g.

a

directly
driven
member

h

Mg

hard fixed surface
the collision-engaged member

(a)

equivalent representation
of surface at vicinity of
impact

(b)

FIGURE 6-36

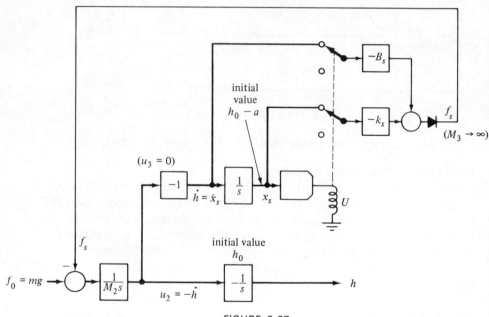

FIGURE 6-37

The analog-computer simulation of this effect is obvious and hence
will not be shown here. Tests on such a simulation program show that k_s
determines the amount that the ball "penetrates" the surface, i.e., how
much the value of h will be less than the distance a. (As $k_s \rightarrow \infty$, $h_{min} \rightarrow a$.)
B_s will determine the decrement of each successive bounce; if B_s were zero,
the ball would bounce in a steady-state manner, always regaining the same
maximum height.

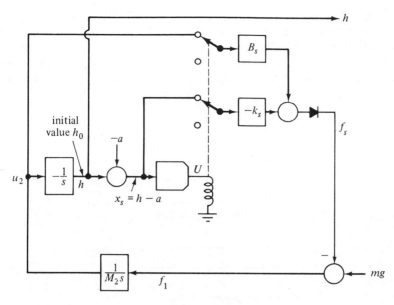

FIGURE 6-38

A digital-computer program for simulating this problem appears in flow-diagram form in Figure 6-39. The comparator shown in Figure 6-38 is represented by the comparator module in that program. In addition to establishing the surface-force reaction f_s when it exists during engagement of the surfaces (U is false), this module also serves one other important function. It establishes a much smaller iteration interval $\Delta t = \Delta t_{\min}$ during periods of engagement than would be required during periods of disengagement, when $\Delta t = \Delta t_{\min}$. This is necessary because of the much more rapid dynamics that exist when the surfaces are in contact.

A second comparator module, which was not included in the Figure 6-38 block diagram, is shown in Figure 6-39. This second comparator is actuated by the velocity u_2. Hence its transition, when u_2 changes sign, may be used to indicate instants of maximum and minimum h. Special printouts are called for at instants of engagement, disengagement, maximum h, or minimum h, in addition to the regular printouts at the normal specified printout interval.

A typical result of such a program is shown in Figure 6-40. Here the damping constant B_s has been chosen so that the maximum value of x_s (the spacing between ball and surface) decreases by roughly a factor of 2 after each bounce. As this is a nonlinear problem, the percentage decrement increases somewhat with successive bounces; furthermore, the interval between bounces decreases (as may be noted by observation of the real situation).

It is useful to test such a program when $B_s = 0$. Then there is no energy loss and a periodic response should result. Any increment or decrement in the maximum value of h between cycles is a measure of program imperfection (insufficiently small Δt's or inappropriate integration subroutines). Such a test run is similar to the sinusoidal test procedure discussed in Section 3-12.

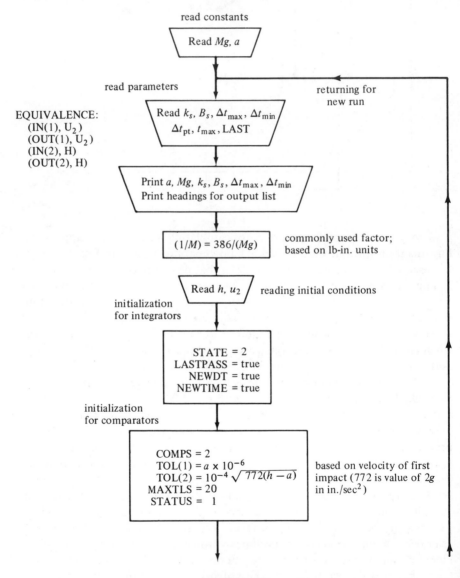

FIGURE 6-39

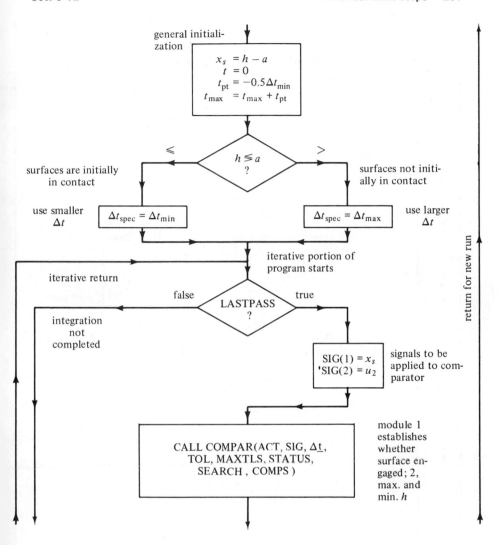

FIGURE 6-39 (cont'd)

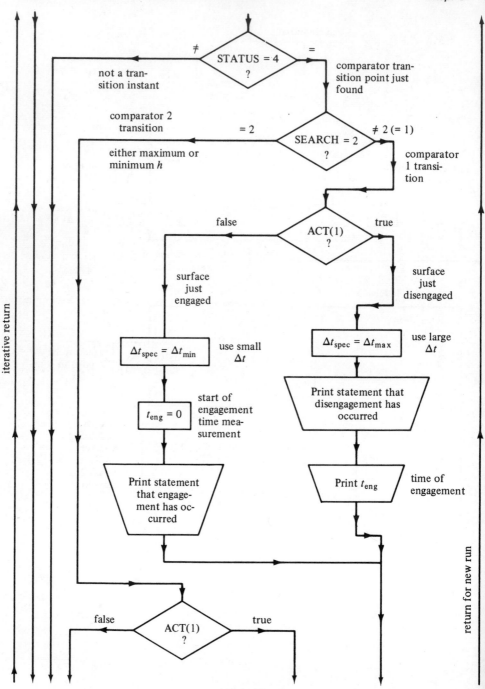

FIGURE 6-39 (cont'd)

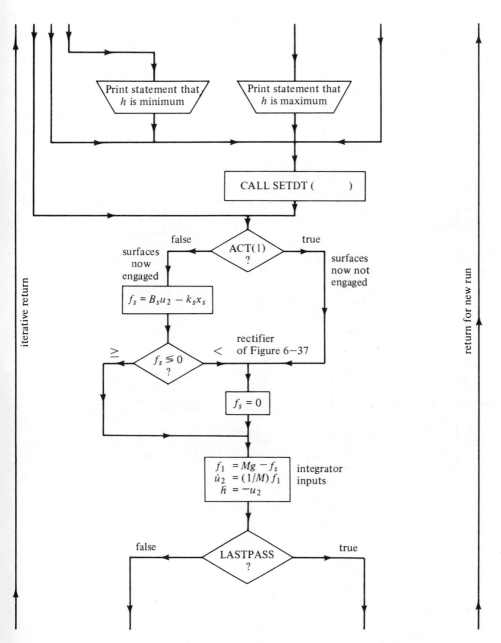

FIGURE 6-39 (cont'd)

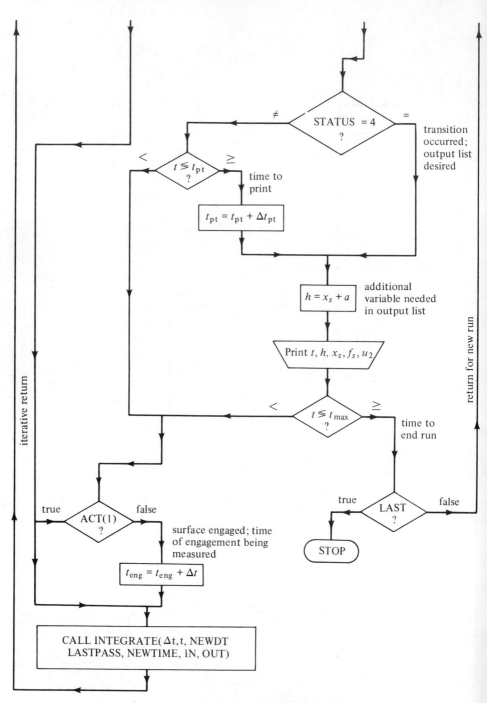

FIGURE 6-39 (cont'd)

```
A=          1.00 INCHES      MG=          1.00 LBS
KS=1000000. LB/IN      BS=       10.0 LB-SEC/IN
DTMAX=  0.10E-01 SECS        DTMIN=  0.50E-05 SECS
```

T	H	XS	FS	U2
SEC	IN	IN	LB	IN/SEC
0.0	5.00000	0.400E 01	0.0	0.0
	MAXIMUM H AT NEXT POINT			
0.0	5.00000	0.400E 01	0.0	0.00000
0.02000	4.92280	0.392E 01	0.0	7.72001
0.04000	4.69120	0.369E 01	0.0	15.44002
0.06000	4.30519	0.331E 01	0.0	23.16002
0.08000	3.76479	0.276E 01	0.0	30.88002
0.10000	3.06999	0.207E 01	0.0	38.60002
0.12000	2.22079	0.122E 01	0.0	46.32002
0.14000	1.21719	0.217E 00	0.0	54.04002
	SURFACE ENGAGED AT NEXT POINT			
0.14396	1.00000	-0.270E-07	0.556E 03	55.56967
	MINIMUM H AT NEXT POINT			
0.14404	0.99755	-0.245E-02	0.245E 04	0.00004
	SURFACE DISENGAGED AT NEXT POINT			
	TIME OF ENGAGEMENT WAS 0.00016066 SECONDS			
0.14412	1.00000	0.114E-08	0.0	-41.54492
0.16000	1.61108	0.611E 00	0.0	-35.41501
0.18000	2.24218	0.124E 01	0.0	-27.69498
0.20000	2.71888	0.172E 01	0.0	-19.97495
0.22000	3.04118	0.204E 01	0.0	-12.25492
0.24000	3.20908	0.221E 01	0.0	-4.53491
	MAXIMUM H AT NEXT POINT			
0.25175	3.23572	0.224E 01	0.0	0.00000
0.26000	3.22257	0.222E 01	0.0	3.18517
0.28000	3.08167	0.208E 01	0.0	10.90518
0.30000	2.78637	0.179E 01	0.0	18.62518
0.32000	2.33666	0.134E 01	0.0	26.34518
0.34000	1.73255	0.733E 00	0.0	34.06519
	SURFACE ENGAGED AT NEXT POINT			
0.35938	1.00000	-0.445E-09	0.415E 03	41.54477
	MINIMUM H AT NEXT POINT			
0.35945	0.99817	-0.183E-02	0.183E 04	0.00005
	SURFACE DISENGAGED AT NEXT POINT			
	TIME OF ENGAGEMENT WAS 0.00016068 SECONDS			
0.35953	1.00000	0.125E-08	0.0	-31.04613
0.36000	1.01444	0.144E-01	0.0	-30.86610
0.38000	1.55456	0.555E 00	0.0	-23.14607

0.40000	1.94028 0.940E 00 0.0		-15.42605
0.42000	2.17160 0.117E 01 0.0		-7.70604
	MAXIMUM H AT NEXT POINT		
0.43996	2.24852 0.125E 01 0.0		0.00000
0.44000	2.24852 0.125E 01 0.0		0.01401
0.46000	2.17104 0.117E 01 0.0		7.73402
0.48000	1.93916 0.939E 00 0.0		15.45403
0.50000	1.55288 0.553E 00 0.0		23.17403

FIGURE 6-40

EXAMPLE 2 Collision Engagement of a Third Member

Figure 6-41 shows another example of a collision process where the block diagram of Figure 6-35 is applicable. In Figure 6-41 only horizontal translational motion is being considered. A time-varying displacement x_0 is imposed at point 0 of the mechanism, presumably part of the driving member. This portion is directly coupled with another mechanism, the directly driven member whose displacement is described in terms of x_2. At an intermediate point, another collision engaged member may also be engaged by the driving member; the displacement of this is described as x_3. All displacements are described with respect to a fixed reference frame and arbitrarily are zero when the system is in static equilibrium (all spring forces zero). The spacing between the engaging surfaces x_s is described as x_{s_0} under such an equilibrium condition (when $x_2 = x_3 = 0$). Hence $x_s = x_{s_0} + x_3 - x_2$.

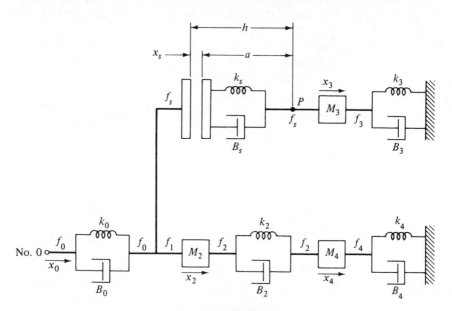

FIGURE 6-41

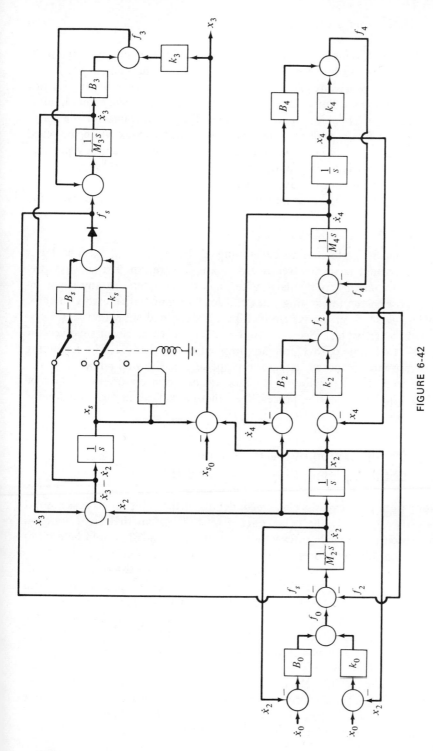

FIGURE 6-42

Figure 6-42 shows the block diagram describing this situation. It admittedly is complicated but not complex. Nevertheless, the implementation of the simulation procedure is straightforward; hence neither the digital nor analog programs are shown here. It is especially easy to make errors in algebraic sign when simulating such a system. Tracing through all the loops that appear in Figure 6-42 does show that negative feedback will be involved in each instance. This is to be expected, as the system is entirely passive; hence such a test is an indication that such algebraic errors *probably* (it is not a complete guarantee) have not been made.

It should also be noted that the displacement x_3 is developed from the relation

$$x_3 = x_2 + (x_s - x_{s_0})$$

This is done in preference to developing x_3 by integrating $\dot{x}_3$. The latter procedure would have involved a redundant integration. It is always preferable to avoid this (particularly with analog computers) as any slight inherent error in the integrating rates can lead to cumulative errors in some problems. A study of the system of Figure 6-42 would show that it is a system with seven states. (See Section 1-4.) One of these seven involves the integration relating x_0 to $\dot{x}_0$, already implied in Figure 6-42. The remaining six correspond to the six integration operations shown in that diagram. As has been stated previously, no more integration operations should be employed in the simulation process than there are states in the system being represented.

6-13   Determination of the Parameters of the Colliding Surfaces (k_s and B_s)

In simulation problems the exact *local* details of the collision process are not of interest; it is only the effect on the overall system that is of concern. As has been mentioned, an exact evaluation of k_s and B_s would be a complicated and tedious process; fortunately, this is not often required.

It is, however, possible to determine the effective values of k_s and B_s from experimental studies of the collision process when this is feasible with the system being simulated. One test involves determining the *coefficient of restitution*, μ_s, of the colliding surfaces. To explain this coefficient, let the situation shown in Figure 6-34 be considered with the external forces f_0, f_2, and f_3 all zero; this is then described as a *free-body problem*. Prior to collision the mass M_2 is considered to be moving at a constant velocity $u_2(0)$, and M_3 at a constant velocity $u_3(0)$. Upon collision the surfaces remain engaged for an interval of time t_s. During this interval a compression force f_s exists between the surfaces. The interval ends when f_s becomes zero (corresponding to the rectifier in the Figure 6-35 block diagram ceasing to conduct). Engagement then has ended (even though x_s will not yet have become positive). Mass M_2 will now have a new velocity $u_2(t_s)$, and M_3 a new velocity $u_3(t_s)$. These will be related to the original velocities as follows:

$$u_2(t_s) = u_2(0) - \frac{M_3}{M_2 + M_3}(1 + \mu_s)[u_2(0) - u_3(0)] \tag{6-10}$$

$$u_3(t_s) = u_3(0) + \frac{M_2}{M_2 + M_3}(1 + \mu_s)[u_2(0) - u_3(0)] \tag{6-11}$$

These relations define μ_s. Its value will always be between zero and unity; it is dependent only on the nature of the engaging surfaces and independent of the masses or velocities involved.

The significance of the coefficient of restitution might be clarified further if the case is considered where M_3 is held stationary; this corresponds to $u_3(0) = 0$, and $M_3 \rightarrow \infty$. Relation (6-10) then becomes

$$u_2(t_s) = -\mu_s u_2(0) \tag{6-12}$$

In other words, the mass M_2 would then bounce off the stationary surface with which it had collided and acquire a negative velocity that is a fraction, μ_s, of its original velocity. This suggests one experimental technique for determining μ_s.

The actual mechanics of the collision process may be analyzed proceeding from Figure 6-35 and employing methods of operational calculus. This analysis is straightforward, but it is tedious and will not be described here. The results can be described in terms of ζ_s, the damping ratio existing during the engagement interval and defined as

$$\zeta_s = \frac{B_s}{2\sqrt{\dfrac{M_2 M_3}{M_2 + M_3}} k_s} \tag{6-13}$$

The coefficient of restitution can then be determined from ζ_s by means of the following relations:

$$\mu_s = \begin{cases} \exp\left[-\dfrac{\zeta_s}{\sqrt{1-\zeta_s^2}}\cos^{-1}(2\zeta_s^2 - 1)\right] & \text{for } \zeta_s < 1 \\[2ex] \exp(-2) & \text{for } \zeta_s = 1 \\[2ex] \dfrac{1}{(2\zeta_s^2 - 1 + 2\zeta_s\sqrt{\zeta_s^2 - 1})^{(\zeta_s/\sqrt{\zeta_s^2 - 1})}} & \text{for } \zeta_s > 1 \end{cases}$$

A plot of μ_s versus ζ_s is shown in Figure 6-43. It may be seen that $\mu_s = 1$, representing a perfectly elastic collision, corresponds to $\zeta_s = 0$, and hence to $B_s = 0$. $\mu_s = 0$ represents a perfectly inelastic collision or what also is called a perfectly viscous collision, where $\zeta_s \rightarrow \infty$ and $k_s = 0$.

Relation (6-14) can be used to evaluate ζ_s from experimental tests by which μ_s has been determined. However, ζ_s cannot be expressed explicitly in terms of μ_s; relation (6-14) must be employed implicitly, by graphical methods, or by using a digital program of the type discussed in Section 5-10.

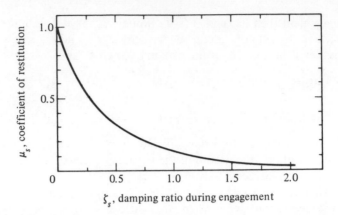

FIGURE 6-43

The spring constant k_s, describing the resilience of the colliding surfaces, determines the duration of the engagement interval t_s. This will be given by the relation

$$t_s = \begin{cases} \sqrt{\dfrac{M_2 M_3}{(M_2 + M_3)k_s}} \; \dfrac{\cos^{-1}(2\zeta_s^2 - 1)}{\sqrt{1 - \zeta_s^2}} & \text{for } \zeta_s < 1 \\[3ex] 2\sqrt{\dfrac{M_2 M_3}{(M_2 + M_3)k_s}} & \text{for } \zeta_s = 1 \quad (6\text{-}15) \\[3ex] \sqrt{\dfrac{M_2 M_3}{(M_2 + M_3)k_s}} \; \dfrac{\ln(2\zeta_s^2 + 2\zeta_s\sqrt{\zeta_s^2 - 1} - 1)}{\sqrt{\zeta_s^2 - 1}} & \text{for } \zeta_s > 1 \end{cases}$$

If t_s has been determined experimentally and ζ_s determined from a knowledge of μ_s, then, from relations (6-13) and (6-15), the values of k_s and B_s may be established.

6-14   Simulation of a Perfectly Elastic Collision

In the case of a perfectly elastic collision, B_s would be zero. Hence $\zeta_s = 0$ and the coefficient of restitution μ_s is unity. The duration of engagement t_s then is simply

$$t_s = \pi \sqrt{\frac{M_2 M_3}{(M_2 + M_3)k_s}} \tag{6-16}$$

For the free-body-collision situation described (no external forces on the colliding members; hence in Figure 6-34, $f_0 = f_2 = f_3 = 0$), the engagement force f_s is

$$f_s = \sqrt{\frac{M_2 M_3 k_s}{M_2 + M_3}} \, [u_2(0) - u_3(0)] \sin \sqrt{\frac{M_2 M_3}{(M_2 + M_3)k_s}} \, t \qquad \text{for } 0 < t < t_s$$

$$\tag{6-17}$$

and its maximum value, therefore, will be

$$f_s = \sqrt{\frac{M_2 M_3 k_s}{M_2 + M_3}} [u_2(0) - u_3(0)] \qquad (6\text{-}18)$$

Relation (6-18) is useful in all collision situations, not simply those when the collision is perfectly elastic and when there are no external forces. Even in these other cases *it is a useful approximation for determining the expected peak magnitude of f_s when scaling analog-computer programs.*

When the situation is one of free bodies colliding, it is interesting to note what occurs in this situation of a perfectly elastic collision. If in relation (6-10) μ_s is set equal to unity, there results

$$u_2(t_s) = \frac{M_2 - M_3}{M_2 + M_3} u_2(0) + \frac{2M_3}{M_2 + M_3} u_3(0) \qquad (6\text{-}19)$$

$$u_3(t_s) = \frac{2M_2}{M_2 + M_3} u_2(0) + \frac{M_3 - M_2}{M_2 + M_3} u_3(0) \qquad (6\text{-}20)$$

From this it will be found that both the momentum and the kinetic energy are preserved for this perfectly elastic case.

As an example of the result, let the case be considered where the overtaken mass M_3 initially is stationary $[u_3(0) = 0]$. Then if the overtaking mass is greater ($M_2 > M_3$), its velocity will be reduced but not reversed in direction following collision. M_3 will be imparted part of the forward velocity. This is shown in Figure 6-44a.

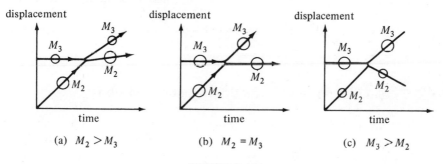

(a) $M_2 > M_3$ (b) $M_2 = M_3$ (c) $M_3 > M_2$

FIGURE 6-44

If the two masses are equal, the overtaking mass will be brought to a halt and the overtaken mass will acquire all its momentum. (This occurs in a straight short in billiards when no English is employed.) On the other hand, if the overtaken mass is the greater ($M_3 > M_2$), u_2 is reversed in direction while M_3 acquires a forward velocity. Simulation studies based on Figure 6-35 should verify these analytically derived conclusions.

In some simulation applications it may be preferred to assume that the collision is perfectly elastic and that $k_s \rightarrow \infty$ (nonresilient surfaces). This has the effect of reducing the engagement time t_s to zero and of making f_s and f_1 impulses (i.e., of infinite magnitude). This can be simulated without overload only if the production of the signals indicating f_s and f_0 can be avoided. Therefore, such an assumption is difficult to achieve exactly with analog simulation and usually is simply approached by making k_s as high as scaling provisions will permit. On the other hand, the perfectly elastic nonresilient situation can be represented in a digital program as follows:

1. During each iteration the portion of the program preceding the collision simulation will provide values of the velocities u_2 and u_3.
2. The spacing between engaging surfaces, x_s, is computed by integrating $(u_3 - u_2)$.
3. As long as this spacing x_s remains positive, no collision situation will have occurred and the values of u_2 and u_3 do not require modification.
4. When this spacing falls to zero or becomes negative, relations (6-19) and (6-20) are applied to modify the velocities u_2 and u_3 to the values $u_2(t_s)$ and $u_3(t_s)$.

Relations (6-19) and (6-20) will be applicable in such a simulation program even when M_2 and M_3 are not free bodies. (They may be subject to gravity or coupled to other elements.) This is true because the momentum transfer is assumed to have occurred in an infinitesimal time interval during which none of the finite forces involved will have had time to affect the velocities.

An example of this procedure will be shown in the simulation of backlash.

6-15   Simulation of a Perfectly Inelastic Collision

A perfectly inelastic collision corresponds to the case of zero resilience; the engaging surfaces exhibit only viscous damping effects, as though an ideal linear shock absorber were involved. Under such circumstances k_s is zero and $\zeta_s \rightarrow \infty$. The coefficient of restitution μ_s becomes zero. From relations (6-10) and (6-11),

$$u_2(t_s) = u_3(t_s) = \frac{M_2 u_2(0) + M_3 u_3(0)}{M_2 + M_3} \qquad (6\text{-}21)$$

There is no loss in momentum caused by this type of collision, but there naturally is a loss in kinetic energy resulting from the viscous forces. The two colliding bodies remain together (in the free-body situation) since they acquire the same velocity.

Relation (6-21) applies to the free-body situation. Under such circumstances t_s would be infinite as the bodies never separate. When this situation exists in a non-free-body situation (i.e., when the collision occurs within a larger system where there are other forces applied, these other forces might, of course, ultimately cause separation).

Such a perfectly inelastic collision may be simulated simply by making k_s zero in the block diagram of Figure 6-35 and applying this to either an analog or digital simulation program.

As in the instance of a perfectly elastic collision, it may be preferred to assume that B_s approaches an infinite value. This reduces to zero the time required for the momentum transfer. In an analog simulation program this is accomplished by setting B_s as high as the scaling limitations imposed on f_s and f_0 will permit. In a digital program it is feasible to employ the procedure described in the preceding section with the one change that in step 4 of that procedure, relation (6-21) is employed rather than relations (6-19) and (6-20).

6-16   Backlash

Backlash, or free play, occurs when two coupled mechanical elements are not coupled rigidly but rather through an inactive zone of displacement within which no direct mechanical coupling exists. This effect occurs often, in both the rotational and translational sense, in mechanical systems. The most commonly observed version of this effect occurs in conjunction with gearing.

Excessive backlash can cause control difficulties in mechanical systems. On the other hand, most procedures used to reduce the amount of backlash can, when carried too far, result in excessive friction instead. In design, some type of "trade-off" is often necessary. Because of the difficulties involved in predicting the effects on the system dynamics by purely analytic techniques, simulation procedures are often necessary to study this effect.

Simply because it is easier to show backlash diagramatically for the translational version, this is the form that is illustrated in Figure 6-45. Conclusions reached from it may, of course, be applied to the rotational version as well.

Figure 6-45 is an extension of Figure 6-34. x_2 and x_3 are measures of the displacements of the driving and collision-engaged members. Actually, only their difference, $x_3 - x_2$, is significant here. This governs the two engagement gap spacings x_{s1} and x_{s2}. These are given by

$$x_{s1} = x_{s1}(0) - (x_3 - x_2) \qquad (6\text{-}22)$$

$$x_{s2} = x_{s2}(0) + (x_3 - x_2) \qquad (6\text{-}23)$$

where $x_{s1}(0)$ and $x_{s2}(0)$ are the *neutral settings* of the gaps (i.e., the values

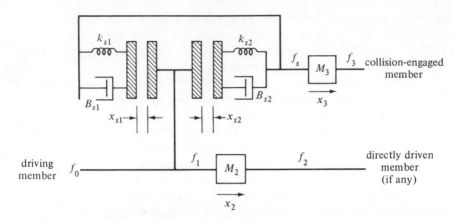

FIGURE 6-45

when $x_3 = x_2$). The total *backlash range*, therefore, is $x_{s1}(0) + x_{s2}(0)$. The engagement force will be given by the relation

$$
f_s = \begin{cases}
-\left(k_{s2} + B_{s2}\dfrac{d}{dt}\right)x_{s2} & \text{when } x_{s2} < 0 \\[2mm]
0 & \text{when } x_{s1} \geq 0 \text{ and } x_{s2} \geq 0 \qquad (6\text{-}24) \\[2mm]
+\left(k_{s1} + B_{s1}\dfrac{d}{dt}\right)x_{s1} & \text{when } x_{s1} < 0
\end{cases}
$$

[Normally, $x_{s1}(0)$ and $x_{s2}(0)$ will be positive; hence the condition that $x_{s1} < 0$ and $x_{s2} < 0$ simultaneously will not arise.] Usually, $k_{s1} = k_{s2}$, $B_{s1} = B_{s2}$, and x_2 and x_3 may be defined so that $x_{s1}(0) = x_{s2}(0)$. In that event the numerical subscripts need no longer be employed; they are included here only for the purpose of greater generality.

From relations (6-22) to (6-24), the relationship between the force f_s and the relative displacement $x_2 - x_3$ will appear as in Figure 6-46 for *static conditions*. It may be seen that an inactive-zone effect is involved.

The block-diagram representation of this general backlash effect is shown in Figure 6-47. This diagram is simply an extension of Figure 6-35. The analog or digital implementation is straightforward, following principles that have already been discussed.

Figure 6-47 represents the correct *general* picture of backlash. A number of simpler simulations have been proposed in the literature; their validity is based upon the validity of the simplifying assumptions upon which they depend. In some instances the assumption is made that the collisions are perfectly elastic. In that instance the collision force f_s will become zero at the same instant that x_s becomes positive, and the diodes shown in Figure 6-47 are superfluous. Furthermore, as B_{s1} and B_{s2} are zero, the comparators function as simple diodes and may be replaced by them. Further simplifica-

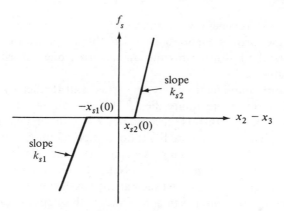

FIGURE 6-46

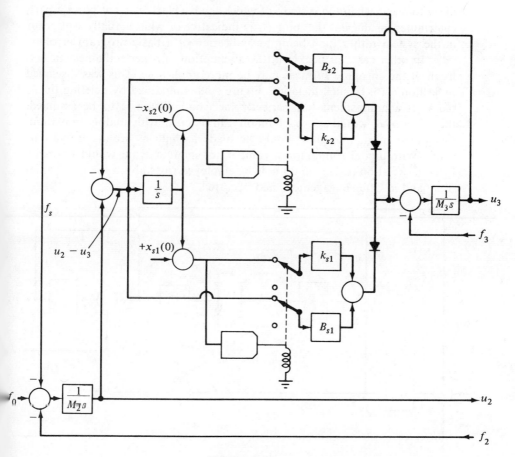

FIGURE 6-47

tion is possible if, as generally is the case, $k_{s1} = k_{s2}$. Figure 6-47 then becomes modified to the form of Figure 6-48. When this simplification is permissible, one of the methods for simulating an inactive zone described in Section 6-5 may be applied.

Often this simplification may be carried still further by assuming that the colliding surfaces are nonresilient. This was discussed in Section 6-14. As mentioned there, this is accommodated with analog simulation by making k_s as high as the scaling limitations imposed on f_s and f_1 will permit. With digital simulation the use of a comparator module is desirable to establish when surface engagement has occurred with either of the limit stops [when $x_2 - x_1$ equals $\pm x_s(0)$]. At such an instant of time the values of the velocities u_2 and u_3 are modified in accordance with relations (6-19) and (6-20).

Often the use of such a simulation program will show a repeated bouncing back and forth between the engaging surfaces. This is particularly likely to occur when the system, of which the backlash element plays a part, contributes insufficient damping. It is indicative of what actually will occur in the system rather than being an indication of a basic program error.

In other cases of backlash, the assumption of a perfectly inelastic collision of the engaging surfaces may be more applicable. This was discussed in Section 6-15. In such instances Figure 6-48 is modified by deleting the k_s block. If a nonresilient but perfectly inelastic collision is to be assumed, the values of B_s would approach infinity. In practice, with analog simulation, this would mean that they would be made as high as scaling limitations allow. With digital simulation a comparator module again would normally be used. Relation (6-21) would now be employed to establish the new values of u_2 and u_3 after engagement had occurred.

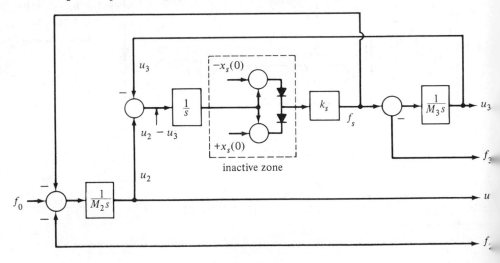

FIGURE 6-48

There will be a number of instances when this assumption of a non-resilient but perfectly inelastic collision may be assumed in connection with backlash phenomena. There will be far fewer instances when it can also be assumed that the driven mass M_3 is negligible and that it is coupled to members that also have negligible inertia. When this is the case, the situation describing the effect of backlash reduces to the very simple one on which Problem 4-4 was based. Unfortunately, this very special case has been presented by a number of writers as describing the general picture of backlash. A. C. Jackson [1] has aptly named this special case "pseudobacklash" to warn the reader that its validity is greatly limited.

6-17   Friction

The term friction has many varied connotations. Some forms of friction give rise to forces or moments that are continuous functions of the velocity. These functions may have various forms; for example, friction caused by energy losses in a fluid, as with fans or propellers, may often be represented, at least approximately, by the *absquare function* (i.e., $f_f = ku|u|$, or $m_f = k\omega|\omega|$) or by more complicated relationships if the more exact fluid dynamics are to be taken into account. Such relationships may be handled readily by diode function generators when analog simulation is being employed, or by appropriate analytic approximations or tabulated data when digital techniques are being used.

As in the example treated in Chapter 1, some forms of friction may be approximated as linear or viscous (i.e., $f_f = Bu$ or $m_f = B\omega$). This form is, of course, the simplest to represent in a simulation program. Such linear friction arises with fluid-type dampers such as dashpots provided only viscous fluid-flow conditions exist (a less-than-critical Reynolds number). However, it should be noted that many damping elements purported to be linear may often operate in the turbulent-flow region where the absquare relationship is more appropriate. Hydraulic shock absorbers may or may not be linear; often they include devices such as check valves so that the force relationship is different for positive and negative velocities. Some types of electrical dampers, such as eddy-current brakes, present essentially linear-friction characteristics over limited ranges of velocity.

Two very common discontinuous types of friction occurring when mechanical surfaces are in direct contact (e.g., not separated by a viscous film of lubricant) are *Coloumb friction* and *stiction*. The former, also called dry friction, is very simple to represent, being given by the following relationship for the translational case:

$$f_f = F_c \operatorname{sgn} u \tag{6-25}$$

or, for the rotational case,

$$m_f = M_c \text{ sgn } \omega \tag{6-26}$$

where sgn is simply the algebraic sign function; e.g.,

$$\text{sgn } u = \begin{cases} +1 & \text{for } u > 0 \\ 0 & \text{for } u = 0 \\ -1 & \text{for } u < 0 \end{cases}$$

Relations (6-24) and (6-25) may appear to be similar to that of the two-position contactor shown in Figure 6-12. Actually, there is a significant difference because that contactor relationship allows for only two values of the function while, on the other hand, the Coloumb-friction force will fall to zero when there is exactly zero velocity. Hence, with analog simulation, circuits as shown in Figure 6-13 should be employed (where there is no true discontinuity at zero) rather than relay comparators.

In many instances the type of friction occurring will be a combination of a number of the types discussed here. It is especially true that when Coulomb friction exists, stiction will exist as well. Therefore, these two types should be simulated specifically as a combination. This is discussed in the section to follow.

In any event, it should be pointed out that friction, in general, is a very variable effect. Different mechanical elements off the same production line may exhibit markedly different characteristics, and the same element may itself at different times exhibit markedly different characteristics, dependent upon such factors as past wear and tear, state of lubrication, and operating temperature. Hence any simulation of a friction effect is necessarily approximate, based upon "typical" values.

6-18   Stiction

As just stated, stiction as well as Coulomb friction occurs whenever two surfaces are in sliding contact. It is easier to describe the effects of stiction in verbal rather than strictly mathematical form.

1. Whenever the velocity is zero, the stiction effect will come into play. The application of any force or torque to the member involved will result in the development of a stiction force or torque of exactly equal magnitude and opposing direction, so that the velocity will continue to be zero.
2. When the applied force (torque) reaches a critical value, F_s or M_s, the stiction limit, then this opposing stiction force (torque) will disappear suddenly, corresponding to *breakaway*, and an immediate acceleration of the member results.

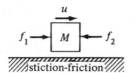

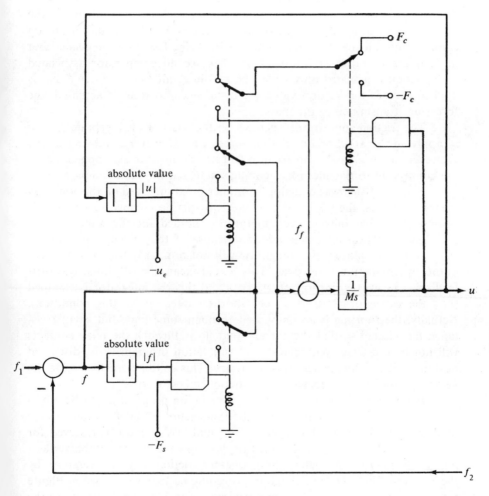

FIGURE 6-49

3. Once motion does occur following breakaway, the Coulomb or sliding-friction effect described previously will apply (i.e., $f_f = \pm E_c$ or $m_f = \pm M_c$). Stiction will not reoccur until the velocity falls again to zero.

Figure 6-49 is a block diagram for representing the *combination* of *stiction* and *friction*. f_1 is the force applied to the mass and f_2 is the total force reaction caused by the mass velocity and/or displacement. The two stiction comparators function on the basis of the logic described above. The comparator having the u (velocity) input is deactuated whenever the absolute value of u, or $|u|$, is zero; in practice, with either digital or analog computation, this must be interpreted as $|u|$ being less than some small but finite tolerance range or *threshold*, u_ϵ. The second comparator associated with stiction is actuated only when the absolute value of the force f that is applied exceeds the stiction value F_s. If *either* comparator is actuated, the forces are transmitted to the mass.

The friction comparator operates on the basis of the algebraic sign of u, applying the appropriate friction force $\pm F_c$ whenever a velocity exists. However, when $|u| < u_\epsilon$, no friction force is assumed to be applied, hence the connection to the additional contacts actuated by the u comparator.

Figure 6-50 shows an analog-computer program based on this logic. By means of diodes, the OR feature of the two stiction comparators shown is combined so that only one comparator is needed for this function. An additional practical feature is added; because of the velocity threshold u_ϵ that must be employed, the integrator will not ordinarily have *exactly* zero output when stiction takes over. This would mean a small, fallacious drift in displacement (the integral of u). To avoid this the integrator is clamped (i.e., the capacitor C is effectively short-circuited under this condition). Actually, the shorting is accomplished through some finite but small resistance R_f selected so that the current that flows through the relay contacts will not be excessive. With the digital simulation program to be discussed next, a similar clamping action is necessary. This will be done by setting the velocity u to exactly zero whenever stiction takes over.

Figure 6-51 shows how a general simulation program might be modified to account for a combination of stiction–friction effect. Two comparator modules, numbered by the integers $COMP_u$ and $COMP_f$, must be reserved for this purpose. The signal actuating $COMP_u$ is simply the velocity u; that actuating $COMP_f$ is $|f| - F_s$, determining whether stiction may be overcome by the available force. The initialization procedure necessary is shown in Figure 6-51. The simulation program then proceeds as in Figure 6-8, just up to the point where the integrator inputs are to be established. At this point, the stiction–friction subprogram to be described below is called. The program then returns to the normal pattern of Figure 6-8.

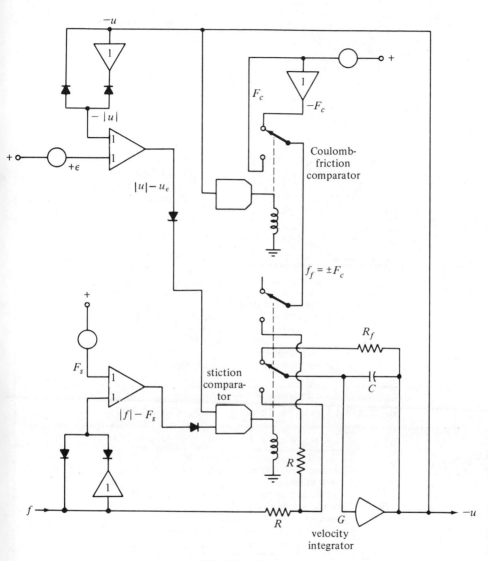

FIGURE 6-50

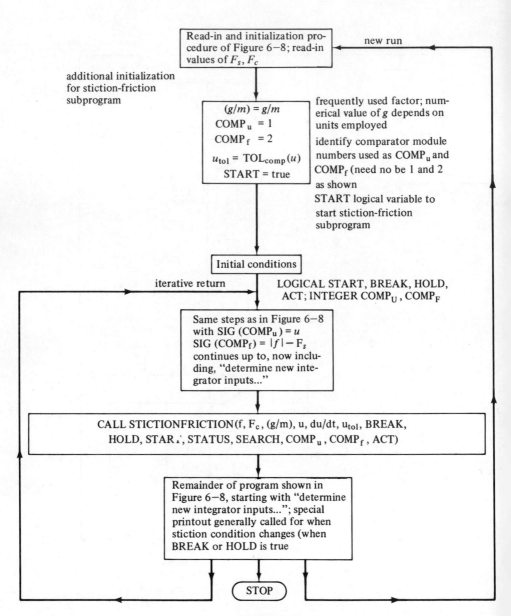

FIGURE 6-51

SUBROUTINE STICTIONFRICTION(f, F_c, (g/m), u, du/dt, u_{tol}, BREAK,
HOLD, START, STATUS, SEARCH, $COMP_u$, $COMP_f$, ACT)

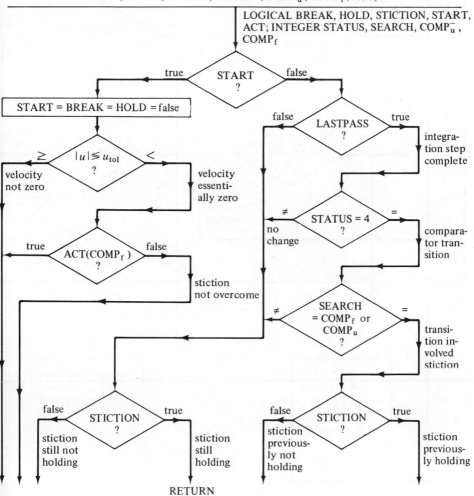

LOGICAL BREAK, HOLD, STICTION, START,
ACT; INTEGER STATUS, SEARCH, $COMP_u^-$,
$COMP_f$

FIGURE 6-52

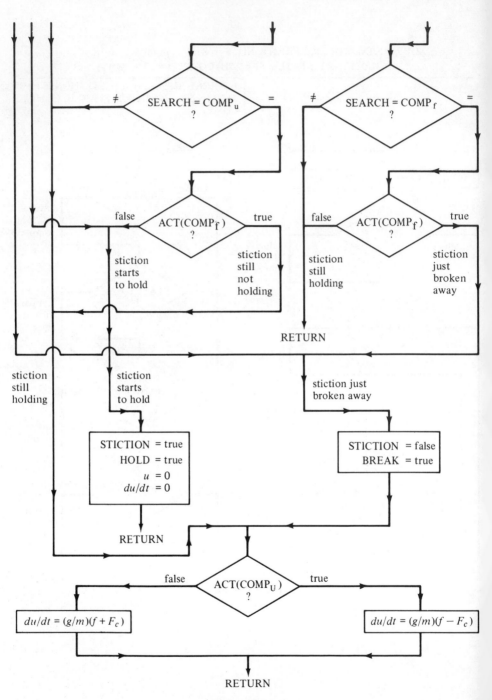

FIGURE 6-52 (cont'd)

Figure 6-52 is a flow diagram of the stiction–friction subprogram. During the first iteration ($\text{START} = \text{true}$) the initial stiction state (whether stiction has broken away or is holding) is established. Thereafter, the program follows one of two alternative courses.

1. If STICTION originally was false (i.e., stiction has already been broken away), a change in condition is considered only when the COMP_u comparator has changed state, indicating a condition of zero velocity. Then, if and only if the COMP_f comparator is not actuated ($|f|$ does not exceed F_s), will stiction be assumed to start to hold. The logical variables involved are modified accordingly.
2. If STICTION originally was true (i.e., stiction had been holding), a change in condition is considered only when the COMP_f comparator becomes actuated, meaning that the force available has finally exceeded the stiction limit F_s. The logical variables involved are then modified accordingly.

Under the conditions when stiction is not in effect (STICTION is false) the acceleration of the associated mass is determined in the last step of the subprogram. Here Coulomb friction F_c is taken into account; the sign by which it enters into the relationship is determined by the algebraic sense of the velocity u (i.e., by the actuation state of the comparator labeled COMP_u).

Figure 6-53 illustrates a simple mechanical situation involving static friction. Here the displacement x of the free end of a spring k is given as some function of time. The resulting displacement y of the mass m is of interest.

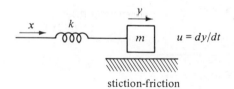

FIGURE 6-53   stiction-friction

Figure 6-54 is a flow diagram of a simulation program to represent this situation, following the general pattern of Figure 6-51.

Figure 6-55 shows a typical response when x is a triangular function of time (i.e., a ramp function followed by a later reversal in direction of motion). The alternate holding and releasing action of the stiction effect may readily be seen and conforms with the situation that is actually observed physically.

Another representation of stiction–friction sometimes used with analog simulation when comparators are not available consists of generating the function shown in Figure 6-56 by means of diode function generators. In that diagram, ϵ_1 and ϵ_2 are maintained as small as the slope limitations

STICTION-FRICTION example of Figure 6—53

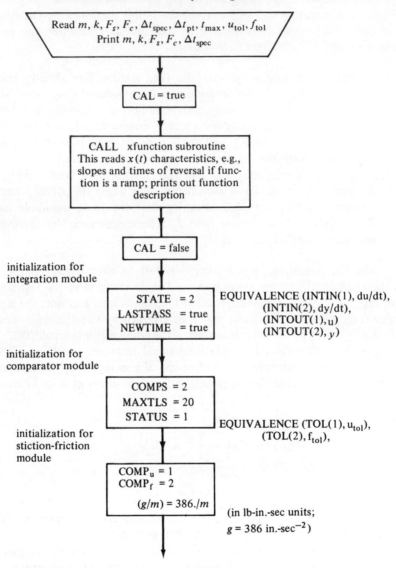

FIGURE 6-54

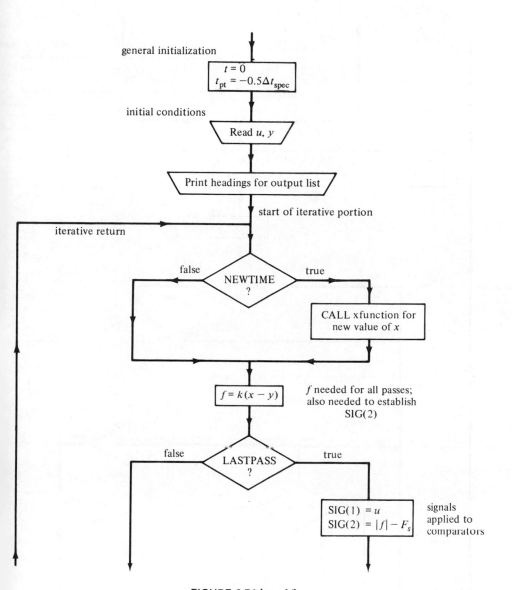

FIGURE 6-54 (cont'd)

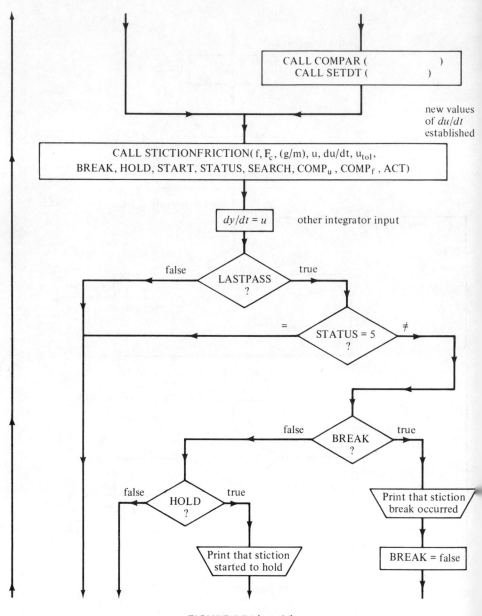

FIGURE 6-54 (cont'd)

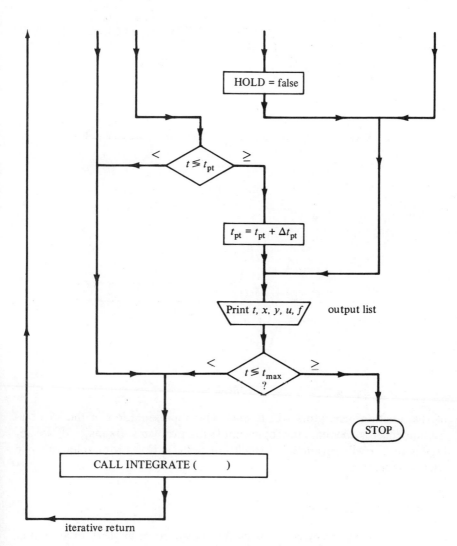

iterative return

FIGURE 6-54 (cont'd)

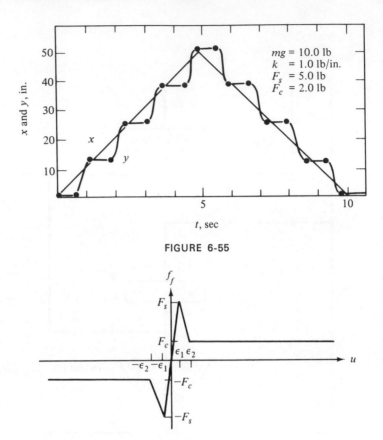

FIGURE 6-55

FIGURE 6-56

of the function generators will permit. This representation of the stiction–friction effect is adequate for some simulation problems. Its major disadvantage is that it will permit some small but finite indication of velocity while stiction is in effect.

Suggested Problems

6-1. A servomechanism system is used to position the angle θ_c of an output load to some desired value θ_r. This system employs the speed-control system of Problem 1-3 and is represented by Figure P6-1. The servomechanism's closed loop is completed by adding, to the arrangement of Problem 1-3, an angle-error detector that senses the actual load angle θ_c, compares it with the desired angle θ_r, and establishes the angle error $\theta_e \triangleq \theta_r - \theta_c$. (Various types of mechanisms, e.g., synchros, might be used for this purpose.) In any event, the associated control preamplifier produces a signal:

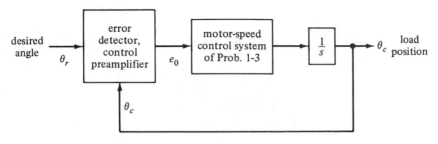

FIGURE P6-1

$$e_0 = \begin{cases} \mu\theta_e \text{ volts} & \text{for } -e_L < \mu\theta_e < e_L \\ e_L \text{ volts} & \text{for } \mu\theta_e > e_L \\ -e_L \text{ volts} & \text{for } \mu\theta_e < -e_L \end{cases}$$

In other words, there is hard limiting imposed on what otherwise would have been a linear control relationship. The limit e_L is 200 V.

(a) Simulate this system by analog means, supplementing the program developed to handle Problem 1-3. Then investigate the relationship between the gain μ and the stability of the system when step changes of θ_r are applied.

(b) Repeat, employing a digital program.

6-2. In the servomechanism described for Problem 6-1, a two-position contactor is substituted for the continuous controller. That is

$$e_0 = \begin{cases} e_L & \text{when } \theta_e > 0 \\ -e_L & \text{when } \theta_e \leq 0 \end{cases}$$

where, again, $e_L = 200$ V.

Using both analog and digital programs, investigate the performance of this system.

6-3. Again, for the servomechanism described for Problem 6-1 a contactor control is substituted. However, in this case

$$e_0 = \begin{cases} e_L & \text{when } \theta_e \geq \theta_\Delta \\ 0 & \text{when } -\theta_\Delta < \theta_e < \theta_\Delta \\ -e_L & \text{when } \theta_e \leq -\theta_\Delta \end{cases}$$

where e_L again is 200 V, and where θ_Δ is an adjustable inactive zone, measured in radians of angle. Use both an analog and a digital program to determine the effect of the adjustment of θ_Δ on the response of this system to step-function changes in θ_r.

6-4. This is an extension of the previous problem. In reality the contactor operation described is being established by an electromechanical relay system that has 20 per cent hysteresis. That is, the relationship between e_0 and

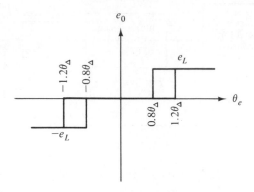

FIGURE P6-4

θ_e is as plotted in Figure P6-4. Again, $e_L = 200$ V. Repeat the work of Problem 6-3 for this new condition.

6-5. This refers back to Problem 6-1 (linear control with hard limiting), except that the position of the output angle θ_c is restrained from motion beyond ± 1.0 rad by hard limit stops, approximately represented as being perfectly elastic but of zero resilience ($B_s = 0$, $k_s \rightarrow \infty$). The range of θ_r is limited to within ± 1.0 rad. Investigate the response when θ_r is changed in step fashion from -0.9 to $+0.9$ rad for various values of the gain μ. Simulate with both analog and digital programs.

6-6. This problem is the same as Problem 6-5 except that now the limit stops are assumed to be perfectly inelastic but with zero resilience ($k_s = 0$, $B_s \rightarrow \infty$).

6-7. Refer to Problem 6-1. Both backlash and resilience effects exist in the gearing coupling the motor and load. Both of these effects are, of course, distributed through the various stages of the gearing, but can be represented as lumped equivalents, an effective torsional spring of constant $k_2 = 1.6 \times 10^7$ kg-cm/rad as referred to the output shaft, and by a backlash range of ± 0.001 rad, also as referred to the output shaft. Repeat Problem 6-1 with these effects added.

6-8. This is a repetition of Problem 6-7 except that there also exists a stiction–friction load given by

$$M_s = 15,000 \quad \text{kg-cm}$$
$$M_c = 5,000 \quad \text{kg-cm}$$

Determine what effect this has on the servomechanism system.

6-9. Establish by analytic methods (not experimental) the y versus x relationship that will result for the analog computer program shown in Figure P6-9.

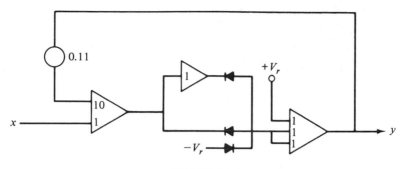

FIGURE P6-9

6-10. The simulation of the vertical motion of a four-wheeled vehicle traveling over a rough road is a somewhat complicated but practical problem. A less complicated version does provide some insight into this, and involves a theoretical "one-wheeled" vehicle. This is represented by Figure P6-10a. y_e is the *equivalent* vertical displacement of the road in feet, with a correction made for the tire radius. y_v and y_w are the vertical displacements in feet of the vehicle and wheel, respectively, and considered to be zero when in static equilibrium (with gravity force) with y_e zero.

The horizontal travel of this vehicle is measured in terms of x in feet. The vehicle is traveling at V ft/sec and hits the curbing shown in Figure P6-10b. y_r represents the actual road profile. However, since the tire is assumed to have a mean radius of 1.1 ft, the equivalent road displacement y_e appears as in Figure P6-10c, where

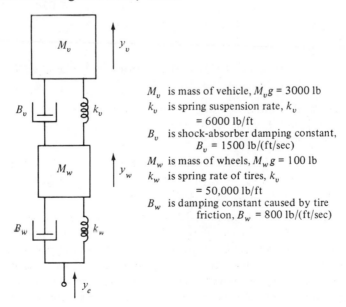

M_v is mass of vehicle, $M_v g$ = 3000 lb
k_v is spring suspension rate, k_v
     = 6000 lb/ft
B_v is shock-absorber damping constant,
     B_v = 1500 lb/(ft/sec)
M_w is mass of wheels, $M_w g$ = 100 lb
k_w is spring rate of tires, k_v
     = 50,000 lb/ft
B_w is damping constant caused by tire
     friction, B_w = 800 lb/(ft/sec)

FIGURE P6-10a

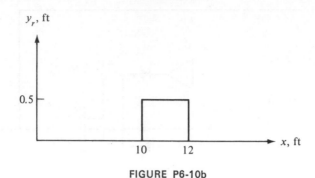

FIGURE P6-10b

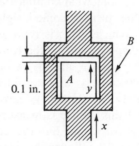

FIGURE P6-10c

$$y_e = \begin{cases} 0 & \text{for} \quad x > 9.078 \\ \sqrt{1.21 - (10 - x)^2} - 0.6 & \text{for } 9.078 < x < 10 \\ 0.5 & \text{for} \quad 10 < x < 12 \\ \sqrt{1.21 - (x - 12)^2} - 0.6 & \text{for} \quad 12 < x < 12.922 \\ 0 & \text{for} \quad x > 12.922 \end{cases}$$

Simulate this situation for various horizontal velocities V ranging from 5 to 100 ft/sec. Keep in mind that the road surface cannot exert tension on the tires, pulling them downward.

6-11. Consider Problem 6-10 again but with limit stops added to the suspension system so that $|y_v - y_w|$ may not exceed 0.5 ft. Assume a perfectly elastic collision with negligible resilience ($B_s = 0, k_s \rightarrow \infty$).

6-12. As illustrated in Figure P6-12, a member A of mass M rests inside another member B that has a relative displacement x. The only forces on A are gravity and the engagement force of B on either the upper or lower surface of A. The vertical displacement of A is described as y, equal to zero when A is resting on the lower surface and x is zero. There is a vertical clearance space of 0.1 in. between A and B. B moves with a vertical sinu-

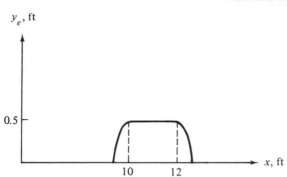

FIGURE P6-12

soidal motion of 0.5 in. amplitude, or

$$x = 0.5 \sin 2\pi f t \qquad \text{inches}$$

where f may be any frequency between 0.1 to 100 Hz. B has sufficient mass so that its motion is assumed unaffected by the motion of A.

It is assumed that the engaging surfaces have zero resilience; i.e., the transfer of momentum is approximated as instantaneous. The coefficient of restitution will have different values between zero and unity. Simulate this situation on both analog and digital computers and determine the steady-state response of y to this sinusoidal variation of x for various frequencies f and values of coefficient of restitution equal to 0.0, 0.25, 0.5, 0.75, and 1.0

References

1. A. C. Jackson, *Analog Computation* (New York: McGraw-Hill, Inc., 1960).

Additional Reading

2. M. G. Rekoff, Jr., *Analog Computer Programming* (Columbus Ohio: Charles E. Merrill Books, Inc., 1967), Chaps. 10 and 11.

Boundary-Value Problems 7

7-1 Occasions When Boundary-Value Problems Arise

In many situations to be simulated, specific conditions are to be met at specific values of the basic independent variable and either the initial conditions or the value of one or more parameters is to be determined so that these conditions will be met. Problems in simulation described by this general statement are called *boundary-value problems*. [1, 2] This definition might be clarified by specific examples.

1. The problem of static bending of a simple beam, where the basic independent variable is distance along the beam, x (rather than time, t, as in dynamic problems). As will be explained in this chapter, this will be describable by a fourth-order differential equation. To simulate this by conventional methods, four initial conditions must be established: the deflection at $x = 0$, the slope at $x = 0$, the shear force at $x = 0$, and the bending moment at $x = 0$. Normally, not all these four initial conditions would be known in such a problem. Instead, for example, deflections, slopes, moments, or shear forces might be specified at some other points along the beam; this is dependent on the manner in which the beam is supported. The unspecified initial conditions must be established so that they will satisfy the other specified boundary conditions. In simple beam

problems this can be handled analytically, but in more complicated situations trial-and-error solutions are required. Such solutions can be performed most expeditiously by negative-feedback techniques using either analog or digital computers. In summary, this particular example represents a case where it is some of the initial conditions that are not known.

2. The problem of determining the actual interest rate applicable when a loan is paid according to an established schedule, where the noninitial boundary condition is the fact that the principle will become zero at the termination date of the loan. The unknown quantity is the interest rate, a parameter. Here again, a solution is effected most expeditiously by trial-and-error methods.

3. The problem of determining optimum parameters of a control system so that a certain objective will be attained at a specified instant of time. Such a system might, for example, be responsible for moving an object in space from one point to another so that, at the specified instant of time, the object will have arrived at exactly that point with zero velocity and acceleration; these latter conditions are the boundary values. Here again, the problem is one of determining the values of the parameters necessary so that these boundary conditions will be satisfied. (When this problem is extended to one of determining the parameters for making the time of attaining these conditions a minimum, the problem then becomes an optimization problem, the subject of Chapter 8.)

4. Distributed parameter problems such as those involving transmission lines, heat flow, and distributed mass and resilience systems, will involve boundary conditions to be satisfied at various points. This is covered in more detail in Chapter 10.

The general approach to be employed when handling such boundary-value problems is illustrated best by example, using 1, 2, and 3 as illustrations.

7-2   General Example of Static Bending of a Simple Beam

The horizontal beam considered will be assumed to be subjected to only vertical forces and associated moments. These forces and moments may be divided into two categories:

1. Concentrated forces and/or moments at a point (this is, of course, an approximation of the real situation).

2. Distributed forces.

Because of the assumption of *point forces*, the axial points, x_p, at which these forces will be applied will be of special interest. These points can be classified among the five types shown in Figure 7-1.

The distributed loading, described as $w(x)$, is such that on any given span, say from x_1 to x_2, the load would be

Type 1. Simple force-application point

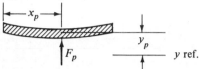

the deflection y_p is not specified; it must be determined

Type 2. Point support from above

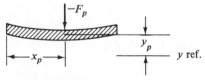

Type 3. Point support from below

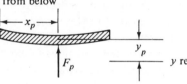

the deflection y_p is specified; the force F_p must be established

Type 4. Support from both above and below, or pin support

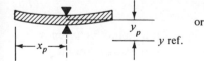   or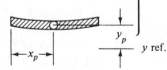

Type 5. Cantilever support, constraining both deflection, y_p, and slope, $(dy/dx)_p$

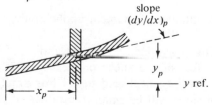

slope $(dy/dx)_p$

the deflection y_p and the slope $(dy/dx)_p$ are specified; both force F_p and moment M_p must be established

FIGURE 7-1

$$\int_{x_1}^{x_2} w(x)\,dx$$

$w(x)$ may be various functions of x, as shown in Figure 7-2. (Such loading generally is downward, and hence would appear as shown.) $w(x)$ would, of course, include the effects of the beam's own weight. The point forces, considered previously, could be considered as impulse functions superimposed on $w(x)$.

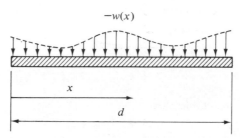

FIGURE 7-2

If, as rarely is the case, the only force-application points are of Type 1, the analysis problem then becomes straightforward. The axial distance x is measured from the left-hand end. Vertical beam deflections y are measured from some reference level with upward deflections being considered as positive. Such deflections are measured to the *neutral axis* of the beam; this roughly is the center of the cross-sectional area, although more rigorous definitions are required for complicated and nonsymmetrical cross-sectional shapes. The analysis steps would be as follows.

1. The shear force along the beam is established by the relation

$$S(x) = \int_0^x w(x)\,dx + \sum_{i=1}^m F_p(i) \tag{7-1}$$

   where m is the number of force-application points between $x = 0$ and $x = d$ and $F_p(t)$ is the force applied at the ith point.
2. The bending moment along the beam is established by the relation

$$M(x) = \int_0^x S(x)\,dx + \sum_{i=0}^j M_p(i) \tag{7-2}$$

   where j is the number of moment-application points between zero and d.
3. Simple bending is assumed where the radius of curvature will be EI/M. (The effect of the shear on deflection is usually relatively negligible and will be neglected here.) For practical beams where the change in slope will be small, the radius of curvature is essentially $1/(d^2y/dx^2)$; hence

$$\frac{d^2y}{dx^2} = \frac{M(x)}{EI(x)} \tag{7-3}$$

where E is the coefficient of elasticity of the material and I is the beam cross-sectional area moment of inertia about the neutral axis. For the case of varying cross sections, EI will be a function of x.

4. The slope dy/dx is then computed as

$$\frac{dy}{dx} = \int_0^x \frac{d^2y}{dx^2} dx \tag{7-4}$$

5. The deflection itself is simply

$$y = \int_0^x \frac{dy}{dx} dx \tag{7-5}$$

Four integration operations, therefore, are necessary; the variable of integration (the basic independent variable) of the simulation process, therefore, is x rather than time, as in the examples considered previously.

The above operations are straightforward and are handled readily by analog or digital computers. With analog computers x is scaled to machine time t_m; with digital computers any of the integration methods mentioned in Chapter 3 may be used. (Other integration methods could also be employed as the future values of the integrands will be known in advance, in contrast to problems in dynamics.)

No boundary-value problems arise with this simple example. The necessary boundary conditions at the right-hand end of the beam where $x = d$ are

$$S(d) = 0 \tag{7-6}$$

$$M(d) = 0 \tag{7-7}$$

These will, however, be met automatically if the sum of the forces and of the moments applied to the beam each total zero, as they would have to if static equilibrium were to apply.

In more typical cases, however, boundary-value problems do arise. Normally, not all the force-application points are of Type 1 but consist rather of various types of supports, Types 2 to 5. These will apply forces that initially are unknown; for a Type 5 support an unknown moment will be applied as well. The supports will specify the deflections y existing at the support points and, for a Type 5 cantilever support, will specify the slope dy/dx as well. These specified deflections and moments are, in addition to the conditions of relations (7-6) and (7-7), the *boundary conditions* to be met. The forces imposed by each support and the moment imposed by a Type 5 support will, in addition, represent the *boundary inputs* to be established so that the boundary *conditions* will be met. Furthermore, if the first force-application point, always designated as point 1, at $x = 0$, should be of Type 1, the initial values of both deflection $y(0)$ and slope $\dot{y}(0)$[1] will be boundary inputs, to be established. If this point is of Type 2, 3, or 4, on the other hand, only the initial slope will be a boundary input. In any event, there will always turn out to be exactly the same number of boundary conditions and inputs.

For ease of describing this further, the *specified* boundary conditions to be met will be given the symbol B_{spec}. The *actual* boundary values, observed during the trial-and-error process of adjusting the boundary inputs, will be called B_{obs}. The boundary inputs to be established will be called B_{in}. When the proper values of B_{in} have been established, the values of B_{spec} and B_{obs} will be equal.

To describe the operations to be performed, consider the force-application points to be numbered sequentially (in order of increasing x) from 1 to N. The point $x = 0$ will always be called point 1 [if no force is applied there, $F_p(1)$ will simply be zero]. Similarly, the point $x = d$ will always be called point N [again, if no force is applied, $F_p(N) = 0$]. The ith point has associated with it forces designated as $F_p(i)$, possibly (for Type 5 supports) moments designated as $M_p(i)$, deflections designated as $y_p(i)$, and slopes designated as $(dy/dx)_p(i)$. The general sequence of operations then is as follows:

1. Consider point 1 ($x = 0$).
   (a) If this point is of Type 1, then

$$B_{\text{in}}(1) = y_p(1)$$

$$B_{\text{in}}(2) = \left(\frac{dy}{dx}\right)_p(1)$$

   The known initial conditions are

$$S(0) = 0$$

$$M(0) = 0$$

   (b) If this point is of Type 2, 3, or 4, then

$$B_{\text{in}}(1) = \left(\frac{dy}{dx}\right)_p(1)$$

$$B_{\text{in}}(2) = F_p(1)$$

   The known initial conditions are

$$y(0) = y_p(1)$$

$$M(0) = 0$$

   (c) If this point is of Type 5, a cantilever support, then

$$B_{\text{in}}(1) = F_p(1)$$

---

[1] Dot notation will be used here to signify derivatives with respect to x rather than to time t.

$$B_{in}(2) = M_p(1)$$

The known initial conditions are

$$y(0) = y_p(1)$$

$$\dot{y}(0) = \left(\frac{dy}{dx}\right)_p(1)$$

2. Now all other force-application points from $i = 2$ to $N - 1$ are considered in turn.

   (a) If point i is of Type 1, then the value of $F_p(i)$ is simply added to the value of shear force in accordance with relation (7-1) when that point is reached. No new boundary conditions or inputs are involved.

   (b) If the point is of Type 2, 3, or 4, then the deflection of this point has been specified and

$$B_{obs}(k) = y[x_p(i)]$$
$$B_{spec}(k) = y_p(i)$$

[The observed boundary conditions and specifications will be subscripted (k) in the order in which they appear.] The presently unknown boundary input, to be established, is

$$B_{in}(j) = F_p(i)$$

[Similarly, boundary inputs will be subscripted (j) in the order in which they appear. The boundary inputs for $j = 1$ and $j = 2$ were already established at point 1.] The trial value of $F_p(i)$ is added to the shear force at this point.

   (c) If the point is of Type 5, then both the deflection and slope at this point have been specified and

$$B_{obs}(k) = y[x_p(i)] \qquad B_{spec}(k) = y_p(i)$$

$$B_{obs}(k + 1) = \dot{y}[x_p(i)] \qquad B_{spec}(k + i) = \left(\frac{dy}{dx}\right)_p(i)$$

The previously unknown boundary inputs, to be established, are

$$B_{in}(j) = F_p(i)$$
$$B_{in}(j + 1) = M_p(i)$$

3. Finally, at the end of the beam the following conditions are imposed:

   (a) If this end point is of Type 1, then the boundary conditions to be met are

$$B_{obs}(k) = S(d) \qquad\qquad B_{spec}(k) = 0$$
$$B_{obs}(k + 1) = M(d) \qquad B_{spec}(k + 1) = 0$$

Prior to computing $S(d)$, the value of $F_p(N)$ is added to the accumulated value of shear force.

(b) If the end point is of Type 2, 3, or 4, the boundary conditions to be met are

$$B_{obs}(k) = y(d) \qquad\qquad B_{spec}(k) = y_p(N)$$
$$B_{obs}(k + 1) = M(d) \qquad B_{spec}(k + 1) = 0$$

The values of $F_p(N)$ must equal the value of shear stress accumulated up to this point since the shear at the very end of the beam must be zero.

(c) If the end point is of Type 5, then the boundary conditions are described by

$$B_{obs}(k) = y(d) \qquad\qquad B_{spec}(k) = y_p(N)$$
$$B_{obs}(k + 1) = \dot{y}(d) \qquad B_{spec}(k + 1) = \left(\frac{dy}{dx}\right)_p (N)$$

Both the shear and the moment at the very end of the beam must be zero. Hence $F_p(N)$ must be equal to minus the value of S accumulated up to that point, and $M_p(N)$ must be minus the value of M so accumulated.

The difference between force-application points Types 2, 3, and 4 has still to be considered. It is obvious that Type 2 supports can exert only negative forces and Type 3 only positive forces.

7-3   Specific Example of a Simple Beam with Cantilever Support at $x = 0$ and One Other Support Point

For the beam shown in Figure 7-3, the block diagram of the simulation model would appear as in Figure 7-4. Note that three boundary conditions are specified:

$$B_{spec}(1) = y_p(2) \qquad \text{position of center support}$$
$$B_{spec}(2) = 0 \qquad\qquad \text{as } S(d) = 0$$
$$B_{spec}(3) = 0 \qquad\qquad \text{as } M(d) = 0$$

The actual observed boundary conditions resulting from the model are

$$B_{obs}(1) = y[x_p(2)] \qquad \text{indicated position of beam at center support}$$
$$B_{obs}(2) = S(d)$$
$$B_{obs}(3) = M(d)$$

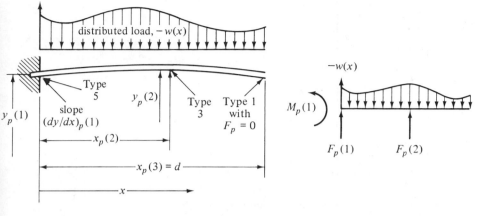

FIGURE 7-3

The error in boundary conditions is, in general,

$$B_{\text{error}}(i) = B_{\text{spec}}(i) - B_{\text{obs}}(i)$$

Some process is required for automatically adjusting the boundary inputs until the error is made zero. These boundary inputs are

$$B_{\text{in}}(1) = F_p(1)$$
$$B_{\text{in}}(2) = M_p(1)$$
$$B_{\text{in}}(3) = F_p(2)$$

Note that there are as many boundary inputs as there are conditions to be adjusted.

Normally, with the center support in contact, there are three boundary inputs with this example and three boundary errors to be made zero. However, for the Type 3 support being considered, the force $F_p(2)$ can never be negative. This fact is shown in Figure 7-4 by the comparator having $B_{\text{in}}(3) = F_p(2)$ as an input. If $F_p(2) < 0$, this force is held at zero instead. Furthermore, one boundary-error signal, designated as $B_{\text{error}}(1) = y[x_p(2)] - y_p(2)$, no longer applies.

The relationship between the required correction of the boundary inputs, designated as ΔB_{in}, and the boundary errors represents a set of simultaneous algebraic equations. That is, these relationships may be represented by the matrix relation

$$[\Delta B_{\text{in}}] = [A][B_{\text{error}}] \tag{7-8}$$

In the above example this A matrix is of dimension 3×3 until the center support loses contact with the beam; it then becomes 2×2.

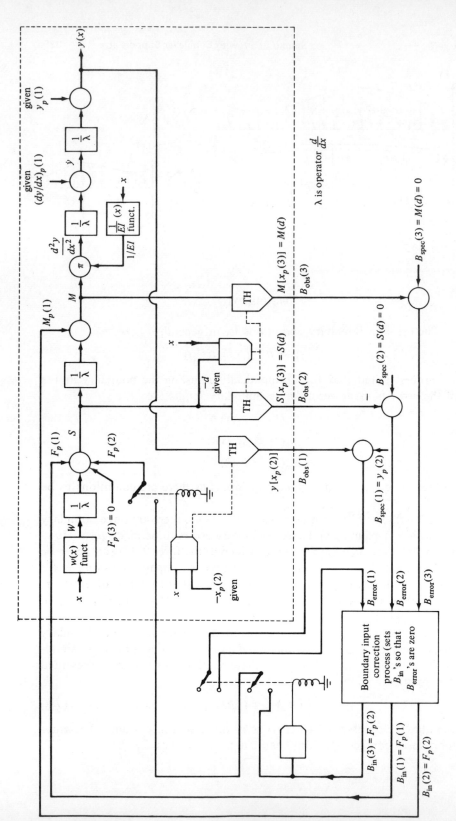

FIGURE 7-4

7-4   Analog Approach Toward Boundary-Input Adjustment

A repeated trial simulation of the beam model is easy to accomplish when dynamic-storage methods are available in an analog computer. For the example of Section 7-3, the block diagram of Figure 7-4 directly suggests the configuration. The repeated trial-and-error simulation of the beam would be performed in the high-speed-repetitive mode; the correction of boundary inputs, in the normal time mode. The more difficult problem is the handling of the boundary-input corrections.

　　The obvious analysis method to be used would be based upon the implicit methods discussed in Chapter 5. The existence of boundary errors would result in rates of change of the boundary inputs until all errors were zero. The question arises, however, which error should cause a rate of change of which boundary input, and in what direction? The answer is not necessarily obvious from physical considerations.

　　One relatively crude approach would be to use a series of console switches to make this decision. For the example of Section 7-3 with the analog arrangement of Figure 7-4, the procedure might be as shown in Figure 7-5. By this arrangement, a trial-and-error selection of the best feedback arrangement, including the relative gains of the three correction channels (set by the three potentiometers), can be established. Note that there is no choice

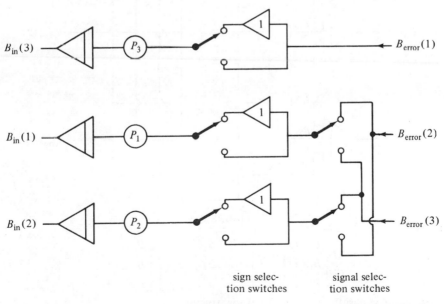

FIGURE 7-5

with regard to the establishment of $B_{in}(3)$; it must be established by $B_{error}(1)$ because, when the central support no longer engages the beam, both signals disappear.

It will be found that unless a correct selection is made the correction process will be unstable. To obtain a reasonably fast, stable, and well-damped correction, it will be necessary to adjust the relative gains rather carefully. The correction problem here is an example of the general feedback-control problem involving multiple inputs and multiple outputs; a correct choice of "what controls what, and how much" must be made if instability or poor response is to be avoided.

A far better correction of boundary inputs could be established if all errors affected all inputs, using the analog scheme shown in Figure 7-6, where the operations described can be represented in matrix form by the relation

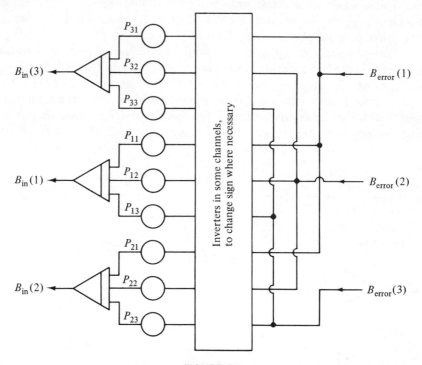

FIGURE 7-6

$$\frac{d}{dt}\begin{bmatrix} B_{in}(1) \\ B_{in}(2) \\ B_{in}(3) \end{bmatrix} = k \begin{bmatrix} a_{11} & a_{12} & a_{13} \\ a_{21} & a_{22} & a_{23} \\ a_{31} & a_{32} & a_{33} \end{bmatrix} \begin{bmatrix} B_{error}(1) \\ B_{error}(2) \\ B_{error}(3) \end{bmatrix} \tag{7-9}$$

or, more generally and more compactly, by

$$\frac{d}{dt}[B_{in}] = k[A][B_{error}] \qquad (7\text{-}10)$$

In Figure 7-6, the potentiometer settings in connection with the integrator gains establish the constant k and the elements a_{ij} of the A matrix. (Diagrams of the type shown in Figure 7-6 become cumbersome if there are a large number of boundary conditions and boundary inputs to be considered. Under such circumstances the use of block diagrams is generally avoided and the matrix description is alone employed to describe the interconnections.)

It can be established by feedback-control theory that the most effective correction of the boundary errors will be obtained when the A matrix is determined by the following procedure:

1. The effect of *changes* in the boundary inputs ΔB_{in} upon *changes* in the boundary errors ΔB_{error} are established by *perturbation tests* (i.e., by making such changes in each input, one at a time, and observing the effect upon the error). This will lead to a set of relations that can be expressed in matrix form as

$$[\Delta B_{error}] = [C][\Delta B_{in}] \qquad (7\text{-}11)$$

   where C will be a square matrix with each dimension equal to the number of boundary conditions involved.

2. The *optimum* A matrix, referring to relation (7-10), then is *the inverse* of the C matrix. When only analog equipment is available, this inversion procedure may have to be performed by pencil-and-paper methods. (There are analog techniques of matrix inversion available but rather elaborate programming is required.) Such a method of matrix inversion could prove extremely tedious when the number of boundary conditions is high; for the specific example shown in Figure 7-3, however, the labor involved is not excessive. Once the inverse, A, matrix has been established, each potentiometer shown in Figure 7-6 is then set so that, for example,

$$P_{ij} = k\,|a_{ij}| \qquad (7\text{-}12)$$

   Whether or not an inverter is required depends upon the sign of a_{ij}. As the integrators already provide a sign inversion, an inverter is required only when a_{ij} is positive.

The result of this technique is a *noninteracting feedback system*. That is, a given boundary error $B_{error}(j)$ will give rise to corrections of boundary inputs that are so proportioned that there will be no effect on the other boundary errors being corrected separately. Stability problems then no longer arise; the adjustment of the boundary conditions will occur according to an exponential time relationship and, as k is increased within reasonable limits (because the data sampling effect of the high-speed-repetitive operation could cause other stability problems if k were too high), the rate of boundary-input correction will become increasingly rapid.

Figure 7-4 shows that the boundary input $B_{in}(3) = F_p(2)$ is removed when the support at point 2 loses contact with the beam [i.e., when $F_p(2)$ tries to become negative]. The boundary error designated as $B_{error}(1)$ then is no longer considered. The matrix acquires a smaller dimension, 2×2, and the four elements of the A, inverse, matrix are then computed differently. Referring now to Figure 7-6, when $B_{in}(3)$ and $B_{error}(1)$ are removed, the only significant potentiometers are P_{12}, P_{13}, P_{22}, and P_{23}. However, their optimum settings for such a noninteracting-control type of convergence will now change radically and will be based, by relation (7-12), on the new smaller A matrix.

This particular example shows the advantage of hybrid analog–digital simulation. The many repeated trial integrations over the span of the beam are performed most expeditiously, and certainly most rapidly, by analog means. The matrix inversion necessary to obtain the optimum boundary-condition corrections is, on the other hand, performed much more readily by digital computers. Furthermore, the various logical operations necessary to establish the effect of a Type 2 or Type 3 support losing contact with the beam is handled most easily by digital logic. Such a hybrid simulation could produce an almost instantaneous display of the changing conditions along the beam as various factors, such as loading and the position of supports, were varied.

A discussion of the techniques necessary to establish such a hybrid simulation must be deferred until a later chapter. Next to be discussed is the purely digital approach for simulating not only the specific situation represented by Figure 7-3 but also the general problem of beam bending.

7-5   Digital Simulation of Beam Bending

Digital simulation of beam bending is quite straightforward and can make effective use of the subroutine modules INTEGRATE, SIMULTANEOUS, SIMQ, COMPAR, and SETDT mentioned in previous chapters. Any of the integration modules discussed in Chapter 3 that do not involve extrapolation (the extrapolating type b modules are unsuitable because of the discontinuities that occur at the special force-application points) may be used for integrating along the length of the beam in accordance with relations (7-1), (7-2), (7-4), and (7-5). Of course, the variable of integration now is, the distance x rather than time t.

The integration problem actually is somewhat different and also simpler than those involved in the dynamic problems discussed in the preceding chapters. Here the future (meaning higher values of x) values of the integrand are known in advance and do not depend on what the integral turns out to be. There are other methods of integration (e.g., Simpson's rule) that can be employed effectively under such circumstances. However, all of the non-extrapolating methods mentioned in Chapter 3 will be suitable, although they may require longer execution times (for a specified degree of accuracy) than these other methods.

With the analog simulation of this general problem, analog comparators were used to locate the force-application points. Similarly, the COMPAR module may be used for this same purpose. It is true that the use of this module will increase execution time somewhat, because of the search procedures involved. However, unless the location of each of these points, the $x_p(i)$'s, corresponds to an even number of iteration intervals, Δx, the use of this subroutine is the most convenient.

The SIMULTANEOUS subroutine is ideally suited for solving the boundary inputs, the B_{in}'s. Referring to this subroutine, as described in Chapter 5, the x array corresponds to the B_{in} array here; the y_{sp} array becomes the B_{spec} array; the y array, the B_{obs} array. The subroutine itself computes B_{error} and adjusts the B_{in} array so that these errors are made smaller than the specified error tolerances. When this subroutine indicates that FINISH = true, the correct boundary conditions have been obtained.

The algebraic relationship between boundary conditions and boundary inputs is a linear one in the type of beam-bending problem discussed thus far; hence, in theory, only one trial of the SIMULTANEOUS subroutine should be required. However, because of round-off errors, a second trial is often necessary before error tolerances are met and FINISH = true. If the problem was a nonlinear one, as it would be if the factor EI was a function of M(true with many materials, and with any material once the elastic limited has been exceeded), such linear relations would no longer apply and more trials would be required of the SIMULTANEOUS subroutine.

The digital simulation program must also accommodate the possibility of a Type 2 or Type 3 support's losing contact (i.e., disengaging with the beam). This is taken care of by observing the algabraic sign of the forces applied at such points (these will be boundary inputs B_{in}). As soon as the value of the corresponding B_{in} assumes the wrong sign, the value of B_{in} is set to zero and this B_{in} is removed as a boundary input; the height of the support point y_p is also removed as a boundary-condition specification, B_{spec}. The number of boundary conditions to be accommodated is therefore reduced accordingly

It is convenient to use a logical array, ENGAGE(i), to indicate whether there is an engagement of the Type 2 or Type 3 support with the beam at the ith force-application point. ENGAGE(i) initially is assumed true; it is changed to false when loss of engagement is observed. Provisions must be made to observe a possible reengagement during the trial runs; this could occur only if more than one support were in this type category. Tests for engagement or disengagement are not made during perturbations of the SIMULTANEOUS subroutine, only during actual trial runs following such perturbation tests.

Figure 7-7 is a general flow diagram illustrating the basic operations involved. A more detailed version, in the form of a Fortran IV program, is shown in Appendix 7A. This program is general in the sense that it can handle any number of force-application points (within the range of computer storage capacity) of any of the five types described. Figure 7-8 illustrates one test case, employing this program, involving a 10-ft beam with a cantilever support at $x = 0$ (where y is defined as zero) and Type 2 support points at $x = 2.5$ and 7.5 ft. Figure 7-9 is a typical printout for one case. Figure 7-10 shows how the beam deflection changes as the two point supports are being progressively lowered. Both supports are initially at the same level as the left-hand cantilever support ($y = 0$). First the outer support is progressively lowered to -0.04 ft. By this time, as shown, it loses contact with the beam. Then the inner support is lowered progressively to -0.01 ft; during this process the outer support first regains contact and then the inner support loses contact. The outer support is then lowered progressively to -0.08 ft; the outer support again loses contact and the only support remaining is the cantilever support at $x = 0$.

It should be pointed out that the program shown in Figure 7-7, and in more detail in Appendix 7A, represents a compromise between ease of programming by making use of standard subroutine modules already available and speed of execution; in many problems of this type, not enough different runs are to be made for the latter to be an important consideration for a modern high-speed computer. When the program is to be used repeatedly, there are a number of modifications (that do complicate the program) that could reduce execution time.

7-6   Example of a Position-Control System

This present example of a boundary-value problem is a relatively classical one used to show how parameters rather than initial conditions may require adjustment to establish prescribed boundary conditions. To avoid undue complication of the explanation, a simple version of this general problem has been chosen which does have a ready analytic solution. However, the approach used is generally applicable to other more complex versions where analytic solutions are not feasible.

The problem consists of that of positioning a mass M along linear

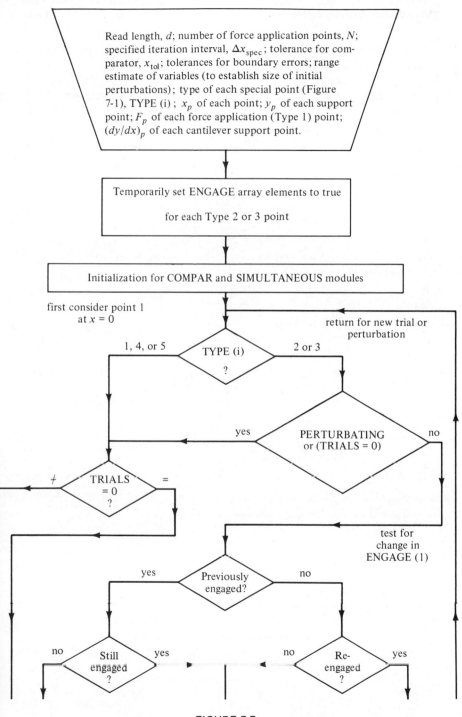

Read length, d; number of force application points, N; specified iteration interval, Δx_{spec}; tolerance for comparator, x_{tol}; tolerances for boundary errors; range estimate of variables (to establish size of initial perturbations); type of each special point (Figure 7-1), TYPE (i); x_p of each point; y_p of each support point; F_p of each force application (Type 1) point; $(dy/dx)_p$ of each cantilever support point.

Temporarily set ENGAGE array elements to true

for each Type 2 or 3 point

Initialization for COMPAR and SIMULTANEOUS modules

first consider point 1
at $x = 0$

return for new trial or
perturbation

TYPE (i)
?

1, 4, or 5

2 or 3

PERTURBATING
or (TRIALS = 0)

yes

no

TRIALS
= 0
?

$\neq$

=

test for
change in
ENGAGE (1)

Previously
engaged?

yes

no

Still
engaged
?

no

yes

Re-
engaged
?

no

yes

FIGURE 7-7

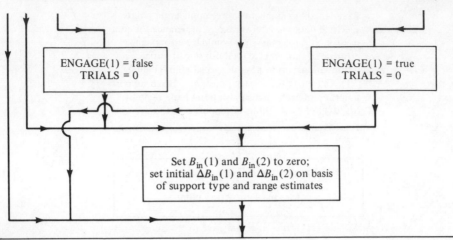

Set initial conditions for point 1 at $x = 0$:

Type 1	Type 2 or 3 if ENGAGE(1) = false	Type 2 or 3 if ENGAGE(1) = true; Type 4	Type 5
$S = F_P(1)$	$S = 0$	$S = B_{in}(1)$	$S = B_{in}(1)$
$M = 0$	$M = 0$	$M = 0$	$S = B_{in}(2)$
$y = B_{in}(1)$	$y = B_{in}(1)$	$y = y_p(1)$	$y = y_p(1)$
$dy/dx = B_{in}(2)$	$dy/dx = B_{in}(2)$	$dy/dx = B_{in}(2)$	$dy/dx = (dy/dx)_p(1)$

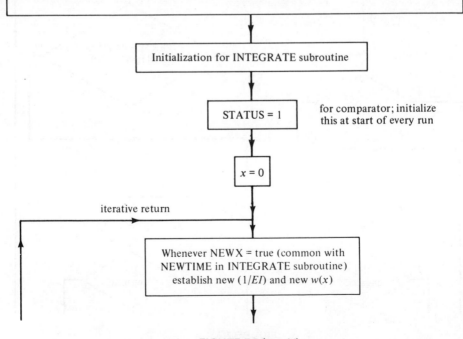

FIGURE 7-7 (cont'd)

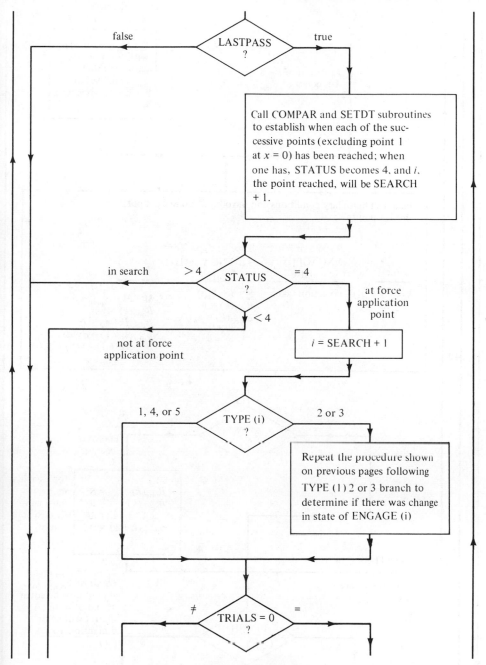

FIGURE 7-7 (cont'd)

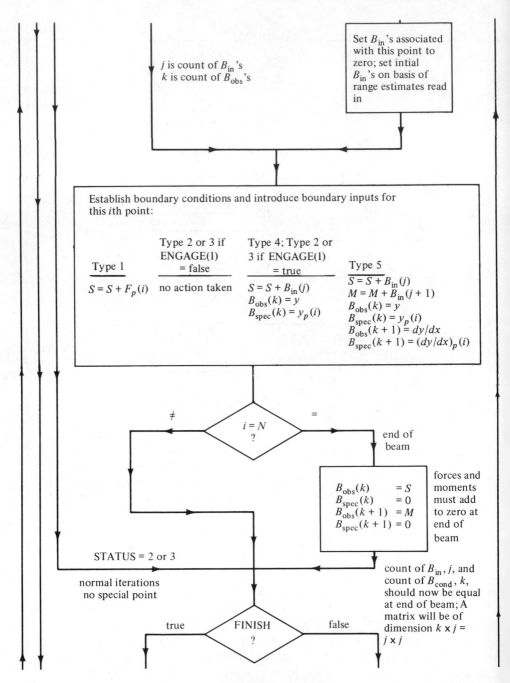

FIGURE 7-7 (cont'd)

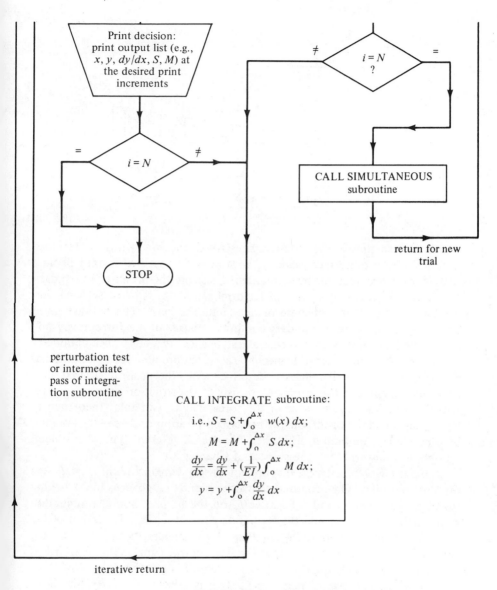

FIGURE 7-7 (cont'd)

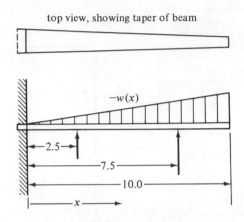

top view, showing taper of beam

$-w(x)$

2.5

7.5

10.0

x

FIGURE 7-8

coordinates so that it will attain a prescribed position within a tolerance $\pm e_\Delta$ and also a prescribed velocity, both at some specified instant of time t_r after correction first has been initiated. These are the prescribed boundary conditions. To this end a force of fixed magnitude f_m is to be selected that can be used to either accelerate or decelerate the mass. The parameters to be selected to meet these boundary conditions consist of this force magnitude f_m and the time of its sign reversal, as established by a controller parameter a. Figure 7-11 illustrates the mechanical situation described. The actual position of the controller mass is described as c; the position desired as r. (A revised version of this problem consists of the situation where f_m is prescribed as the maximum value of the force that is available; then time t_r, when the boundary conditions of prescribed position and velocity are met, is to be made a minimum. This then becomes a different type of problem, an optimization problem, the subject of Chapter 8.)

Figure 7-12 is a block diagram of this system including a suggested form of controller. The proposed controller is one that governs the switching between a positive f_m and a negative f_m on the basis of some combination of the error $e = r - c$, and the error rate $\dot{e} = \dot{r} - \dot{c}$. In this version of the problem, in order to limit the number of parameters to be adjusted, the combination of e and $\dot{e}$ used is linear (i.e., the control signal m that established the sign of f is made equal to $e + a\dot{e}$). When m is positive, a positive f_m is applied; when negative, a negative f_m. If a is selected properly, the force will switch algebraic signs at the proper instant to meet the boundary conditions. The value of a necessary to accomplish this will naturally depend upon the disturbance of r that is applied.

In Figure 7-12 the contactor has been modified to represent a more practical situation. After correction has been accomplished, there should be some provision for the force f being zero as well as $\pm f_m$. (Failing to provide for this could result in a rapid oscillation between plus and minus values of

X	W	EI	Y	DY/DX	M	S

CANTILEVER SUPPORT OF HEIGHT 0.0 AND SLOPE 0.0
PRODUCING MOMENT 51881. AND FORCE -60754.1

X	W	EI	Y	DY/DX	M	S
0.0	-0.0	0.500E 08	0.0	0.0	51881.	-60754.1
0.250	-120.00	0.494E 08	0.00003	0.00022	36691.	-60769.0
0.500	-240.00	0.487E 08	0.00011	0.00037	21494.	-60814.0
0.750	-360.00	0.481E 08	0.00021	0.00044	6282.	-60889.0
1.000	-480.00	0.475E 08	0.00032	0.00044	-8953.	-60994.0
1.250	-600.00	0.469E 08	0.00042	0.00035	-24218.	-61129.0
1.500	-720.00	0.463E 08	0.00049	0.00018	-39520.	-61294.0
1.750	-839.99	0.456E 08	0.00050	-0.00008	-54867.	-61489.0
2.000	-959.99	0.450E 08	0.00044	-0.00043	-70267.	-61714.0
2.250	-1079.99	0.444E 08	0.00028	-0.00086	-85727.	-61969.0
2.500	-1200.00	0.437E 08	0.00000	-0.00139	-101255.	-62254.0

POINT SUPPORT OF HEIGHT 0.0 WITH FORCE 84754.5

X	W	EI	Y	DY/DX	M	S
2.500	-1200.00	0.437E 08	0.00000	-0.00139	-101255.	22500.5
2.750	-1320.00	0.431E 08	-0.00042	-0.00196	-95669.	22185.5
3.000	-1440.00	0.425E 08	-0.00098	-0.00250	-90165.	21840.5
3.250	-1559.99	0.419E 08	-0.00167	-0.00302	-84751.	21465.5
3.500	-1679.99	0.413E 08	-0.00249	-0.00351	-79434.	21060.5
3.750	-1799.99	0.406E 08	-0.00342	-0.00398	-74223.	20625.5
4.000	-1919.99	0.400E 08	-0.00448	-0.00443	-69124.	20160.5
4.250	-2039.99	0.394E 08	-0.00564	-0.00485	-64145.	19665.5
4.500	-2159.98	0.388E 08	-0.00690	-0.00524	-59293.	19140.5
4.750	-2279.98	0.381E 08	-0.00825	-0.00561	-54577.	18585.5
5.000	-2399.98	0.375E 08	-0.00970	-0.00596	-50003.	18000.5
5.250	-2519.98	0.369E 08	-0.01123	-0.00628	-45579.	17385.5
5.500	-2639.98	0.363E 08	-0.01284	-0.00658	-41313.	16740.4
5.750	-2759.98	0.356E 08	-0.01452	-0.00685	-37211.	16065.4
6.000	-2879.97	0.350E 08	-0.01626	-0.00710	-33282.	15360.4
6.250	-2999.97	0.344E 08	-0.01806	-0.00732	-29534.	14625.4
6.500	-3119.97	0.338E 08	-0.01992	-0.00753	-25972.	13860.4
6.750	-3239.97	0.331E 08	-0.02183	-0.00771	-22606.	13065.4
7.000	-3359.97	0.325E 08	-0.02377	-0.00787	-19442.	12240.4
7.250	-3479.96	0.319E 08	-0.02576	-0.00801	-16488.	11385.4
7.500	-3600.00	0.312E 08	-0.02778	-0.00813	-13751.	10500.1

DISENGAGED POINT SUPPORT OF HEIGHT -0.0400

X	W	EI	Y	DY/DX	M	S
7.500	-3600.00	0.312E 08	-0.02778	-0.00813	-13751.	10500.1
7.750	-3720.00	0.306E 08	-0.02982	-0.00823	-11240.	9585.1
8.000	-3840.00	0.300E 08	-0.03189	-0.00831	-8961.	8640.1
8.250	-3959.99	0.294E 08	-0.03398	-0.00838	-6922.	7665.1
8.500	-4079.99	0.288E 08	-0.03608	-0.00843	-5131.	6660.1
8.750	-4199.99	0.281E 08	-0.03819	-0.00847	-3594.	5625.1
9.000	-4319.99	0.275E 08	-0.04031	-0.00849	-2321.	4560.1
9.250	-4439.98	0.269E 08	-0.04244	-0.00851	-1317.	3465.1
9.500	-4559.98	0.263E 08	-0.04457	-0.00852	-591.	2340.1
9.750	-4679.98	0.256E 08	-0.04670	-0.00852	-149.	1185.1
10.000	-4800.00	0.250E 08	-0.04883	-0.00852	-1.	-0.1

FIGURE 7-9

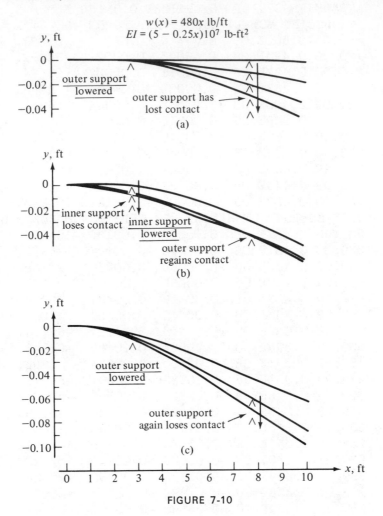

FIGURE 7-10

f_m after the boundary conditions have been met.) This provision is shown in Figure 7-12 by introducing an inactive zone (as discussed in Chapter 6), designated as e_Δ, in the contactor operation.

In Figure 7-12 the parameters a and f_m are shown as signals entering their respective blocks. This is done to indicate that these parameters are to be adjustable. They will be adjusted to satisfy the stated boundary conditions,

$$e(t_r) = 0$$
$$\dot{e}(t_r) = 0 \qquad\qquad (7\text{-}13)$$

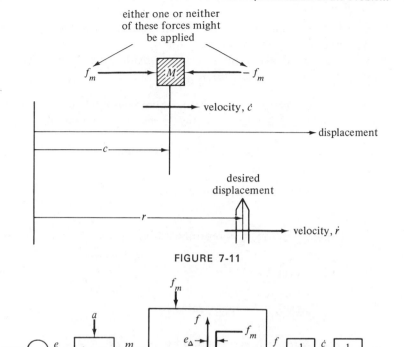

FIGURE 7-11

FIGURE 7-12

7-7   Dimensionless Representation of the Problem

If this example is to be considered as representing a general problem, rather than involving only specific ranges of r and $\dot{r}$ and a specific mass M, it will be convenient to present it in a *dimensionless* form. The results obtained would then be of more general utility. Furthermore, this procedure will simplify greatly the problem of machine-variable scaling when an analog computer is used for the purpose of simulation, and it will avoid the necessity of changing machine scale factors when the size of the mass or the range of r and $\dot{r}$ should be changed.

The dimensionless representation will be based upon the value of the mass M and the following two constants:

1. r_m, which is equal to or somewhat greater than the maximum magnitude of the reference position r.
2. t_m, which is equal to or somewhat greater than the maximum magnitude of the prescribed response time t_r.

Both r_m and t_m should be selected as round numbers in whatever units are employed to simplify the conversion between real and dimensionless quantities.

The dimensional variables involved in the problem are converted to a dimensionless form as follows:

controlled position, c, is represented by

$$\gamma = \frac{c}{r_m} \qquad (7\text{-}14\text{a})$$

reference position, r, is represented by

$$\rho = \frac{r}{r_m} \qquad (7\text{-}14\text{b})$$

error, e, is represented by

$$\epsilon = \frac{e}{r_m} \qquad (7\text{-}14\text{c})$$

control signal, m, is represented by

$$\mu = \frac{m}{r_m} \qquad (7\text{-}14\text{d})$$

applied force, f, is represented by

$$\phi = \frac{t_m^2}{Mr_m}f \qquad (7\text{-}14\text{e})$$

controlled velocity, $\dot{c}$, is represented by

$$\dot{\gamma} = \frac{t_m}{r_m}\dot{c} \qquad (7\text{-}14\text{f})$$

reference position velocity, $\dot{r}$, is represented by

$$\dot{\rho} = \frac{t_m}{r_m}\dot{r} \qquad (7\text{-}14\text{g})$$

elapsed time, t, is represented by

$$\tau = \frac{t}{t_m} \qquad (7\text{-}14\text{h})$$

time derivative operator, s, is represented by

$$\lambda = t_m s \qquad (7\text{-}14\text{i})$$

The adjustable parameters will be represented in dimensionless form as follows:

controller rate constant, a, is represented by

$$\alpha = \frac{a}{t_m} \qquad (7\text{-}15\text{a})$$

control force magnitude, f_m, is represented by

$$\phi_m = \frac{t_m^2}{Mr_m}f_m \qquad (7\text{-}15\text{b})$$

Also, the inactive zone introduced, e_Δ, equal also to the error tolerance range, is represented in dimensionless form as

$$\Delta = \frac{e_\Delta}{r_m} \qquad (7\text{-}16)$$

On this basis the block diagram of Figure 7-12 may be converted to one of simpler form, shown in Figure 7-13. The operation $(1 + \alpha\lambda)$ in Figure 7-13 implies differentiation, usually inadvisable with either analog or digital simulation. For this reason the modification of the block diagram to the form shown in Figure 7-14 is proposed as a model for purposes of simulation.

In Figure 7-14, ρ and $\dot{\rho}$ will be functions of τ, established either as input data or derived from another program.

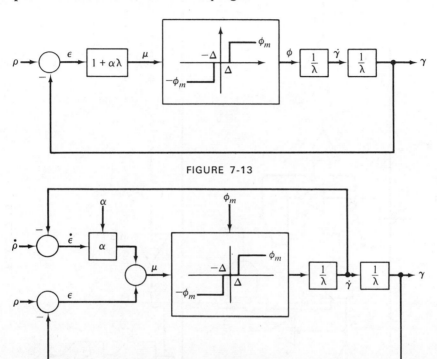

FIGURE 7-13

FIGURE 7-14

7-8   Analog Simulation of the Problem

Figure 7-15 illustrates the analog simulation of this problem. It should be noted that since all quantities are expressed in a dimensionless form, appropriate machine variables may be determined simply by multiplying these quantities by V_R, the computer's reference voltage. This is, for example,

$$\gamma_m - \gamma V_R$$

It should also be noted that since α is adjustable, it is introduced by means of a multiplier rather than by a potentiometer. (Since this program

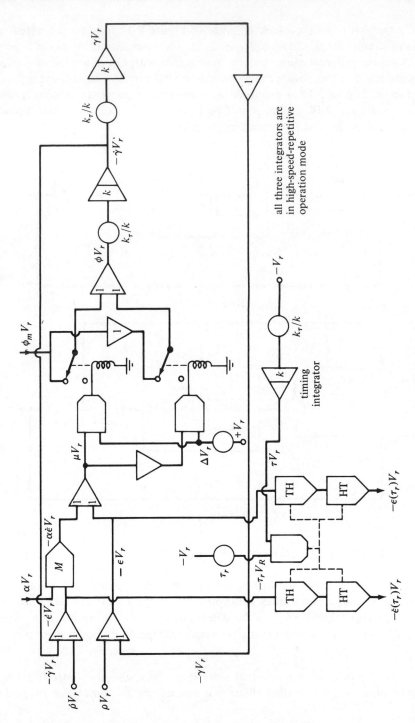

all three integrators are
in high-speed-repetitive
operation mode

timing
integrator

FIGURE 7-15

348

is to be operated in a high-speed-repetitive mode, a quarter-square type of multiplier might be the most appropriate.)

The contactor operation indicated is accomplished most easily by means of comparators, as shown in Figure 7-15. Since these must operate in a high-speed-repetitive mode, conventional electromechanical comparators may not be suitable. When they are not, electronic gating circuits equivalent to the comparator arrangement shown may be employed instead. Another alternative is the use of a combination inactive zone and switching circuit, as discussed in Section 6-7.

A time-scale factor k_τ should be chosen so that $1/k_\tau$ is less than the period of the computer when in the high-speed-repetitive mode (so that the simulation will be completed before the period of interest has expired and the reset period has begun).

It is also necessary to represent, in equivalent machine volts, an indication of elapsed time τ. This is accomplished by the additional integrator that develops the voltage τV_R. This integrator is used to actuate the track–hold combination when τ attains its specified value τ_R. The values of ϵ and $\dot{\epsilon}$, the two pertinent boundary conditions, are then sampled and held once each repetitive cycle, as they apply when $\tau = \tau_R$.

7-9 Adjusting Parameters to Satisfy Boundary Conditions

The outer (parameter-adjustment) loop is closed in a manner similar to that shown in the previous example of Figure 7-6. For the example now being considered, a program to accomplish this is shown in Figure 7-16. Again, since an intuitive selection of the algebraic sign associated with parameter correction may be deceptive, sign-reversal switches are provided. Because there are only four possible feedback loops involved here for parameter adjustment, trial-and-error adjustment to achieve a stable and reasonably rapid correction of parameters is more feasible than with the preceding example (where there were nine such possible loops).

Optimum correction of boundary errors is obtained only by using the procedure described in Section 7-3, employing the noninteracting-control concept. In order to find the optimum potentiometer settings, test perturbations are necessary.

7-10 Digital Simulation of the Positional-Control-System Problem

Digital simulation for this problem follows the same general principles that were described for the beam-bending problem; the correct boundary inputs,

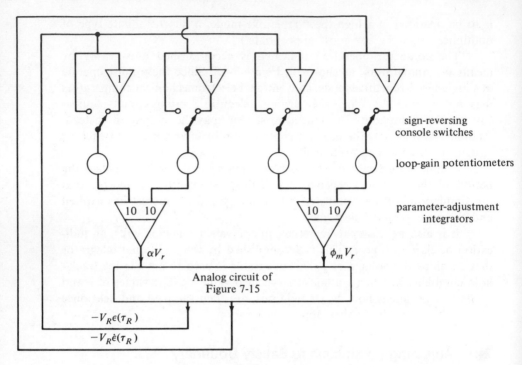

sign-reversing
console switches

loop-gain potentiometers

parameter-adjustment
integrators

αV_r

$\phi_m V_r$

Analog circuit of
Figure 7-15

$-V_R \epsilon(\tau_R)$

$-V_R \dot{\epsilon}(\tau_R)$

FIGURE 7-16

α and ϕ_m, are established by the simultaneous-equation module so that the boundary conditions $\epsilon(\tau_r)$ and $\dot{\epsilon}(\tau_r)$ both attain their specified values of zero. Three comparators may be employed, just as Figure 7-15 shows. Two would be employed to establish the inactive-zone boundaries at $\pm\Delta$ and to determine when they are crossed by the actuating signal μ. The third could be used to establish when $\tau = \tau_r$. This third comparator would not be needed if τ_r were made to equal some integer number of interation intervals, $\Delta\tau$; then a simple termination of the run when $\tau = \tau_r$ would suffice. Greater flexibility without this restriction on τ_r is, however, achieved by using the third comparator, even though it does involve some cost of speed of execution.

Figure 7-17 shows a flow diagram for simulating this problem. Note that to accommodate the possibility of the input $\rho(\tau)$ being various functions of τ, $\rho(\tau)$ and $\dot{\rho}(\tau)$ are established by a special command-function subroutine.

It has been mentioned that one of the advantages of using such a dimensionless version of the problem is the avoidance of scaling difficulties. Note that such difficulties also arise with digital simulation as far as tolerances of comparators and of simultaneous-equation modules are concerned. Here such difficulties could be avoided.

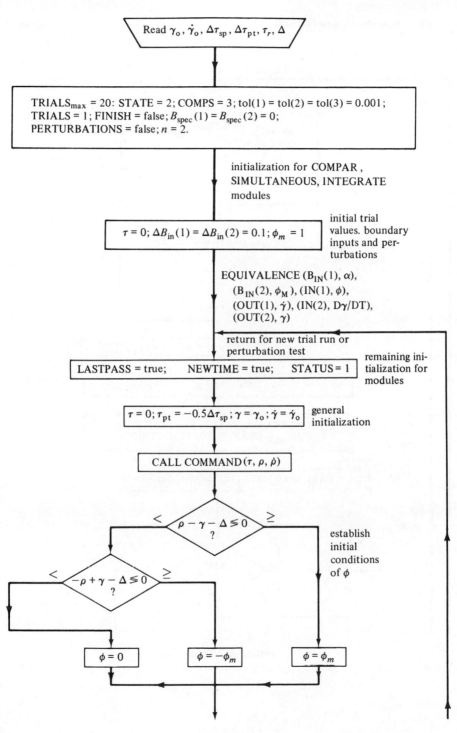

FIGURE 7-17

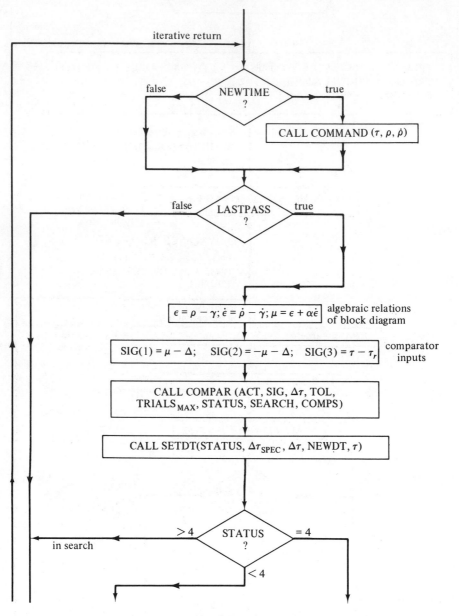

FIGURE 7-17 (cont'd)

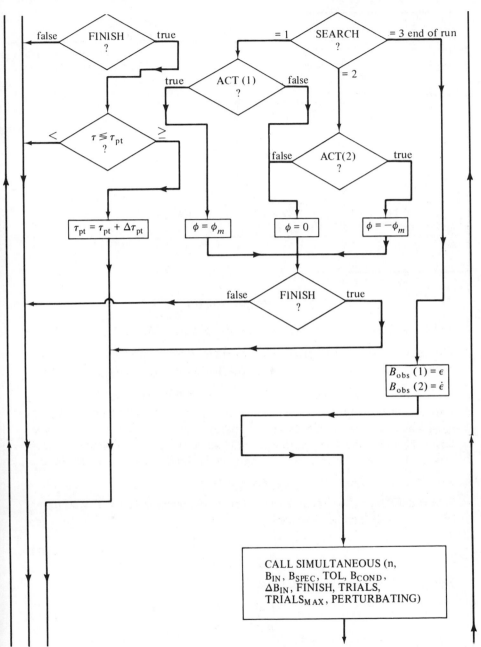

FIGURE 7-17 (cont'd)

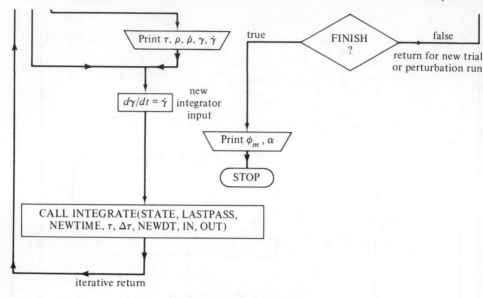

FIGURE 7-17 (cont'd)

7-11   Alternative Procedure for Parameter Correction

The analog and digital programs described here, applying to this second example, were based upon meeting the following boundary conditions:

$$\epsilon(\tau) = 0 \quad \text{and} \quad \dot{\epsilon}(\tau) = 0 \qquad \text{when} \quad \tau = \tau_r$$

This is a direct expression as the conditions were specified and hence the most obvious basis of a program for parameter correction. It is not necessarily the most effective approach as far as convergence of solution is concerned. First, a new variable, τ_0, may be defined implicitly as follows:

$$\epsilon(\tau_0) = 0 \tag{7-17}$$

This is defining τ_0 as the value of τ when ϵ first becomes zero. The boundary conditions will then be described as

$$B_{obs}(1) = \tau_0 \qquad B_{spec}(1) = \tau_r$$
$$B_{obs}(2) = \dot{y}(\tau_0) \qquad B_{spec}(2) = \dot{p}(\tau_0) \tag{7-18}$$

The boundary inputs still remain

$$B_{in}(1) = \alpha$$
$$B_{in}(2) = \phi_m \tag{7-19}$$

7-12   Application of Boundary-Value Problems

In general, boundary-value problems arise whenever physical situations are to be simulated that can be described by differential equations and not as many initial conditions are known as there are states. In addition, in Chapter 8 is discussed the determination of the optimum parameters to minimize certain *cost functions* or to maximize certain *merit functions*. These functions are in a sense boundary conditions, and the methods described here will be applicable.

Chapter 10 deals with the simulation of distributed parameter systems, describable by partial differential equations. Under these circumstances, the initial conditions will rarely coincide with the specified boundary conditions and, again, the techniques just described will be necessary.

Suggested Problems

7-1.
(a) Prepare and execute an analog program for handling the second example of this chapter when the alternative technique for parameter correction suggested in Section 7-11 is employed.
(b) Repeat (a), this time with a digital program.

7-2. A perfectly flexible cable of weight w lb/ft is stretched between two horizontal support points, both at the same level, and located l ft apart. The cable supports two concentrated loads of W_1 and W_2 lb located at distances x_1 and x_2, respectively, from the left-hand support. The right-hand end of the cable is tightened by a winch until the lowest point on the cable sags no more than d ft below the support points. Find the tension force that must be applied by the winch and the contour of the cable. Typical values for scaling:

$$l = 150 \text{ ft}$$
$$d = 0.5 \text{ ft}$$
$$w = 0.1 \text{ lb/ft}$$
$$W_1 = W_2 = 5 \text{ lb}$$
$$x_1 = 30 \text{ ft}$$
$$x_2 = 90 \text{ ft}$$

7-3. Figure P7-3 illustrates the situation where 50 liters/min of liquid is to be poured into the first of three differently shaped tanks connected in cascade. Each tank has a bottom outlet furnished with a valve whose flow resistance, R, is to be established. Since the valves are essentially sharp-edged orifices, the relationship between the head (height of liquid in the tank involved) and flow from that tank will be

$$\text{head:} \quad h = RQ^2 \qquad \text{cm}$$

with Q in liters/min.

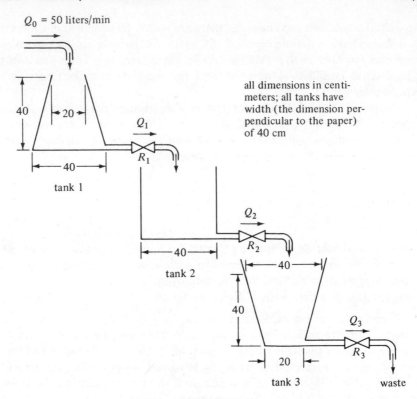

Q_0 = 50 liters/min

all dimensions in centimeters; all tanks have width (the dimension perpendicular to the paper) of 40 cm

tank 1

tank 2

tank 3   waste

FIGURE P7-3

The required valve resistances R_1, R_2, and R_3 are to be established to meet the requirement that with the tanks initially empty the liquid level in all three will be exactly 40 cm in T minutes. Establish both analog and digital programs for finding the necessary values of R. (There will be a minimum value of T below which this requirement can never be satisfied; find this value as well.) Note that the R's must remain constant for $0 < t < T$; this rule prevents the application of an obvious control strategy.

References

1. Zdenek Kopal, *Numerical Analysis* (New York: John Wiley & Sons, Inc., 1961), Chap. 5.

2. W. E. Grove, *Brief Numerical Methods* (Englewood Cliffs, N.J.: Prentice-Hall, Inc., 1966), Chap. 8.

Appendix 7A:
Fortran IV Program
That Produced Results
of Figure 7-9

```
C      BEAM BENDING SIMULATION 1/14/69 RJK
       INTEGER TYPE,COMPS,MAXTLS,STATE,TRIALS,STATUS,
      1SEARCH
       REAL M,MTOL,INTIN,INTOUT
       LOGICAL FINISH,PERT,LSTPAS,NEWX,NEWDX,ACT,
      1ENGAGE,MORE
       DIMENSION TYPE(10),FP(10),YP(10),DYDXP(10),
      1DBIN(18),BIN(18),XP(10),JLOC(10),KLOC(10),
      2BSPEC(18),BTOL(18),A(18,18),ACT(10),SIG(10),
      3TOLC(10),INTIN(10),INTOUT(10),BCOND(18),XLAST
      4(10),YLAST(10),ENGAGE(10)
       EQUIVALENCE(INTOUT(1),S),(INTIN(2),SHEAR),
      1(INTOUT(2),M),(INTOUT(3),DYDX),(INTIN(4),
      2SLOPE),(INTOUT(4),Y)
       READ 100,D,N,DXSPEC,DXPT,TOLX,TOLY,TOLF,TOLM,
      1RANGEY,RANGEF,RANGEM
  100  FORMAT(F10.3,I10,3F10.3,/F10.5,F10.3,F10.1,
      1F10.3,2F10.0)
```

```
201     READ 101,MORE,(TYPE(I),I=1,N)
101     FORMAT(L2,I3,9I5)
        DO 4 I=1,N
        L=TYPE(I)
        GO TO (1,2,2,2,3),L
1       READ 103,XP(I),FP(I)
103     FORMAT(F10.3,2F10.5)
        GO TO 4
2       READ 103,XP(I),YP(I)
        ENGAGE(I)=.TRUE.
        GO TO 4
3       READ 103,XP(I),YP(I),DYDXP(I)
4       CONTINUE
        MAXTLS=20
        STATE=4
        COMPS=N-1
        DO 5 I=1,COMPS
5       TOLC(I)=TOLX
        TRIALS=0
        FINISH=.FALSE.
        PERT=.FALSE.
        PRINT 108
108     FORMAT(1H1,17X,1HX,8X,1HW,7X,2HEI,11X,1HY,6X,
       15HDY/DX,8X,1HM,9X,1HS)
C       RETURN FOR NEW TRIAL RUN
6       L=TYPE(1)
        GO TO (9,7,7,12,15),L
7       IF(.NOT.ENGAGE(1))GO TO 8
        IF(PERT.OR.(TRIALS.EQ.0)GO TO 12
        IF((TYPE(1).EQ.3).AND.(BIN(1).GE.0))GO TO 12
        IF((TYPE(1).EQ.2).AND.(BIN(1).LE.0))GO TO 12
C       FIRST POINT SUPPORT JUST FOUND DISENGAGED
        ENGAGE(1)=.FALSE.
        TRIALS=0
        FP(1)=0.
        BIN(1)=YP(1)
        GO TO 10
8       IF(PERT.OR.(TRIALS.EQ.0))GO TO 9
        IF((TYPE(1).EQ.3).AND.(Y.GE.YP(1)))GO TO 9
        IF((TYPE(1).EQ.2).AND.(Y.LE.YP(1)))GO TO 9
C       POINT SUPPORT JUST FOUND REENGAGED
        ENGAGE(1)=.TRUE.
        TRIALS=0
```

```
        GO TO 13
9       IF(TRIALS.NE.0)GO TO 11
        BIN(1)=0.
        DBIN(2)=.1*RANGEY/D
        BIN(2)=0.
10      DBIN(I)=.1*RANGEY
11      S=FP(1)
        M=0.
        Y=BIN(1)
        DYDX=BIN(2)
        IF(.NOT.FINISH)GO TO 17
        IF(TYPE(1).EQ.1)PRINT 105,FP(1)
105     FORMAT(10X,20HFORCE APPL. POINT OF,F10.1,5H
       1LBS.)
        IF(TYPE(1).NE.1)PRINT 109,YP(1)
109     FORMAT(10X,34HDISENGAGED POINT SUPPORT OF
       1HEIGHT,F8.4)
        GO TO 17
12      IF(TRIALS.NE.0)GO TO 14
13      BIN(1)=0.
        DBIN(1)=.1*RANGEF
        BIN(2)=0.
        DBIN(2)=.1*RANGEY/D
14      S=BIN(1)
        M=0.
        Y=YP(1)
        DYDX=BIN(2)
        IF(FINISH)PRINT 106,YP(1),BIN(1)
106     FORMAT(10X,23HPOINT SUPPORT OF HEIGHT,F10.5,11H
       1WITH FORCE,F10.1)
        GO TO 17
15      IF(TRIALS.NE.0)GO TO 16
        BIN(1)=0.
        BIN(2)=0.
        DBIN(1)=.1*RANGEF
        DBIN(2)=.1*RANGEM
16      S=BIN(1)
        M=BIN(2)
        Y=YP(1)
        DYDX=DYDXP(1)
        IF(FINISH)PRINT 107,YP(1),DYDXP(1),BIN(2),
       1BIN(1)
107     FORMAT(10X,28HCANTILEVER SUPPORT OF HEIGHT,
```

```
         1F10.5,10H AND SLOPE,F10.5,/10X,16HPRODUCING
         2MOMENT,F10.0,10H AND FORCE,F10.1)
   17    K=0
         J=2
         LSTPAS=.TRUE.
         NEWX=.TRUE.
         STATUS=1
         X=0.
         XPT=-.5*DXSPEC
C        ITERATIVE RETURN
   18    IF(.NOT.NEWX)GO TO 19
         EI=EIFUNC(X)
         REI=1./EI
         W=WFUNC(X)
   19    IF(.NOT.LSTPAS)GO TO 37
         DO 20 I=1,COMPS
   20    SIG(I)=X-XP(I+1)
         I=0
         CALL COMPAR(ACT,SIG,DX,TOLC,MAXTLS,STATUS,
         1SEARCH,COMPS,X)
         CALL SETDT(STATUS,DXSPEC,DX,NEWDX,X)
         IF(STATUS-4)35,21,37
C        IF CONTINUES ON TO 21,NEW SPECIAL POINT ON BEAM
         1HAS BEEN REACHED
   21    I=SEARCH+1
         IF(FINISH)PRINT 104,X,W,EI,Y,DYDX,M,S
  104    FORMAT(10X,F10.3,F10.2,E11.3,2F10.5,F10.0,
         1F10.1)
         L=TYPE(I)
         GO TO (24,22,22,27,27),L
   22    IF(.NOT.ENGAGE(I))GO TO 23
         IF(PERT.OR.(TRIALS.EQ.0))GO TO 27
         IF((TYPE(I).EQ.2).AND.(BIN(J+1).LE.0))GO TO 27
         IF((TYPE(I).EQ.3).AND.(BIN(J+1).GE.0))GO TO 27
C        THIS POINT SUPPORT JUST FOUND TO BE DISENGAGED
         ENGAGE(I)=.FALSE.
         TRIALS=0
         FP(I)=0.
         GO TO 25
   23    IF(PERT.OR.(TRIALS.EQ.0))GO TO 24
         IF((TYPE(I).EQ.3).AND.(Y.GE.YP(I)))GO TO 24
         IF((TYPE(I).EQ.2).AND.(Y.LE.YP(I)))GO TO 24
C        THIS POINT SUPPORT JUST FOUND REENGAGED
```

```
         ENGAGE(I)=.TRUE.
         TRIALS=0
         BIN(J+1)=0.
         GO TO 27
   24    S=S+FP(I)
   25    IF(I.NE.N)GO TO 30
         K=K+1
         BCOND(K)=S
         IF(TRIALS.NE.0)GO TO 26
         BTOL(K)=TOLF
         BSPEC(K)=0.
   26    K=K+1
         BCOND(K)=M
         IF(TRIALS.NE.0)GO TO 30
         BTOL(K)=TOLM
         BSPEC(K)=0.
         GO TO 30
   27    J=J+1
         K=K+1
         BCOND(K)=Y
         IF(TRIALS.NE.0)GO TO 28
         BTOL(K)=TOLY
         BSPEC(K)=YP(I)
         DBIN(J)=.1*RANGEF
         BIN(J)=0.
   28    S=S+BIN(J)
         IF(TYPE(I).LT.5)GO TO 291
         J=J+1
         K=K+1
         BCOND(K)=DYDX
         IF(TRIALS.NE.0)GO TO 29
         BTOL(K)=TOLY/D
         BSPEC(K)=DYDXP(I)
         DBIN(J)=.1*RANGEM
         BIN(J)=0.
   29    M=M+BIN(J)
  291    IF(I.NE.N)GO TO 30
         K=K+1
         BCOND(K)=S
         K=K+1
         BCOND(K)=M
         IF(TRIALS.NE.0)GO TO 30
         BTOL(K)=TOLF
```

```
        BTOL(K+1)=TOLM
        BSPEC(K)=0.
        BSPEC(K+1)=0.
30      IF(.NOT.FINISH)GO TO 361
        L=TYPE(I)
        GO TO (31,32,32,33,34),L
31      PRINT 105,FP(I)
        GO TO 36
32      IF(ENGAGE(I))GO TO 33
        PRINT 109,YP(I)
        GO TO 36
33      PRINT 102,YP(I),BIN(J)
        GO TO 36
34      PRINT 107,YP(I),DYDXP(I),BIN(J-1),BIN(J)
        GO TO 36
35      IF((.NOT.FINISH).OR.(X.LT.XPT))GO TO 37
        XPT=XPT+DXPT
36      PRINT 104,X,W,EI,Y,DYDX,M,S
        IF(FINISH.AND.(I.EQ.N))GO TO 38
361     IF(I.NE.N)GO TO 37
        CALL SIMEQ(J,BIN,BSPEC,BTOL,BCOND,FINISH,A,
       1TRIALS,MAXTLS,DBIN,PERT)
        GO TO 6
37      SHEAR=S
        INTIN(1)=W
        INTIN(3)=M*REI
        SLOPE=DYDX
        CALL INT(STATE,DX,X,NEWDX,LSTPAS,NEWX,XLAST,
       1YLAST,INTIN,INTOUT)
        GO TO 18
38      IF(MORE)GO TO 201
        STOP
        END
```

Optimization of Simulated Systems   8

8-1 Cost Functions and Merit Functions

A system is said to be optimized with respect to its parameters when all its adjustable parameters are adjusted so that a cost function is minimized or a merit function is made a maximum. To clarify this further, cost functions and merit functions must be explained. This is done best by example.

Suppose, in the last example of Chapter 7, illustrated by Figure 7-11, that it was desirable to move the mass M to its desired displacement in the *minimum* possible time (i.e., τ_r, rather than being made to attain some specified value, is to attain a minimum possible value). [It will be assumed, for the purpose of this discussion that $r(t)$ and hence $\rho(\tau)$ are step functions (i.e., ρ is constant and $\dot{\rho}$ is zero for all positive τ).] If this is the only requirement imposed on the system, then the meeting of this requirement will result in what is called *optimum performance* and the *cost function*, C, will be simply

$$C = \tau_r(\alpha, \phi_m) \tag{8-1}$$

This function is described as a function of the parameters α and ϕ_m on the basis of the assumption that these are the only parameters to be adjusted. (Let it be assumed that the inactive zone Δ has been specified and is not considered adjustable.)

The example up to this point is not completely realistic. No finite optimum values of α and ϕ_m will exist for this particular problem as it will be found that C can always be made smaller by increasing ϕ_m and then re-adjusting α. Obviously, the cost function as so defined is inadequate. Not all factors have been taken into consideration. In a practical situation there must be some limit imposed on ϕ_m. This could be handled in either of two ways.

The first method for making C, as defined in relation (8-1), a realistic cost function is to apply a *constraint* to ϕ_m, as by adding the condition

$$\phi_m \leq \phi_L \tag{8-2}$$

where ϕ_L is some specified limit. With such a constraint optimum values of ϕ_m and α can be found. The results of an optimization study will show that

$$\phi_{m_{opt}} = \phi_L \tag{8-3}$$

The optimum α may then be established.

The second method is based on recognizing that the value of ϕ_m given by (8-3) should be employed so that maximum use is being made of the corrective action available in this system. Then the cost function would have been considered from the start as a function of only one parameter, α. That is,

$$C = \tau_r(\alpha) \tag{8-4}$$

Either viewpoint will lead, of course, to the same result.

This example is an oversimplified one and the optimum conditions could readily have been established by pencil-and-paper analysis. The reason for developing computer methods of optimization is, of course, to be able to optimize the more complicated systems usually encountered in practice that are not susceptible to such pencil-and-paper techniques. Nevertheless, it is advantageous to pursue this oversimplified example still further simply because the expected results are known and can be used to check any computer method of optimization that might be proposed.

What the computer optimization procedure will actually accomplish will be to survey the relationship between cost function and the remaining adjustable parameter α. It will see a relationship that, when plotted, appears roughly as in Figure 8-1. The optimum value of α is obviously that which makes C a mathematical minimum; i.e., $C_{opt} = C(\alpha_{opt}) = C_{min}$. Optimization in this case involves the finding of *extrema*.

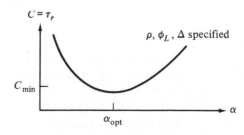

FIGURE 8-1

The above example as discussed here illustrates a cost function. It could have been described as well as the problem of establishing the conditions for making a merit function a maximum. The merit function would have been $M = 1/\tau_r$. As another example, in a chemical-processing problem the merit function might have been the yield of the desired product.

8-2 Problem of Finding Extrema

The discussion will be confined to those cases where there is only one adjustable parameter, or where the problem has been reduced to that of adjustment of only one parameter, as in the case illustrated by Figure 8-1. This is the simplest type of optimization problem but may, even so, become complicated when the relationship between cost function and the parameter show more than one mathematical minimum, as in Figure 8-2. α_1 obviously represents the optimum α. It can easily be seen that unless precautions are taken a computer program searching for α_{opt} might erroneously decide on α_2 instead.

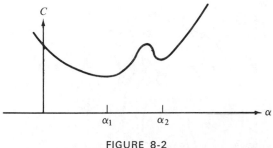

FIGURE 8-2

Another problem that might result is that an imposed constraint might prevent a true mathematical minimum from being attained. Suppose, in the example of Figure 8-1, that some constraint is imposed so that $\alpha \leq \alpha_L$,

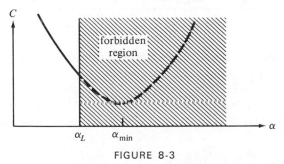

FIGURE 8-3

where $\alpha_L < \alpha_{min}$. This situation is shown in Figure 8-3. Obviously, the optimum value of α will then be α_L.

8-3 Optimization with More than One Adjustable Parameter

Very often the cost function will remain a function of more than one adjustable parameter and the problem cannot be described as a simple relationship that plots as in Figure 8-1. Suppose, for example, that the next degree of complication was involved, where there were two parameters to be adjusted, say $\alpha(1)$ and $\alpha(2)$. The cost-function relationship might then be described mathematically as

$$C = C[\alpha(1), \alpha(2)] \tag{8-5}$$

A three-dimensional plot would now be required to show this relationship in a manner similar to that of Figure 8-1. It can be pictured more readily, on paper, by plotting *contours* of constant C, as in a contour map. In a typical problem such a map might appear as in Figure 8-4. Although C is assumed

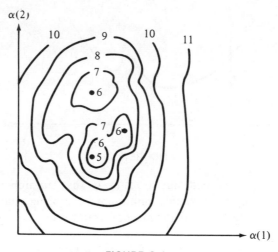

FIGURE 8-4

to be a continuous function of $\alpha(1)$ and $\alpha(2)$, contours are shown for integer values of C only. The optimum values of $\alpha(1)$ and $\alpha(2)$ are those where $C = 5$; this is at one of the minimum points on the contour. However, there are at least two other mathematical minima, both resulting in a C of 6, and possibly other less apparent minima not discernible because of the coarseness of the plot. This indicates that some definition of a practical minimum is necessary. (For example, in a geographical-contour problem, is every pothole considered a minimum point?) In any event, it is important that any optimization procedure arrive at the lowest minimum—in this example, where $C = 5$.

The more general problem may involve still more adjustable parameters and it is no longer possible to discuss the problem graphically. The problem can still be considered in the mathematical sense and computer solutions may be feasible. A combination of n parameters, described as $\alpha(1), \alpha(2), \ldots, \alpha(n)$, may be considered as an n-state *vector* and C as a scalar function of that vector. Again, constraints may be applied to some of the α's, or to combinations of them, which will affect the methods of solution and the results that are obtained.

8-4 General Survey of Techniques for Finding Optimum Parameters

A host of literature has been written about optimization methods; not all of it is pertinent to the problems being discussed here. For example, many of the techniques proposed depend upon knowledge of the analytic form of C so that the partial derivatives of C with respect to the parameters may be expressed analytically instead of being determined, experimentally and approximately, by perturbation methods.

As an example, optimization techniques are often used as the basis of methods for finding the complex roots of polynomials, as in the determination of root loci for control systems. This problem does not relate directly to simulation but would be of interest, nevertheless, to those readers interested in feedback-control theory. The problem here is to find the roots of an equation of the form

$$a_n s^n + a_{n-1} s^{n-1} + \ldots + a_1 s + a_0 = 0$$

In general, the values of s that will satisfy this equation (i.e., the roots) will be complex. They are described best in terms of their magnitude, $|s|$, and argument, $\underline{/s}$. (This is preferable from a computation standpoint to a resolution into real and imaginary parts, α and $j\omega$.) These two quantities are the parameters to be varied in a trial-and-error search for the roots. In general, for trial values of $|s|$ and $\underline{/s}$, a nonzero result will be obtained when the polynomial terms are added; i.e.,

$$a_n s^n + a_{n-1} s^{n-1} + \ldots + a_1 s + a_0 = \epsilon$$

where ϵ is the error which, for the correct root, should be zero. ϵ also will in general be complex and can be expressed in terms of its real and imaginary parts:

$$\epsilon = u + jv$$

Any positive definite function of u and v will be an appropriate cost function for the purpose of finding the roots. One possible cost function [1] is

$$C = u^2 + v^2$$

Another possibility, claimed to result in a more rapid convergence of solution [2], is

$$C = |u| + |v|$$

In any event, once an appropriate cost function has been defined, the problem becomes one of optimization. In the process of search for the parameters $|s|$ and $\underline{/s}$ that result in minimum C (minimum C is, of course, zero), the roots will be found.

Because the relationship between C and the parameters can be expressed in analytic form, this problem can make use of optimization techniques that depend upon this knowledge; these techniques are, however, not of value in the optimization of most simulated systems where no such analytic form is possible. In the simulation problems of the type of concern here, the relationship between C and the parameters can be established only by perturbation tests performed on a simulation model. The optimization techniques to be discussed here will assume that that is the case. These techniques could also be used to find the roots of polynomials according to the procedure discussed above but would result in longer execution times than when those techniques are employed that rely on the analytic knowledge of the relationships involved.

Parameter optimization techniques may be divided into three general categories:

1. The method of steepest descent (or steepest ascent when dealing with a merit rather than cost function).
2. Relaxation methods.
3. Random-scan methods.

The method of steepest descent is based upon making the path of the parameter corrections, when considered in the parameter space, *orthogonal* to the constant C contours and, naturally, in the direction of decreasing C. When finite trial adjustments of the α's are made, as in digital optimization, these adjustments are made in a direction opposite to that of the vector representing the gradient of $C([\alpha])$. That is, proceeding from trial starting values of the α's, changes are made simultaneously in all the α's so that

$$\Delta[\alpha] = \begin{bmatrix} \Delta\alpha(1) \\ \Delta\alpha(2) \\ . \\ . \\ . \\ \Delta\alpha(n) \end{bmatrix} = -k \begin{bmatrix} \dfrac{\partial C}{\partial\alpha(1)} \\ \dfrac{\partial C}{\partial\alpha(2)} \\ . \\ . \\ . \\ \dfrac{\partial C}{\partial\alpha(n)} \end{bmatrix} \tag{8-6}$$

The more "daring" the steps, the greater the value of k. As convergence is being reached, k should be decreased to avoid overshooting the correct solution and then oscillating about it.

The procedure is the same for analog simulation, except that a continuous rather than stepwise adjustment of the parameters might then be feasible. The above relation still applies if the operator d/dt is substituted for Δ. Actual execution of these methods will be explained in more detail in the section to follow.

Relaxation methods are based on finding the minimum C with respect to one parameter with all others kept constant. Then minimization is repeated with the next parameter varied, etc. The cycle is repeated until C is recognized as a minimum within the specified region of tolerance. In other words, the following sequence of operations is employed:

$$\Delta\alpha(1) = -k\frac{\partial C}{\partial\alpha(1)}$$

$$\Delta\alpha(2) = -k\frac{\partial C}{\partial\alpha(2)}$$

$$\vdots \tag{8-7}$$

$$\Delta\alpha(n) = -k\frac{\partial C}{\partial\alpha(n)}$$

$$\Delta\alpha(1) = -k\frac{\partial C}{\partial\alpha(1)}$$

etc.

There are a number of random-scan techniques. In their crudest form they consist of assigning a series of random combinations of values to the α's until all of the n-dimensional $[\alpha]$ space within the range of interest has been reasonably filled. For each point (matched set) in the $[\alpha]$ space so established, the value of C is computed. Whenever the value of C is lower than any previously observed value, it is tentatively considered to represent the minimum.

This random-scan method, while seemingly crude, is surprisingly effective for problems where the cost function is computed easily with short execution time. It becomes inefficient when the C computation is complex, as it is in most simulation problems. However, it does possess the advantage of not being fooled by mathematical minima that do not represent the extreme minimum. Steepest-descent and relaxation methods are, on the other hand, easily fooled and will converge on a false minimum unless the correct initial trial values are specified. *Hence random-scan methods may be useful for providing a proper starting point for these other, more rapidly convergent, techniques.*

8-5   Optimization Technique with One Adjustable Parameter—Analog Means

When there is only one adjustable parameter α the situation may be described in terms of a plot of cost function versus α, as in Figures 8-1, 8-2, and 8-3. Then the steepest-descent methods simply amount to finding the algebraic sign of $\alpha C/\partial \alpha$ and varying α in the opposite sense. The relaxation method amounts to the same thing; i.e., there is no distinction between these two methods when only one adjustable parameter is involved.

With analog techniques being used to find the conditions for minimum C, this minimum is in theory being approached continuously and there would be no danger of missing the minimum by going beyond it, as might be the case when finite increments are employed. In practice this is not completely true. Normally, the cost function C is computed by a simulation program performed in high-speed-repetitive operation; its value is held from cycle to cycle of the repetitive process by track–hold means. As a consequence, finite increments of α actually do result; however, they may be made exceedingly fine by employing a high frequency of repetition and by making the analog optimization process occur reasonably slowly. Then no special precautions need be taken to slow down the rate at which α is varied as the minimum is approached. When it is sensed that the slope magnitude $|dC/d\alpha|$ is less than some specified tolerance value, a minimum point is considered to have been reached and the search is halted.

Figure 8-5 shows an analog program for accomplishing this. The actual process being optimized is simulated in a high-speed-repetitive mode and two cascaded ratchet circuits, actuated by the comparator marking the end of the trial run (actuated in turn by the timing integrator within the high-speed-repetitive program), store $C(n)$ and $C(n-1)$. Their difference, $\nabla C(n)$, is then obtained. When $\{[\nabla C(n) > 0] \cap [\dot{\alpha}(n) > 0]\} \cup \{[\nabla C(n) < 0] \cap [\dot{\alpha}(n) < 0]\}$ [i.e., when $\nabla C(n)$ and $\dot{\alpha}(n)$ possess the same algebraic sign], a positive slope of the C versus α relationship is indicated for that operating point and a negative $\dot{\alpha}$ is called for during the next, $(n + 1)$th, trial; other-

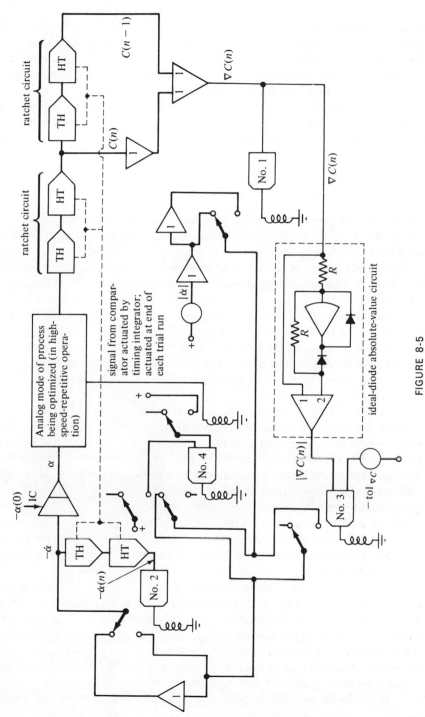

FIGURE 8-5

wise, a positive $\dot{\alpha}$ is called for. In Figure 8-5 this logic is handled by comparators 1 and 2; 1 determines the sign of $\nabla C(n)$ and 2 the sign of $\dot{\alpha}(n)$. A fixed magnitude for the rate of change of α is established by the associated potentiometer, and the combination of these two comparators establishes the proper algebraic sign for the next trial.

The search procedure should be terminated and the value of α then in effect should be accepted as the optimum when $|dC/d\alpha|$ is less than some specified tolerance value. $dC/d\alpha$ is related to the values of $\nabla C(n)$, t_h, and $\dot{\alpha}$ as follows:

$$\frac{dC}{d\alpha} = \frac{\nabla C(n)}{\dot{\alpha} t_h}$$

where t_h is the period of repetition of the high-speed-repetitive operation. Hence the tolerance range, within which the minimum may be assumed to have been found, may be expressed as some value of $\nabla C(n)$, or tol_{VC}. Comparator 3, therefore, is included to interrupt the input to the integrator producing α and essentially to place it in hold when this final condition has been reached.

Further complications are introduced by the fact that until the first trial run of the HRO circuit has been completed (while $n = 0$), comparator 3 would not be actuated [as $\nabla C(n) = \nabla C(0) = 0$] and the correction procedure would be interrupted at its very start. Hence, comparator 4 is also needed to bypass the interrupting action of comparator 3 during this first interval only.

Figure 8-5 represents a rather complicated arrangement employing a sizable number of comparators in consideration of those usually available with a purely analog computer. It is becoming obvious that, as the optimization problem grows in complexity, more sophisticated logic hardware will be necessary. An otherwise purely analog computer that possessed a reasonable number of logic-circuit elements, such as AND, OR, NOR, and NAND gates, would permit a much simpler configuration. With still increasing complication, such as an increase in the number of parameters to be optimized, actual digital-computer operations become desirable and the need for hybrid facilities becomes obvious if the speed advantages of analog computation (when establishing C for various values of α) are to be realized.

In any event, the arrangement shown in Figure 8-5 will converge on a mathematical minimum cost function. If the C versus α relationship appears as in Figure 8-1, this solution will constitute the optimum. If, on the other hand, the relationship has more than one minimum, as in Figure 8-2, whether the minimum found corresponds to the extreme minimum and hence to the optimum will depend upon the initial value of α (i.e., α_0) that is introduced at the integrator producing the signal α.

It would be possible to prepare a random-scan program that would be applied prior to the operations shown in Figure 8-5; this would require the generation of a sequence of random values of α, With a purely analog machine, such a sequence could be produced by techniques discussed in Chapter 9. Additional comparators and track–hold circuits would then be required to store the lowest value of C that resulted and the corresponding α. With a sufficient number of such random values of α employed, it could be assumed that the value of α finally being so stored would represent a starting value for the procedure of Figure 8-5, so the minimum reached would be the true optimum.

The above procedure is entirely feasible with a sufficiently extensive analog machine. However, it is becoming obvious that except for the simplest optimization problems hybrid facilities should be used if analog computation is to be employed during the trial runs.

8-6   Optimization Technique with One Adjustable Parameter—Digital Means

With digital simulation, or hybrid simulation where the computation of C as a function of α is performed by analog means but all other computations are performed digitally, a different strategy is preferred. The procedure for finding the minimum then is as follows:

1. An initial trial value of α first is specified; then the corresponding value of C is established. α is then increased by a specified increment $\Delta\alpha$ and the next value of C is computed.

2. If the second value of α results in a lower value of C than did the first, α continues to be increased by the increment $\Delta\alpha$. On the other hand, if the second C is greater, the direction of change of α should be reversed. Therefore, the next increment will be $-2\Delta\alpha$ and, for subsequent increments, $\Delta\alpha$ is changed to minus its original value. In any event, the desired progression is toward lower and lower values of C.

3. Eventually, if a minimum exists, C should at some time be observed to increase again as this progression of α is continued. As soon as this is observed to occur, a search is conducted for the minimum point. Let the interval at which this occurs be called the nth interval. Then $C(n) > C(n-1)$ and $C(n-1) < C(n-2)$. This situation is illustrated in Figure 8-6. (This diagram is based on $\Delta\alpha$ being positive; however, the procedure is valid when it is negative as well.)

   In Figure 8-6, $C(n) < C(n-2)$; this is not always the case. In any event, from these three point a quadratic algebraic relationship between C and α may be established and the value of α where

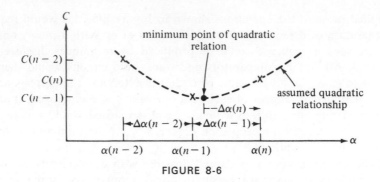

FIGURE 8-6

C would be a minimum, *if* such a relationship were valid, may be found. The algebra involved in establishing the increment necessary to arrive at this value of α is completely straightforward but somewhat tedious and will not be included here. It results in the following suggested value of the next, nth, increment:

$$\Delta\alpha(n) = \frac{1}{2} \frac{[\Delta\alpha(n-1)]^2[\Delta C(n-2)] + [\Delta\alpha(n-2)]^2[\Delta C(n-1)]}{[\Delta\alpha(n-1)][\Delta C(n-2)] - [\Delta\alpha(n-2)][\Delta C(n-1)]}$$
$$- \Delta\alpha(n-1) \tag{8-8}$$

4. α is increased by the increment proposed in the above relation (which will always be algebraically negative during the first try); that increment then is defined as $\Delta\alpha(n-1)$ and the preceding increment now becomes $\Delta\alpha(n-2)$. C is evaluated again with this new α. The previous increment in C, $\Delta C(n-1)$, is renamed $\Delta C(n-2)$, and the new increment now resulting, $\Delta C(n-1)$. Relation (8-8) is applied again for the increment in α that is to follow.

5. If the C versus α relationship were truly of a quadratic form, the increment of α obtained from relation (8-8) the second time it was applied would, theoretically, be zero and in practice (because of roundoff errors) would be very small. Hence the next time C is computed, $\Delta C(n-1)$ would be practically zero. The minimum is assumed to be found when $\Delta C(n-1)$ falls to within some specified tolerance range of C, tol_C.

   As in general the relationship will not be quadratic, relation (8-8) will usually have to be applied more than twice before this tolerance is met and the minimum is found.

6. In any practical situation there will be some constraints applied to the permissible range of α, designated as $\alpha_{\max}$ and $\alpha_{\min}$. If, while stepping along according to part 2 above, C is never observed to ascend before $\alpha_{\max}$ or $\alpha_{\min}$ is reached, the minimum point (not a true mathematical minimum in the sense of there being zero slope) is assumed to exist there.

The above procedure can be handled as a subprogram, shown in flow-diagram form in Figure 8-7. All the common arguments of this subprogram have already been mentioned except for the integer and logical variables that are used. FINISH indicates that the minimum has been found. MAXHOLD or MINHOLD indicates that the optimum lies at the α_{max} or α_{min} value and is not a true mathematical minimum. TRIALS is the count of the number of search trials made plus the two necessary at the beginning of the program to assure the correct initial direction of progress of α; TRIALS is initialized as 1 in the calling program. MAXTRIALS is the maximum number of search trials permitted, to be named in the main program; when this number of trials must be exceeded to find the optimum, EXCESS is made true; this informs the main program of this event so that a corrective operation, or else a termination of operation, may be called for.

The procedure shown in Figure 8-7 is self-explanatory for the most part. The computation of C with the suggested starting value of α before calling this subroutine for the first time normally would be the first trial. However, it is necessary, as the easiest way to prevent programming difficulties that could occur, to assure that this starting α will lie at least $2\Delta\alpha$ increments away from the α_{max} and α_{min} boundaries (and, naturally, between these boundaries). Therefore, during the first call with TRIALS = 1, a test is made to determine whether this is the case. If it is not, the value of α is reset to comply with this condition and TRIALS remains 1 so that the first initializing pass is repeated. In any event, once this requirement is met during either the initial or second pass the value of C is saved (as C_{last}), α is incremented the prescribed initial amount, and TRIALS is made equal to 2.

After TRIALS becomes 2, it is observed whether α has been progressing in the proper direction (so that C will decrease). If this is not the case, the sign of $\Delta\alpha$ is reversed; a double negative increment of α is made just this one time; the first observed value of C is treated as the second and the second as the first [for the purpose of application of relation (8-8)].

From TRIALS = 3 on, α is progressed at the same constant increment in the direction just established until C is observed to increase again. If before this happens α_{max} or α_{min} is reached, the value of C then resulting is considered to be the minimum; LAST is made true; either MAXHOLD or MINHOLD is also made true. The value of α is then made equal to either α_{max} or α_{min} and the operation returned to the calling program for one last computation of C. The next time this subroutine is called, since LAST is true, FINISH will be made true and the final return to the calling program is made.

Once C is observed to increase, SEARCH is made true. Relation (8-8) is applied repeatedly until the increment of C is within the tolerance range. Once it is, the value of α and C last established are considered to correspond

SUBROUTINE MINIMA (C, tol_C, α, $\Delta\alpha$, α_{max}, α_{min}, FINISH, MAXHOLD
MINHOLD, TRIALS, MAXTRIALS, EXCESS)

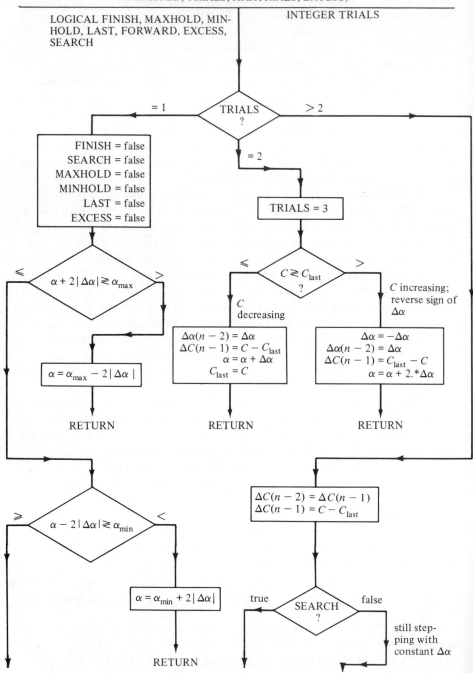

FIGURE 8-7

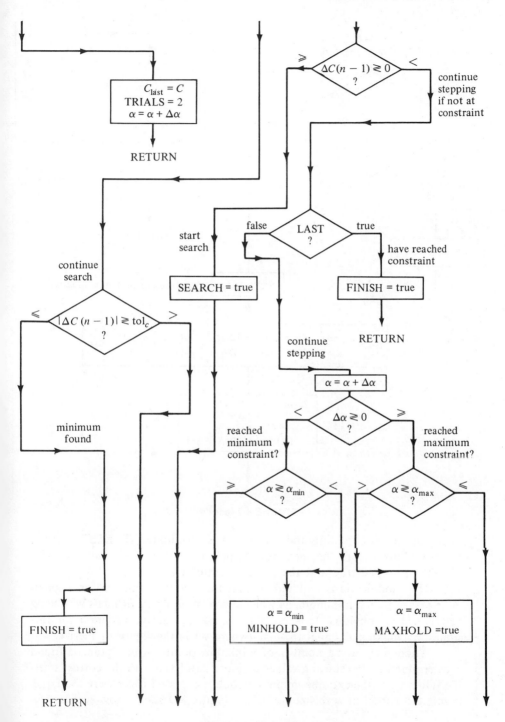

FIGURE 8-7 (cont'd)

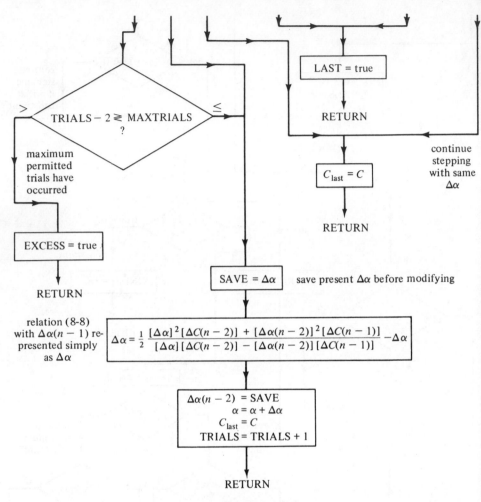

FIGURE 8-7 (cont'd)

to the optimum condition and the search is terminated (FINISH = true). If before this occurs the maximum stipulated number of trials is made, EXCESS is made true and the search terminated.

The modifications required so that the search would be for a maximum rather than a minimum, as when a maximum figure of merit was being determined, is obvious. It is possible to use the above program for this simply by making C equal to $-M$ (where M is the figure of merit).

When there are a number of minimum points, which point is found is determined by the starting values of α and $\Delta\alpha$. Even with the correct starting values of α, the extreme minimum could be missed if $\Delta\alpha$ were too large. Figure 8-8 shows how this could occur. Figure 8-9 shows how such a sub-

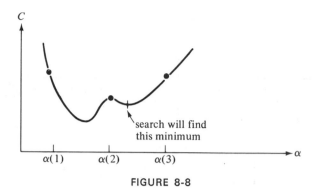

FIGURE 8-8

program could be employed in connection with a simulation program to find an optimum parameter α.

8-7 Use of Random-Search Technique to Find Optimum Parameter

Chapter 9 will discuss both analog and digital techniques for generating random variables. For the purpose of random search, usually a uniform probability density over the complete range of α from α_{min} to α_{max} is desired. This simply means that the probable frequency of occurrence of the variable in a given range, say $\Delta\alpha$, is independent of the magnitude of α. How such uniform probability-density variables might be generated is also discussed in the Chapter 9.

Figure 8-10 shows an analog arrangement for effecting optimization by such a means. The source of random values of α, or $\alpha(t)$, would be adjusted to cover the range from α_{min} to α_{max}. At the end of each trial the ratchet circuit holds a new value of α, or $\alpha(n)$. The resulting cost function $C(n)$ is sampled by a second ratchet circuit, similarly actuated. Comparator 5 compares each $C(n)$ with what has been established as C_{opt}; whenever $C(n)$ is of a smaller magnitude than the present C_{opt}, this comparator becomes actuated and, by means of the ratchet circuit that it controls, $C(n)$ becomes the new C_{opt}. At the same time, by another ratchet circuit controlled by the same comparator, $\alpha(n)$ becomes the new α_{opt}. Comparator 4 serves a function similar to that of Figure 8-5; it causes $\alpha(1)$ and $C(1)$ to be tentatively accepted as the optimum values when the search procedure first starts.

With a sufficient number of such trials, a reasonably close optimum might be found with the advantage, mentioned previously, that no confusion is caused by nonextreme minima. It is also possible to combine the arrangements of Figures 8-5 and 8-10 so that the random search just described will be conducted first and, when a sixth comparator indicates that sufficient time has elapsed (this comparator being actuated by a relatively slow timing inte-

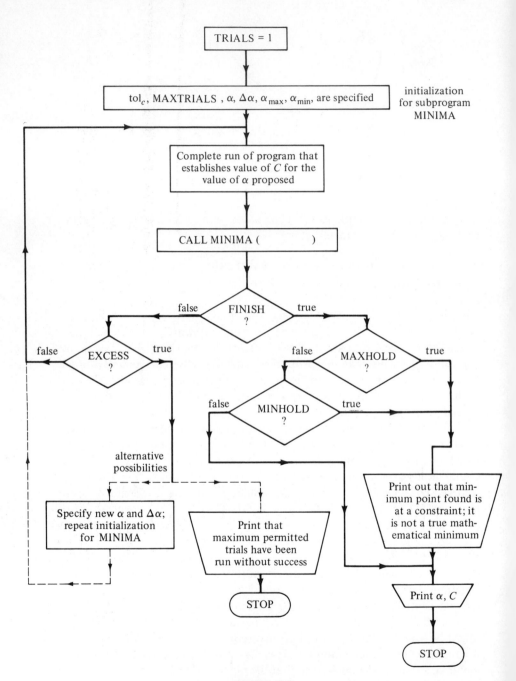

FIGURE 8-9

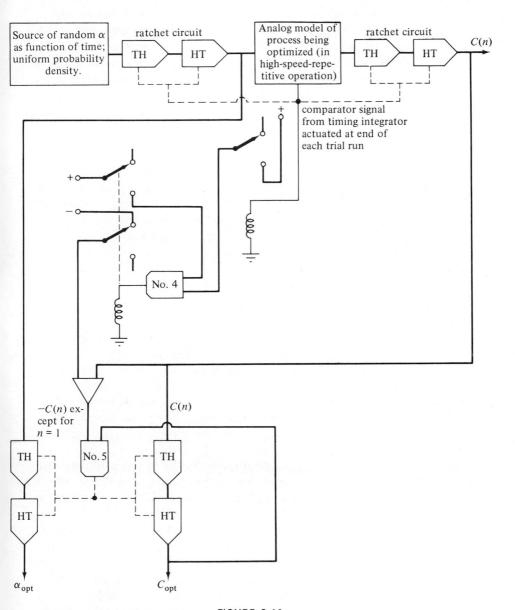

FIGURE 8-10

grator), the configuration is switched to that of Figure 8-5. The value of α_{opt} being held at the end of the random-search portion of the program would be used as the initial α_0 value applied as the initial condition to the integrator that develops the parameter α.

The procedure that would be used for effecting a random search by digital means is obvious. Either a user-provided or library subroutine would be employed to provide a new random number every time it was called. As mentioned earlier, this subroutine should be of the type that provides numbers with a uniform probability density. For example, this random source[1] might provide numbers in decimal form, from zero to 1. Suppose that the number provided between zero and 1 is a. The parameter α could then be established as

$$\alpha = \alpha_{min} + a(\alpha_{max} - \alpha_{min})$$

The problem then becomes simply that of saving the number pair, (α, C), and calling them α_{opt} and C_{opt} whenever the results of a given trial run provide a lower value of C than has been achieved previously. Again this method could be used as a starting technique for a limited number of trials, after which the program of Figure 8-7 might be employed.

8-8   Method of Steepest Descent with More Than One Adjustable Parameter

The general problem of optimization with more than one adjustable parameter has been discussed in Section 8-3 and illustrated in Figure 8-4 (for the special case of there being two adjustable parameters). One method mentioned, the method of steepest descent, was described by relation (8-6). Returning again to that relation, it is seen that the partial derivatives of the cost function with respect to each of the adjustable parameters must be established in order to reestablish, in turn, the direction of the next trial $[\Delta\alpha]$ vector. With the type of simulation problems we are concerned with here, this cannot be done analytically, only by means of test perturbations.

It is possible to employ an analog computer that is equipped with a sufficient number of comparators and track–hold circuits to effect such a type of operation. However, this would be somewhat foolish unless there were no other hardware available; everything involved in such an operation is essentially of a digital nature except for, possibly, the actual trial run of the analog model itself. Hence the type of program that might be used will be discussed here only in its digital version, it naturally being understood that if hybrid analog–digital facilities should be available, the trial runs might be conducted more effectively (and rapidly) by analog means. The method is based on trial iterations of $|\Delta\alpha|$, where $|\Delta\alpha|$ is the *magnitude* of the $[\Delta\alpha]$ vector. When there are n parameters to be adjusted [i.e., $\alpha(1)$

---

[1]For example, the IBM Scientific Subroutine Package includes a subroutine, RANDU, that will furnish such numbers.

to $\alpha(n)$], $|\Delta\alpha|$ would be given by the relation

$$|\Delta\alpha| = \sqrt{[\Delta\alpha(1)]^2 + [\Delta\alpha(2)]^2 + \cdots +]\Delta\alpha(n)]^2}$$
$$= \sqrt{\sum_{i=1}^{n} [\Delta\alpha(i)]^2} \tag{8-9}$$

Two considerations are involved here:

1. The relative values of each trial parameter change, $\Delta\alpha(i)$, must satisfy relation (8-6) so that progress will be exactly opposite to the direction of the gradient vector; that is, each $\Delta\alpha$ must have a relative magnitude that is proportional to the partial derivative relating it to the cost function $\partial C/\partial\alpha(i)$.
2. The magnitude of the trial change in the parameters $|\Delta\alpha|$ should be adjusted so as to converge upon the minimum value of the cost function C. The procedure used in Section 8-6, employing the subprogram shown in Figure 8-7 and called here SUBROUTINE MINIMA, is still useful for this purpose.

The first of these considerations can be seen most readily in an example where the number of parameters to be varied, n, is only two. The effect of $\alpha(1)$ and $\alpha(2)$ on the cost function may then be pictured by means of contour maps, as was illustrated in Figure 8-4. Trial increments of $|\Delta\alpha|$ will appear simply as two-dimensional vectors on the $\alpha(2)$ versus $\alpha(1)$ plane. The effect of complying with relation (8-6) is the maintenance of these vectors in a direction perpendicular to the contours and always in the direction of decreasing C. This procedure is analogous to that of a person lost in a fog who is attempting to find his way to the point of lowest elevation. As he can sense only the gradient (slope and direction of slope) of the ground in his immediate vicinity, his natural course is to always proceed in the direction of steepest descent. This procedure may not take him to the point of the extreme minimum of elevation, or optimum point, but it will take him to some minimum.

This example may also be extended to cover the second consideration mentioned above. As the rate of change of the slope of the ground becomes less and less, the person involved would anticipate that he is reaching the minimum and would take progressively shorter steps, finally coming to halt when the minimum has been reached (and possibly deciding to engage in some sort of random search if he discovers that the minimum found is not his destination). The equivalent of this would be the procedure of minimization discussed in Section 8-6.

One difficulty that may be encountered when optimizing with respect to more than one adjustable parameter is caused by the possibility that the different parameters involved may have vastly different orders of magnitude.

Suppose, for example, that $\alpha(1)$ was a voltage of range from zero to 100 V, and $\alpha(2)$ a current of range from zero to 10^{-4} A. The magnitude of the vector change $|\Delta\alpha|$ would then be

$$\sqrt{[\Delta\alpha(1)]^2 + [\Delta\alpha(2)]^2}$$

but $\alpha(2)$ would have a negligible effect on the computation of $|\Delta\alpha|$ in spite of the possibility that, from a relative standpoint, $\alpha(2)$ might be the most significant factor in determining the cost function. If the *roundoff error* associated with digital computers is considered, the computation difficulties that could arise from such vastly different orders of magnitude of the α's can be appreciated. (Here a scaling problem has arisen with digital computers, where, up to now, the impression may have been created that such problems arise only with analog computation.)

A difficulty such as that mentioned can be handled by the obvious procedure of *normalization*. One convenient normalization technique consists of representing each α by a corresponding dimensionless β defined as

$$\beta(i) = \frac{\alpha(i) - \alpha_{\min}(i)}{\alpha_{\max}(i) - \alpha_{\min}(i)} \tag{8-10}$$

where $\alpha_{\max}(i)$ and $\alpha_{\min}(i)$ are either constraints imposed on $\alpha(i)$ or else the minimum and maximum values of the anticipated range. $\beta(i)$ would then vary in magnitude from zero to 1 as α varied from $\alpha_{\min}$ to $\alpha_{\max}$. The minimization procedure would be carried out with respect to the normalized parameter value β. Steepest descent (i.e., the minimum gradient) would follow the relationship

$$[\Delta\beta] = \begin{bmatrix} \Delta\beta(1) \\ \Delta\beta(2) \\ . \\ . \\ . \\ \Delta\beta(n) \end{bmatrix} = -k \begin{bmatrix} \dfrac{\partial C}{\partial\beta(1)} \\ \dfrac{\partial C}{\partial\beta(2)} \\ . \\ . \\ . \\ \dfrac{\partial C}{\partial\beta(n)} \end{bmatrix} \tag{8-11}$$

where k is a constant selected so that the magnitude of $[\Delta\beta]$, or $|\Delta\beta|$ will be of the size desired. This constant will be

$$k = \frac{|\Delta\beta|}{\sqrt{\sum\limits_{i=1}^{n} [\partial C/\partial\beta(i)]^2}} \tag{8-12}$$

$|\Delta\beta|$, in turn, may be established by the minimum-seeking program of the type discussed in Section 8-6 and employing the interpolating relationship of relation (8-8).

This minimization procedure may also be complicated by the consideration of the constraints $\alpha_{max}(i)$ and $\alpha_{min}(i)$ imposed on some of the adjustable parameters. In terms of the β's these constraints may be expressed simply as

$$0 < \beta(i) < 1 \tag{8-13}$$

as far as the normalized parameters are concerned. Therefore, when establishing each trial increment of β, it will be necessary to observe whether the above limits are being violated. Suppose that when a given increment $|\Delta\beta|$ is applied, the limits constraining the jth parameter do turn out to be violated. It will then be necessary to reduce the magnitude of $|\Delta\beta|$ so that the boundary at $\beta(j) = 0$ or at $\beta(j) = 1$ is just reached. During future increments $|\Delta\beta|$, the particular value of $\beta(j)$ that would be called for by relation (8-11) is observed. If the sign of this is such as to penetrate the boundary [i.e., $\Delta\beta(j) > 0$ when $\beta(j) = 1$, or $\Delta\beta(j) < 0$ when $\beta(j) = 0$], then the increment $\Delta\beta(j)$ is not applied, but the other, unconstrained parameters are incremented in such a way that the proposed magnitude of $|\Delta\beta|$ is maintained. Of course, if all parameters become so constrained, the minimum (not the true mathematical minimum since the gradient is not zero) will be considered to have been reached. If, however, during any subsequent iterations it develops that the change in $\beta(j)$ recommended by relation (8-11) should tend to move its value away from the boundary into the unconstrained region, the constraint again is removed and $\beta(j)$ is again progressively adjusted during the optimizing process.

The procedure discussed above is illustrated by Figure 8-11 for the example of two adjustable parameters, $\alpha(1)$ and $\alpha(2)$, which are represented here by their normalized values, $\beta(1)$ and $\beta(2)$. The proposed starting values

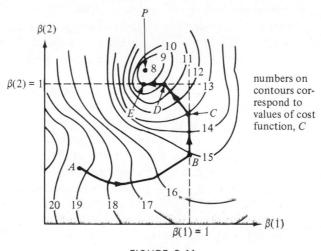

FIGURE 8-11

of $\alpha(1)$ and $\alpha(2)$ are converted to their corresponding normalized values, $\beta(1)$ and $\beta(2)$. In Figure 8-11 this corresponds to starting point A The steepest-descent approach involves progressing in a direction normal to the contours and in a sense to decrease C, until finally, at point B, the maximum value of $\beta(1)$, or unity, is encountered. $\beta(1)$ is then held at unity; only $\beta(2)$ is changed and the progress is in the direction shown until point C, where it is observed that again progressing in the steepest-gradient direction would cause the operating point to leave the $\beta(1) = 1$ boundary. The $\beta(1)$ constraint is no longer applied and progress again continues perpendicular to the contours until, at D, the constraint at $\beta(2) = 1$ is reached. $\beta(2)$ is then held constant and only $\beta(1)$ is varied until the optimum point E is reached. E represents the true optimum in consideration of the $\alpha(2)_{\max}$ constraint. Had it not been imposed, point P would, of course, have represented the optimum conditions.

From Figure 8-11 it is obvious that the shortest route was not taken. However, as with the analogy of the man lost in a fog who is attempting to find the point of lowest elevation, the procedure followed here is one of the most effective ones when the cost function can be found only by trial-and-error simulation runs.

A parameter constraint should not cause the type of limiting described here unless it represents a true physical constraint. Some parameters will not be constrained at all, in a practical sense. True, their physical manifestation must have some reasonable maximum and minimum values, but these may be far removed from the range of values within which these parameters would normally be adjusted. In such instances $\alpha_{\max}$ and $\alpha_{\min}$ are specified only to provide a basis for normalization; they should be established at sufficiently high and sufficiently low values so that these constraints are never reached during the optimizing search procedure.

The program for employing the method of steepest descent is complicated mostly by the constraints placed on the α's; without these it would be fairly simple. It will be explained first as though there were no constraints to be considered.

The tolerance imposed to establish when the minimum C has been reached, the starting value of each α, the maximum and minimum values of each α, the initialization of the count of trials, and the number of adjustable parameters involved are all in common with the main program and are established by it. Also specified there are the initial values of the first increments, the $\Delta\alpha(i)$'s, expressed in normalized form as $\Delta\beta_{\text{start}}$ and applicable to all of the $\Delta\beta(i)$'s during the first trial increment. A typical starting value for $\Delta\beta_{\text{start}}$ might be 0.05, The corresponding vector length for this first increment would be $|\Delta\beta| = \Delta\beta_{\text{start}}\sqrt{\text{NPARAM}}$, where NPARAM is the number of adjustable parameters involved.

A very considerable amount of research has been done on the optimum method for determining step size and for determining when the optimum has been found when the steepest-descent technique is employed. From this no conclusions can be drawn as to which are the best methods. Ones that prove superior for one type of C versus $[\alpha]$ relationship may fail completely with other types. One method is to keep the step size (as measured by the length of the vector, $|\Delta\beta|$) constant until C again is observed to increase. Whenever this occurs, $|\Delta\beta|$ is multiplied by a reduction factor k_r. As a result, there will be progressively smaller and smaller increments taken as the optimum is approached. Some trial-and-error procedure may be required to establish the best size of this reduction factor; values between 0.5 and 0.8 have been found successful in practice, the lower values providing a slower and more cautions approach to the minimum (and also a greater possibility of a computer underflow as $|\Delta\beta|$ becomes too small).

The determination of when the optimum has been found is done by means of the specified tolerance, tol_c. This tolerance is applied to the magnitude of the change of C during a given increment. It should be noted that the meeting of this tolerance merely once is no indication whatsoever that the optimum has been found. This is illustrated in Figure 8-12 for the special case of one adjustable parameter. This tolerance must be met *twice* in a row; after it has been met the first time the increment size is halved. As a result, as Figure 8-13 shows, the tolerance normally would not be met the second time if a true minimum had not been encountered.

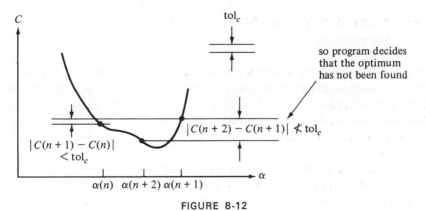

FIGURE 8-12

This simplified approach of using a tolerance imposed on C as a criterion may be criticized in that it will not locate the optimum parameters very precisely when the minimum is a very flat one. The answer to this argument would be simply that the precise location of the parameters becomes less and less important as the minimum becomes flatter and flatter.

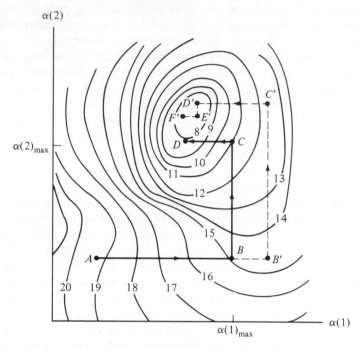

FIGURE 8-13

8-9 Relaxation Method for Finding the Optimum Parameters

Properly speaking, *the* relaxation method consists of determining at the start the steepest-descent direction, and then continuously varying all parameters without changing that direction until a minimum has been found. The new steepest-descent direction is then determined and the process is repeated. This is continued until the criterion for establishing the optimum has been met.

Almost as effective is the method to be discussed here, often called the *modified relaxation method*. (As there is no official terminology, this is only one of several methods so designated.) It was discussed in Section 8-4 and consists of varying each parameter in turn. As far as required execution time is concerned, it often proves more effective than *the* relaxation method because the much simpler programming and computation involved compensate for the increased number of steps that may be required for convergence.

Figure 8-13 illustrates how this method might operate for the special case of there being two adjustable parameters. It portrays the same type of contour map as was shown in Figure 8-11, where the steepest-gradient approach was illustrated. There is no need for normalization of parameters; hence, the axes are labeled directly in terms of the α's. The solid-line paths show the path that would be traveled with the α_{max} constraints imposed. Starting at point A, $\alpha(1)$ is varied first until $\alpha(1)_{max}$ is encountered at point B. $\alpha(2)$ is then varied until $\alpha(2)_{max}$ is encountered at point C. $\alpha(1)$ is varied again until the minimum (in consideration of the constraints) is found.

The dotted-line path illustrates the path that would be followed had there been no maximum constraints on the α's. The first search ends at B', then successively at C', D', E', to F' where the optimum is found.

The program for optimization using this relaxation method is simpler than that of the steepest-descent method as the gradient need not be evaluated at every step, and since at any time optimization is being performed with respect to only one parameter, SUBROUTINE MINIMA, described in Section 8-6 and shown in flow-diagram form in Figure 8-7, may be employed. Still, it is complicated somewhat by the necessity of considering constraints.

Figure 8-14 is a flow diagram for this relaxation-method subprogram. It is mostly self-explanatory. One complete series of optimization operations with each of the NPARAM parameters is called a ROUND. ROUNDS are counted, and some limit, MAXROUNDS, is imposed so that the program does not run indefinitely should it fail to find the optimum within a reasonable execution time. MAXTRIALS is also specified to limit the permissible number of search trials each time the subroutine MINIMA is called. A tolerance, tol_c, is imposed as usual to decide when the subroutine MINIMA has found the local minimum (on the basis of varying only one parameter); this is explained in Section 8-6. When the difference between the minima found at the end of each trial for each parameter is less than tol_c for NPARAM *successive* trials, it is then decided that the optimum has been found. NCONVERGE is the variable that counts the number of successful trials to apply this criterion.

The actual operation of the program is simple to explain if the constraints first are not considered. The single adjustable parameter of SUBROUTINE MINIMA, called α in that program, is in common with the variable called A here. This is set equal to the value of α for the parameter being adjusted [i.e., to $\alpha(1)$ at the very start]. Also, at the start, the starting $\Delta\alpha$'s are all proportioned by the single variable established in the main program, called $\Delta\beta_{start}$. For the ith parameter this would be

$$\Delta\alpha(i) = \Delta\beta_{start}[\alpha_{max}(i) - \alpha_{min}(i)]$$

This initialization is done by SUBROUTINE RELAX when ROUNDS = 0. At this time also, all logical variables involved initially are set to false. Further initialization is then performed with regard to the particular parameter to be next adjusted [i.e., to $i = 1$ at the very start]. Then, this first time only (because START is true), SUBROUTINE MINIMA is called at this point to start the minimization procedure on the basis of the value of C

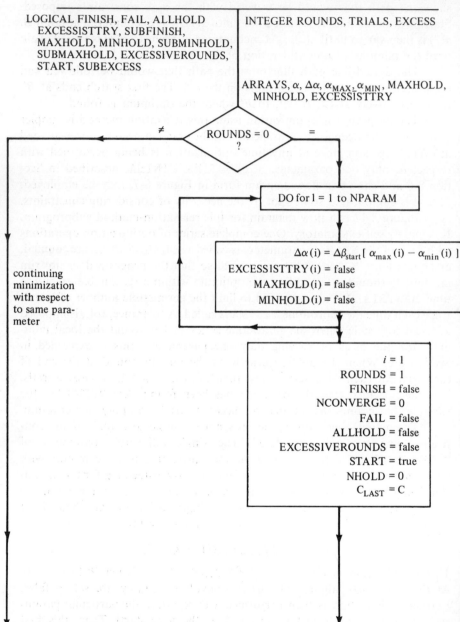

SUBROUTINE RELAX (C, tol $_C$, α, $\Delta\beta$, α_{max}, α_{min}, ROUNDS, MAXROUNDS,
NPARAM, FINISH, EXCESSIVEROUNDS, FAIL, ALLHOLD, MAXTRIALS, EXCESS)

LOGICAL FINISH, FAIL, ALLHOLD
   EXCESSISTTRY, SUBFINISH,
   MAXHOLD, MINHOLD, SUBMINHOLD,
   SUBMAXHOLD, EXCESSIVEROUNDS,
   START, SUBEXCESS

INTEGER ROUNDS, TRIALS, EXCESS

ARRAYS, α, $\Delta\alpha$, α_{MAX}, α_{MIN}, MAXHOLD,
   MINHOLD, EXCESSISTTRY

$\neq$ ROUNDS = 0   =
                     ?

continuing
minimization
with respect
to same para-
meter

DO for l = 1 to NPARAM

$\Delta\alpha(i) = \Delta\beta_{start}[\ \alpha_{max}(i) - \alpha_{min}(i)\ ]$
EXCESSISTTRY(i) = false
MAXHOLD(i) = false
MINHOLD(i) = false

$i = 1$
ROUNDS = 1
FINISH = false
NCONVERGE = 0
FAIL = false
ALLHOLD = false
EXCESSIVEROUNDS = false
START = true
NHOLD = 0
$C_{LAST} = C$

FIGURE 8-14

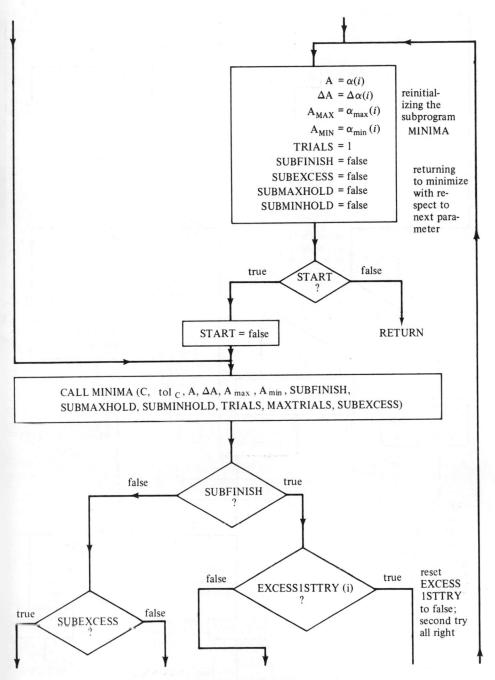

FIGURE 8-14 (cont'd)

FIGURE 8-14 (cont'd)

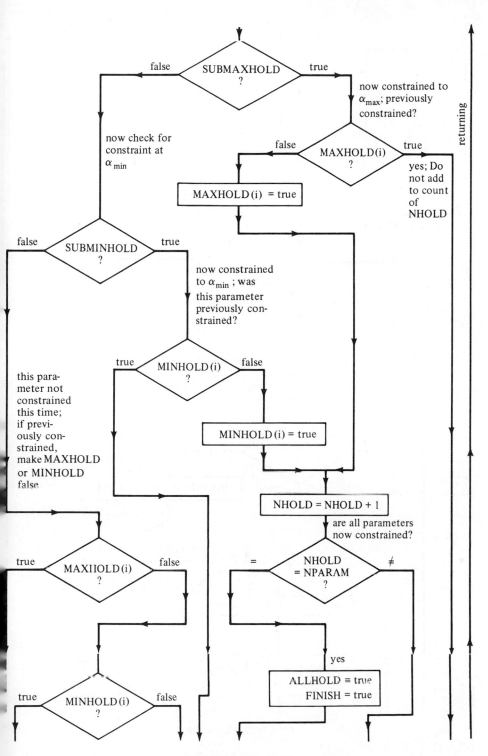

FIGURE 8-14 (cont'd)

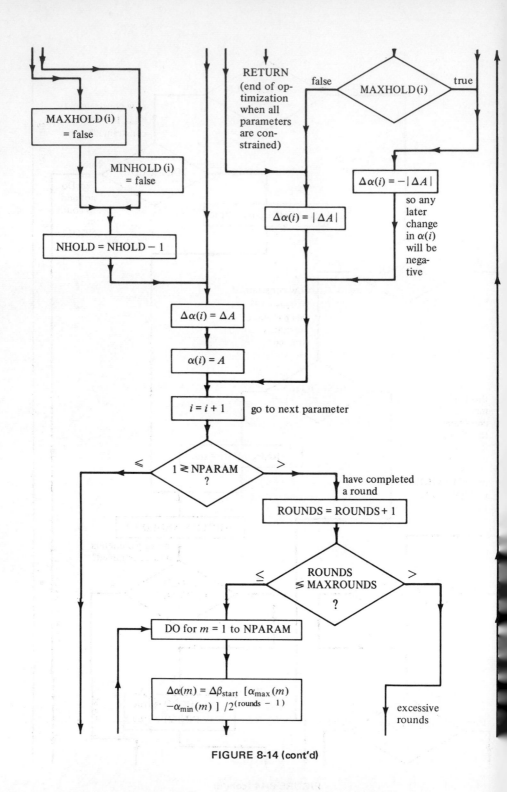

MAXHOLD (i) = false

MINHOLD (i) = false

NHOLD = NHOLD − 1

RETURN (end of optimization when all parameters are constrained)

MAXHOLD(i)

false

true

$\Delta\alpha(i) = -|\Delta A|$ so any later change in $\alpha(i)$ will be negative

$\Delta\alpha(i) = |\Delta A|$

$\Delta\alpha(i) = \Delta A$

$\alpha(i) = A$

$i = i + 1$ go to next parameter

1 ≧ NPARAM ?

≦

>

have completed a round

ROUNDS = ROUNDS + 1

ROUNDS ≦ MAXROUNDS ?

≦

>

DO for m = 1 to NPARAM

$\Delta\alpha(m) = \Delta\beta_{start}\ [\alpha_{max}(m) - \alpha_{min}(m)\ ]\ /2^{(rounds\ -\ 1)}$

excessive rounds

FIGURE 8-14 (cont'd)

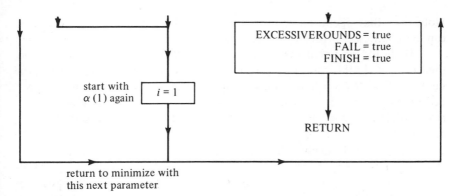

FIGURE 8-14 (cont'd)

already computed for the first trial values of the α's. When the return is made from SUBROUTINE MINIMA, which provides the new suggested value of $\alpha(1)$ as the variable, A, as SUBEXCESS (in common with EXCESS in MINIMA) and SUBFINISH (in common with FINISH in MINIMA) will not be true, this relaxation subroutine simply will set $\alpha(1)$ equal to A and then return to the main program for another trial computation of C. When RELAX is called again, and during all future calls, MINIMA will immediately be called in turn. This process continues until either SUBFINISH or SUBEX-CESS becomes true.

If MINIMA should make SUBFINISH true, meaning it has found the minimum successfully, any previous record of excessive trials with this parameter is erased (EXCESSISTTRY is made false) and a check is made to see whether the change in C resulting from this parameter adjustment is within the tolerance. If it is, the count of convergences, NCONVERGE, has one added to it. If it is not, NCONVERGE is reset to zero as these successful trials must be consecutive.

On the other hand, if MINIMA should instead make SUBEXCESS true, a check is made to establish whether the condition of excessive trials happened also during the preceding adjustment of this parameter. If it did, the optimization task is considered to have failed; FAIL and FINISH are made true and the integer EXCESS is set equal to i to identify the parameter involved in the difficulty. If this was the first failure (EXCESSISTTRY is false), another chance is given; EXCESSISTTRY is set to true and the operation proceeds with minimization with respect to the next parameter.

At the start of minimization with the next parameter, the value of C applying prior to the adjustment is saved as C_{last}. Then the proposed values of α and $\Delta\alpha$, established as A and ΔA, are set into the values of $\alpha(l)$ and $\Delta\alpha(i)$. Finally, i is moved up one so that the next parameter will be adjusted. The operation then returns to the beginning of the subroutine where re-initialization again takes place for the adjustment of the next parameter.

Note then that operation returns directly to the main program so that C can be computed before again calling MINIMA.

It should be noted that when i exceeds NPARAM after the operation, then $i = i + 1$; this indicates that a round has been completed. Hence, the number of ROUNDS has one added to it. A check is made to see if the specified maximum number of rounds has been exceeded. If it has, the program is considered to have failed; EXCESSIVEROUNDS, FAIL, and FINISH are all made true and the operation terminated. Otherwise, i is reset equal to 1 so that $\alpha(1)$ will again be adjusted—the start of a new round.

As has been mentioned, every successful convergence upgrades NCONVERGE by one; these must be consecutive. When NCONVERGE becomes equal to NPARAM, the optimum is assumed to have been found, FINISH is made true. Note that because of this criterion of successive convergences all satisfying tol_c, the actual precision of computation of the optimum will ordinarily be much finer than the amount specified by this tolerance range.

Now the complicating factor of considering constraints should be discussed. The engagement of a constraint is first noted by MINIMA, which makes either SUBMAXHOLD or SUBMINHOLD true. If either are, then either MAXHOLD(i) or MINHOLD(i) is correspondingly made true, and NHOLD is upgraded by one. If all parameters should become constrained, this is the end of the optimization procedure; ALLHOLD and FINISH are made true and a return is made to the main program. Otherwise, operation continues with adjustment of the next parameter.

If, on the other hand, a parameter just adjusted is found to have not engaged a constraint, a check is made to establish whether it previously had been constrained. If it had been, that constraint indication, MAXHOLD(i) or MINHOLD(i), is made false, and NHOLD downgraded by one. Note that a constrained parameter still is retested each round; SUBROUTINE MINIMA will automatically commence the test two $\Delta\alpha$ increments away from the constraint bound.

Figure 8-15 is a general flow diagram of a program that would call this SUBROUTINE RELAX. Since most initialization takes place within the subroutine itself, only a few initialization operations are required here. The starting α's, the values of α_{max} and α_{min} for each α, and the proportion of initial increment $\Delta\beta_{start}$ must all be established in the calling program. The logical variables FINISH, FAIL, EXCESSIVEROUNDS, and ALLHOLD inform the calling program of the status once operation is terminated; the calling program may take different recourses as a result, depending on the application.

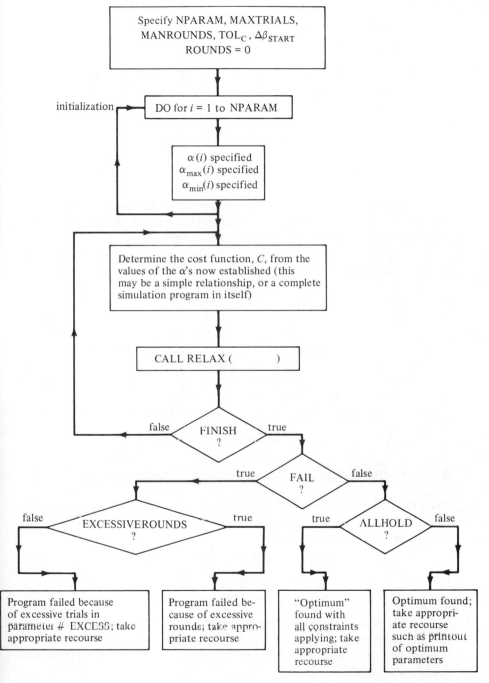

FIGURE 8-15

8-10   Analog Method for Applying the Relaxation Technique

The relaxation method of optimization is more adaptable to analog computation than is the steepest-descent approach. When using digital means, such as SUBROUTINE RELAX, most of the actual work of optimization was done by SUBROUTINE MINIMA. The analog arrangement shown in Figure 8-5 is the equivalent of MINIMA and may be similarly employed. The major modification of the program shown there involves the input and control of the integrator that develops the parameter α. Track-and-hold circuits are required that will hold each value of α as the others are being adjusted. When its turn comes, this value of α is applied to this integrator as a new initial condition. The integrator output is reconnected to the appropriate input terminal of the analog of the process being optimized.

The switching operations described above could all be accomplished by means of comparators. The duration of time that optimization is allowed to take place with respect to each parameter during each round could also be specified and controlled by a timing integrator and comparator. This is equivalent to specifying MAXTRIALS with the digital approach. Another method might consist of switching to the adjustment of the next parameter when $|\dot{\alpha}|$ becomes sufficiently small. All these operations would be expedited, of course, by the availability of hybrid facilities.

With such analog optimization schemes, scaling of the parameters is, of course, necessary. It should be noted that this is similar to conversion of the parameters to the normalized β parameters represented by relation (8-10).

8-11   Optimization with More General Constraints

The only constraints discussed thus far have been maximum and minimum constraints applied to each parameter. The more general situation will involve constraints of the form

$$f(j)[\alpha(1), \alpha(2), \ldots, \alpha(n)] \leq H(j)$$

or

$$f(j)[\alpha(1), \alpha(2), \ldots, \alpha(n)] \geq L(j)$$

or possibly both. This is the situation in what are called programming problems in operations research. If $f(j)$ is a linear function, then the problem is described as being one in *linear programming*; otherwise it is called *nonlinear programming*.

A general approach to all such programming problems is beyond the intended scope of this chapter. (After all, many books have been devoted to this one subject.) However, one approach is suggested here that is applicable to most of the cases that arise in practice. It is illustrated best by example.

Example of a Nonlinear Constraint. Suppose that there are only two adjustable parameters, $\alpha(1)$ and $\alpha(2)$; three constraint variables, $f(1)$, $f(2)$, and $f(3)$; and five constraints:

$$f(1)[\alpha(1), \alpha(2)] = \alpha(1)$$

$$f(2)[\alpha(1), \alpha(2)] = \alpha(2)$$

$$f(3)[\alpha(1), \alpha(2)] = \alpha(1)^2 + 2\alpha(2)^2$$

$$0 \leq f(1) \leq 1 \quad \text{or} \quad f(1)_{\min} = 0 \quad\quad f(1)_{\max} = 1$$

$$0 \leq f(2) \leq 1 \quad \text{or} \quad f(2)_{\min} = 0 \quad\quad f(2)_{\max} = 1$$

$$f(3) \leq 1 \quad \text{or} \quad\quad\quad\quad\quad\quad f(3)_{\max} = 1$$

These constraints plot on the $\alpha(2)$ versus $\alpha(1)$ plane as shown in Figure 8-16. It is obvious from the diagram that the $f(1)_{\max}$ and $f(2)_{\max}$ constraints

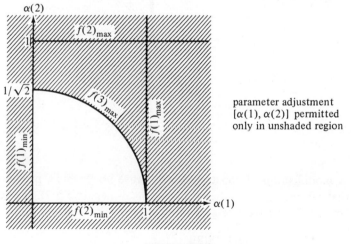

parameter adjustment $[\alpha(1), \alpha(2)]$ permitted only in unshaded region

FIGURE 8-16

play no role. To be able to use such optimization techniques as RELAX, theses constraints must be converted to constraints of the maximum and minimum type only. It would first occur that this might be accomplished by optimizing with respect to the adjustable parameter $\alpha(1)$ and with respect to $f(3)$, considered as though it, also, was an adjustable parameter. After the optimum $\alpha(1)$ and $f(3)$ have been found, the corresponding value of $\alpha(2)$ may be readily determined. The constraints would be expressed as

$$\alpha(1)_{\min} = 0 \quad \alpha(1)_{\max} = 1 \quad f(3)_{\min} = 0 \quad f(3)_{\max} = 1$$

The constraint $\alpha(1)_{max}$ is a completely artificial one and is used only because the optimizing subroutines require some indication of all maximum and minimum values of the parameters. Still referring to the $\alpha(2)$ versus $\alpha(1)$ plane, these constraints would now appear as shown in Figure 8-17. It should be noted that the constraint corresponding to $\alpha(2)_{min}$ has been lost and parameter adjustment is permitted anywhere in the unshaded portion of the $\alpha(2)$ versus $\alpha(1)$ plane; an additional unwanted quarter-circle has been added to the allowable region.

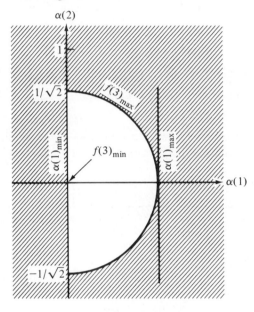

FIGURE 8-17

This modification of constraints will cause no problem provided it is assured that no minimum exists in this region of negative $\alpha(2)$. If one does, an additional obvious parameter modification is necessary:

$$f(4)[\alpha(1), \alpha(2)] = \tan^{-1}\frac{\sqrt{2}\,\alpha(2)}{\alpha(1)}$$

with the maximum and minimum limits

$$f(4)_{max} = \frac{\pi}{2} \qquad f(4)_{min} = 0$$

Minimization would then take place as though $f(3)$ and $f(4)$ were the parameters with the limits as described. Whenever the optimization subroutine returned to the calling program for evaluation of C, this program would be required to compute $\alpha(1)$ and $\alpha(2)$ from the values of $f(3)$ and $f(4)$ proposed by the subroutine, and then, in turn, compute C. For the example here, the computation of the α's from the f's is simply

$$\alpha(1) = f(3) \cos f(4)$$

$$\alpha(2) = \frac{1}{\sqrt{2}} f(3) \sin f(4)$$

The example above involved constraint functions, $f(3)$ and $f(4)$, that were expressible in algebraic–trigonometric form; furthermore, the inverse operations for obtaining the α's from the f's were also so expressible. Not all constraint relations are of this type; some may consist simply of a list of tabulated values of the f's versus the α's with the implication that interpolation is to be used between such values. Even such constraints could be handled by the method suggested. Given the values of the f's, the values of the α's could be obtained by means of the SIMULTANEOUS subroutine described in Chapter 5. This approach would, of course, consume more execution time than when the method could be performed by means of simple algebraic–trigonometric relations, as in the example above.

8-12 Random-Search Optimization with More than One Parameter

Whenever there is a suspicion that nonextreme minima may result in a solution at a false optimum, an initial random-search optimization procedure should be employed first to assure that the starting values of the parameters for subroutine RELAX will arrive at the true optimum. Section 8-7 discussed this for the case of there being only one adjustable parameter. The method with more than one adjustable parameter is essentially the same except that, instead of calling for just one random value to establish a parameter for each trial, n such random values must be called for each trial, where n is the number of parameters to be adjusted.

8-13 Optimization of Configuration—Dynamic Programming

Optimization has been handled here from a very restrictive viewpoint, which is, however, the simplest viewpoint to consider first. It is assumed that the rules that determine the cost function have already been established and that nothing remains except the choosing of optimum values of various constants (i.e., parameters) involved in this relation.

Optimization in the broader sense involves optimization of configuration (e.g., configuration of the block diagram describing a system) or optimal strategy. Three general techniques (all basically related) have been proposed for this purpose:

1. Techniques based upon the calculus of variations.
2. Use of the maximum principle proposed by Pontryagin [3].
3. Dynamic programming, as first proposed by Bellman [4].

Of the three methods, dynamic programming appears to be most adapted to computer optimization. A discussion of this technique, however, would be beyond the intended scope of this book, but the reader certainly is encouraged to pursue this field further as a logical extension of what was treated here.

Suggested Problems

8-1. Figure P8-1 is the block diagram of a very simple control system. K_c is to be selected to meet the criterion that, for r being the step function indicated, of magnitude r_m, the following cost function will be minimized:

$$C = \int_0^\infty e^2 \, dt$$

To make this problem more general it is suggested that time be normalized; i.e.,

$$\tau = \frac{t}{T} \qquad \text{dimensionless time}$$

$$\lambda = Ts = T\frac{d}{dt} \qquad \text{dimensionless operator}$$

$$\mu = K_c K_p T \qquad \text{dimensionless gain}$$

The problem then becomes one of finding the optimum μ. (This problem does have a not too difficult analytic solution.) Find the optimum μ by either analog or digital means.

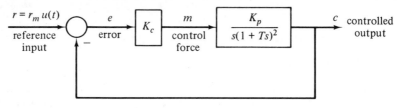

FIGURE P8-1

8-2. Repeat Problem 8-1 for the following definitions of the cost function:

(a) $C = \int_0^\infty |e| \, dt$

(b) $C = \int_0^\infty (|e| + K_p T |m|) \, dt = \int_0^\infty (1 + \mu) |e| \, dt$
    (A penalty is now imposed for excessive control force, m.)

8-3. Repeat Problem 8-1 with the original cost criterion but with a limiter added to the configuration as in Figure P8-3. That is,

$$m = \begin{cases} a & \text{for} \quad -m_L < a < m_L \\ m_L & \text{for} \quad a \ge m_L \\ -m_L & \text{for} \quad a \le -m_L \end{cases}$$

Find the optimum μ as a function of the normalized ratio $K_p T m_L / r_m$.

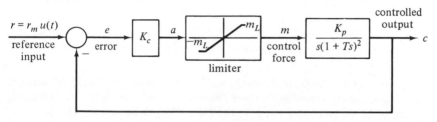

FIGURE P8-3

8-4. [2] Four hundred cubic yards of gravel are to be moved across a river. It is to be shipped in one open box, making as many round trips as necessary. The box dimensions will be length $a(1)$, width $a(2)$, and height $a(3)$. The sides and bottom of the box will be made of material costing \$10 per square yard; the ends of material costing \$20 per square yard. The box will have no salvage value when the job is done. Each round trip across the river will cost 10 cents.

With no constraints imposed on any of the dimensions, use a general computer technique (analog or digital) to determine the values of the a's that will minimize cost.

8-5. Problem 8-4 is to be modified by the addition of one constraint. The length $a(1)$ is to be limited to a maximum value of 1.5 yards. Now find the optimum dimensions.

8-6. Problem 8-4 again is considered but now modified by the constraint that the maximum diametrical length, i.e.,

$$\sqrt{a(1)^2 + a(2)^2 + a(3)^2}$$

is to be 1.5 yards. Now find the optimum dimensions.

8-7. The control system of Problem 8-1 is now modified so that the controller, previously designated simply by the transfer constant K_c, now becomes

$$K_c \frac{1 + T_1 s}{1 + 0.1 T_1 s}$$

[2] From *R & D Letter*, April–May 1964, Westinghouse Electric Co., Technical Information Dept.

Use a computer optimization method to find the optimum K_c and T_1 in terms of normalized expressions for these parameters, μ and $\beta = T_1/T$.

References

1. L. Levine and H. F. Meissinger, An Automatic Analog Computer Method for Solving Polynomials and Finding Root Loci, *IRE Convention Record*, part IV (1957), 164–172.

2. J. A. Ward, The Downhill Method of Solving a Polynomial Equation, *Proceedings of the Eleventh Annual Meeting of the Association for Computing Machinery*, Los Angeles, 1956.

3. L. S. Pontrayagin, V. G. Boltyanskii, R. V. Gamkrelidze, and E. F. Mishenko, *The Mathematical Theory of Optimal Processes* (translation by K. N. Trirogoff, edited by L. W. Neustadt) (New York: John Wiley & Sons, Inc., 1962).

4. R. Bellman, *Dynamic Programming* (Princeton, N.J.: Princeton University Press, 1957).

Additional Reading

Leon Levine, *Methods for Solving Engineering Problems Using Analog Computers* (New York: McGraw-Hill, Inc., 1964), Chap. 8.

Simulation of Random
Disturbances and Their Effects

9

9-1 Circumstances Giving Rise
to Random Disturbances

It is more likely that systems being simulated will be subjected to disturbances (i.e., independent variables affecting the response) that are of a
random nature than to those of a deterministic nature. A *deterministic*
function is one whose value can be defined at any instant of time.[1] Examples
are classical transient forms such as step functions, ramps, exponential
functions, and classical steady-state (stationary) forms such as sinusoidal
functions. For example, the characteristics of communications systems are
generally described in terms of the response to sinusoidal disturbances (e.g.,
the frequency response). In practice the disturbances likely to be applied
to such systems are more likely to be of a random nature, with regard to
both the useful signal being transmitted and the noise.

Other examples of random disturbances that may be important in
certain systems are the variation of outdoor wind velocity, the surface height
of the water at a given point on a rough sea, the outdoor temperature at
a given location, the degree of daily activity of trading in the N.Y. Stock

[1]In this chapter it will be assumed that *time* is the basic independent variable; when
the word "time" is used, it actually implies the basic independent variable involved in the
simulation problem, whatever that might be.

Exchange, etc. In each of these instances the instantaneous values of the disturbance will not be predictable. The simplest qualitative definition of a random disturbance is simply that it is a disturbance that is not deterministic. This is not, of course, a rigorous mathematical definition of a random disturbance, but it should suffice for the purposes here. It will be assumed that the reader does have some other background in this subject. In any event, much more rigorous and hence much more lengthy definitions of a random variable and related definitions are given in a number of textbooks on this subject.

From the examples given above it may appear that natural phenomena generally lead to random forms of disturbances. This is not always the case. As an example, the angular elevation of the sun above the horizon represents a function of time that is deterministic, at least within the time of observation of interest to us. Other random disturbances may not be completely random in nature. As an example of this, the outside air temperature at a given location will prove to have an annual periodic cycle, which is essentially deterministic, superposed on the random fluctuations, and, in addition, a shorter diurnal cycle. One of the functions often assigned to computers is the separation of the deterministic portion of a disturbance from the purely random part.

It will require little imagination to see how random disturbances might arise in practical situations. Mechanical structures are subject to random forces resulting from wind velocities. Airborne and seaborne vehicles are subject to random disturbances caused by sea turbulence. Chemical processes may be subject to random variations of the properties of the entering constituents. The random nature of the forces acting on an economic or biological system is obvious.

Fortunately, in spite of the uncertain nature of a random disturbance at any given instant of time, it is possible to describe such disturbances from a statistical standpoint. It is possible to describe, quantitatively, the *size* of a random disturbance. For example, the height of random sea waves on a calm day naturally is generally less than on a rough day; this fact can be expressed in quantitative as well as qualitative form. The manner of time variation of a random disturbance can also be described quantitatively. As an example, the random variation of outdoor air temperature above the surface of the ground is known to be not only larger but also faster than the temperature 3 ft below the surface of the ground. This difference in *rate* of variation may also be described in a quantitative sense. Fortunately, there are methods available for describing the *general statistical nature* of random disturbances so that it will be possible to represent them reasonably faithfully in a simulation problem.

9-2 Stationary Random Disturbances

The types of disturbances to be discussed in this chapter will be confined to those described as either stationary or semistationary. Again, a rigorous definition of these terms would require more space than is practical in this book. It will suffice to describe a *stationary* disturbance as one whose statistical properties do not change with time. For example, the instantaneous wave height in a disturbed sea might be considered as a stationary random variable if the wind remains steady and the sea state does not change. On the other hand, if the wind velocity was continuously increasing, giving rise to a progressively rougher sea state, the wave height could no longer be represented as a stationary random variable. In practice many random variables may be considered as stationary for only limited durations of time. They may be mathematically represented as stationary within a reasonable degree of approximation if the variation in statistical properties is minor during the time of interest and during the statistical averaging time (to be described later).

Random disturbances may be described, loosely, as *semistationary* as well. These simply are stationary disturbances that are "turned on" at $t = 0$ (i.e., they are mathematically represented as the product of a stationary disturbance and a unit step function).

The analytic treatment of nonstationary disturbances is, in general, much more difficult and will not be discussed here. However, it will be obvious to the reader how simple cases of such nonstationary disturbances, such as a noise signal having statistical properties that are uniform except for a slowly but uniformly increasing intensity, might be handled for simulation purposes.

9-3 Describing the Magnitude of Stationary Disturbances—Probability Density

If there is no concern regarding the manner of time variation, the amplitude characteristics of a random variable can be described by its *probability density*. Most readers undoubtedly are already familiar with this concept, but, for purposes of review, it is expressed here when applying to a random variable $\mathbf{x}(t)$ as

$$f(x) = \lim_{\Delta x \to 0} \left[\frac{P\{x \leq \mathbf{x}(t) < x + \Delta x\}}{\Delta x} \right] \tag{9-1}$$

In the above expression the symbol P represents the probability of the event described in the braces that follow. In this application it is implied to mean the probability that $\mathbf{x}(t)$ meets the inequality condition stated when t is randomly selected. (Again a more precise definition would be required for complete mathematical rigor.)

When $\mathbf{x}(t)$ is a stationary random variable, the probability of the event referred to above may be reexpressed as

$$P\{x \leq \mathbf{x}(t) < x + \Delta x\} = \lim_{T \to \infty}\left[\frac{t_\Delta(x)}{T}\right] \tag{9-2}$$

where $t_\Delta(x)$ is the duration of time that the event $\{x \leq \mathbf{x}(t) < x + \Delta x\}$ is satisfied during a given test measurement of the random variable, of *duration T*.

Relation (9-2) indicates that this time-averaging method for determining the probability P becomes valid only as T approaches infinity. In practice, if a running record of the ratio expressed by relation (9-2) were kept with T finite and increasing, it would be found that as T became sufficiently long, relation (9-2) would be fulfilled to a reasonable degree of approximation. This ratio would approach a constant value with eventually only minor fluctuations about this value during such a measurement procedure.

Relations (9-1) and (9-2) suggest methods for measuring the probability density by computer means. An analog technique for doing this is shown in Figure 9-1. The integrator shown that produces the signal V_T measures the elapsed time of the test run. If the associated potentiometer setting is k_2, this time will be limited to $T = V_r/k_2$ sec because of the time-limiting comparator. When this time has elapsed, both integrators will be placed in a hold mode. The other integrator, producing the signal $V_{t\Delta}$, measures t_Δ [i.e., the duration of time that $\mathbf{x}(t)$ is within the prescribed limits]. Hence $V_{t\Delta} = k_1 t_\Delta$ and

$$P\{x \leq \mathbf{x}(t) < x + \Delta x\} = \frac{t_\Delta}{T} = \frac{V_{t\Delta}/k_1}{V_r/k_2} = \frac{k_2}{k_1}\frac{V_{t\Delta}}{V_r} \tag{9-3}$$

Relation (9-3) is approximate in the sense that T necessarily must be finite. Substituting (9-3) in (9-1) yields the result,

$$f(x) = \frac{k_2 V_{t\Delta}}{k_1 V_r \Delta x} \tag{9-4}$$

Relation (9-4) is approximate, not only because T is finite but also because Δx necessarily must be finite rather than infinitesimal. As a result, a *granulated* relation for $f(x)$ will be obtained.

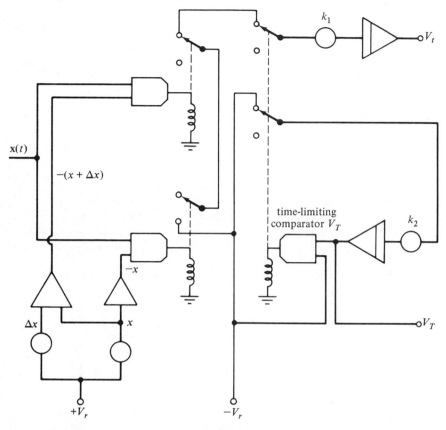

FIGURE 9-1

9-4   Classical Forms of the Probability-Density Function

There are a number of classical forms of the function $f(x)$ that appear frequently when dealing with natural phenomena. A few of these that might be encountered will be mentioned here.

If $x(t)$ should happen to have a finite probability of acquiring a specific discrete value of x, say x_a, then $f(x)$ will include an *impulse function* (Dirac function) as shown in Figure 9-2. Of course, measurements made as described on such a random disturbance, with a necessarily finite Δx, would appear as a large pulse of finite magnitude rather than as an actual impulse.

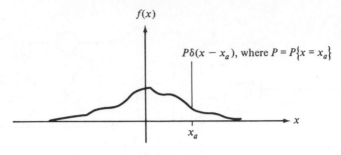

FIGURE 9-2

In many instances $f(x)$ will be a constant within some specified range of x between $x = x_a$ and $x = x_b$ $(x_b > x_a)$. That is, $P\{x \leq \mathbf{x}(t) < x + \Delta x\}$ is constant for a given Δx, provided that $x_a \leq x$ and $x + \Delta x < x_b$. This is called a *uniform probability density*; a plot of $f(x)$ versus x would then appear as in Figure 9-3, where it should be noted that the magnitude of

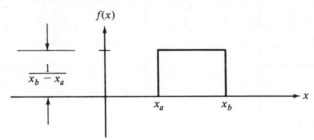

FIGURE 9-3

$f(x)$ between $x = x_a$ and $x = x_b$ is given as $1/(x_b - x_a)$. This must necessarily be the case since

$$\int_{-\infty}^{\infty} f(x)\, dx = P\{-x_c \leq \mathbf{x}(t) < x_c\}_{x_c \to \infty} = 1 \qquad (9\text{-}5)$$

As the above probability represents the probability of $\mathbf{x}(t)$ having some value between minus and plus infinity, this must certainly represent a certainty and the probability must be unity. Relation (9-5) applies to any probability-density function.

One very common classical form of probability-density function is the *normal* or *Gaussian* form, where

$$f(x) = \frac{1}{\sqrt{2\pi}\sigma_x} \exp\left[-\frac{1}{2}\left(\frac{x - x_0}{\sigma_x}\right)^2\right] \qquad (9\text{-}6)$$

The general shape of this function is shown, when plotted versus x, in Figure 9-4. The quantity σ_x is called the *mean deviation*; the quantity x_0 the *mean value*, the *expected value*, or the *average value* of $\mathbf{x}(t)$.

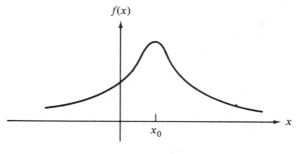

FIGURE 9-4

A basic theorem of statistics, the *central-limit theorem*, shows that if a large number of random variables arising from *independent* sources are added, the result will approach a random variable having such a normal or Gaussian probability distribution as the number of sources becomes increasingly large. In practice it will be found that even if a relatively small number, say 10, of such independent random variables are added, the probability density of the resulting sum will bear a surprisingly close resemblance to the normal form. This fact explains why the normal density function is so often encountered with random disturbances arising in nature. Such disturbances usually represent the net effect of many independent random disturbances (e.g., Brownian motion, thermal noise, air turbulence). Hence the disturbances to be simulated in many practical simulation problems will be of a normal or Gaussian form.

There are a number of other classical forms of probability-density functions encountered often in simulation problems. Among them are the Poisson and binomial density functions applying to random variables that may partake of only discrete values, and also the gamma, beta, Laplace, Cauchy, Rayleigh, and Maxwell forms. These are discussed in many textbooks that deal with random variables in more detail [1].

9-5   Digital Measurement of the Probability Density

The digital program to determine the value of $f(x)$ for some given digital record of a random disturbance is reasonably simple. It is assumed that there is some portion of the program producing the random signal $\mathbf{x}(t)$ in a sequential fashion. The main program then would simply call a subprogram, called here PROBDENSITY, every time a new value of $\mathbf{x}(t)$ was produced. The features that would be added to such a main program for this purpose are shown in Figure 9-5.

At the beginning of the program, the logical variables START and FINISH are made true and false, respectively. The maximum and mini-

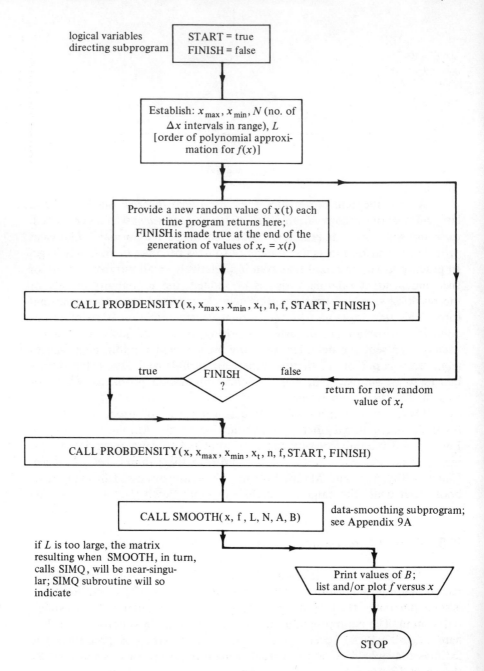

logical variables directing subprogram

START = true
FINISH = false

Establish: x_{max}, x_{min}, N (no. of Δx intervals in range), L [order of polynomial approximation for $f(x)$]

Provide a new random value of x(t) each time program returns here; FINISH is made true at the end of the generation of values of $x_t = x(t)$

CALL PROBDENSITY(x, x_{max}, x_{min}, x_t, n, f, START, FINISH)

true   FINISH ?   false

return for new random value of x_t

CALL PROBDENSITY(x, x_{max}, x_{min}, x_t, n, f, START, FINISH)

CALL SMOOTH(x, f, L, N, A, B)   data-smoothing subprogram; see Appendix 9A

if L is too large, the matrix resulting when SMOOTH, in turn, calls SIMQ, will be near-singular; SIMQ subroutine will so indicate

Print values of B; list and/or plot f versus x

STOP

FIGURE 9-5

mum expected values of $\mathbf{x}(t)$, $x_{\max}$ and $x_{\min}$, are established, as is N, the number of increments Δx into which the range from $x_{\min}$ to $x_{\max}$ is to be divided. These values should be selected so that the middle of each increment Δx will be based on some reasonably round series of decimal values for the purpose of listing and plotting.

Every time a new random $\mathbf{x}(t)$ is produced (called x_t in the flow diagrams), the subprogram PROBDENSITY is called. Finally, when all values of $\mathbf{x}(t)$ have been generated, FINISH is made true and the subprogram PROBDENSITY called for the last time. The result will then be values of the probability density $f(k)$ versus the values $x(k)$ corresponding to the middle of each Δx interval, with values for k from 1 to N.

The probability-density subroutine itself is shown in Figure 9-6. The first time it is called, when START is true, the counters for COUNT (the number of values of $\mathbf{x}(t)$ furnished) and for $f(k)$ are set to zero. Although $f(k)$ eventually will be the probability density at each value of $x(k)$, it will initially be simply a count of the number of times that $\mathbf{x}(t)$ falls within the kth interval. At the start of the use of the subprogram, the values of $x(k)$ are also established. START is then made false so that these computations will not be repeated unnecessarily.

During the first and each subsequent call on this program, until FINISH is made true, COUNT is advanced one and location k of the Δx interval in which $\mathbf{x}(t)$ falls is established; the count $f(k)$ for this interval is then advanced by one. At the end of this part of the operation, f will constitute a record of the number of times $\mathbf{x}(t)$ has fallen within that Δx range.

When FINISH is true and the subprogram PROBDENSITY is called for the last time, the number of times $\mathbf{x}(t)$ has fallen within a given range, the present $f(k)$, is divided by COUNT$*\Delta x$ [number of Δx intervals multiplied by the total number of $\mathbf{x}(t)$ values]. The result now becomes the new $f(k)$ and corresponds to the probability density as defined by relation (9-1) with, however, Δx remaining finite (although preferably as small as storage limitations will permit) rather than truly approaching zero.

If the probability density $f(x)$ of the signal involved, $\mathbf{x}(t)$, were truly a smooth function of x (as it very well might be) and *if an infinite number of values of* $\mathbf{x}(t)$ *could have been furnished*, it would be expected that the relationship between f and x, while discrete, would nevertheless be smooth. However, because the number COUNT of values furnished must be reasonable, although preferably as large as is practical, the actual relationship obtained will probably be quite irregular when observed from interval to interval. It might be difficult under these circumstances to determine the true functional nature of f. For this reason a *smoothing* operation is usually desirable. It should be realized, however, that such an operation never adds but rather always detracts from the statistical accuracy of the results; the

SUBROUTINE PROBDENSITY$(x, x_{max}, x_{min}, x_t, n, f, \text{START}, \text{FINISH})$

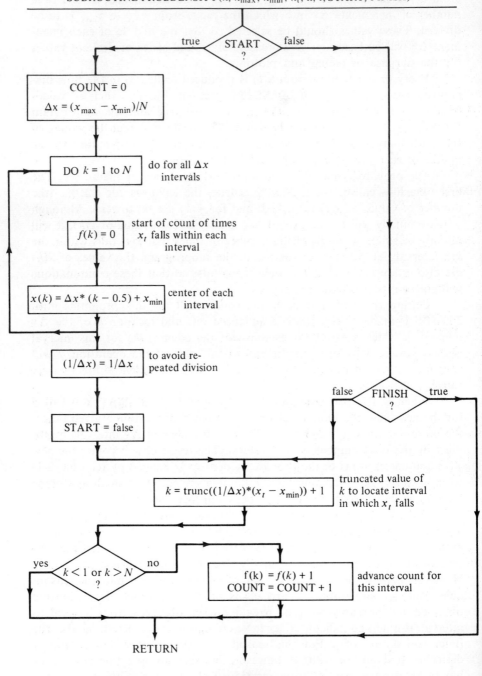

FIGURE 9-6

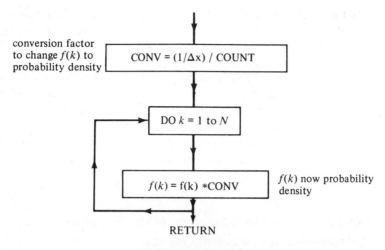

FIGURE 9-6 (cont'd)

only justification for its use is the fact that it does permit a more understandable description of $f(x)$.

In the particular type of program shown for example here, the smoothing operation approximates $f(x)$ as a polynomial in x having L terms (i.e., of order $L - 1$). Note that L was also established at the start of the main program. The method of least-mean-squares fit is employed. If computer roundoff errors and the limitations imposed on floating-point ranges were not a problem, L preferably should be as large as possible (but less than N). Actually, if L is made too large, a near-singular matrix results when an attempt is made to find the polynomial's coefficients. For this reason L is practically never made greater than 6, the best value depending on the degree of irregularity of $f(x)$.

Hence, after the last call of the subprogram PROBDENSITY has been made, a smoothing operation is performed by calling another subprogram, called SMOOTH, which is designed for this general purpose. As the algorithms for this latter subprogram are only incidental to the subject matter here, they will be discussed in Appendix 9A.

Subroutine SMOOTH involves a common logical argument, called SINGULAR. If the matrix involved is near-singular, this will be set to true and, as Figure 9-5 shows, a printout explaining this difficulty is obtained instead of the results desired. The usual cure is to make L smaller.

If the above difficulty is not encountered, an array B of dimension L is obtained after the subprogram SMOOTH has been called. This array will represent the coefficients of the approximating polynomial, which is of the form

$$f(x) = B(1) + B(2)x + \cdots + B(L)x^{L-1}$$

Sometimes the interest is in the values of these polynomial coefficients; at other times it will be in providing either a listing and/or plot of $f(x)$ versus x as based on these coefficients. What the main program does at this final stage, therefore, depends upon the application involved.

There will be times when a finite probability exists of $\mathbf{x}(t)$ having a specific value x; $f(x)$ will then contain an impulse at this value of x. This has been discussed in the preceding section. The nature of the problem will indicate when this is expected to be the case [e.g., when $\mathbf{x}(t)$ has been subjected to hard limiting]. Under such circumstances, the value of the probability density computed for this value of x should be omitted from the smoothing operation.

9-6   Describing the Time Variation of the Random Variable—Power-Spectral Density

The probability density or distribution discussed above describes only the *amplitude* characteristics of the random time function. For faithful simulation in a dynamic problem, the manner by which the variable *varies with time* must also be represented. This manner of variation can be described conveniently (but not completely for all purposes) by the power-spectral density, $\Phi_{xx}(\omega)$. This concept is described in many textbooks dealing with random variables and only certain basic features of the power-spectral density will be reiterated here.

$\Phi_{xx}(\omega)$, the power-spectral density of the random variable $\mathbf{x}(t)$, describes the frequency content of $[\mathbf{x}(t)]^2$. The word power appears in the description because the square of many physical variables does happen to be indicative of power. Its significance may be explained by a hypothetical experiment.

Suppose that the random time variable $\mathbf{x}(t)$ was applied to a band-pass filter that has a pass range from the frequency ω to $\omega + \Delta\omega$. Within this pass range the transmission is assumed to be unity; outside of it, zero. (The fact that such an ideal filter cannot be built because of certain basic limitations of network theory is the reason why this experiment is described as hypothetical.)

The output of this filter, described as $\mathbf{x}_f$, would contain only the frequency components of the random variable that lie within this frequency range. This output is then squared and the average value of this result is determined, the averaging being conducted over a sufficiently long time period. What will be obtained will be represented here as $\overline{(\mathbf{x}_f)^2}$, the bar over the symbol indicating the process of time averaging. Figure 9-7 illustrates this experimental procedure. The time constant of the averaging filter must be such that $\omega\tau \gg 1$, where ω is the lower band limit of the filter.

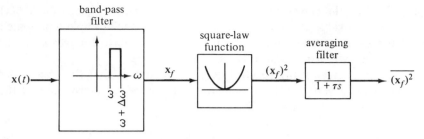

FIGURE 9-7

The quantity obtained when $\overline{(x_f)^2}$ is divided by the filter bandwidth, $\Delta\omega$, is an approximate indication of $\Phi_{xx}(\omega)$ for the value of ω employed in the filter. As $\Delta\omega$ is made progressively smaller, this ratio approaches a constant value and, in the limit, as $\Delta\omega \longrightarrow 0$, it becomes exactly $\Phi_{xx}(\omega)$. That is,

$$\Phi_{xx}(\omega) = \lim_{\Delta\omega \to 0} \left[\frac{\overline{(x_f)^2}}{\Delta\omega} \right] \qquad (9\text{-}7)$$

The above process may then be completed over the significant range of ω to obtain the complete spectrum.

Power-spectral densities of typical random variables may take on a number of forms. One common one is

$$\Phi_{xx}(\omega) = \frac{2\sigma_x^2 \omega_0}{\omega^2 + \omega_0^2} \qquad (9\text{-}8)$$

Such a spectrum would appear when plotted as in Figure 9-8. In relation

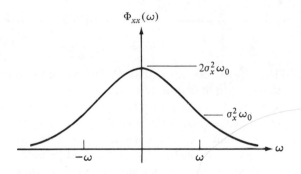

FIGURE 9-8

(9-8), ω_0 is called the half-power frequency for reasons obvious from the plot. σ_x is the mean deviation of the random signal $x(t)$, generally defined for all random functions by

$$\sigma_x^2 = E[x^2] - [E(x)]^2 \qquad (9\text{-}9)$$

where $E[x^2]$ is the expected value of x^2 (i.e., the mean-square value). $E(x)$ is the expected value of x itself (i.e., its average). In the example represented by relation (9-8), the average value of $\mathbf{x}(t)$ must be zero (for reasons to be discussed below); hence, for this case, $\sigma_x^2 = E[x^2]$.

One property of any spectral density function is that the area under it, when plotted versus x, is an indication of the mean-square value of the function (i.e., $E[x^2]$). Specifically,

$$E[x^2] = \frac{1}{2\pi} \int_{-\infty}^{\infty} \Phi_{xx}(\omega)\, d\omega \qquad (9\text{-}10)$$

Substitution of relation (9-8) in (9-10) would indicate, after performing the integration operation, that for this particular example the expected result would be obtained that $E[x^2] = \sigma_x^2$.

Another form of power-spectral density discussed frequently is *white noise*, where

$$\Phi_{xx}(\omega) = n = \text{constant for all } \omega\text{'s} \qquad (9\text{-}11)$$

The power spectrum for white noise appears as in Figure 9-9. Substitution

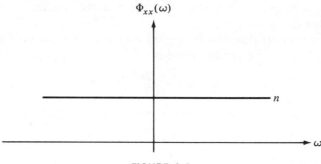

FIGURE 9-9

of relation (9-11) in (9-10) will show that $E[x^2]$ becomes infinite, indicating a random disturbance of infinite intensity. Hence ideal white noise is a strictly theoretical concept. What usually is meant by white noise, as in commercially available white-noise generators, is that the power-density spectrum remains essentially constant within the frequency range of interest; of course, it must approach zero as ω approaches $\pm\infty$. (It should be noted that although it is a mathematical convenience to consider ω as possessing both positive and negative values, as is done when employing the Fourier transform of deterministic functions, the power-spectral density of *real* random variables will always be an even function of ω.)

Another typical form of power-spectral density might appear as in Figure 9-10. A random function described by such a spectral density would have most of its frequency components in the *vicinity* of ω_a, and would possess

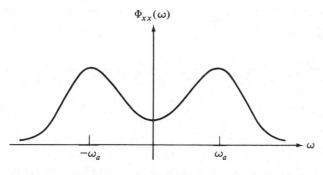

FIGURE 9-10

what at first appeared to be a periodic component; however, further inspection would, show that this apparently periodic portion also was random in both phase and frequency. A power-spectral density of the type shown could result from the amplitude modulation of a carrier signal, at frequency ω_a, by a random modulating signal. As another example, sea waves sometimes exhibit almost sinusoidal swells in the vicinity of some particular frequency.

A limiting case of the example shown in Figure 9-10 exists when a truly sinusoidal signal of one specific frequency exists mixed with the remainder of the random signal. In this case an impulse function of ω appears in the spectrum at $\pm\omega_a$. This is shown in Figure 9-11. The existance of an average value, $E(x)$, or the d.c. component, corresponds to the above instance where ω_a is zero. The impulse would then appear at $\omega = 0$.

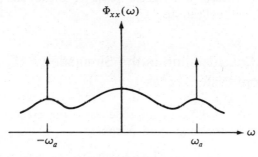

FIGURE 9-11

The discussion of the significance of the power-spectral density has been presented because, in simulation problems, it is always important that the spectral density of the simulated disturbance match that of the disturbance being simulated. This is a *necessary* condition for faithful simulation. As a matter of fact, when the performance of *linear* systems is being investigated, it also is a *sufficient* condition. For this reason the ability to evaluate the power-spectral density of random signals produced by experimental observations or by other simulations is discussed next.

9-7   Evaluation of the Power-Spectral Density

It is not feasible to evaluate the power-spectral density of random signals by analog methods *alone*. Until a few years ago evaluation by digital means was a tedious process, involving first the evaluation of the inverse transform of the power-spectral density (i.e., the *autocorrelation function*). However, new direct and efficient algorithms have been developed based on a general technique known as the *fast Fourier transform* (FFT). The paper by E. O. Brigham and R. E. Morrow [2] provides a good general survey of these methods.

Because the algorithms used for this purpose are still in such a rapid stage of development, nothing could be said about them in any book that would not be very out of date by the time of publication. Use of the most efficient algorithm is important because evaluation of the spectral density of a random signal will, in any event, consume excessive expensive execution time; hence these newer algorithms have been concentrating primarily on ways of reducing execution time. Quite possibly the most efficient and economical methods will involve the use of hybrid analog–digital computers. In any event, anyone interested in employing the FFT should examine the current literature to find the most efficient technique applicable to his needs. No attempts will be made to describe the method here. Hopefully, the latest FFT programs will become standard parts of digital-computer libraries devoted to scientific applications.

9-8   General Consideration in the Simulation of Random Disturbances

There are a number of different approaches to the problem of supplying random disturbances for simulation purposes.

1. The disturbance to be simulated itself, if available and occurring concurrently, may be applied to the simulation model, usually in the form of an equivalent electrical voltage or equivalent digital indication. This implies real-time simulation.
2. A recording of the actual disturbance may be used, as in the form of an analog or digital recording on magnetic tape. As the play-back rate of such a record need not necessarily be the same as the

recording rate, real-time simulation is not necessarily required with this method.

3. An equivalent random disturbance may be generated in analog form by one of the means to be discussed in the section to follow.
4. The distubance may be derived from a series of random numbers generated in digital from, either from a random-number library program or from special program devised fo this purpose.
5. A pseudorandom signal designed to match the power-spectral density and probability density in an at least approximate sense might be created to match the actual disturbance. One way of accomplishing this is by adding the outputs of a series of independently generated sinusoidal signals having frequencies that bear no integer relationship with each other. This method will also be described in more detail.

An important distinction must be made between *repeatable* and *nonrepeatable* random disturbances. Usually the purpose of simulating systems subject to random disturbances is for the comparison of different system-design techniques, such as specific mechanical design features or parameter adjustments in control systems. If the various techniques to be investigated are compared by sequential test, it is important that they be subjected to random disturbances of the same degree of severity. Even though the same random disturbance is applied (in the sense that it has the same amplitude probability density and the same power-spectral density), and even though this disturbance is truly stationary, a series of such tests, each of limited duration, may result of some of the models being tested being subjected to more severe phases of the disturbances than others. This disadvantage, which can affect the validity of comparison, can be overcome only by

1. individual test runs, each of an unusually long duration (with obvious disadvantages, including expense of testing), or
2. applying the same disturbance in turn to each model.

Recourse 2 is generally the most practical but places restrictions on the choice of methods, as listed from 1 to 5 above, that might be employed. A *repeatable* source of random disturbance is required. Method 1, involving the actual disturbance itself or its electrical indication, will not suffice for obvious reasons. This very fact is what often makes computer simulation of systems desirable for comparison purposes, even when direct tests on the equipment being simulated are a practical possibility. For example, when comparing the effectiveness of different aircraft-autopilot designs by means of actual flight tests, the apparent superiority of one design over another might simply be due to the more favorable air-turbulence conditions at the time the better system was tested.

Method 2 obviously fulfills the repeatability requirement when such a requirement is applicable. Method 3, involving analog generation of random disturbances, does not. Method 4, involving digital generation of random disturbances, may or may not fulfill the repeatability requirement, depending on the technique of random-number generation used. Method 5, in theory, will fulfill this repeatability requirement and will do so in fact when implemented by digital methods. When analog methods are used, however, slight drifting in the frequencies of the sinusoidal signal generators from one run to another may result in imperfect repeatability unless the durations of the runs are fairly short.

Methods 1 and 2 as techniques for supplying random disturbances to a simulation program are self-explanatory and will not be discussed further here. Methods 3, 4, and 5 have in common the fact that the disturbance is created as part of the computer simulation process. These methods will require further explanation, to be given in the sections that follow.

9-9   Generation of Random Signals in Analog Form

This relates to method 3 of Section 9-8. A number of experimental techniques have been proposed and tried, but the two employed most frequently are

1. The use of gas-tube noise generators.
2. The use of pulses generated by a Geiger–Müller counter exposed to a radioactive source.

Method 1 is used frequently in commercially made noise generators. The random fluctuations in ion density about the cathode of a gas tube (e.g., thyratron) result in noise signals being created that have a normal probability density and a power-density spectrum ranging from about 30 Hz to about 2 kHz. These signals are modified by a variety of electronic means, including means for introducing a frequency shift, so that the output spectrum will be essentially flat (i.e., white) from zero to anywhere from 50 to 200 Hz, depending on the design of the equipment. The actual electronic circuitry necessary to produce a good source of Gaussian white noise is fairly complicated; this is generally the concern of the equipment manufacturer, not of the persons preparing the simulation program.

Method 2 is illustrated in Figure 9-12. The radiactive source emits particles that actuate the Geiger–Müller (G–M) tube and result in a train of pulses, $e_1(t)$. The arrival time of each pulse is independent of that of any

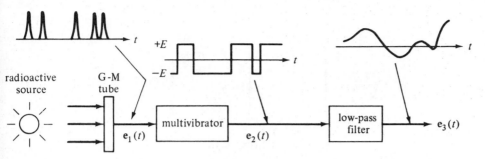

FIGURE 9-12

other pulse and can be described statistically by the *Poisson probability distribution*. This means simply that the probability of n pulses arriving during a specified time interval t_a will be

$$P\{n, t_a\} = \frac{(\lambda t_a)^n}{n!} \exp(-\lambda t_a) \tag{9-12}$$

where λ will be the *mean frequency* of pulse arrival, a function of the intensity of the radioactive source and of its proximity to the Geiger–Müller tube. For example, the probability of *no* pulses arriving in a time interval t_a is $P\{0, t_a\} = \exp(-\lambda t_a)$.

For some simulation applications the output of the Geiger–Müller tube shown in Figure 9-12 may be directly representative of the type of random signal desired, but for most purposes this signal must be shaped to another form. This is done most readily if the output of the Geiger–Müller tube, $e_1(t)$, is first used to trigger a multivibrator that has an output switching alternately between $+E$ and $-E$ V. (Such a circuit is easily constructed from analog-computer elements; see Chapter 6.) The output of such a multivibrator circuit, $e_2(t)$, will now be described by an amplitude probability density expressed as

$$P\{e_2\} = 0.5[\delta(e_2 - E) + \delta(e_2 + E)] \tag{9-13}$$

and appears, when plotted, as in Figure 9-13. The power density spectrum of such a signal can be shown to be expressed as

$$\Phi_{e_2 e_2}(\omega) = \frac{2E^2\lambda}{\omega^2 + \lambda^2} \tag{9-14}$$

The plot of this power-spectral density function will appear as in Figure 9-8, with the half-power frequency appearing as the mean frequency of pulse arrival λ.

Again, although it is possible that the random-signal output of the multivibrator may be directly suitable for some simulation applications, in most cases a different form of amplitude probability and/or power-spectral density will be required. This will be accomplished by applying the output

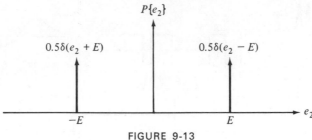

FIGURE 9-13

of the multivibrator, $e_2(t)$, to the low-pass filter shown in Figure 9-12, obtaining the actual random signal desired for simulation purposes, $e_3(t)$. The design of this filter depends upon the power spectral density $\Phi_{e_3 e_3}(\omega)$ that is desired and is based upon the considerations discussed in the next section.

In most applications it will be desired that the amplitude probability density of $e_3(t)$ be of the normal or Gaussian type. Although a rigorous proof is tedious, it can be shown that *a normal form of amplitude probability density will be approached as the amplitude response of the shaping filter approaches zero for frequencies of a magnitude equal to or greater than the mean frequency of pulse arrival λ.* In practice this means that the transmission of the filter should be negligible in this frequency range, or, conversely, that λ should be chosen to be significantly greater than the bandwidth of the filter. If this is done, the output $e_3(t)$ will be of essentially Gaussian form, subject, however, to the inevitable limitations on the amplitude range of the electronic equipment (since a truly Gaussian or normal density implies some exceedingly small but finite probability of signals beyond the normal signal-handling range). This necessary relationship between filter bandwidth and the frequency λ is why the shaping filter shown in Figure 9-12 is described as low pass.

There are a number of other methods of analog generation of random signals that have also been employed. More detailed treatment of these, as well as the two techniques that have just been described, are discussed in the literature [3].

9-10   Analog Techniques for Shaping Power-Spectral Densities

The relationship upon which the design of the shaping filter is based is quite simple. If, with reference to Figure 9-12, $e_2(t)$ is the random input to the filter and $e_3(t)$ is the random output, and if the transfer function relating them is designated as $G_{32}(s)$; i.e., if

$$E_3(s) = G_{32}(s)E_2(s) \tag{9-15}$$

then it will be true that

$$\Phi_{e_3e_3}(\omega) = G_{32}(j\omega)G_{32}(-j\omega)\Phi_{e_2e_2}(\omega) \tag{9-16}$$

or

$$\Phi_{e_3e_3}(\omega) = |G_{32}(j\omega)|^2\Phi_{e_2e_2}(\omega) \tag{9-17}$$

This is one of the basic relations of random-signal theory and its proof will not be repeated here.

Suppose, for example, that a power-density spectrum of the form of relation (9-8), shown plotted in Figure 9-8, was desired for $e_3(t)$; i.e.,

$$\Phi_{e_3e_3}(\omega) = \frac{2\sigma_e^2\omega_0}{\omega^2 + \omega_0^2} \tag{9-18}$$

when, as given in relation (9-14),

$$\Phi_{e_2e_2}(\omega) = \frac{2E^2\lambda}{\omega^2 + \lambda^2} \tag{9-19}$$

[In relation (9-18), σ_e is the mean deviation desired of the signal $e_3(t)$.]

Practically by inspection it can be established that the necessary filter will be of the form

$$\begin{aligned}
G_{32}(s) &= \frac{\sigma_e}{E}\sqrt{\frac{\omega_0}{\lambda}}\left(\frac{s+\lambda}{s+\omega_0}\right) \\
&= \frac{\sigma_e}{E}\sqrt{\frac{\lambda}{\omega_0}}\left(\frac{1+s/\lambda}{1+s/\omega_0}\right)
\end{aligned} \tag{9-20}$$

Such a transfer function is simply represented by basic linear analog-computer elements. For $\omega_0 < \lambda$ the filter would have the amplitude characteristic shown plotted in Figure 9-14. If $\lambda \gg \omega_0$, the effect of this low-pass filtering would practically result in the amplitude probability density of $e_3(t)$ being Gaussian, as discussed in the preceding section. However, also as mentioned previously, the amplitude probability density of the simulated disturbance is usually important only when nonlinear systems are being evaluated.

Relation (9-20) was obtained by inspection. Actually, a simple mathe-

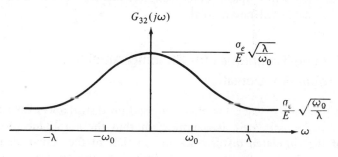

FIGURE 9-14

matical procedure may be employed for determining $G_{32}(s)$ in a more formal manner that does not depend on intuition. Both of the power-spectral densities can be expressed as the product of two conjugate functions of $(j\omega)$. For example,

$$\Phi_{e_2e_2}(\omega) = F_{e_2}(j\omega)F_{e_2}(-\omega) \tag{9-21}$$

where

$$F_{e_2}(j\omega) = \frac{\sqrt{2}\,E\sqrt{\lambda}}{\lambda + j\omega} \tag{9-22}$$

(In general, the above result may be obtained by factoring the denominator, expressing the power-density function as partial fractions, and using the method of undetermined coefficients to find the numerator terms.)

Also,

$$\Phi_{e_3e_3}(\omega) \quad F_{e_3}(j\omega)F_{e_3}(-j\omega) \tag{9-23}$$

where

$$F_{e_3}(j\omega) = \frac{\sqrt{2}\,\sigma_e\sqrt{\omega_0}}{\omega_0 + j\omega} \tag{9-24}$$

The correct $G_{32}(j\omega)$ function then is

$$G_{32}(j\omega) = \frac{F_{e_3}(j\omega)}{F_{e_2}(j\omega)} \tag{9-25}$$

where, for this specific example,

$$G_{32}(j\omega) = \frac{\sigma_e}{E}\sqrt{\frac{\omega_0}{\lambda}}\left(\frac{\lambda + j\omega}{\omega_0 + j\omega}\right) \tag{9-26}$$

If in the above $(j\omega)$ becomes s, relation (9-20) is obtained.

This method for finding the proper transfer function of the shaping filter may be used whenever the power-spectral densities involved are of a form that can be expressed as the ratio of polynomials in ω^2. When this is not the case, more ingenious techniques beyond the scope of this chapter are required. When one of the power-spectral density functions is empirical, it first is necessary to employ curve-fitting techniques in order to express it in the above-described polynomial form.

9-11   Analog Techniques for Shaping Amplitude Probability Densities

As stated previously, when the effect of random disturbances on nonlinear systems is to be simulated, it is important that the amplitude probability density of the simulated disturbance match that of the actual disturbance being simulated. Therefore, *after* the desired power-spectral density has been obtained by a shaping filter, as described in the preceding section, a second amplitude-shaping filter should be used to assure that the probability density is of the desired form as well. It is important that this amplitude-shaping filter *follow* the operation of the spectrum shaping filter because the former would modify the probability density.

The problem becomes that of the situation pictured in Figure 9-15. A random signal $x(t)$ of known (or determinable) probability density $f_x(x)$ is to be applied to a zero-memory filter (having no dynamics) that establishes the functional relationship $y = g(x)$. The output of this filter, $y(t)$, should have some specified probability density $f_y(y)$. The problem specifically is that of finding the necessary function $g(x)$.

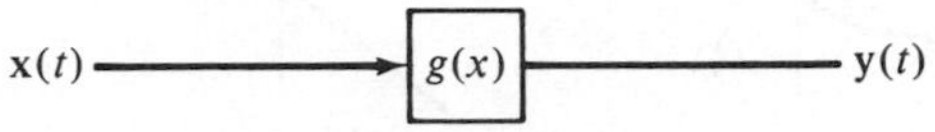

$$x(t) \longrightarrow \boxed{g(x)} \longrightarrow y(t)$$

FIGURE 9-15

There is no *unique* answer to the problem of determining $g(x)$; an infinite number of suitable functions exist. However, if it is specified that $g(x)$ must be a single-valued function of x (i.e., a true function) of a slope that is never negative, then a unique solution does exist for this condition. The solution, will, in fact, result in a simpler shaping filter than with any of the other solutions.

The relation between the probability densities $f_x(x)$ and $f_y(y)$ and the function $g(x)$ is more easily handled in terms of the *probability distributions* $F_x(x)$ and $F_y(y)$, instead. The probability distribution $F_x(x)$ is related to a corresponding probability density $f_x(x)$ as follows:

$$F_x(x) = \int_{-\infty}^{x} f_x(x)\, dx \tag{9-27}$$

Hence, of course,

$$f_x(x) = \frac{dF_x(x)}{dx} \tag{9-28}$$

and it is easily shown that

$$F_x(x) = P\{x(t) < x\} \tag{9-29}$$

As x approaches infinity, $F_x(x)$ must, of course, approach unity.

With the restriction on $g(x)$ stated above it can be shown that

$$F_x(x) = F_y[g(x)] \tag{9-30}$$

Figure 9-16 illustrates the graphical (nomographical) procedure that might be employed to determine $g(x)$, given $f_x(x)$ and $f_y(y)$. The relationships for $f_x(x)$ and $f_y(y)$ are integrated to obtain $F_x(x)$ and $F_y(y)$. Then, in step (1), a given value of x is selected. Projecting upward to (2), the corresponding $F_x(x)$ is found. Projecting horizontally, in accordance with relation (9-30), the corresponding y is found at (3). This is projected onto the $g(x)$

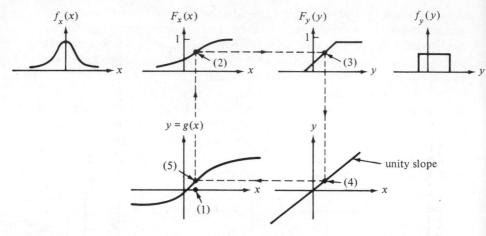

FIGURE 9-16

plot by first projecting downward to (4), and then horizontally to point (5), aligned vertically with the initial starting point (1). By repeating this procedure for a number of values of x, a curve of y versus x [i.e., the $g(x)$ relationship] may be drawn.

In some instances an analytic expression for x is possible. For example, if the available random signal $\mathbf{x}(t)$ is Gaussian with zero mean value, and [from relation (9-6)] is described by a probability density

$$f_x(x) = \frac{1}{\sqrt{2\pi}\sigma_x} \exp\left[-\frac{1}{2}\left(\frac{x}{\sigma_x}\right)^2\right]$$

and if the desired signal $\mathbf{y}(t)$ is to have a uniform probability density between $y = -a$ and $y = b$, then

$$f_y(y) = \frac{1}{a+b} \qquad \text{for } -a < y < b$$

$$= 0 \qquad \text{for } y \leq -a \text{ or } y \geq b$$

This is essentially the situation pictured in Figure 9-16.

In this example the required shaping function $g(x)$ can be determined directly. This is done by first expressing the corresponding probability distributions:

$$F_x(x) = \frac{1}{2} + \text{erf}\left(\frac{x}{\sigma_x}\right)$$

$$F_x(y) = \begin{cases} 0 & \text{for } y \leq -a \\ \dfrac{y+a}{b+a} & \text{for } -a < y < b \\ 1 & \text{for } y \geq b \end{cases}$$

Relation (9-30) may then be applied directly:

$$F_x(x) = \frac{1}{2} + \text{erf}\left(\frac{x}{\sigma_x}\right) = F_y(y) = \frac{y+a}{b+a} \qquad \text{for } -a < y < b$$

where y in the above is the required function, $g(x)$. Solving for y in the range where $f(y)$ is nonzero yields

$$y = -a + (a+b)\left[\frac{1}{2} + \text{erf}\left(\frac{x}{\sigma_x}\right)\right]$$

$$= \frac{b-a}{2} + (a+b)\,\text{erf}\left(\frac{x}{\sigma_x}\right)$$

or

$$g(x) = \frac{b-a}{2} + (a+b)\,\text{erf}\left(\frac{x}{\sigma_x}\right)$$

The general shape of this function is shown in Figure 9-17.

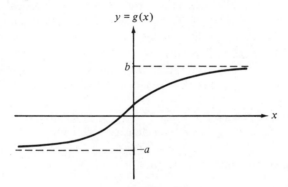

FIGURE 9-17

    With other probability densities it may not be possible to obtain a direct algebraic expression for $g(x)$, but it may be possible to obtain one for the inverse function, $g^{-1}(y) = x$. In some cases, however, no algebraic expression is obtainable and it is necessary to resort to the graphical operations shown in Figure 9-16, or their equivalent.

    It might be noted that to be "shapable" to other probability density forms, the input signal $x(t)$ should not consist of only discrete values [i.e., $f_x(x)$ should not contain *only* impulses]. For this reason the output of the multivibrator in Figure 9-12 would not be directly adaptable to probability-density shaping. However, if (as has been recommended above) the *spectral-density-shaping* filter was used first, its output would no longer contain discrete values and could be shaped to other probability-density forms.

    The operations indicated in Figure 9-16 are accomplished most easily by digital-computer means (unless a simple algebraic solution is obtainable as in the example just given). For purposes of analog simulation, this could be used as the basis of setting up a diode function generator that performed that shaping-filter function.

9-12   Digital Methods for Generating Random Disturbances

The subject of producing random variables by digital-computer means is one that has received wide attention and study [4]. The need for such methods arose originally not in connection with simulation, but rather in connection with the Monte Carlo method of problem solution.

A number of techniques have been proposed. Most but not all are repeatable, and therefore meet that usual requirement discussed in Section 9-8. Only such repeatable techniques will be discussed here. It may be argued that such repeatable random variables are, in the true statistical sense, deterministic, and not random at all. This is true, but it constitutes no impediment to their use in simulation problems. All such methods have a *period* at which their pattern will repeat. This also is no disadvantage, provided that the period is sufficiently long. Four criteria usually are employed to evaluate the suitability of random-variable generation techniques:

1. Length of the period.
2. Uniformity of the amplitude-density spectrum.
3. Small degree of autocorrelation.
4. Speed of computer execution.

The first criterion simply means that the period should be larger than the intended test duration. The second implies that a uniform probability density (Figure 9-3) is to be obtained and that the degree of true uniformity is to be a measure of quality. Of course, digital-computer programs cannot produce variables having other than a possibly large, but nevertheless finite, number of discrete values and the probability-density curve would consist only of impulses. The probability *distribution* would be a staircase type of function, as pictured in Figure 9-18. If this staircase function follows sufficiently closely a straight line of slope equal to $1/x_{\max}$, it is then an adequate approximation for the probability distribution of a random variable with a truly uniform density. It should be noted that in Figure 9-18 only positive values of the random variable are produced. This is the case for purposes of computational convenience; obviously the range can be shifted to negative values, just as the scale can easily be modified.

The third criterion, if met perfectly, would mean that zero correlation would result, corresponding to true white noise. This will not be the case with

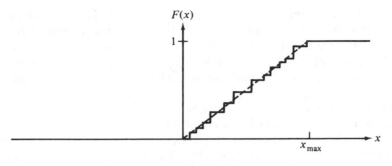

FIGURE 9-18

any of the methods that have been proposed, but only a reasonably small amount of autocorrelation (and consequent deviation of the power-spectral density from a white-noise form) should be considered allowable. The significance of the fourth criterion is obvious from the standpoint of economy of time and expense.

The only true criterion of merit is the applicability of the method used to the problem at hand. From this viewpoint it will be found that methods that are very satisfactory for some applications will show marked defects when applied to others. The person concerned with preparing the simulation program will consider random-variable generation to be a *tool*, not an end in itself. Hence, he ordinarily will care to devote little time to research on what is the best method for his purposes. A method that is adequate and does not present unexpected pitfalls will generally be all that he asks for. Fancier and faster methods may exist, but one apparent characteristic of such methods is their tendency to get into trouble when various situations arise, such as looping (i.e., suddenly encountering a repetitive pattern of very short period).

With these considerations in mind, the method to be suggested here for general simulation purposes is the one imposingly described as the *multiplicative congruent method."* The operation is described mathematically as follows:

$$x_{i+1} = ax_i(\text{mod } m) \tag{9-31}$$

This terminology, used in number theory, means simply that the last value of the variable, or x_i, is multiplied by a constant a and then divided, in the integer sense, by m; the next value of the variable, or x_{i+1}, is the *remainder*. For example, if $a = 8$, $m = 64$, $x_i = 11$, then x_{i+1} would be the remainder resulting when ax_i, or 88, is divided by 64, or $x_{i+1} = 24$.

In practice, it is recommended for binary machines [5] that

1. The starting value, x_0, be some odd number less than m.
2. $m = 2^i$, where i is some integer, naturally selected within the range

of the computer and in consideration of the fact that the period will be $m/4$. This period should be substantially larger than the expected duration of the run.

3. a should be of the order m (i.e., approximately $2^{1/2}$). It should also meet the criterion that $a = 8k \pm 3$, where k is any integer.

As an example, if it is expected that a series of 10,000 random numbers will be required, a reasonable value of m should be greater than 40,000, or, say, $m = 2^{15} = 32,768$. a should be in the vicinity of $2^{7.5}$ or 181. The closest value to this that satisfied the form $8k \pm 3$ is the integer 179; hence a is so selected. The random pattern developed will depend upon the starter x_0. Say $x_0 = 11$. Then

$$x_1 = 179 \cdot 11 (\text{mod } 32768) = 1969$$

$$x_2 = 179 \cdot 1969 (\text{mod } 32768) = 24,771$$

$$\text{etc.}$$

The range of x_i will be between zero and m (i.e., 0 to 32,768) but with it being noted that all the random numbers produced will be odd integers. The result can be translated and scaled to any range desired.

To obtain the fastest machine speed, the instructions for such a program should be given in binary-integer form, preferably in machine language.[2] Various techniques can be used to obtain a rapid execution, such as by utilizing register overflow to obtain the necessary remainder. The method best employed will depend upon the computer being used, and instructions are often furnished by the computer manufacturer for the most efficient utilization of this standard type of program.

When employing decimal-type machines, the rules for most efficient utilization of this method vary somewhat. Then:

1. The starting value x_0 again must be some odd number less than m.
2. $m = 10^i$, where again i is an integer, now selected on the basis of the period being $m/20$.
3. a should again be of the order of $\sqrt{m}$. It now should meet the requirement that $a = 200k \pm r$, where k may be any positive integer and r is 3, 11, 13, 19, 21, 27, 29, 37, 53, 59, 61, 67, 69, 77, 83, or 91.

Let the same situation be considered as before where a series of 10,000 random numbers is required. Since the period is $m/20$, m should be greater

---

[2]With user-oriented languages such as Fortran or Algol, the number of significant digits handled is usually inadequate unless special forms of operation, such as double precision, are employed or unless the mod function is available in the program library.

than 200,000. Hence $m = 10^6$ is chosen. a should be of the order of $\sqrt{m}$, or 1000. To meet the recommended form $a = 200k \pm r$, let $k = 5$ and $r = 3$; then $a = 5 \cdot 200 + 3 = 1003$. Then, with $m = 10^6$ and $a = 1003$, let the first two steps be considered with $x_0 = 11$:

$$x_1 = 10003 \cdot 11 (\text{mod } 10^6) = 11{,}033$$

$$x_2 = 1003 \cdot 11033 (\text{mod } 10^6) = 66{,}099$$

etc.

The range of x_i will now be between zero and m (i.e., between 0 and 1,000,000). Again, only odd interger values of x will result.

Again, the most effective programming of such a decimal digital operation is often furnished by the computer manufacturer. This has been studied by many, and there are published reports describing the most effective techniques for executing such a program [6].

Often the computer being used will contain one or more programs for random-number generation in its library, and use of one of these will relieve the person preparing the simulation program from the necessity of preparing the random-number generation program as well. However, many of these library programs were designed with Monte Carlo methods in mind, where the white-noise requirement generally is not as important as it is in simulation studies. For this reason, before employing such a program, it may be well to examine both the probability density and spectral density by the general approach discussed in Section 9-7.

9-13   Autocorrelation Function

To analyze the statistical nature of random-number sequences, it is most convenient to consider the inverse transform of the spectral density (i.e., the *autocorrelation function*). This probably will be well known to many readers in far greater detail than the brief description that follows here.

As mentioned, the autocorrelation function $\psi_{xx}(\tau)$ is the inverse Fourier transform of $\Phi_{xx}(\omega)$; i.e.,

$$\psi_{xx}(\tau) = \frac{1}{2\pi} \int_{-\infty}^{\infty} \Phi_{xx}(\omega) e^{j\omega\tau} \, d\tau \tag{9-32}$$

and, conversely,

$$\Phi_{rr}(\omega) = \int_{-\infty}^{\infty} \psi_{xx}(\tau) e^{-j\omega\tau} \, d\tau \tag{9-33}$$

If we are willing to assume that the signal being dealt with is stationary, then the autocorrelation function may be determined from the relation

$$\psi_{xx}(\tau) = E[\mathbf{x}(t)\mathbf{x}(t + \tau)] = \overline{\mathbf{x}(t)\mathbf{x}(t + \tau)} \tag{9-34}$$

where E represents the expected value (i.e., the average value of the product as averaged over a statistically sufficiently long averaging time).

For theoretical analysis purposes, it is frequently simpler to employ relation (9-34) first, and then to obtain the power-spectral density by means of relation (9-33). (Prior to the development of the FFT algorithms, this procedure was also that used for the analysis of empirical data.)

9-14   Statistical Nature of Random-Number Generator Outputs

Before considering means by which the outputs of digital random-number generators may be shaped to represent the disturbance being simulated, the statistical nature of the random signals produced by these generation procedures should be understood. All the procedures mentioned produce what is, at least approximately, a uniform probability density of integers ranging from $x = 1$ to $x = m$. That is,[3]

$$f(x) = \begin{cases} \dfrac{1}{m} & \text{for } 0 < x \le m \\ 0 & \text{for } x \le 0 \text{ or } x > m \end{cases} \tag{9-35}$$

The mean value of any random variable may be computed from its probability density as follows:

$$E(x) = \int_{-\infty}^{\infty} x f(x)\, dx \tag{9-36}$$

Applying this relation to (9-35) yields the obvious result

$$E(x) = \int_{0}^{m} x \frac{1}{m}\, dx = \frac{m}{2} \tag{9-37}$$

The mean-squared value of any random signal may be determined by the relation

$$E(x^2) = \int_{-\infty}^{\infty} x^2 f(x)\, dx \tag{9-38}$$

Applying this to relation (9-35) yields the result

$$E(x^2) = \int_{0}^{m} x^2 \frac{1}{m}\, dx = \frac{m^2}{3} \tag{9-39}$$

The mean deviation is defined as the mean-square value *after* the mean value has been removed, or is

$$\sigma_x^2 = \int_{\infty}^{\infty} [x - E(x)]^2 f(x)\, dx \tag{9-40}$$

and can easily be shown to be

$$\sigma_x^2 = E(x^2) - [E(x)]^2 \tag{9-41}$$

[3]It is assumed that the output of the random-number generator has been modified by an obvious algorithm to include even as well as odd integers from 1 to m.

Hence the random signal produced by the digital means described has a mean deviation of

$$\sigma_x^2 = \frac{m^2}{3} - \left(\frac{m}{2}\right)^2 = \frac{m^2}{12} \tag{9-42}$$

Therefore, the first step to produce a purely random signal from the random sequence of numbers generated is to remove the d.c. (i.e., subtract the mean value). The signal remaining after this is done will be designated as $x(t)$. Its autocorrelation function and corresponding power-spectral density are now to be determined.

Since whatever signal is produced by the digital signal generator at the beginning of an iteration interval Δt is assumed to apply throughout the interval, such a random signal is equivalent to a stepwise continuous signal as shown in Figure 9-19.

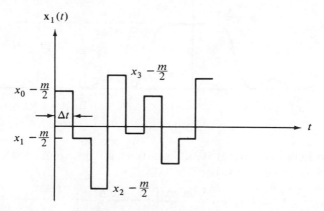

FIGURE 9-19

If each number generated, x_i, is statistically independent, then the autocorrelation function of the above signal can be determined by use of relation (9-34), which is of the form shown in Figure 9-20. Inevitable imperfections in the white-noise properties of the random-number generation process will result in the presence of some amount of autocorrelation for values of $|\tau|$ greater than Δt.

By employing relation (9-33), the corresponding power-spectral density of the random signal $x_1(t)$ may be established as

$$\Phi_{x_1 x_1}(\omega) = \sigma_x^2 \, \Delta t \frac{1 - \cos(\omega \, \Delta t)}{\frac{1}{2}(\omega \, \Delta t)^2}$$

$$= \frac{m^2 \, \Delta t}{12} \left[\frac{1 - \cos(\omega \, \Delta t)}{\frac{1}{2}(\omega \, \Delta t)^2} \right] \tag{9-43}$$

When plotted, this spectral density will appear as in Figure 9-21.

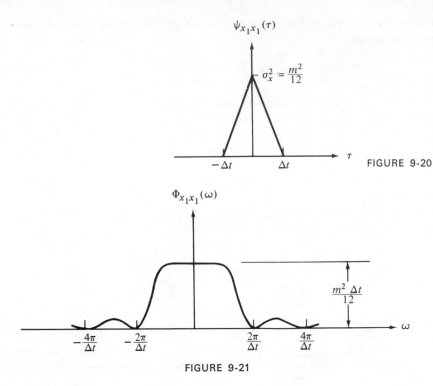

FIGURE 9-20

FIGURE 9-21

If the iteration interval is sufficiently small (i.e., $\omega\,\Delta t \ll 1$), relation (9-43) becomes approximately

$$\Phi_{x_1 x_1}(\omega) = \frac{m^2\,\Delta t}{12}\left[1 - \frac{(\omega\,\Delta t)^2}{12}\right] \tag{9-44}$$

and if $\omega\,\Delta t$ is small enough, for the range of frequencies ω involved in the simulation problem, it may be considered that operation takes place on the flat part of the spectrum curve near $\omega = 0$; i.e., it may be considered that the signal is white noise with a constant spectrum of

$$\Phi_{x_1 x_1}(\omega) = \frac{m^2\,\Delta t}{12} \tag{9-45}$$

It is on this basis that shaping filters will be designed to determine the actual power-spectral density desired to represent the disturbance.

9-15 Shaping the Spectral Density of Random Disturbances in Digital Form

The same general principles are employed for the purpose of shaping the spectral density of random disturbances when they appear in digital form as are used for those appearing in analog form. These principles have been discussed in Section 9-10. The necessary modifying-filter transfer function, $G_{yx_1}(s)$, is determined. From this the digital counterpart is established most easily by means of z-transform theory, as discussed in Chapter 3.

Suppose, for example, that the power-spectral density of the actual disturbance to be simulated, $y(t)$, is to be of the form illustrated in Figure 9-8 and as described mathematically in relation (9-8). The shaped random-output signal then has a spectral density

$$\Phi_{yy}(\omega) = \frac{2\sigma_y^2 \omega_0}{\omega^2 + \omega_0^2} \tag{9-46}$$

where σ_y is the mean deviation desired of the random signal and ω_0 is the desired half-power frequency. The input signal to the filter is $x_1(t)$, whose spectral density has been described in relation (9-45).

Factoring $\Phi_{x_1x_1}(\omega)$ and $\Phi_{yy}(\omega)$ into a product of conjugate functions of $j\omega$, as discussed in Section 9-10, leads to

$$\Phi_{x_1x_1}(\omega) = E_{x_1}(j\omega)F_{x_1}(-j\omega)$$
$$\Phi_{yy}(\omega) = F_y(j\omega)F_y(-j\omega)$$

where

$$F_{x_1}(j\omega) = m\sqrt{\frac{\Delta t}{12}} \tag{9-47}$$

and

$$F_y(j\omega) = \frac{\sigma_y\sqrt{2\omega_0}}{j\omega + \omega_0} \tag{9-48}$$

Then, from relation (9-25), the necessary shaping-filter transfer function is

$$G_{yx_1}(j\omega) = \frac{\sigma_y}{m}\sqrt{\frac{24\omega_0}{\Delta t}}\left(\frac{1}{j\omega + \omega_0}\right) \tag{9-49}$$

or, in operational form,

$$G_{yx_1}(s) = \frac{\sigma_y}{m}\sqrt{\frac{24\omega_0}{\Delta t}}\left(\frac{1}{s + \omega_0}\right) \tag{9-50}$$

The last expression is the transfer function desired. However, it is recalled that this shaping operation is to be carried out by digital means. One way of doing this is by drawing the block diagram representing this transfer function and then, when integration is called for, using one of the methods of numerical integration discussed in Chapter 3. However, an easier method, which will produce more satisfactory results, is to determine the z transform of the transfer function [i.e., $G_{yx_1}(z)$]. By employing the procedure of Appendix 3A, the time-domain version of $G_{yx_1}(s)$, or $g_{yx_1}(t)$, is first expressed as

$$g_{yx_1}(t) = \frac{\sigma_y}{m}\sqrt{\frac{24\omega_0}{\Delta t}}\, e^{-\omega_0 t} \tag{9-51}$$

or in terms of the number of iteration intervals, n,

$$g_{yx_1}(n) = \frac{\sigma_y}{m}\sqrt{\frac{24\omega_0}{\Delta t}}\,e^{-\omega_0\Delta t n} \tag{9-52}$$

Then by employing tabulation (2) of Table 3A-1,

$$G_{yx_1}(z) = \frac{\sigma_y}{m}\sqrt{\frac{24\omega_0}{\Delta t}}\left(\frac{z}{z - e^{-\omega_0\Delta t}}\right) = \frac{Y(z)}{X_1(z)} \tag{9-53}$$

This can be expressed in operational ($\mathfrak{z}$) form as

$$\frac{y(n)}{x_1(n)} = \frac{\sigma_y}{m}\sqrt{\frac{24\omega_0}{\Delta t}}\left(\frac{\mathfrak{z}}{\mathfrak{z} - e^{-\omega_0\Delta t}}\right)$$

$$= \frac{2\sigma_y}{m}\sqrt{\frac{6\omega_0}{\Delta t}}\left(\frac{1}{1 - e^{-\omega_0\Delta t}\mathfrak{z}^{-1}}\right)$$

or as

$$y(n) = e^{-\omega_0\Delta t}y(n-1) + \frac{2\sigma_y}{m}\sqrt{\frac{6\omega_0}{\Delta t}}\,x_1(n) \tag{9-54}$$

The procedure for generating this disturbance is pictured in block-diagram form in Figure 9-22.

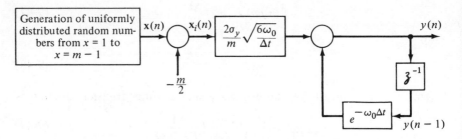

FIGURE 9-22

As a specific numerical example, let it be supposed that the numbers are being generated on a decimal machine where m has been selected as 10^6. The time-iteration interval being used in the simulation process is, for example, $\Delta t = 0.001$ sec. A random disturbance $y(t)$ is desired with a power-spectral density of the form expressed in relation (9-46) with $\sigma_y = 100$ and $\omega_0 = 5$ sec^{-1}. Relation (9-54) would then become

$$y(n) = 0.995y(n-1) + 0.03464x_1(n)$$

With this decimal-machine procedure, the period of random-number repetition is $m/20$ or, for this example, 50,000 numbers, representing a problem time duration of 50,000 $\Delta t = 50$ sec. Since $\omega_0 = 5$, this duration corresponds to $\omega_0 t = 250$, probably an adequate statistical averaging time for many problems. However, if this problem-time duration should prove to be inadequate, it would be necessary to select a higher value of m.

9-16 Shaping the Probability Density of Random Disturbances

Exactly the same procedures apply for shaping the amplitude probability density of random disturbances when they are presented in digital form as have been discussed for those in analog form in Section 9-11. Again, such shaping, when necessary, should take place *after* the power-spectral density has been shaped.

      Although the output of the random-number generator is usually of the type with a uniform probability density (as it is with the specific methods described previously here), the effect of most spectral-shaping operations will be to modify this probability density to an essentially Gaussian form. This will be the case whenever the spectral-density-shaping feature has a low-pass effect, as it will in most applications, and as it certainly would for the specific example of the preceding section. Then if, for example, a uniform probability density was desired, it would be necessary to employ the type of shaping function shown in Figure 9-17. When the shaping function cannot be expressed in an analytic form involving functions available as subroutines in the digital-computer library, it will be necessary to prepare an empirical look-up table, supplemented by suitable interpolation procedures.

9-17 Generation of Pseudorandom Disturbances by Superposing Sinusoids

One method, often very convenient, for simulating random disturbances is by means of superposed sinusoidal signals. This procedure has the advantage of providing directly the spectral density desired and eliminating the need for a later shaping filter. It also produces what is essentially a Gaussian form of amplitude probability density.

      This sinusoidal method is based upon a discrete frequency sampling of the power-spectral density. As an example, let a spectral density as plotted in Figure 9-23 represent the spectrum desired. For both the positive and negative ranges of ω, the area under the curve is divided into m parts of equal area. This is shown in Figure 9-24 with $m = 5$; in practice a higher value of m would normally be employed.

      For each of the ranges of ω when so divided, this portion of the curve

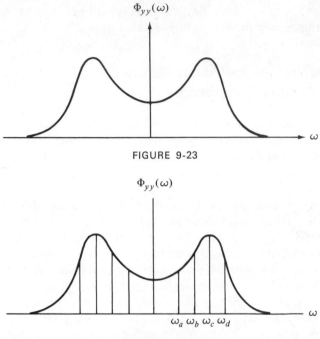

FIGURE 9-23

FIGURE 9-24

is now replaced by an impulse function located at the frequency that divides each of these areas into two equal parts; this impulse replaces the portion of the spectrum whose area it bisects. The total area under the curve will be $2\pi\sigma_y^2$; this area is divided into $2m$ portions (considering the negative as well as positive range of ω). Hence the size of each impulse should be $\pi\sigma_y^2/m$. This is shown in Figure 9-25. Every spectrum line so created, designated as being at the frequency ω_k, is matched by a corresponding spectrum line at the frequency $-\omega_k$. The pair of positive and negative spectra for each value of k comprises a steady-state sinusoidal component of frequency ω_k of a fixed but randomly selected phase angle and with a mean deviation (i.e., rms value) equal to $\sigma_y^2/\sqrt{m}$. That is, the approximation of the random disturbance with a spectral density as pictured in Figure 9-23 consists of the sum of such sinusoids, or

$$\mathbf{y}(t) = \frac{\sqrt{2}\,\sigma_y}{\sqrt{m}} \sum_{k=1}^{m} \sin{(\omega_k t + \phi_k)} \qquad (9\text{-}55)$$

ϕ_k is any randomly selected phase angle, different for each of the m sinusoidal components.

If m could be increased without limit while the above procedure was followed, a truly random signal having exactly the desired spectral density of Figure 9-23 could be generated in this fashion. Actually, a relatively small

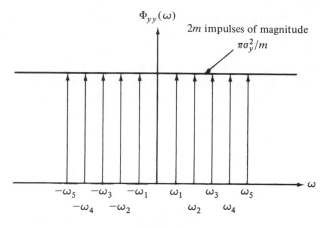

FIGURE 9-25

value of m (e.g., $m = 10$) will result in approximations that are adequate for many simulation purposes. The actual signal produced is, of course, deterministic (just as it was when random numbers were generated by digital techniques), but for simulation purposes it may be considered as random.

This technique may be employed with both analog and digital simulation methods. With analog methods it is necessary to establish m different and independent sine-wave generators (each requiring two integrators and one inverter). It is obvious that with analog simulation a considerable amount of equipment might be required when this method is used. With digital simulation this method places no great demand on computer storage facilities; however, it does require the program's "looking up" m sinusoidal functions for every time iteration, a somewhat slow process.

To avoid a pattern repetition during the simulation process, the frequencies ω_1 to ω_m should not bear an integer relationship with each other (i.e., they should have no subharmonics in common). With analog techniques the fact that the sinusoidal generators are independent will ordinarily guarantee this. With digital generation of random signals by this method, special precautions should be observed in this regard.

As an example, suppose it is found that the frequencies required to simulate a given random disturbance are

$$\omega_1 = 0.50 \qquad \omega_5 = 1.75$$
$$\omega_2 = 1.20 \qquad \omega_6 = 1.80$$
$$\omega_3 = 1.50 \qquad \omega_7 = 1.95$$
$$\omega_4 = 1.65$$

It ordinarily would not be satisfactory to employ the above list of frequencies directly, expressed to merely two places after the decimal point as listed (in spite of the fact that this represents the highest degree of precision warranted by the data). If these specific frequencies were employed, there would be a common subharmonic of $\omega = 0.05$ rad/sec and hence a period of pattern repetition of $2\pi/0.05 = 31.4$ sec. To extend this repetition period by a considerable factor, the frequencies are expressed to one additional decimal place and the last digit is then adjusted so that the complete series of digits representing any one frequency (neglecting the decimal point) is a prime number. For example, the above list would be modified to

$$\omega_1 = 0.499 \qquad \omega_5 = 1.753$$
$$\omega_2 = 1.201 \qquad \omega_6 = 1.801$$
$$\omega_3 = 1.499 \qquad \omega_7 = 1.951$$
$$\omega_4 = 1.657$$

All the digital sequences listed above [e.g., the numbers 499, 1201, etc.] are prime numbers. The only common factor is 0.001; hence this is the basic subharmonic. The period of repetition will be $2\pi/0.001 = 6280$ sec. If this still should prove to be too short, it would be necessary to express the frequencies to more decimal places.

Another question of importance with this method relates to its repeatability (see Section 9-8). When this is a consideration, analog methods employing this technique may not suffice. Even with supposedly the same adjustments, the actual frequencies and phase relations produced by the various analog sine-wave generators may differ slightly from one run to the next because of minor variations in voltage, temperature, etc. Hence, unless the runs were unusually short, the random signal produced would not be repeated exactly every time a run was made. With the digital generation of random signals by this method, on the other hand, the results obtained will be exactly repeatable.

As the number of sinusoids employed, m, is increased indefinitely, the probability density of their sum approaches a Gaussian form. This results from the *central-limit theorem* of statistics. In practice, however, it can be shown that even a small number of sinusoidal components (e.g., $m = 10$) will result in a reasonably good approximation of a Gaussian probability density.

9-18   Evaluation of Systems Subjected
to Random Disturbances

The purpose of applying simulated random disturbances to models of systems is almost always for the purpose of comparison (i.e., to compare one system technique with another or to determine the optimum adjustment of parameters). To accomplish such comparisons, some *figure of merit* or *figure of demerit* must be established.

Depending upon the problem, various figures of merit (or demerit) are proposed. For example:

1. The time average value of some function, $w(t)$, or

$$w = \lim_{T \to \infty} \frac{1}{T} \int_0^T w(t)\, dt$$

where $w(t)$ is a *weighting function*. $w(t)$ may represent a favorable condition; in this case the maximum obtainable value of the average is desired, the average being a figure of merit. It may represent an unfavorable condition; then the minimum obtainable average value is desired and this average used as a figure of demerit.
2. The *proportion* of time that some critical boundary value is exceeded by a variable of interest.
3. The *number* of times that some critical boundary value is crossed by a variable of interest.

Other criteria might also be employed in other problems. The significance of the three types listed above is explained best by example.

If the problem is one of control, quality is often measured by the control error or difference between the ideal value of the output being controlled and the actual value; it is this error that is to be minimized. This error, in response to stochastic disturbances, will be a function of time and hence might be expressed as $e(t)$. What the minimization of $e(t)$ actually means is to be established; this depends upon the criterion employed. It would not suffice to use $e(t)$ itself as the weighting function $w(t)$, because then the figure of demerit corresponding to the integral expression above would be

$$W = \lim_{T \to \infty} \frac{1}{T} \int_0^T e(t)\, dt = E[e(t)]$$

(where $E[e(t)]$ denotes the mean or expected value of $e(t)$). This integral simply corresponds to the average value; making the average value of error zero certainly is no indication of satisfactory performance because it does not account for large but compensating positive and negative errors.

A more realistic weighting function sometimes employed is the *absolute* value of the error; i.e., $w(t) = |e(t)|$ and the figure of demerit to be minimized is

$$W = \lim_{T \to \infty} \frac{1}{T} \int_0^T |e(t)|\, dt = E[|e(t)|]$$

Another weighting function used still more frequently is based on $w(t) =$

$e^2(t)$. The figure of demerit then is

$$W = \lim_{T \to \infty} \frac{1}{T} \int_0^T e^2(t)\, dt = E[e^2(t)]$$

The figure of demerit thus obtained is the mean-square value of the error.

All the figures of demerit expressed above correspond to *expected values* of various functions of $e(t)$. These time-averaging relations are based upon the error $e(t)$ being an *ergodic* function of time as this term is defined in statistical theory. For our purposes here, it means simply that probability averages may be measured in terms of time averages.

Often, more complex weighting functions are used. In a control system, for example, it may be desirable to minimize the error $e(t)$ but not at the expense of unreasonable fuel consumption $f(t)$. The weighting function might then be some positive definite function of both $e(t)$ and $f(t)$ with proper relative weights applied to each of these; it might, for example, be represented by a cost function $ae^2(t) + bf^2(t)$, integrated and averaged over a sufficiently long period of time.

It is not the purpose here to go into details of how the weighting function might be selected to constitute an adequate criterion of merit or cost. This consideration will vary from one application to the next and considerable judgment and knowledge of the application will be required if a meaningful cost function is to be developed; without this the most sophisticated and elaborate of computer evaluation or optimization programs would produce results of little significance.

9-19   Techniques for Measuring the Time Average of a Weighting Function

The relationship for the time average of a weighting function,

$$W = \lim_{T \to \infty} \frac{1}{T} \int_0^T w(t)\, dt = E[w(t)]$$

implies averaging over an interval T of infinite duration. In practice, of course, this not only is impossible but unnecessary; it merely is necessary that T exceed what loosely has been called the *statistical averaging time*. This time can be determined by experiment.

With analog equipment, averaging is generally accomplished by applying the signal representing $w(t)$ to a low-pass filter. A simple filter, adequate for this purpose, has the transfer function

$$\frac{1}{1 + \tau_f s}$$

where τ_f is of the order of the statistical averaging time. With τ_f sufficiently long, an observation of the filter's output eventually will indicate (in a time interval roughly equal to $10\tau_f$) a steady value (if the random disturbance applied is truly stationary). This value denotes the average that is desired. The analog arrangement for accomplishing this is pictured in Figure 9-26. As stated above, the adjustment of τ_f is conducted most easily on an experimental basis. If τ_f is too low, the output indication of the average value will not settle down but will fluctuate with a significant amplitude. If too high, it will take too long a time before the final steady-state value of W is reached.

With digital simulation it might be thought that finding the average value of a function by means of the straightforward arithmetic approach (i.e., by summing all values and then dividing by the number of items entered) would be adequate. In practice this has several disadvantages when dealing with random functions. First, it assumes a stationary random function and will not exhibit any lack of this property that might exist. Also, after a certain point in the summing operation, which may not have been carried far enough to represent an adequate statistical averaging time, the effect of the later entries may be partially or completely nullified by roundoff errors. For this reason some other averaging technique is preferred.

One simple and generally adequate averaging technique is simply the digital counterpart of the method shown in Figure 9-26. Figure 9-27 is the block diagram that corresponds to this analog filter. Because normally $\tau_f \gg \Delta t$, simple rectangular integration, method 1a-1, will suffice to handle the time integration indicated. Assuming here that the values of $w(t)$ are supplied at some uniform interval Δt, the block diagram for this digital procedure will be as shown in Figure 9-28.

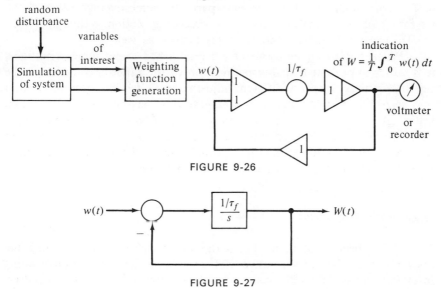

FIGURE 9-26

FIGURE 9-27

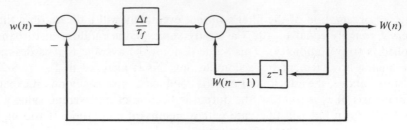

FIGURE 9-28

The actual operation is described by

$$W(n) = \frac{W(n-1) + (\Delta t/\tau_f)w(n)}{1 + \Delta t/\tau_f} \tag{9-56}$$

Relation (9-56) represents a relatively simple algorithm that may be used for this digital filtering operation. In view of its simplicity, no flow chart is shown here and, as a matter of fact, the use of a special subprogram module for this purpose would hardly be justified.

9-20   Optimization of Systems Subject to Random Disturbances

When systems are subject to random disturbances or random variations of parameters, these may be simulated by the methods described in this chapter Optimum adjustments may then be established, using the methods of Chapter 8. The cost function will be, at least partially, some average value of the weighting function as discussed in the preceding section, although it may involve some determinate (nonrandom) factors as well.

When optimizing adjustments are established under these conditions, it is rather important that the specification of the random disturbances be repeated exactly for every different adjustment. Otherwise, even after what may seem like a sufficiently long averaging time has been used, the actual statistical properties of what are supposedly disturbances of the same statistical nature actually will be sufficiently different so that it will be difficult to find a true optimum. In other words, one of the repeatable methods mentioned at the start of Section 9-8 should be employed.

Suggested Problems

9-1. It has been established that a random disturbance representing the instantaneous height of a sea wave, $y(t)$, under a particular situation resulting in almost sinusoidal swells has a normal probability density and a power-spectral density given by

$$\Phi_{yy}(\omega) = \frac{20\omega^2}{\omega^4 + 2.04\omega^2 + 1} \text{ ft}^2\text{-sec}$$

This disturbance is to be represented for the purpose of computer simulation.

(a) Assume that an analog simulation program is being prepared employing a 10 V computer. One volt is to represent one foot of instantaneous wave height. A random-signal generator is available that produces essentially white noise up to 100 Hz and has an essentially normal probability density. The output of this generator is adjustable but not calibrated.

   Establish a program for producing a simulation of this disturbance. Include a procedure for establishing the proper amplitude.

(b) Assume that a digital-computer simulation program is to be prepared and that a source of random numbers is available in the computer library ranging from 1 to 9999. These numbers have a uniform probability density and may be considered as white noise. The iteration interval Δt is to be 0.001 sec. Prepare a digital program for shaping the signal produced by the random-number generator so that the result will simulate this sea wave.

9-2. A milling machine feeds the work at a constant rate and the cutter is adjusted by an automatic control system to cut for a desired depth (command) x, where $x = x(t)$. Considering an ensemble of parts to be machined, it is found that the function x is random and can be described by a triangular probability density ranging from zero to 0.3 in. as shown in Figure P9-2. For this feed speed the time variation of $x(t)$ is described by a power-spectral density as follows:

$$\Phi_{xx}(\omega) = 0.2\pi\delta(\omega) + \frac{10^{-4}}{\omega^2 + 10^{-4}} \quad \text{in.}^2\text{-sec}$$

This command signal is to be simulated on a computer.

(a) Assume that an analog simulation program is to be prepared using a 100 V computer where 1 V is to represent a command of $x(t) = 5 \times 10^{-3}$ in. The same type of signal generator is available

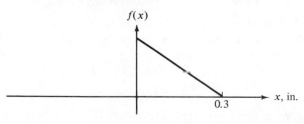

FIGURE P9-2

as is described in Problem 9-1(a). Prepare a program for producing this simulated signal.

(b) Assume that a digital simulation program is to be prepared for this problem. The same source of random numbers is available as is described in Problem 9-1(b). The iteration interval Δt is to be 10^{-5} sec. Prepare a digital program for shaping the signal produced by the random-number generator so that the result will simulate this sine wave.

9-3. In Problem 9-1 it has been decided to employ the principle of superposed sinusoidal signals to simulate the sea-wave effect rather than employing truly random sources. Because the spectral density is concentrated about the frequency $\omega = 1$, it is considered appropriate to employ only five sinusoidal components. Prepare both analog and digital programs for simulating $x(t)$ in this manner. The repetition period of the random disturbance produced should not be less than 5,000 sec.

9-4. In an information-transmission system the problem is one of separating signal and noise. Some separation is possible because the noise consists of sharp impulses of high amplitude but short duration, while the signal is of a more continuous nature. Both the signal and noise have essentially normal probability densities. The power-spectral density of the noise, $\mathbf{n}(t)$, has been established as

$$\Phi_{nn}(\omega) = \frac{2 \times 10^8 \omega^2}{\omega^4 + 10^{12}\omega^2 + 10^{18}} \quad \text{V}^2\text{-sec}$$

The useful signal to be transmitted, $\mathbf{x}(t)$, is statistically independent and its power-spectral density has been established as

$$\Phi_{xx}(\omega) = \frac{2 \times 10^6}{\omega^2 + 10^8} \quad \text{V}^2\text{-sec}$$

It is proposed that the transmission error resulting from noise be reduced by simple limiting; i.e., a limiting filter will be employed having an output of

$$\mathbf{y}(t) = \begin{cases} \mathbf{x}(t) + \mathbf{n}(t) & \text{when } |\mathbf{x}(t) + \mathbf{n}(t)| < y_L \\ y_L & \text{when } |\mathbf{x}(t) + \mathbf{n}(t)| \geq y_L \\ -y_L & \text{when } |\mathbf{x}(t) + \mathbf{n}(t)| \leq -y_L \end{cases}$$

where y_L is the adjustable limit of the filter.

The block diagram describing the problem appears in Figure P9-4. The difference between the output signal $\mathbf{y}(t)$ and the useful input signal $\mathbf{x}(t)$ is described as the error $\mathbf{e}(t)$. The figure of demerit is

$$W = E[\mathbf{e}^2(t)]$$

A program is to be prepared to evaluate W as a function of y_L so that the optimum value of y_L might be established. Assume that provisions have

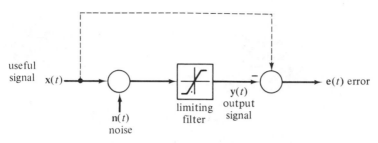

FIGURE P9-4

already been made for furnishing the signals $\mathbf{x}(t)$ and $\mathbf{n}(t)$ with their correct power-spectral densities and probability density.

    (a) Prepare an analog program for handling this problem. Assume that a 100 V computer is available and that one machine volt corresponds to one "problem volt."

    (b) Prepare a digital-computer program for handling this problem.

9-5. Prepare a digital program that will automatically find the optimum conditions for the program done in Problem 9-4.

References

1. A. Papoulis, *Probability, Random Variables, and Stochastic Processes* (New York: McGraw-Hill, Inc., 1965).

2. E. O. Brigham and R. E. Morrow, The Fast Fourier Transform, *IEEE Spectrum* (Dec. 1967).

3. H. Low, Noise and Statistical Techniques, *Handbook of Automation, Computation and Control* (New York: John Wiley & Sons, 1959), Vol. 2, Chap. 26.

4. R. P. Chambers, *Random-Number Generation on Digital Computers, IEEE Spectrum* (Feb. 1967), 48–56.

5. V. D. Barnett, The Behavior of Pseudo-Random Sequences Generated on Computers by the Multiplicative Congruential Method, *Mathematical Computation*, Vol. 16 (1962), 63–69.

6. J. L. Allard, A. R. Dobell, and T. E. Hull, Mixed Congruential Random Number Generators for Decimal Machines, *Journal of the Association of Computing Machinery*, Vol. 9 (1966), 432–33.

Appendix 9A:
Data-Smoothing Algorithm

The subject of data smoothing is part of the broader subject of *regression analysis* used extensively in statistics and many sophisticated techniques have been developed.[4] The method described here, leading to the subprogram called SMOOTH, is one of the most elementary methods and is based on obtaining the coefficients of an approximating polynomial of a prescribed order, $L - 1$, that will provide the least-mean-squares fit.

Say that there are N number pairs corresponding to N coordinate points relating y to x. It is desired to obtain some polynomial relationship $f(x)$ so that $f(x)$ will be the best approximation of y. Just what is meant by best depends upon the application, but it is assumed here that the best fit will be obtained when the sum of the squares of the discrepancy between y and $f(x)$ at each abscissa value x is a minimum. This discrepancy might be called d and would be computed as:

[4]B. W. Arden, *Digital Computing* (Reading, Mass.: Addison-Wesley Book Company Inc., 1963), Chap. 15.

$$d_1 = f(x_1) - y_1$$
$$d_2 = f(x_2) - y_2$$
$$d_3 = f(x_3) - y_3$$

$$\cdot$$
$$\cdot \tag{9A-1}$$

$$d_i = f(x_i) - y_i$$

$$\cdot$$
$$\cdot$$

$$d_L = f(x_L) - y_L$$

The sum of the squares of the discrepancies might then be written as σ^2:

$$\sigma^2 = \sum_{k=1}^{N} d_k^2 = \sum_{k=1}^{N} [f(x_k) - y_k]^2 \tag{9A-2}$$

$f(x)$ is to be such that σ^2 is a minimum. As we are restricting $f(x)$ to a polynomial form (with no evidence whatsoever that this form is the most applicable; it simply is the easiest to use), $f(x)$ may be written as[5]

$$f(x) = \sum_{j=1}^{L} a_j x^{j-1} \tag{9A-3}$$

Relation (9A-2) then becomes

$$\sigma^2 = \sum_{k=1}^{N} \left(\sum_{j=1}^{L} a_j x_k^{j-1} - y_k \right)^2 = \text{minimum} \tag{9A-4}$$

These minimum conditions are obtained only if the partial derivative of σ^2 with respect to each a, from a_1 to a_L, equals zero; i.e., if

$$\frac{d\sigma^2}{da_i} = \frac{d}{da_i} \sum_{k=1}^{N} \left(a_j x_k^{j-1} - y_k^2 \right)^2 = 0$$

for all values of i from 1 to L, or if

$$\sum_{k=1}^{N} 2 \left(\sum_{j=1}^{L} a_j x_k^{j-1} - y_k \right)^2 = 0 \tag{9A-5}$$

for all values of i from 1 to L.

The above may be simplified by omitting the common factor 2 and writing it as

$$\sum_{k=1}^{N} \sum_{j=1}^{L} x_k^{j-1} x_k^{i-1} a_j = \sum_{k=1}^{N} x_k^{i-1} y_k$$

[5] It would be more logical to write $f(x)$ as

$$\sum_{j=0}^{L} a_j x^j$$

The form of (9A-3) was used instead because of the subscript limitations of Fortran; these limitations do not apply to Algol 60 or PL/1.

for all values of i from 1 to L. In the above the order of summation may be interchanged:

$$\sum_{j=1}^{L} \sum_{k=1}^{N} x_k^{j-1} x_k^{i-1} a_j = \sum_{k=1}^{N} x_k^{i-1} y_k \tag{9A-6}$$

for all values of i from 1 to L. The above represents L simultaneous equations with L unknowns and corresponds to the matrix relationship

$$\left[A \right] \begin{bmatrix} a^1 \\ \cdot \\ \cdot \\ \cdot \\ a_L \end{bmatrix} = \begin{bmatrix} B \end{bmatrix} \tag{9A-7}$$

where A is an $L \times L$ matrix, the element in the ith row and jth column being

$$A_{ij} = \sum_{k=1}^{N} x_k^{j-1} x_k^{i-1} \tag{9A-8}$$

and B is a vector array of L elements where the $i$the element would be

$$B_i = \sum_{k=1}^{N} x_k^{i-1} y_k \tag{9A-9}$$

As an oversimplified example, suppose that the four abscissa-ordinate pairs were

k	x_k	y_k
1	2	1
2	3	2
3	4	2
4	5	4

as shown in Figure 9A-1 with the points represented by the symbol *. Suppose that this set of abscissa–ordinate pairs, presumably obtained from experimental observation, is to be represented by a quadratic relation ($L = 3$). The matrix relations would then be

$$\begin{bmatrix} (\sum 1) & (\sum x_k) & (\sum x_k^2) \\ (\sum x_k) & (\sum x_k^2) & (\sum x_k^3) \\ (\sum x_k^2) & (\sum x_k^3) & (\sum x_k^4) \end{bmatrix} \begin{bmatrix} a_1 \\ a_2 \\ a_3 \end{bmatrix} = \begin{bmatrix} (\sum y_k) \\ (\sum x_k y_k) \\ (\sum x_k^2 y_k) \end{bmatrix}$$

where $\sum$ represents the summation $\sum\limits_{k=1}^{4}$. Numerically, for this example, this is

$$\begin{bmatrix} 4 & 14 & 54 \\ 14 & 54 & 224 \\ 54 & 224 & 938 \end{bmatrix} \begin{bmatrix} a_1 \\ a_2 \\ a_3 \end{bmatrix} = \begin{bmatrix} 9 \\ 36 \\ 154 \end{bmatrix}$$

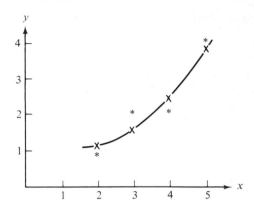

FIGURE 9A-1

The solution for these simultaneous equations is

$$a_1 = 1.85$$
$$a_2 = -0.85$$
$$a_3 = 0.25$$

In other words, $f(x)$ is

$$f(x) = 1.85 - 0.85x + 0.25x^2$$

The smoothed abscissa–ordinate pairs would be

$$(2, 1.15), (3, 1.55), (4, 2.45), (5, 3.85)$$

These points are shown as the symbol x in Figure 9A-1 with a curve drawn through them conforming to $f(x)$, the smoothed relationship.

The flow diagram used for obtaining A_{ij} and B_i from relations (9A-8) and (9A-9) is shown in Figure 9A-2. Note that after the matrix A has been obtained, the simultaneous subroutine SIMQ is called. This will return the array of solutions of the L polynomial coefficients in the array B.

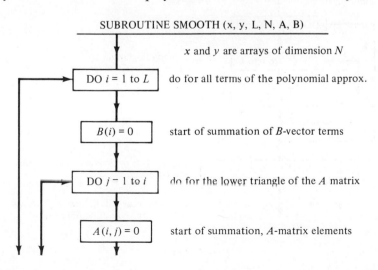

SUBROUTINE SMOOTH (x, y, L, N, A, B)

x and y are arrays of dimension N

DO $i = 1$ to L do for all terms of the polynomial approx.

$B(i) = 0$ start of summation of B-vector terms

DO $j = 1$ to i do for the lower triangle of the A matrix

$A(i, j) = 0$ start of summation, A-matrix elements

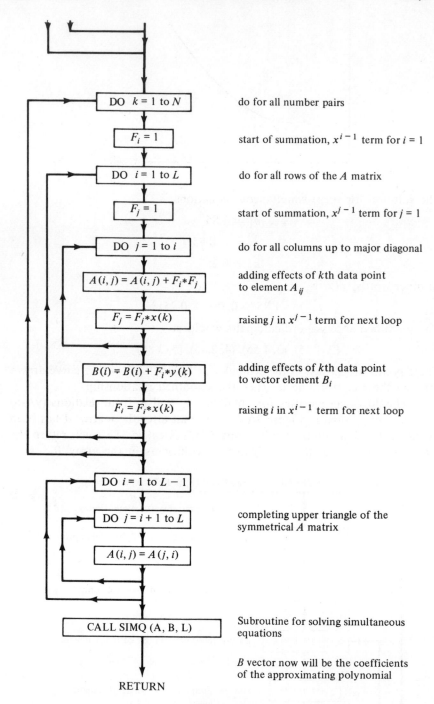

FIGURE 9A-2

Simulation of Distributed-   **10**
Parameter Systems—
Partial Differential Equations

10-1 Circumstances That Lead to Partial
Differential Equations

In all the simulation examples discussed up to now, the systems considered have been describable by differential equations involving only one basic independent variable. Usually this basic independent variable has been *time*; this fact identifies the problem as a dynamic one. However, time need not necessarily be the basic independent variable; in the beam-bending example of Chapter 7 it was instead, x, the distance along the beam.

A number of situations will arise when the differential equations describing the system will involve more than one basic independent variable. This will lead, of course, to *partial differential equations*. For example, if the beam-bending example of Chapter 9 had been a dynamic rather than static one (i.e., if the transient states of the beam when adjusting from one load condition to another had been of interest), then the equations describing the beam bending would have been functions of both x and the elapsed time t. Partial differential equations would have been required to describe such a situation.

Partial differential equations are always involved in *field problems*, such as those describing electrostatic, magnetic, and hydrodynamic fields, and in problems of two- or more-dimensional heat flow. As far as dynamic simulation is concerned, even a one-dimensional problem will involve partial differential equations because of the introduction of time as an additional basic independent variable. In addition to the beam-bending example cited above, many other types of simulation problems will arise that involve a distance variable as well as a time variable. These are generally described as *distributed-parameter problems* for reasons to be clarified by the example to follow.

10-2   Example of a Distributed-Parameter Problem

All the examples of the preceding chapters were based on *lumped parameters*. Referring back to Figure 1-1, the spring shown there, designated as k, was assumed to have negligible mass. If its mass was considered at all, this was done in a very approximate manner by attributing one half to the movable mass M and one half to the bottom support. For rapid changes of the input displacement x, this could lead to significant simulation errors.

In the spring example the only exact approach is to take into account the *distributed* (in contrast to lumped) nature of the spring mass. Suppose that the spring is uniform and that its active portion has a *free length* (length under conditions of zero tension or compression) designated as D. Its mass will be designated as M_k. It will then be said to have a *mass distribution* of $m_k = M_k/D$. The spring's *resilience* (the inverse of the stiffness k) will be $R_k = 1/k$ (e.g., in units of inches per pound or centimeters per kilogram), and the *resilience distribution* will be $r_k = R_k/D$. If any given part of the spring is identified by its free-length distance u from a given end (where $u = 0$), u will range from zero to D. An approximate representation of the spring could be obtained by dividing D into n increments, each of length $\Delta u = D/n$. The spring would then appear as in Figure 10-1. The spring alone would now comprise a $2n$-state system and the complete system of Figure 1-1, a $(2n + 1)$-state system. The total mass M_k and resilience R_k have now been divided into n-finite increments, $\Delta M_k = m_k \, \Delta u$ and $\Delta R_k = r_k \, \Delta u$. The force on each ΔR_k segment is designated as f, a positive force indicating compression. Including the end connections, there are $n + 1$ connection points; the relative displacements of these points will be designated as $x(i)$, with i ranging from zero to n. $x(0)$ corresponds to the displacement of the left-hand end of the spring and would be equivalent to simply x in the example shown in Figure 1-1. The other $x(i)$ displacements would be arbitrarily called zero when $x(0) = 0$ and when the spring is in the static state with neither tension nor compression forces.

In Figure 10-1 there might be some question as to whether the mass

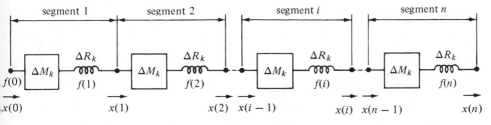

FIGURE 10-1

element ΔM_k or the resilient element ΔR_k should come first in the tandem arrangement shown. The decision in regard to this does, of course, affect the approximation. However, as n becomes sufficiently large, this decision will prove to have negligible effect on the results obtained.

The compression of the resilient element ΔR_k associated with the ith segment will simply be $-\Delta x(i) = x(i-1) - x(i)$, or minus the first difference of $x(i)$. As the spring is assumed to be obeying Hooke's law of linearity, this compression will be equal to $f(i)\Delta R_k$, or $\Delta x(i) = -f(i)r_k\Delta u$, or

$$\frac{\Delta x(i)}{\Delta u} = -r_k f(i) \qquad (10\text{-}1)$$

where

$$\Delta x(i) = x(i) - x(i-1) \qquad (10\text{-}2)$$

The net force acting on the mass element ΔM_k associated with the ith segment (assuming that a positive force acts to the right) will be $-\Delta f(i) = f(i-1) - f(i)$. This net force is simply ΔM_k times the acceleration, $d^2x(i-1)/dt^2$ or $\Delta f(i) = -m_k \Delta u \, d^2x(i-1)/dt^2$, or

$$\frac{\Delta f(i)}{\Delta u} = -m_k \frac{d^2 x(i-1)}{dt^2} \qquad (10\text{-}3)$$

where

$$\Delta f(i) = f(i) - f(i-1) \qquad (10\text{-}4)$$

Of course, this dividing of the spring into only a finite number of segments n will only approximate the true state of affairs; if the mass and resilience distributions are continuous, as they would be here, n properly should be infinite and Δu should approach the differential ∂u. Then $\Delta x(i)$ and $\Delta f(i)$ will also become differentials, ∂x and ∂f. Displacement and force will now become continuous functions of both u and t. As two independent variables are involved, it becomes necessary to employ partial derivative notation, and relation (10-1) attains the form

$$\frac{\partial x}{\partial u} = -r_k f \qquad (10\text{-}5)$$

Relation (10-3) attains the form

$$\frac{\partial f}{\partial u} = -m_k \frac{\partial^2 x}{\partial t^2} \tag{10-6}$$

The above set of equations comprises what are known as *traveling-wave equations* and have standard analytic solutions for classical forms of disturbances. It can be shown that disturbances in force and velocity will propagate along such a spring with a *velocity of propagation* given by the relation

$$v_p = \frac{1}{\sqrt{r_k m_k}} \tag{10-7}$$

This relation is important because it can be used to establish whether the distributed-parameter effect is significant or whether a lumped-parameter approximation will suffice. Suppose, for example, that the active portion of a given spring weighs 0.1 kg, that it has a stiffness of $k = 20.0$ kg/cm, and that it is 5 cm long. Then $R_k = 1/kg$ (the gravity constant g enters in the relation to convert the mass unit of kilograms to units of force) $= 1/(20)(980)$ $= 5.1 \times 10^{-5}$ sec²/kg. $r_k = R_k/D = (5.1 \times 10^{-5})/5 = 1.02 \times 10^{-5}$ sec²-kg⁻¹-cm⁻¹. $m_k = 0.1/5 = 0.02$ kg/cm. Hence

$$v_p = \frac{1}{\sqrt{(1.02 \times 10^{-5})(0.02)}}$$
$$= 2210 \text{ cm/sec}$$

As $D = 5$ cm, it will require $D/v_p = 5/2210 = 2.26 \times 10^{-3}$ sec for force and displacement disturbances to be transmitted the length of the spring.

If the spring so described is that employed in the example of Chapter 1, this distributed-parameter effect could be significant. It should be noted in that example, employing the lumped-parameter approximation, that the undamped natural frequency was

$$\omega_n = \frac{kg}{M} = \frac{(20)(980)}{0.5} = 198 \text{ rad/sec}$$

The significant range of frequencies may be estimated to extend to about $3\omega_n$ or 600 rad/sec. At this latter frequency the phase lag introduced by this propagation delay will be $(600)(2.26 \times 10^{-3}) = 1.35$ rad (about 77°). Such a lag certainly would be significant. Hence, if the spring used in the Chapter 1 example is that meeting the description here, the lumped-parameter approximation employed in that chapter would be far from valid and, for accurate simulation, it would be necessary to take the true, distributed nature of the spring mass and resilience into account.

10-3   Other Cases in Which Distributed-Parameter Situations Occur

A diagram analogous to that of Figure 10-1 applies when the transmission of longitudinal sound waves in a solid or fluid is being considered, provided the losses are assumed to be negligible. Hooke's law is often assumed to apply to the compressibility effects; then linear partial differential equations of the same form as relations (10-5) and (10-6) are still applicable. This approach is the one employed when computing the velocity of sound in various media.

In the case of gases, the compressibility relations may be approximated as linear only when the amplitude of pressure variation is small in comparison to the absolute pressures involved. For large pressure amplitudes, more complicated nonlinear compressibility relations apply. Figure 10-1 is still applicable as a model (provided thermal losses are neglected) but the springs shown in the model now become nonlinear in a nonsymmetrical way. Relations of the form of (10-5) and (10-6) no longer describe the situation and the analysis is considerably more complex. Computer simulation is still feasible, however, as it is relatively simple to take the nonlinear compressibility relationships into account.

An electrical transmission line represents another example of a distributed-parameter system leading to similar traveling-wave types of differential equations. Here the distributed parameters of interest are the series inductance per unit length l, the series resistance per unit length r, the shunt capacitance per unit length c, and the shunt-leakage conductance per unit length g. If such a line were divided into segments of length Δu, a lumped-parameter approximation of the kth segment would appear as in Figure 10-2.

If an analysis similar to that of relations (10-1) to (10-6) is performed as Δu is allowed to approach the differential ∂u, the partial differential equa-

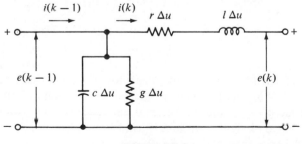

FIGURE 10-2

tions that result are

$$\frac{\partial e}{\partial x} = -ri - l\frac{\partial i}{\partial t} \tag{10-8}$$

$$\frac{\partial i}{\partial x} = -ge - c\frac{\partial e}{\partial t} \tag{10-9}$$

For a lossless line where g and r are negligible, these attain the form of standard traveling-wave equations. That this is the case may be established by comparing these relations with those of relations (10-5) and (10-6), considering i analogous to f and e analogous to dx/dt. Hence, by comparison with relation (10-7), the velocity of propagation here will be

$$v_p = \frac{1}{\sqrt{lc}} \tag{10-10}$$

It can also be shown that l and c will be so related that v_p will be equal to the velocity of light in the medium in which the line exists. The presence of losses (finite g and r) in a real line results in both attenuation effects and in a reduction in this velocity. Such attenuation effects are also readily simulated.

One of the most important types of simulation problems are those involving heat transfer. Nevertheless, it has not been possible to discuss the applications of simulation techniques to these problems prior to this chapter because all heat-transfer problems inevitably involve distributed-parameter effects and lumped-parameter approximations never suffice.

As an example of a heat-transfer problem, a simplified case might be considered where heat is being transmitted through a long thin rod insulated at its sides. This is illustrated in Figure 10-3, where the temperatures

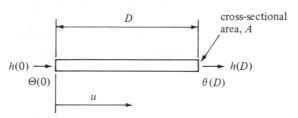

FIGURE 10-3

are designated by the symbol θ and heat flow (e.g., calories per second or Btu per hour) by h. The pertinent properties of the material in the rod are the thermal resistivity p and the thermal capacity per unit volume c. These will be distributed along the rod and it will be assumed that the rod is homogeneous and hence that this distribution is uniform. The rod may be considered to be divided into n axial sections of length $\Delta u = D/n$. If the symbols used for electrical resistance and capacitance are also used for this problem, the kth section of the rod, when so divided, might be represented as shown in Figure 10-4. The temperature change over this segment will be

$$\Delta\theta(k) = \theta(k) - \theta(k-1) = -\frac{\rho}{A}\Delta u h(k) \qquad (10\text{-}11)$$

The change in heat flow over this segment will be

$$\Delta h(k) = h(k) - h(k-1) = -cA\,\Delta u\frac{d\theta(k-1)}{dt} \qquad (10\text{-}12)$$

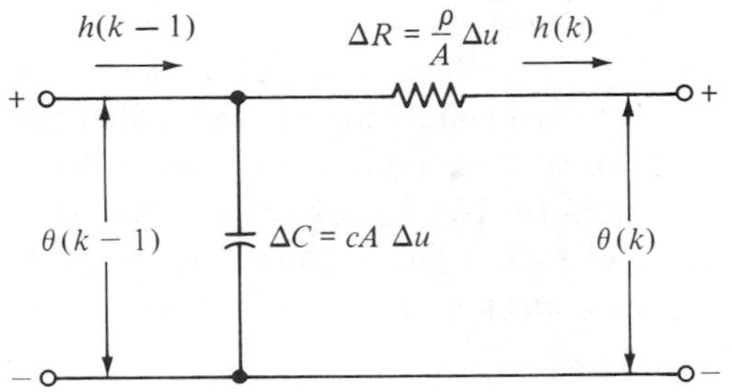

FIGURE 10-4

If n is considered to approach infinity and Δu to approach ∂u, these relations result in the partial differential equations

$$\frac{\partial\theta}{\partial u} = -\frac{\rho}{A}h \qquad (10\text{-}13)$$

$$\frac{\partial h}{\partial u} = -cA\frac{\partial\theta}{\partial t} \qquad (10\text{-}14)$$

These are not traveling-wave equations of the type previously described. They do correspond to the equations for an electrical line given in relations (10-8) and (10-9) when there is negligible inductance l and negligible conductance g. These equations are sometimes described as *diffusion equations* [1] because the same form arises in problems having to do with material being diffused from one medium to another. When the cross-sectional area A, and ρ and c are constant, analytic solutions of problems involving such equations are sometimes feasible. Even then such solutions are difficult; when transform methods are applied, nonrational transforms will result. Computer simulation of such problems usually represents a more practical approach. It becomes a must when additional complicating factors are introduced, such as a variation of cross-sectional area A, of resistivity ρ, or of capacitance c with the location along the line.

10-4   Aritificial-Line Approach
to Distributed-Parameter Problems

One of the earliest simulation techniques employed was that applied to the analysis and study of electrical transmission lines. Here the actual lines being represented involved many miles in length and direct models obviously could not be brought into the laboratory. For this reason the idea was proposed of dividing the line into n sections with each section having attributed to it, in a lumped fashion, the parameters pertaining to that $1/n$th of the line. Circuit models used to represent real lines and constructed in this fashion were described as *artificial lines*. The concept on which they are based may be applied, in general, to the simulation of distributed-parameter systems.

Consider an electrical line, typical of a telephone or power transmission line, that has uniform parameters r, l, g, and c per unit length. The lumped representation of such a line is shown in Figure 10-2; this lumped representation becomes more and more valid as Δu becomes shorter and shorter (and n becomes greater).

An artificial line could be constructed to simulate the real line by connecting in cascade all n such sections of the type shown in Figure 10-2. Actually, it is found that a better model is obtained if either what are called *T sections* or *pi sections* are used instead. Such line sections are shown in Figure 10-5. When n such sections are cascaded, such an artificial line made up of T sections can be distinguished from one made up of pi sections only by the end terminations.

The validity of the approximation represented by an artificial line may be established roughly by considering a *lossless* and properly terminated version of such a line where g and r are zero and the line is terminated in a resistance equal to the *characteristic impedance Z_0*. Z_0 is given by the relation

$$Z_0 = \sqrt{\frac{l}{c}} \tag{10-15}$$

Under such circumstances, an actual uniformly distributed line would result simply in a *transportation lag* (or finite time delay) equal to t_d sec. That is, if the voltage applied to one end of the line (where $u = 0$) is $e(0)$ and the the voltage at the other end (where $u = D$) is $e(D)$, these voltages would be related by $e(D, t) = e(0, t - t_d)$. Relation (10-10) expresses the velocity of propagation for such a line; therefore,

$$t_d = \frac{D}{v_p} = D\sqrt{\frac{l}{c}} \tag{10-16}$$

If the steady-state frequency response is used as the basis for comparing a real line with its artificial model, it will be found that for the real

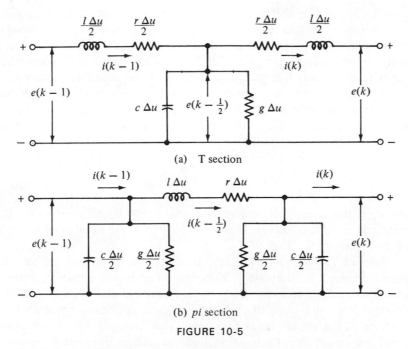

(a)   T section

(b) *pi* section

FIGURE 10-5

line the output voltage (at $u = D$) will be related to the input voltage (at $u = 0$) by the phasor relationship

$$\frac{E(D)}{E(0)} = 1\underline{/-\omega t_d} \tag{10-17}$$

This response may be illustrated by plots of the amplitude and phase response versus the frequency ω, as shown in Figure 10-6. Here the solid lines represent

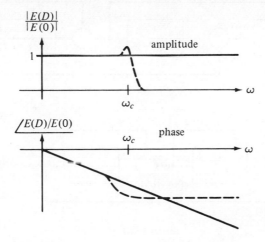

FIGURE 10-6

the performance of a real line, having a constant amplitude and a phase lag proportional to frequency. The artificial line, consisting of n lumped sections, will have phase and amplitude characteristics as shown (qualitatively) by the dashed-line curves of Figure 10-6. These will substantially agree with the actual line until the vicinity of the cutoff frequency ω_c is reached. Upon reaching the vicinity of this frequency, both the amplitude and phase characteristics will deviate markedly from those of the actual line. Therefore, the artificial line may be considered as a reasonable model of the actual line for all frequencies that are somewhat lower than ω_c. It can be shown that this critical frequency ω_c is given by the relation

$$\omega_c = \frac{nv_p}{D} \tag{10-18}$$

where v_p is the velocity of propagation and D the length of the line. It is particularly significant that ω_c is proportional to n, the number of segments used to represent the line.

Relation (10-10) may be used to estimate the number of artificial-line sections required to simulate a distributed-parameter situation with an acceptable degree of accuracy. The critical frequency ω_c should be considerably larger (e.g., by a factor of 3) than the highest significant frequency being considered in the system being simulated. This criterion may be employed for not only electrical transmission lines but other distributed-parameter problems as well. When the system has significant losses (finite values of r and g or their analogs), the velocity of propagation v_p appearing in (10-18) may still be determined approximately on the basis of neglecting these losses and employing such relations as (10-7) or (10-10). It is desirable to make the number of segments employed, n, not only sufficiently large but

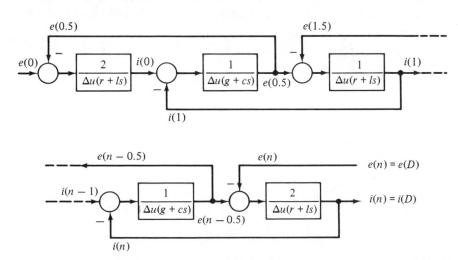

FIGURE 10-7

also not too large. The selection of too large a value for n will use up excessive components when analog-computer simulation is being considered and will result in excessive execution time when digital simulation is considered.

To establish the computer programs for representing the n sections of an artificial-line approximation of a distributed-parameter system, it first will be helpful to consider the block diagrams. Figure 10-7 illustrates the scheme used when T-type sections are employed, and Figure 10-8 the scheme when pi-type sections are used. It should be noted that the T-section termination leads to a block-diagram configuration where the voltages at the ends of the line, $e(0)$ and $e(D)$, must be furnished and where the configuration, in turn, furnishes the currents $i(0)$ and $i(D)$. The converse effect is obtained with the pi-section terminations shown in Figure 10-8.

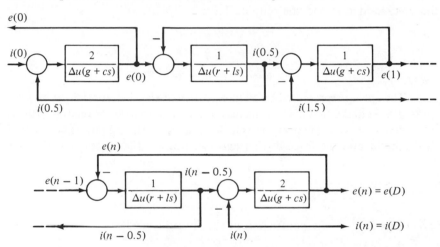

FIGURE 10-8

10-5 General Version of the Artificial Line

In Figure 10-7 voltage at the sending end, $e(0)$, was considered as an input or cause, and current at that end, $i(0)$, as an output or effect. To be general, let the sending-end input variable be denoted as x and the output variable as y. The general relations analogous to relations (10-8) and (10-9) then become

$$\frac{\partial x}{\partial u} = -\alpha y - \beta\frac{\partial y}{\partial t} \tag{10-19}$$

$$\frac{\partial y}{\partial u} = -\gamma x - \delta\frac{\partial x}{\partial t} \tag{10-20}$$

where, for the artificial electrical-line analog, the following correspondences (indicated by the symbol $\sim$) hold:

$$x \sim e \qquad \beta \sim l$$
$$y \sim i \qquad \gamma \sim g$$
$$\alpha \sim r \qquad \delta \sim c$$

For a lossless (and approximately for a low-loss) system, the velocity of propagation v_p is, therefore,

$$v_p = \frac{1}{\sqrt{\beta\delta}} \qquad (10\text{-}21)$$

The dual relations, based on interchanging the functions of relations (10-19) and (10-20), are applicable when the sending-end current is the input and the the voltage at that end the output. Then

$$x \sim i \qquad \beta \sim c$$
$$y \sim e \qquad \gamma \sim r$$
$$\alpha \sim g \qquad \delta \sim l$$

The spring represented by Figure 10-1 may also be represented by relations (10-19) and (10-20). The time derivative of both sides of relation (10-15) must first be taken. Then, if the velocity v at the sending end is considered as the input and the force at that end the output, the correspondence will be

$x \sim v$

$y \sim f$

$\alpha = 0$ if internal friction of the spring is neglected

$\beta \sim r_k$

$\gamma = 0$ if internal friction with respect to stationary members is neglected

$\delta \sim m_k$

If force at the sending end is the input and velocity at that end the output, then

$x \sim f$

$y \sim v$

$\alpha = 0$ if internal friction with respect to stationary members is neglected

$\beta \sim m_k$

$\gamma = 0$ if internal friction of the spring is neglected

$\delta \sim r_k$

The heat-flow equations of relations (10-13) and (10-14) may also use this general form. If sending-end temperature is the input and heat flow at that end the output, then

$$x \sim \theta \qquad \beta = 0$$
$$y \sim h \qquad \gamma = 0$$
$$\alpha \sim \frac{p}{A} \qquad \delta \sim cA$$

If sending-end heat flow is the input and temperature at that end the output, then

$$x \sim h \qquad \beta \sim cA$$
$$y \sim \theta \qquad \gamma \sim \frac{p}{A}$$
$$\alpha = 0 \qquad \delta = 0$$

A general block diagram for the artificial-line approximation may then be drawn by analogy to Figure 10-7 and appears as Figure 10-9.

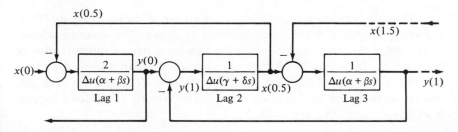

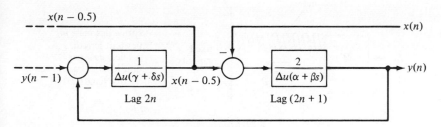

FIGURE 10-9

Which of the two forms of variable (signal) is represented as x and which as y is arbitrary, except that it is desirable to make this decision in such a way that only integrators, not differentiators, will be involved in the block-diagram representation of the other system elements to which this distributed system is coupled.

In some instances the variable designated as *x*, because it is a sending-end input, will appear as an output signal at the receiving end of the distributed system. It will then be necessary to add another half-section so that $D = (n + 0.5) \Delta u$. The *lower* portion of Figure 10-9 would be replaced by the arrangement shown in Figure 10-10. The preceding sections would be identical to those of Figure 10-9.

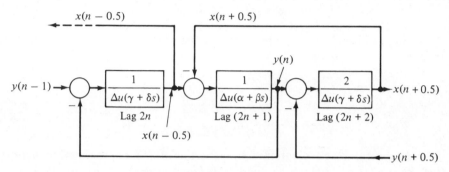

FIGURE 10-10

Consider, for example, a spring–mass system as shown in Figure 10-11. A force f_{in} is applied to the restrained mass as shown. The resulting velocity of the mass, v_m, and corresponding displacement are of interest; also of interest is the force exerted on the fixed support. If distance along the spring free length is measured from left to right, $v_m = v(0)$, $f(0)$ is f_{in} less $M\, dv_m/dt$, and the force on the fixed support is $f(n)$. The velocity of the fixed support is of course zero [i.e., $v(n) = 0$].

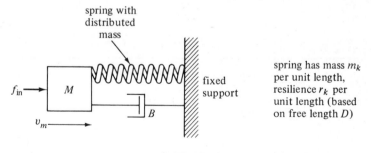

FIGURE 10-11

To include the effect of the lumped mass *M* without requiring differentiation, the block diagram representing the mass should appear as shown in Figure 10-12. Hence, at the sending end of the spring, the input is *v* and the output *f*; hence the analogy based on $x \sim v$ and $y \sim f$ is chosen. At the receiving end the imposed velocity $v(n) = 0$ is the input. Hence, as *v* is the

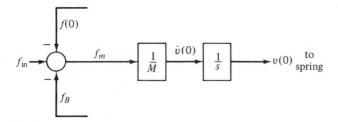

FIGURE 10-12

input at both ends, the configuration of Figure 10-9 is applicable. The complete block diagram representing the system of Figure 10-11 is, therefore,
as shown in Figure 10-13.

Figure 10-14 represents an example where, instead, the block-diagram
arrangement shown in Figure 10-10 is applicable. Here a force f_{in} is imposed
on a member (assumed to have negligible mass) connected to one end of
both the spring and dashpot. The velocity of this member $v(0)$ and of the
mass v_M are of interest. On the sending end of the spring (where $u = 0$),
the input is the force f_0. On the receiving (left-hand) end of the spring, the
block diagram describing the effect of the mass M must be considered. To
avoid differentiation, this must be in the form shown in Figure 10-15. Here
the input at the sending end is the force $f(0)$, while at the receiving end
it is the velocity v_M. Hence, an extra half-section is necessary and the spring
must be represented by the diagram of Figure 10-10.

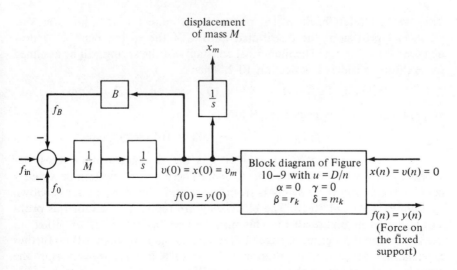

FIGURE 10-13

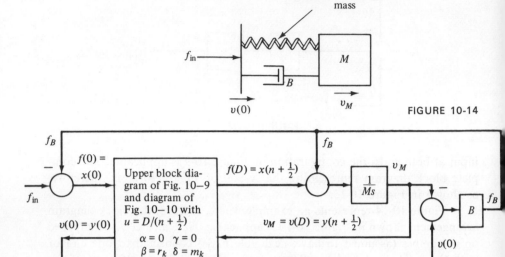

FIGURE 10-14

FIGURE 10-15

10-6   Example : Problem of Chapter 1
with Spring–Mass Distributed

This example refers back to that pictured in Figure 1-1 with, however, one additional provision: the distributed nature of the spring–mass shall now be taken into account. The numerical constants of the spring will be assumed to be those considered in Section 10-2. Then

$$M_k = 0.1 \text{ kg} \qquad R_k = 5.1 \times 10^{-5} \text{ sec}^2/\text{kg} \qquad D = 5 \text{ cm}$$

and spring friction is neglected. Hence

$$m_k = 0.02 \text{ kg/cm} \qquad r_k = 1.02 \times 10^5 \text{ sec}^2/\text{kg-cm}$$

In the example of Chapter 1, x was the displacement of the lower support and y was the displacement of M. These will be written as **x** and **y** here to distinguish these symbols from the x and y used in the sense shown by Figures 10-9 and 10-10. The block-diagram representation for this problem is shown in Figure 10-16. This may be used as the basis of either an analog or digital program. Conversion to an analog program needs no further explanation; for a digital program the use of a general transmission-line module is explained in the section to follow.

Relation (10-18) may be used to determine the number of line segments

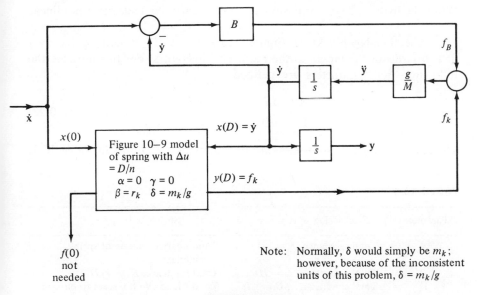

FIGURE 10-16

that are required. The velocity of propagation has already been determined in Section 10-2 as 2210 cm/sec. [Had it not been, it could have been determined from relation (10-21) by substituting r_k for β and m_k/g for δ.] The undamped natural frequency of this system, prior to considering the effect of the spring–mass, was computed as $\omega_n = \sqrt{kg/M} = 198$ rad/sec. It will be desirable to reproduce faithfully the effects of disturbances having frequency content up to about three times this frequency or, roughly, up to 600 rad/sec. In turn, the critical frequency ω_c should be about three times this higher disturbance frequency or about 1800 rad/sec. From relation (10-18),

$$\omega_c = \frac{n(2210)}{5} = 442n$$

Hence five sections would appear to be sufficient. With digital simulation there is less pressure to maintain the number of sections at this minimum because no additional equipment becomes required by being overgenerous; of course, increased time of execution would be the result.

10-7 General-Purpose Module
for Transmission-Line-Type Problems

Figures 10-9 and 10-10 may be used as the general bases for modules for handling such transmission-line types of simulation problems, regardless of whether they are of an electrical, mechanical, hydraulic, or thermal type.

(With the hydraulic type provision generally has to be made for a nonlinear r.)

The time-lag blocks of Figures 10-9 and 10-10 should be redrawn first in terms of the inputs to the required integrators. For this purpose the following total parameters are defined:

$$A = \alpha D \qquad B = \beta D$$
$$\Gamma = \gamma D \qquad \Delta = \delta D$$

(10-22)

The analogs to actual transmission-line situations are shown in Table 10-1.

TABLE 10-1

Parameter	Electrical, $x \sim e, y \sim i$	Spring, $x \sim v, y \sim f$
A	Total resistance, $R = rD$	Total internal friction of spring material
B	Total inductance, $L = lD$	Total resilience, $R_k = r_k D$
Γ	Total conductance, $G = gD$	Total friction with respect to outside members
Δ	Total capacitance, $C = cD$	Total mass, $M_k = m_k D$

The lag blocks of Figures 10-9 and 10-10 then become as shown in Figures 10-17 and 10-18.

A subprogram to represent, in general, any transmission-line type of system, called LINE, has been prepared; its flow diagram is shown in Figure 10-19. It possesses the following arguments in common with the calling program:

n	The number of line sections to be used
HALF	True if an extra half-section is used; otherwise false
NEW	Made initially true by calling program, to set constants and initial integrator outputs
A, B, Γ, Δ	The total parameters
x_0, y_0	Input and output variables at the sending end
x_D, y_D	Input and output variables at the receiving end
INTIN	The array of integrator inputs developed by this subprogram
INTOUT	The array of integrator outputs developed by this subprogram
LASTINT	See explanation below

In the integration module, all integrators, whether used to represent this transmission line or for other parts of the program, are subscripted and

For Lag i with i Odd

(Numerator factor is 2 for $i = 1$ and, for Fig. 10—9 configuration, for $i = 2n + 1$)

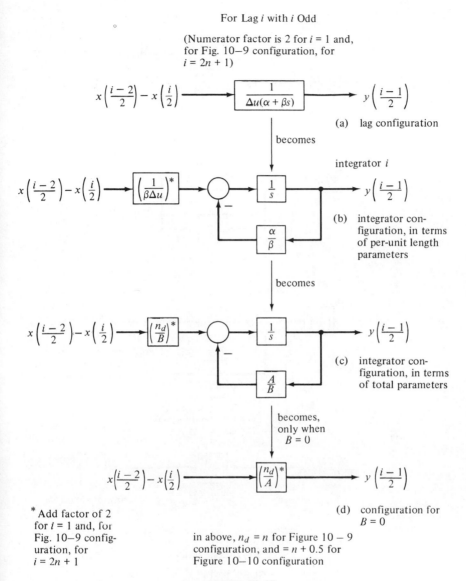

(a)   lag configuration

becomes

integrator i

(b)   integrator con-figuration, in terms of per-unit length parameters

becomes

(c)   integrator con-figuration, in terms of total parameters

becomes, only when $B = 0$

*Add factor of 2 for $i = 1$ and, for Fig. 10—9 config-uration, for $i = 2n + 1$

(d)   configuration for $B = 0$

in above, $n_d = n$ for Figure 10 — 9 configuration, and $= n + 0.5$ for Figure 10—10 configuration

FIGURE 10-17

each pass of the integration routine then handles these sequentially. Other integrators may be employed in the overall program, hence the $i = 1$ integrator developing y_0 is not necessarily integrator 1. All integrators not involved within the line simulation are assigned subscripts first: LASTINT is the last subscript so assigned. Hence integration operation i will be handled

For Lag i with i Even

(For Fig. 10–10 configuration, numerator factor is 2 when $i = 2n + 2$)

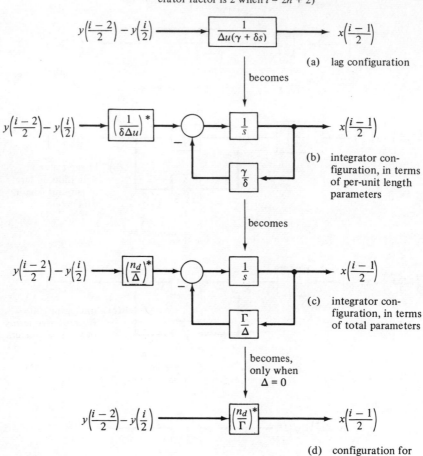

$$y\left(\frac{i-2}{2}\right) - y\left(\frac{i}{2}\right) \longrightarrow \boxed{\dfrac{1}{\Delta u(\gamma + \delta s)}} \longrightarrow x\left(\frac{i-1}{2}\right)$$

(a) lag configuration

becomes

(b) integrator con-
figuration, in terms
of per-unit length
parameters

becomes

(c) integrator con-
figuration, in terms
of total parameters

becomes,
only when
$\Delta = 0$

(d) configuration for
$\Delta = 0$

* For Fig. 10–10
configuration,
add factor of
2 for $i = 2n + 2$

where $n_d = n$ for Figure 10–9 configuration, and $= n + 0.5$ for
Figure 10–10 configuration

FIGURE 10-18

by the integrator subscripted (LASTINT+i). Hence, when i is odd,

$$\text{INTOUT}(\text{LASTINT}+i) = y\left(\frac{i-1}{2}\right)$$

When i is even,

$$\text{INTOUT}(\text{LASTINT}+i) = x\left(\frac{i-1}{2}\right)$$

SUBROUTINE LINE (n, HALF, LASTINT, A, B, Γ, Δ, NEW,
x_0, x_d, y_0, y_d, INTIN, INTOUT)

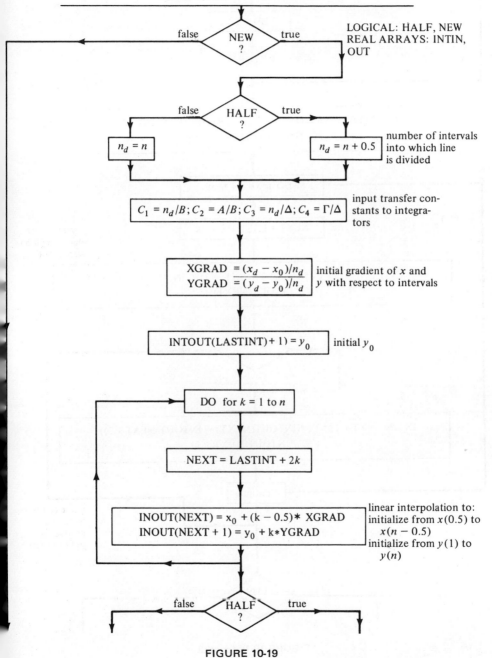

FIGURE 10-19

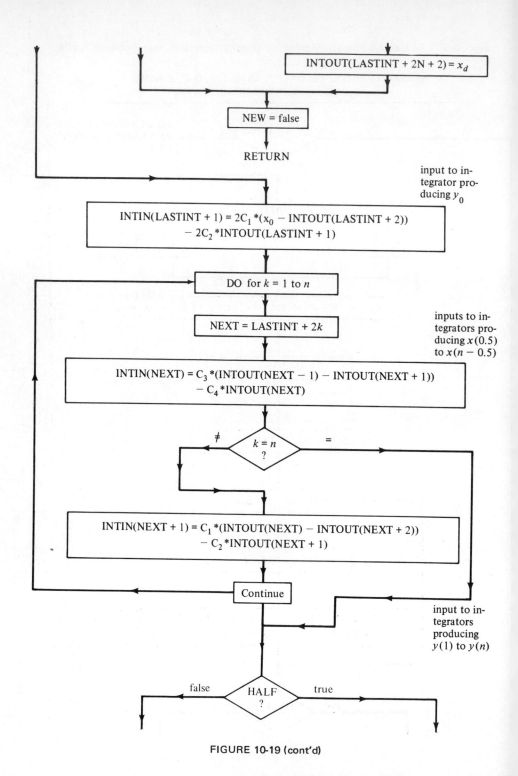

FIGURE 10-19 (cont'd)

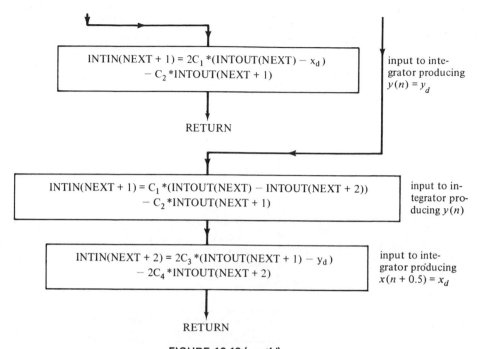

FIGURE 10-19 (cont'd)

At the start of the program, NEW is made true by the calling program prior to starting the time iterations. At that time operation branches to the upper part of the flow diagram shown in Figure 10-18. The value of n_d (see Figures 10-17 and 10-18) is first established. Then the transfer constants establishing the integrator inputs, named C_1 to C_4, are computed.

The initial values of the integrator outputs at the ends of the line, x_0, x_0, x_d, and y_d, will have to be established by the main program. The initial values of all other integrator outputs used in representing the line will have to be established as well. Their distribution is initially assumed to be linear (i.e., the x's may be determined by interpolating between x_0 and x_d and the y's) between y_0 and y_d. (The program may be modified if this linear assumption is not the case.)

After all the above has been done prior to the actual time iterations, NEW is made false by the LINE subroutine and control returned to the main calling program. The LINE subroutine will be called again when $t = 0$ and then at each successive integration pass.

In summary, the major function of this subroutine is to establish the new integrator inputs at each iteration interval. The general configuration of a main program that would call such a subroutine is shown in Figure 10-20.

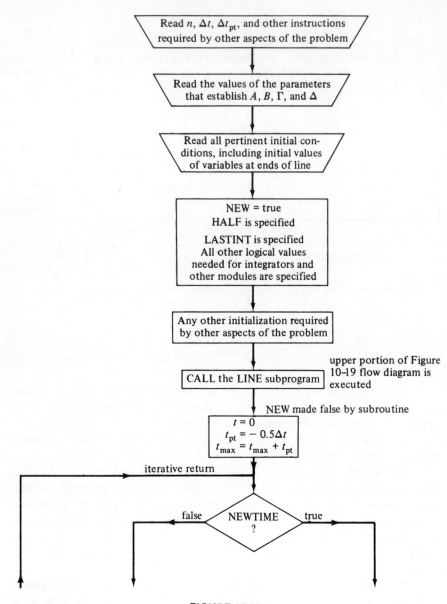

FIGURE 10-20

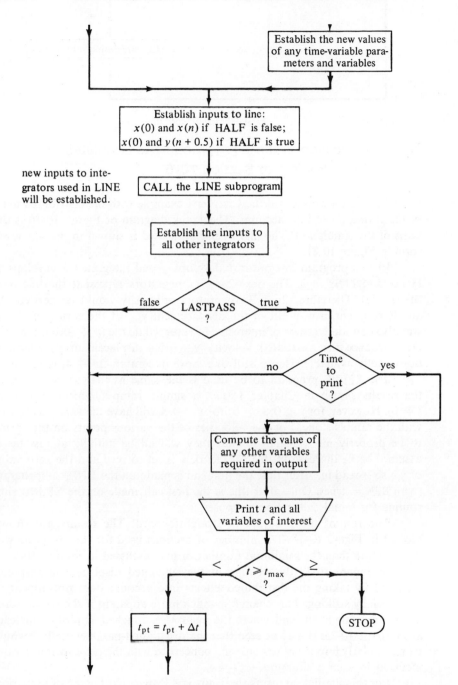

new inputs to inte-
grators used in LINE
will be established.

FIGURE 10-20 (cont'd)

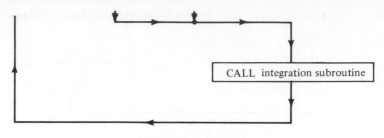

FIGURE 10-20 (cont'd)

10-8 Application of the LINE Module to Simulation of the Problem of Section 10-6

In Section 10-6 we discussed the Chapter 1 example with the distributed mass of the spring taken into account. The block diagram of Figure 10-16 is the basis of the simulation. The digital program used is shown in flow-diagram form in Figure 10-21.

In this program integrator 1 develops $\mathbf{y}$ and integrator 2 develops $\dot{\mathbf{y}}$. Hence LASTINT $= 2$. The next $2n + 1$ integrators represent the line (i.e., the spring). Therefore, $2n + 3$ integrators ordinarily would be needed. As an afterthought, a printout of the displacement $\mathbf{y}_{\text{mid}}$ of the spring midpoint was also considered to be of interest. However, while the $(n + 3)$th integrator does produce the associated velocity $\dot{\mathbf{y}}_{\text{mid}}$, this displacement $\mathbf{y}_{\text{mid}}$ itself is not directly available. Hence still one more integrator, $2n + 4$, is required.

The XFUNC program to be used is the same as that associated with the results shown in Chapter 1 (i.e., a simple ramp function applied at $t = 0$). However, for $t < 0$, $\dot{\mathbf{x}} = 0$; for $t = 0$, $\dot{\mathbf{x}}$ will have the value associated with the ramp's slope. For the velocities of the various points on the spring to be properly interpolated so that they will all be initially at rest (as is assumed to be the case in this problem), $\dot{\mathbf{x}}$ is set to zero and the zero value of $\dot{\mathbf{y}}$ also is read in. After this, the first call is made on the LINE subprogram (with NEW $=$ true). Only after this is the first call made on the XFUNC subroutine for initial calibration purposes.

The rest of the program is straightforward. The results are shown plotted in Figure 10-22. The number of sections used for this example was 33, far more than the minimum number of five discussed in Section 10-6.

In Figure 10-22 the change in the simulated displacement response y caused by taking the distributed effects into account does not appear to be especially striking. This change is much more apparent if the spring force f_k, as it appears at the end where the mass M is attached, is plotted instead, as in Figure 10-23. It may be seen that the distributed-parameter effect would be particularly important to someone concerned with the peak spring stresses incurred in such a situation.

For this simulation, using the four-pass Runge–Kutta type of numerical integration (4A-1), a Δt of 0.0005 was required in order to obtain reasonable

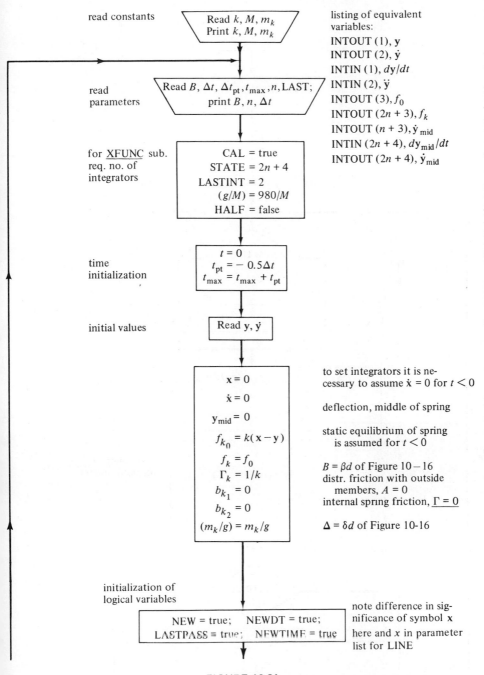

read constants

Read k, M, m_k
Print k, M, m_k

listing of equivalent variables:
INTOUT (1), $\mathbf{y}$
INTOUT (2), $\dot{\mathbf{y}}$
INTIN (1), dy/dt
INTIN (2), $\ddot{\mathbf{y}}$
INTOUT (3), f_0
INTOUT $(2n + 3), f_k$
INTOUT $(n + 3), \dot{\mathbf{y}}_{mid}$
INTIN $(2n + 4), dy_{mid}/dt$
INTOUT $(2n + 4), \dot{\mathbf{y}}_{mid}$

read parameters

Read $B, \Delta t, \Delta t_{pt}, t_{max}, n, LAST$;
print $B, n, \Delta t$

for XFUNC sub. req. no. of integrators

CAL = true
STATE = $2n + 4$
LASTINT = 2
$(g/M) = 980/M$
HALF = false

time initialization

$t = 0$
$t_{pt} = -0.5\Delta t$
$t_{max} = t_{max} + t_{pt}$

initial values

Read $\mathbf{y}, \dot{\mathbf{y}}$

$\mathbf{x} = 0$

$\dot{\mathbf{x}} = 0$

$y_{mid} = 0$

$f_{k_0} = k(\mathbf{x} - \mathbf{y})$

$f_k = f_0$

$\Gamma_k = 1/k$

$b_{k_1} = 0$

$b_{k_2} = 0$

$(m_k/g) = m_k/g$

to set integrators it is necessary to assume $\dot{\mathbf{x}} = 0$ for $t < 0$

deflection, middle of spring

static equilibrium of spring is assumed for $t < 0$

$B = \beta d$ of Figure $10-16$
distr. friction with outside members, $A = 0$
internal spring friction, $\Gamma = 0$

$\Delta = \delta d$ of Figure 10-16

initialization of logical variables

NEW = true;   NEWDT = true;
LASTPASS = true;   NEWTIME = true

note difference in significance of symbol x here and x in parameter list for LINE

FIGURE 10-21

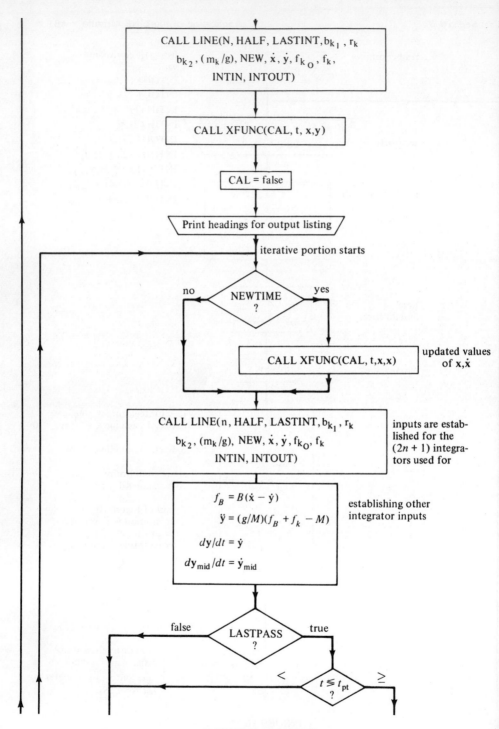

FIGURE 10-21 (cont'd)

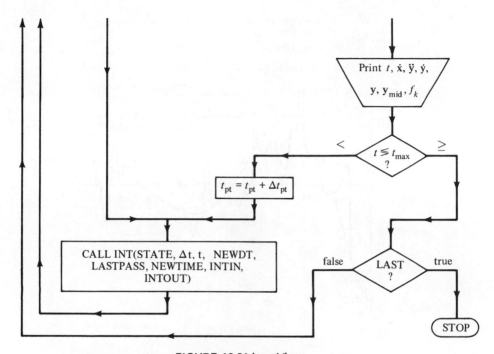

FIGURE 10-21 (cont'd)

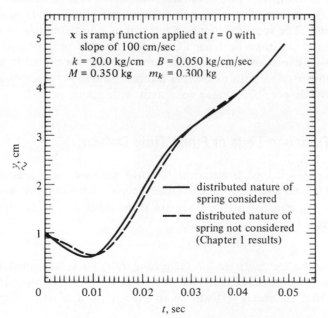

FIGURE 10-22

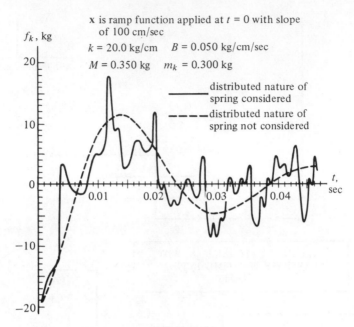

f_k, kg

x is ramp function applied at $t = 0$ with slope of 100 cm/sec

$k = 20.0$ kg/cm $B = 0.050$ kg/cm/sec
$M = 0.350$ kg $m_k = 0.300$ kg

———— distributed nature of spring considered
– – – – distributed nature of spring not considered

FIGURE 10-23

accuracy, as compared with the much coarser interval permissible when the spring was considered as a lumped resilience with half of its mass lumped at each end. The required iteration interval is approximately proportional to $1/n$. Since execution time per iteration is roughly proportional to n (for $n \gg 1$), total execution time will then tend to be proportional to the *square* of the number of sections used. This indicates the importance of selecting n with as low as possible a value consistent with accuracy.

10-9   Transport Lags or Finite Time Delays

In Section 10-4 a lossless electrical line was discussed that was terminated by its characteristic impedance. Under such circumstances disturbances applied at one end, say $x(t)$, will appear at the other end as, say $y(t)$, in such a way that

$$y(t) = x(t - t_d) \tag{10-23}$$

where t_d is the *transport lag*, or *finite time delay*, that was introduced. For this lossless electrical line the value of t_d is given by relation (10-16). It may be noted that the result $y(t)$ will be an exact replica of $x(t)$ except for this delay.

Similar phenomena occur in other types of physical systems. Disturbances in a hydraulic line will travel at the speed of sound (for the medium involved); if the line is terminated in a hydraulic resistance equal to its characteristic impedance there will be no *reflections* (the cause of water-hammer effects) and, again, disturbances applied to one end will appear as an exact replica at the other except for this time delay. Many other forms of transport lag exist because of distributed-parameter effects. Another example where time delays are important is the earth control of a space vehicle. Radio signals between earth and the vehicle will travel at the velocity of light (essentially because of a distributed-parameter effect). Hence important time delays will be apparent in such a control problem. In general, time delays cause serious difficulties in control problems and are best avoided or minimized. However, this is not always possible. In any event, because of their significance, it is important that they be simulated properly.

The examples mentioned up to this point related to time delays resulting from distributed-parameter effects. This is not the only cause; in fact, the alternative term, transport lag, implies that they arise from transport phenomena as well. Processes being simulated will be subject to such lags whenever transport is part of the process, as in conveyor-belt or flow operations. Traffic-control problems, often simulated, always involve such delays because of the time required for a vehicle to travel from one point to another. Heat transmission by convection (as opposed to transmission by conduction, discussed in Section 10-3) involves the transport lag of the convecting medium.

Finite time delays, or transport lags, are usually unwelcome but unavoidable effects to one responsible for preparing a computer simulation program. This is particularly the case when analog simulation is contemplated, since no completely satisfactory analog method for simulating such effects has been developed. The problem is a simpler one when digital-computer simulation is contemplated, but an objection arises again because of the excessive demand that is likely to be placed on the computer's storage facilities. Unfortunately, just those instances when the time delay poses the most severe simulation problems are also those where this time-delay effect is the most significant. Hence the problem cannot usually be "ducked," but must be faced in as satisfactory as possible a manner with the equipment that is available.

10-10   Analog Simulation of Finite Time Delays

Relation (10-23) described the input–output relationship represented by a finite time delay. In operational or transform notation, this would correspond to

$$Y(s) = X(s)e^{-t_d s} \tag{10-24}$$

The transfer function $e^{-t_d s}$ describing this effect is nonrational. The effect cannot be synthesized exactly by any arrangement employing a finite number of lumped elements.

A large number of methods have been proposed for simulating time delays on an analog computer. The four basic methods that are used most frequently are

1. Sampling and capacitor storage.
2. Magnetic-tape storage.
3. Simulation of a properly terminated *distortionless* line.
4. Padé approximations.

The first method simply involves sampling and holding the input $x(t)$ at specified time intervals Δt and then reading them out t_d later. In this respect the method is basically the same that is used with digital simulation, to be discussed in the next section. Various mechanisms have been proposed for this purpose. One of these consists of connecting a large number of capacitors to commutator segments; the other terminal of each capacitor is grounded. A *recording brush* applies the signal $x(t)$ to each capacitor in turn as its commutator segment engages the brush, thus charging it so that it will hold that voltage. This holding operation is continued until the capacitor's commutator segment is engaged by a *playback brush*, which applies the stored voltage to an output amplifier. The speed of commutator rotation and the spacing between the recording and playback brushes establishes the value of t_d.

Method 2 is essentially a continuous version of the above scheme which avoids the time-sampling effect. A continuous belt of magnetic tape first engages a recording head that applies the signal $x(t)$ and later engages a playback head that reads the signal $y(t)$. The speed of the tape and the spacing between recording and playback heads determine t_d. Unfortunately, a number of practical problems enter into the implementation of this scheme so that, although it performs very satisfactorily, it does require complicated, bulky, and expensive equipment. First, the mechanical problems involved for obtaining a value of t_d continuously adjustable over a wide range are obvious. Second, it should be pointed out that magnetic-tape recording is not sufficiently faithful to reproduce analog voltages directly. As a result, frequency-modulation methods are necessary to provide sufficient accuracy. This means that the signal $x(t)$ must be converted to a frequency-modulated form before being applied to the recording head, and that the signal obtained from the playback head must be demodulated before it appears as $y(t)$. Commercially furnished equipment is available for this purpose to supplement analog-computer installations. However, none of this equipment is inexpensive; this presents an especially serious problem when a number of finite time delays must be simulated.

Method 3 is based on the analog of what is called a distortionless electrical line. Because the basic principles of its development are somewhat detailed, the explanation is postponed to Appendix 10A. The basic block diagram describing the application of this method is shown in Figure 10-24. From that block diagram, an analog-computer program may readily be synthesized. One version would appear as in Figure 10-25. This method is probably the most satisfactory known for simulating finite time delays, provided n, the number of sections employed, is sufficiently great. Its one disadvantage is that it is somewhat wasteful of integrators.

Method 4 employs the Padé approximation [2]. The transfer function $Y(s)/X(s) = e^{-t_d s}$ is approximated by the following form:

$$\frac{Y(s)}{X(s)} = \frac{N(s)}{D(s)} \tag{10-25}$$

where, for an nth-order approximation,

$$D(s) = 1 + \frac{t_d s}{2} + \frac{n(n-1)}{2n(2n-1)} \frac{(t_d s)^2}{2!}$$
$$+ \cdots + \frac{n(n-1)\cdots(n-i+1)}{(2n)(2n-1)\cdots(2n-i+1)} \frac{(t_d s)^i}{i!}$$
$$+ \cdots + \frac{n!}{(2n)!}(t_d s)^n \tag{10-26}$$

and

$$N(s) = D(-s) \tag{10-27}$$

For example, for the fourth-order Padé approximation,

$$\frac{Y(s)}{X(s)} = \frac{1 - \frac{t_d s}{2} + \frac{3(t_d s)^2}{28} - \frac{(t_d s)^3}{84} + \frac{(t_d s)^4}{1680}}{1 + \frac{t_d s}{2} + \frac{3(t_d s)^2}{28} + \frac{(t_d s)^3}{84} + \frac{(t_d s)^4}{1680}} \tag{10-28}$$

When viewed in terms of frequency response, it may be noted that the magnitude of $Y(j\omega)/X(j\omega)$ is always unity, agreeing exactly with that of the actual function being approximated, $e^{-jt_d\omega}$. The only approximation error relates to phase. For the fourth-order approximation, given above, the phase response is reasonably faithful for frequencies up to about $t_d = 5$.

A fair basis of comparison between the Padé approximation and the artificial version of a distortionless line, just discussed previously, would be on the basis of assuming the same number of integrators are available in either instance. For example, the artificial-line simulation of Figure 10-25 will employ $(2n + 1)$ integrators; hence, for $n = 5$, 11 integrators are

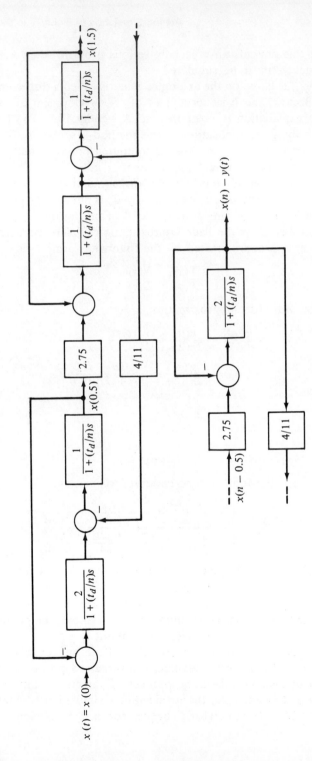

FIGURE 10-24

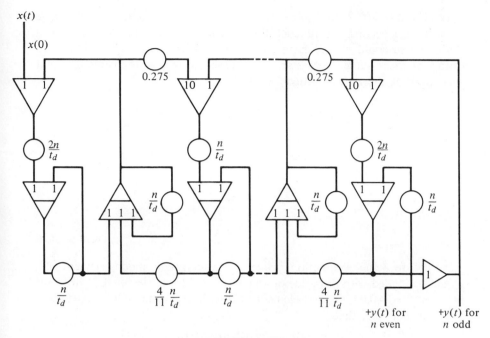

FIGURE 10-25

required. Therefore, such a fifth-order artificial-line simulation should be compared with an eleventh-order Padé approximation.

In general, which technique is superior will depend upon the type of simulation problem encountered. Characteristic of the Padé approximation is the tendency for significant output, $y(t)$, effects to appear almost immediately after the application of a step-function input $x(t)$. This does not occur with the artificial-line technique. There, as Figures 10A-2 and 10A-4 show, no significant output effects appear at all for a substantial portion of the interval $0 < t < t_d$. When this latter feature is desirable, method 3 does appear to be somewhat superior. This particularly will be the case when markedly nonlinear elements, as contactors, follow the time-delay effect.

10-11   Digital Simulation of Finite Time Delays

Because the digital simulator operates on a sampling basis, no particular problems other than those regarding storage requirements are encountered when producing a finite time-delay simulation by digital means. The values of the lag input $x(t)$ are stored for every normal iteration interval Δt. Enough values must be stored so that the range of the time delay t_d is covered.

A very simple example, say $t_d = 0.045$ sec and a normal iteration interval of $\Delta t = 0.02$ sec, will be employed. Then, $0.045/0.02 = 2.25$ storage elements are needed—in practice three elements would be employed in a chain. These could be indicated as shown in Figure 10-26. In addition, a storage element named y_{next} is shown reserved to receive the value of y that will apply at the *next* iteration interval.

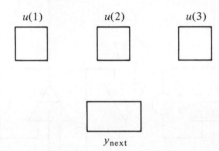

FIGURE 10-26

Before actual simulation, while in the calibrate mode, element $u(3)$ would be loaded with the value of x at $t = -0.02$ sec, element $u(2)$ with the value at $t = -0.04$ sec, and element $u(1)$ with the value at $t = -0.06$ sec. Say, for example, that

$$x = 0 \qquad\qquad t < 0.02$$
$$= 2 + 100t \qquad t \geq 0.02$$

so that $x(t)$ plots as the linear function shown in Figure 10-27. The resulting values of y are also shown plotted in Figure 10-27.

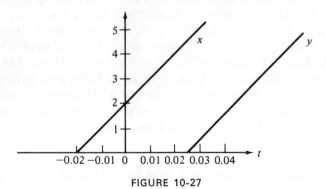

FIGURE 10-27

The initial values held by the memory locations would appear as in Figure 10-28. The interpolation relationship used is

$$y_{next} = 0.25u(1) + 0.75u(2)$$

and, in this example, the result will equal zero.

At $t = 0$, the first iteration of simulation y, the delayed output, is set

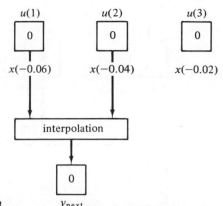

FIGURE 10-28

equal to y_{next} and hence to zero [i.e., $y(0) = 0$]. Memory location $u(1)$ is set to the value $x(0)$. y_{next} is reset by the interpolation relationship

$$y_{\text{next}} = 0.25u(2) + 0.75u(3)$$

The result will still be zero. These procedures are shown in Figure 10-29.

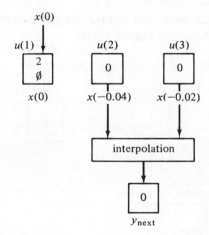

FIGURE 10-29

At $t = 0.02$, the next iteration of simulation, y, is again set to y_{next}, happening to remain zero in this example [i.e., $y(0.02) = 0$]. Memory location $u(2)$ is set to the value of $x(0.02)$. y_{next} is reset by the interpolation relationship

$$y_{\text{next}} = 0.25u(3) + 0.75u(1)$$

The result will be $y_{\text{next}} = 1.5$. Note the recycling. The above-described procedures are shown in Figure 10-30.

At $t = 0.04$, the next iteration of simulation y is again set equal to

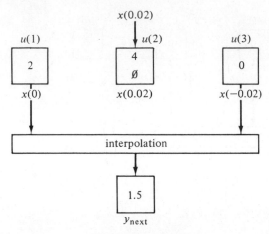

FIGURE 10-30

y_{next}, happening to be 1.5 in this example [i.e., $y(0.04) = 1.5$]. Memory location $u(3)$ is set to the value of $x(0.04)$. y_{next} is reset by the interpolation relationship

$$y_{next} = 0.25u(1) + 0.75u(2)$$

The result will be $y_{next} = 3.5$. Note that the recycling continues. The above-described procedures are shown in Figure 10-31.

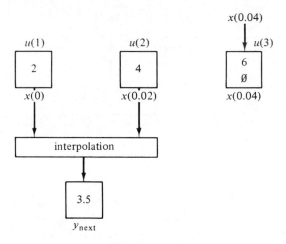

FIGURE 10-31

At $t = 0.06$, y is again set to y_{next}, happening to be 3.5 in the example [i.e., $y(0.06) = 3.5$]. Memory location $u(1)$ is set to the value of $x(0.06)$. y_{next} is reset by the interpolation relationship

$$y_{next} = 0.25u(2) + 0.75u(3)$$

The result will be $y_{next} = 5.5$. Note that the recycling has now been completed. The above-described procedures are shown in Figure 10-32.

Let K denote the index of the u element used for storing the present value of x. L and M would then be the next successive elements. (However, if $K = n - 1$, then $L = n$ and $M = 1$. Also, if $K = n$, then $L = 1$ and $M = 2$. This effects the resequencing operation.) The interpolation relation is

$$y_{next} = c_1 u(L) + c_2 u(M)$$

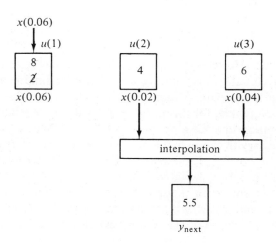

FIGURE 10-32

where

$$c_1 = \frac{t_d}{\Delta t} - (n - 1)$$

$$c_2 = 1 - c_1$$

and

$$n = \text{TRUNC} \frac{t_d}{\Delta t} + 1$$

TRUNC is the operation that truncates a quantity to the highest integer value contained within it. For the example just given the following values would have been obtained:

$$n = 3 \qquad c_1 = 0.25 \qquad c_2 = 0.75$$

In instances when t_d is an integer number of Δt's, interpolation is not necessary. Then

$$c_1 = 1 \qquad c_2 = 0 \qquad n = \frac{t_d}{\Delta t}$$

It is convenient to have a standard subprogram handle such finite time delays. Figure 10-33 is a flow diagram for such a program, called TLAG. This program is designed to handle a number (LAGS) of such delays. Hence $x, y, n, c_1, c_2,$ and IN will be arrays, subscripted in terms of which lag is involved. (IN is the order number of the next memory element to be loaded with the present value of x.) The storage elements described as u will have double subscripts, first in terms of the lag involved, and second in terms of the order number of the element.

Most of Figure 10-33 is self-explanatory in view of the preceding discussion and example. However, the situation of a comparator search or of an intermediate pass in the integration procedure should also be considered. Under these conditions, the value of x should not be stored in the memory elements. However, unless time has not changed (NEWTIME = false), the delayed values of y during these irregular time increments must still be computed by extrapolation. The procedure for this is shown in Figure 10-33a. Note that, for this purpose, the value of y established for the last regular iteration interval must be saved as y_{now}. This also is the reason why it was necessary to compute the delayed output one interval in advance, as y_{next}. The value of y_{next} is needed for purposes of interpolation.

The calling program should include the statements, LASTPASS = true and NEWTIME = true, even though no integration is involved; it should include the statement, STATUS=1, even though no comparators are involved. To illustrate TLAG, the example of the next section will be used.

10-12   Example of a Control Loop
with a Finite Time Delay

Figure 10-34 is an example of a very simple control system susceptible to easy pencil-and-paper analysis that might be used to check the results produced by the TLAG subprogram. It is assumed that a unit step-function input $r(t)$ is applied. (As the system is linear, there is no need to try step inputs of other magnitudes.) It is also assumed that $c(0)$ is zero. The results of this program may be checked, as it is simple to show that the system becomes unstable when the gain K is equal to the value $\pi/2t_d$. Under these circumstances it will exhibit steady-state oscillations at a frequency $f_{osc} = 1/4t_d$ (i.e., the period of oscillations will equal $4t_d$). The flow diagram for the program to simulate this situation is shown in Figure 10-35.

The only subroutines required are TLAG and INTEGRATE. The major point of the program is to note the change in response as K is varied. If the program is correct, steady-state oscillations should be observed when $K = \pi/2t_d$, as was stated above.

SUBROUTINE TLAG(LAGS, CALIBRATE, u, Δt, t_d, t, x, y, STATUS, LASTPASS, NEWTIME)

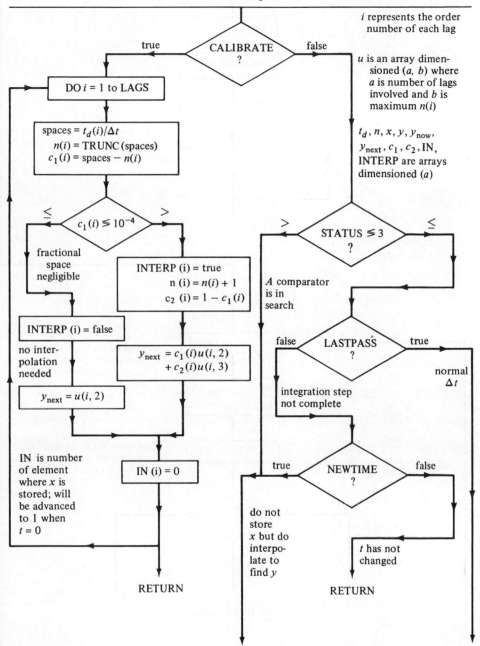

FIGURE 10-33

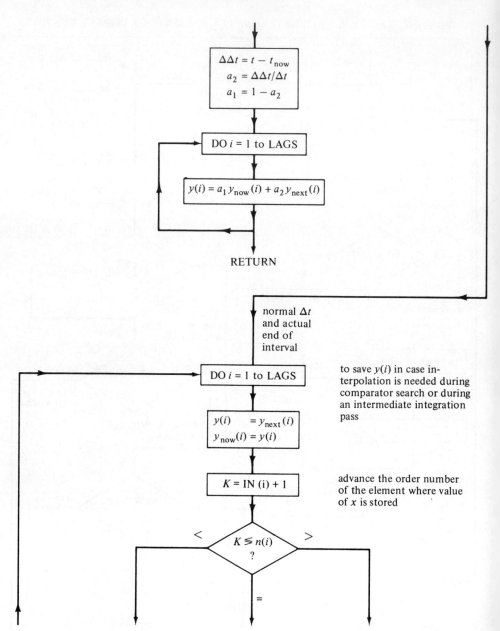

$$\Delta\Delta t = t - t_{now}$$
$$a_2 = \Delta\Delta t/\Delta t$$
$$a_1 = 1 - a_2$$

DO i = 1 to LAGS

$$y(i) = a_1 y_{now}(i) + a_2 y_{next}(i)$$

RETURN

normal Δt
and actual
end of
interval

DO i = 1 to LAGS   to save $y(i)$ in case in-
                                   terpolation is needed during
                                   comparator search or during
                                   an intermediate integration
$$y(i)\qquad = y_{next}(i)$$ pass
$$y_{now}(i) = y(i)$$

$$K = \text{IN}(i) + 1$$ advance the order number
                                   of the element where value
                                   of x is stored

$<$ $K \leqq n(i)$ $>$
                       ?

                      $=$

FIGURE 10-33 (cont'd)

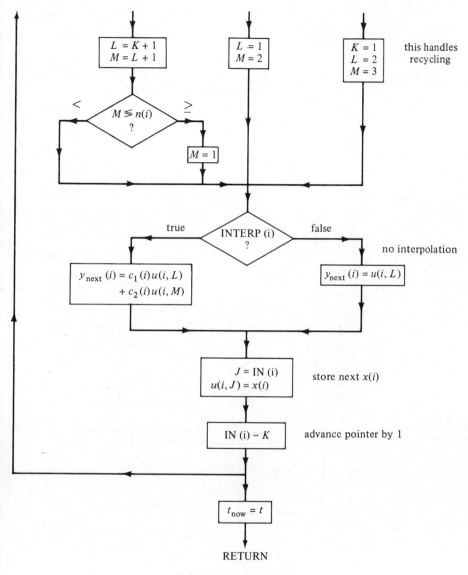

FIGURE 10-33 (cont'd)

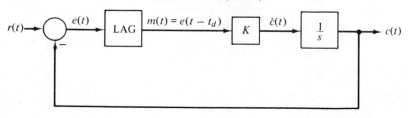

FIGURE 10-34

LOGICAL: LASTPASS, NEWTIME
           CALIBRATE, MORE, NEWDT

INTEGER: STATES

the dimension *a* is chosen to
agree with that used in TLAG

b should be an integer greater
than the maximum value of
$(t_d/\Delta t + 1)$, i.e. the number
of memory locations needed

u is an array dimensioned (a, b)
e, m, t_d, are arrays dimensioned (a)

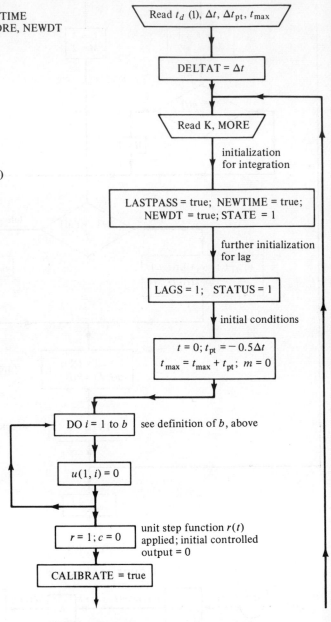

Read t_d (l), Δt, Δt_{pt}, t_{max}

DELTAT = Δt

Read K, MORE

initialization
for integration

LASTPASS = true; NEWTIME = true;
NEWDT = true; STATE = 1

further initialization
for lag

LAGS = 1;   STATUS = 1

initial conditions

$t = 0; t_{pt} = -0.5\Delta t$
$t_{max} = t_{max} + t_{pt};\ m = 0$

DO i = 1 to b see definition of b, above

$u(1, i) = 0$

$r = 1; c = 0$ unit step function $r(t)$
applied; initial controlled
output = 0

CALIBRATE = true

FIGURE 10-35

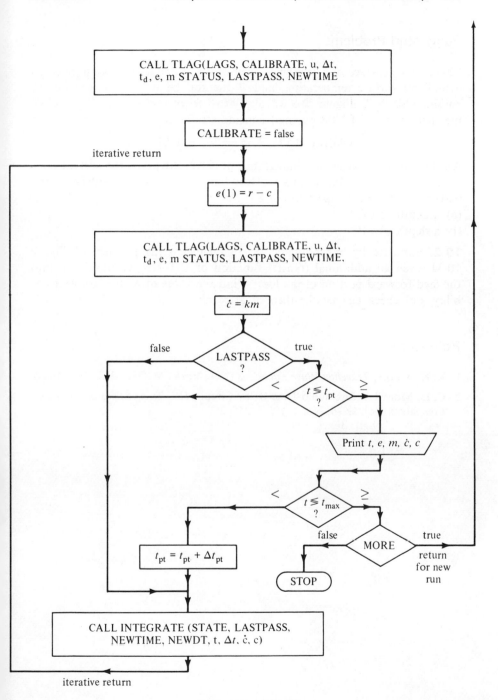

FIGURE 10-35 (cont'd)

Suggested Problems

10-1. If the surface of a section of ground is flat and level, it is subjected to a uniform surface temperature, and if the soil below is homogeneous (a considerable "if"), Figure 10-3 will apply to 1 ft² of surface. u is depth below the surface. For 1 ft² the thermal constants referred to in Section 10-3 are

$$c = 44(\text{Btu}/°\text{F})/\text{ft} \qquad \rho = 2(\text{deg/ft})/(\text{Btu/hr})$$

All the soil is at an initial temperature of 50°F. At $t = 0$ the surface temperature is raised suddenly to 90°. How long will it take a point below the surface to attain a temperature of 85° for
(a) a depth of 1 ft?
(b) a depth of 5 ft?

10-2. Simulate by either analog or digital means the problem of Figure 10-34 when an additional transfer function of $1/(1 + s)$ is introduced into the feed-forward portion of the loop. Find the value of K that causes instability and check against the theoretical result.

References

1. R. K. Moore, *Traveling Wave Equations* (New York: McGraw-Hill, Inc., 1960).

2. C. D. Morrill, A Sub-audio Time Delay Circuit, *IRE Transactions on Electronic Computers*, Vol. EC-6, No. 4 (1957), 255–260.

Appendix 10A:
Applying the Distortionless-Line Principle to Simulation of Finite Time Delays

Figure 10-5 shows the parameters representing one section of an electrical line. Such a line is called a *distortionless* line when

$$\frac{g}{c} = \frac{r}{l} \tag{10A-1}$$

The characteristic impedance of such a line is still given by relation (10-15); that is,

$$Z_0 = \sqrt{\frac{l}{c}} \tag{10A-2}$$

If such a line is properly terminated (i.e., terminated by the characteristic impedance), then voltages applied to the input end will appear at the output end in an undistorted form, differing from the input voltages only because of the finite time delay t_d, and because of a relative attenuation of A nepers. If the input signal is designated as $x(t)$ and the output as $y(t)$, then

$$y(t) = e^{-A}x(t - t_d) \tag{10A-3}$$

where t_d is still given by the relation

$$t_d = \frac{D}{v_p} = \sqrt{lcD} \qquad \text{sec} \tag{10A-4}$$

and A, the attenuation, by

$$A = \frac{rD}{Z_0} = rD\sqrt{\frac{c}{l}} \qquad \text{nepers} \qquad (10A\text{-}5)$$

The only difference between such a distortionless line and the special case of a lossless line is that the latter has no attenuation. An artificial-line version of a distortionless line is just as suitable for the purpose of simulating a finite time delay as is that of a lossless line because the attenuation occurring with the former presents no problem; it can always be compensated by amplification.

With the artificial-live version the critical frequency is still given by relation (10-18); it may also be expressed as

$$\omega_c = \frac{n}{t_d} \qquad (10A\text{-}6)$$

where n is the number of sections used to simulate the line. Figure 10-6 shows a typical frequency-response characteristic and how the artificial-line version differs from the real line in the vicinity of, or beyond, this critical frequency. A circuit analysis of an artificial-line version of a distortionless line, employing T sections, would yield the following transfer function:

$$\frac{Y(s)}{X(s)}$$

$$= \frac{4^n}{\left[\left(\frac{t_d}{n}s\right)^3 + (2+3a)\left(\frac{t_d}{s}s\right)^2 + (4+4a+3a^2)\left(\frac{t_d}{n}s\right) + (4+4a+2a^2+a)^3\right]^n} \qquad (10A\text{-}7)$$

where a is the attenuation per section of line, or

$$a = \frac{A}{n} = \frac{r\,\Delta u}{Z_0} = r\,\Delta u\sqrt{\frac{c}{l}} \qquad (10A\text{-}8)$$

When $a = 0$, the situation then becomes that of a lossless line and relation (10A-7) becomes

$$\frac{Y(s)}{X(s)} = \frac{4^n}{\left[\left(\frac{t_d}{n}s\right)^3 + 2\left(\frac{t_d}{n}s\right)^2 + 4\left(\frac{t_d}{n}s\right) + 4\right]^n} \qquad (10A\text{-}9)$$

This transfer function has nth-order poles at

$$s = -\frac{1.3n}{t_d} \qquad \text{and} \qquad s = -\frac{0.35n}{t_d} \pm \frac{j1.98n}{t_d}$$

The relative pole locations are shown in Figure 10A-1. In consideration of these pole locations, a highly oscillatory transient response can be expected

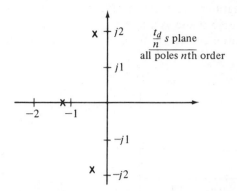

FIGURE 10A-1

with this artificial version of a lossless line. This especially would be the case if $x(t)$ were a step function. Then the response of $y(t)$ to such a step change of $x(t)$ might appear as shown in Figure 10A-2. The oscillatory nature of the response is apparent. This "ringing" effect might be objectionable in situations where $x(t)$ is expected to change rapidly and could cause a transient overloading of the amplifiers. It is to avoid this that the use of an artificial-line model of a *distortionless* line, having some attenuation ($A < 0$), is proposed instead. If n sections of such a line are employed, then the attenuation per section a will be

$$a = \frac{A}{n} \qquad \text{nepers} \qquad (10A\text{-}10)$$

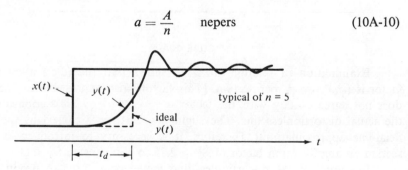

FIGURE 10A-2

The critical frequency ω_c will still be the same. Substituting $a = 1$ in relation (10A-7) yields the following transfer function:

$$\frac{Y(s)}{X(s)} = \frac{4^n}{\left[\left(\dfrac{t_d}{n}s\right)^3 + 5\left(\dfrac{t_d}{n}s\right)^2 + 11\left(\dfrac{t_d}{n}s\right) + 11\right]^n} \qquad (10A\text{-}11)$$

This function has nth-order poles at

$$s = -\frac{2.3n}{t_d} \qquad \text{and} \qquad s = -\frac{1.35n}{t_d} \pm \frac{j1.72n}{t_d}$$

These relative pole locations are shown in Figure 10A-3. Now the response is only slightly oscillatory; it shows a much more satisfactory damping than before. The response, after correction for the attenuation, is shown in Figure 10A-4.

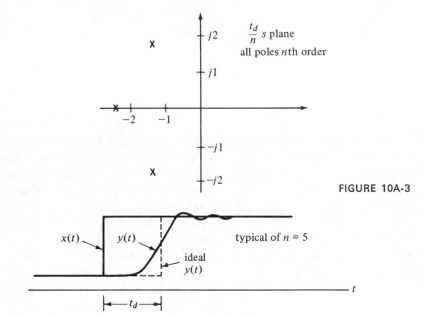

FIGURE 10A-3

FIGURE 10A-4

Examination of relation (10A-11) shows that the (d.c.) attenuation factor is $(\frac{4}{11})^n$, or $\frac{4}{11}$ per section. [This factor, also expressible as $(0.363)^n$, does not agree exactly with the factor $e^{-A} = e^{-an} = (0.368)^n$ applicable to the actual distortionless line. The slight descrepancy is caused by the artificial-line approximation.] Therefore, it is necessary to introduce in each section an amplification factor of $\frac{11}{4} = 2.75$ to compensate for this.

In summary, the distortionless-line model being used to produce the finite time delay should have the following relations between parameters:

$$t_d = n\,\Delta u\sqrt{lc} \qquad (10A\text{-}12)$$

$$a = \frac{A}{n} = \frac{rD}{nZ_0} = \frac{r\,\Delta u}{Z_0} = 1 \qquad (10A\text{-}13)$$

and, from (10A-1),

$$g = r\frac{c}{l} = \frac{r}{Z_0^2} \qquad (10A\text{-}14)$$

where, from (10-15),

$$Z_0 = \sqrt{\frac{l}{c}}$$

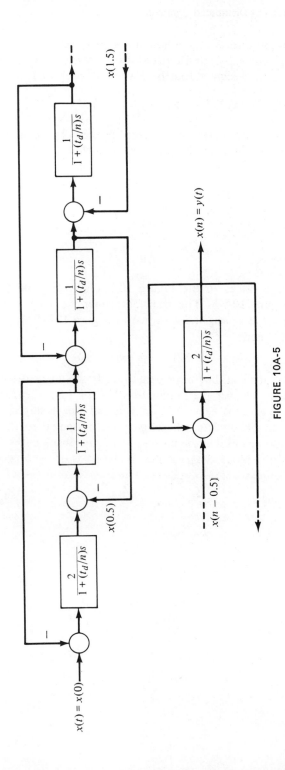

FIGURE 10A-5

As the problem consists of synthesizing a hypothetical line rather than real one, the values of r, l, g, and c need not be realistic of actual lines. Therefore, for ease in design a fourth relation is proposed:

$$Z_0 = \sqrt{\frac{l}{c}} = 1 \tag{10A-15}$$

Now, the four parameters have been defined by relations (10A-12) to (10A-15). The solution of these equations yields

$$r\,\Delta u = 1 \tag{10A-16}$$

$$g\,\Delta u = 1 \tag{10A-17}$$

$$l\,\Delta u = \frac{t_d}{n} \tag{10A-18}$$

$$c\,\Delta u = \frac{t_d}{n} \tag{10A-19}$$

Applying these values to the Figure 10-7 block diagram yields the result shown in Figure 10A-5. The transfer element $Z_0 = 1$ can of course be omitted. With the arrangement shown in Figure 10A-5 the following result should be obtained:

$$y(t) = (\tfrac{4}{11})^n x(t - t_d) \tag{10A-20}$$

subject to the artificial-line approximation. It would be desirable to modify this diagram to recover the attenuation loss of $(\tfrac{4}{11})^n$. This can be done by introducing a gain of $\frac{11}{4} = 2.75$ in each of the n stages. Feedback-loop gains must remain unchanged, so gain factors equal to the reciprocal, or $\frac{4}{11}$, are necessary as well in the corresponding feedback paths. This procedure and the resulting block diagram that is the basis of the analog program are shown in Figure 10-25.

Parallel and Serial Computation: Hybrid Computers

11

11-1 Relative Advantages of Analog and Digital Computers

In comparison with digital computers, analog computers possess the following advantages with respect to the simulation of physical systems:

1. Because of the more direct modeling, greater insight into the problem is possible.
2. Completely parallel operation is the rule. (Why this is an advantage is discussed in the next section.)
3. Continuous rather than step-by-step integration is possible.
4. A complete system response can be simulated in a minute fraction of the time that would be required by the fastest digital computer.

However, the analog computer also suffers the following relative disadvantages:

1. It has less precision.
2. Its memory capacity is much more limited.
3. It finds it difficult to generate functions of more than one variable.

(This even includes the simple arithmetic process of multiplication.)

4. Program control (i.e., change of program configuration) is possible by means of comparators, as discussed in Chapter 4. However, such logical-decision facilities are much more limited in number than with digital computers. Also, time is required to do the necessary patching.

5. Although functions of a single variable can be represented by diode function generators, these are tedious to set up unless the accuracy requirements are such that the method of Figure 4-14 may be employed.

Other relative advantages and disadvantages depend upon whether the digital computer being compared is a large system, such as the IBM 360 series, or a small system such as the PDP-9. Large systems can be operated economically only on the basis of batch processing or conversational programming on a time-shared basis. Small digital computers can be economically devoted to just one simulation problem for a reasonable period of time.

Both analog computers and small digital computers share the following advantages over large digital-computer systems when used for simulation.

1. Parameters are easily varied as soon as the results being obtained indicate that this may be desirable.

2. Man–machine interaction may be simulated.

11-2   Parallel Versus Serial Operation

With parallel operation all computations involved in a problem are carried out simultaneously. This obviously is the case with analog computers during any one simulation run; all integrators integrate simultaneously and all other elements function at the same time; the various steps of computation do not have to take their turn.

In serial operation only one computation is performed at a time. This is why flow diagrams are used to illustrate the algorithms. Serial operation is necessary with the present generation of *general-purpose* digital computers.

A combination of parallel and serial operation *is* possible with special-purpose digital computers equipped with more than one arithmetic processor. This has been done in the case of special-purpose digital computers built to perform only one particular simulation function. In many simulation problems various computation steps were not dependent on some of the steps executed previously. Under such circumstances there is no reason why such independent computations should not be performed simultaneously.

As one example of this, let us suppose that parallel digital processing is possible and the problem of Chapter 1 is being simulated. Figure 1-31 is the original flow diagram for this example, based on simple rectangular integration. Of course, a more sophisticated method of integration would be used instead. Let us say, for example, that we use the trapezoidal method, method 2a-1. (We might prefer Runge–Kutta, but that would make the flow diagram more complicated than it has to be for the purpose of this explanation.) As the computer would be special purpose, we would not be using a general-purpose integration module and the integration will be performed as part of the main program rather than by calling a subroutine.

Figure 11-1 is a flow diagram for such a combination serial–parallel program. Note that during the initializing portion of the program, prior to the iterative portion, there is no parallel operation. Such operation serves a purpose only with computation steps that are performed repetitively where there would be some significant time saving resulting.

The saving in execution time that would result by adding the parallel-operation features in this particular example would be considerable, but not as spectacular as it would be with problems involving many more states. As the number of states increased, the saving of execution time would increase in an approximately proportionate fashion.

Although the flow diagram of Figure 11-1 indicates a user-oriented computer language, normally such special-purpose computer configurations would be written directly in machine language. A simple one, as in this example, would probably not even use a stored program (to eliminate the time required to obtain instructions), but more complicated programs probably would. In any event, if a direct machine language was used, it probably would first have been tested with a user-oriented language on a general-purpose digital computer before the special-purpose computer program was made up.

When parallel processing is performed, not all the parallel computation steps will require exactly the same amount of execution time. Some type of synchronization is necessary to assure that the steps to follow those processed in parallel fashion will not be initiated until all the preceding parallel-processed steps have been completed. This usually is handled by a *digital clock* so that progress to the next step will not occur until a pre-arranged number of clock pulses has occurred to assure that all the preceding processes have been completed.

The discussion here has been on the basis of parallel computations being "good" and serial computations "bad." This is not necessarily true in all computation problems. Although parallel computations do reduce computation time, they add to the number of necessary arithmetic processors and to the responsibilities assigned to the main processor. However, in problems of simulation, the subject of this book, the major cost factor with

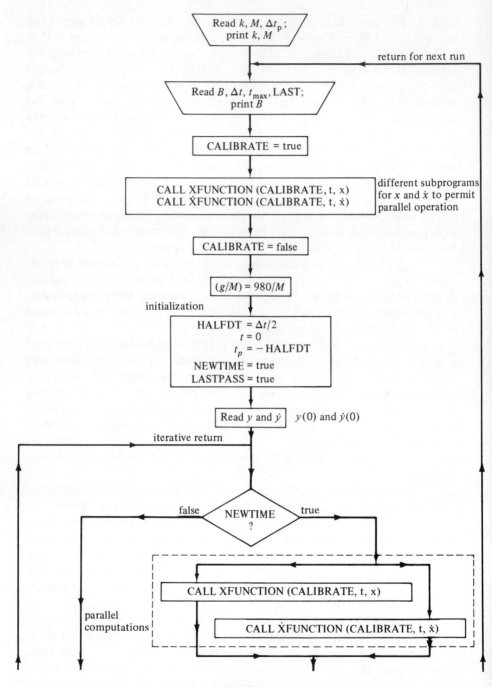

FIGURE 11-1

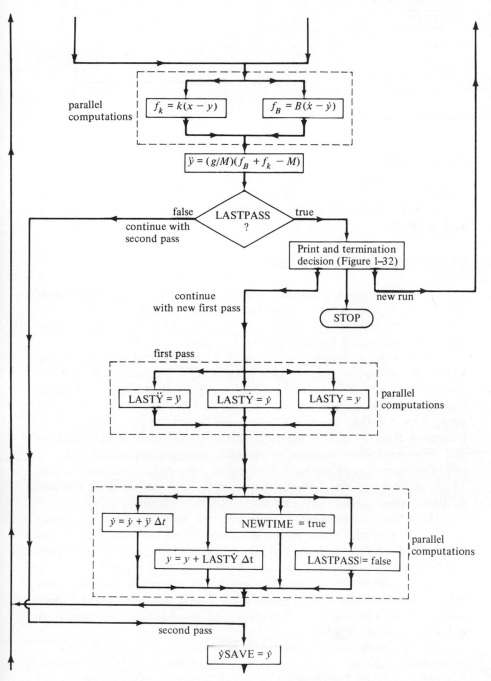

FIGURE 11-1 (cont'd)

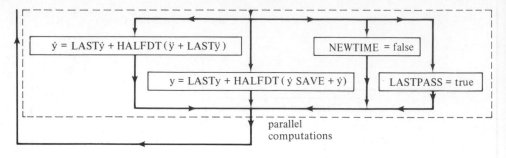

$$\dot{y} = \text{LAST}\dot{y} + \text{HALFDT}(\ddot{y} + \text{LAST}\ddot{y})$$

$$\text{NEWTIME} = \text{false}$$

$$y = \text{LAST}y + \text{HALFDT}(\dot{y}\,\text{SAVE} + \dot{y})$$

$$\text{LASTPASS} = \text{true}$$

parallel
computations

FIGURE 11-1 (cont'd)

digital simulation is the long execution time that is generally required. Besides costing money, this also might negate the possibility of real-time simulation that may be required with many problems. Often the use of parallel processing (when possible) does permit the digital computer to handle such problems.

11-3 Hybrid Analog Computers

The common vocabulary used to describe the degrees of hybridization of an analog computer is apt to be misleading. This might be clarified by describing the step-by-step evolution of what begins as a purely analog computer and finally becomes a completely hybrid system.

When various *logical elements*, to be discussed in the next section, are added, the analog computer starts to become what is called a *hybrid analog computer* (not a "hybrid system"). There are different degrees of hybridization. Even older and now obsolete analog computers could be said to be partly hybrid if they had some relay comparators, since, as discussed in Chapter 4, these do perform logical operations. The degree of hybridization and of sophistication increases as the relay comparators are replaced by solid-state comparators and gates. By the time track–hold elements have been added, introducing the dynamic-storage capability described in Chapter 4, the computer already has been substantially hybridized.

In modern terminology, especially in the sales promotion of analog computers, a hybrid analog computer is one where the hybridization has been carried still further by the addition of digital clocks, logical gates (such as AND or OR), flip-flops, and registers. Output will be displayable by means of a digital voltmeter as well as by means of an oscilloscope. But this is not yet a complete hybrid system because no digital computer has yet been added. There is no arithmetic processor and the digital-storage capability is limited to a few registers.

If this hybrid analog computer is now coupled to a digital computer by means of suitable interface equipment, a complete *hybrid system* results. Normally, the digital computer used in this combination would be a small one with just enough storage capacity for the types of problems likely to be handled (generally about the order of 50K). (The hybrid analog computer would not normally be coupled to a large system, such as the IBM 360 series, or any system that employed time sharing.) Now each of the two computer portions, the analog and the digital, can be assigned the computation functions for which it is best suited.

11-4 Logical Elements

One of the basic logical elements is a simple *digital/analog electronic switch*. These were already discussed in Chapter 4. The switch is simply equivalent to the combination of an input resistance and a single-pole single-throw switch inserted in the analog signal path and controlled by digital logic. The conventional programming diagram appears in Figure 11-2. The electrical connection between points x and y becomes closed when $U = 1$ (true) and becomes open when $U = 0$ (false). (Different hardware systems will have different electrical methods for indicating a zero or 1 condition.)

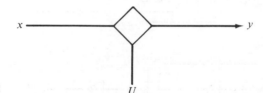

FIGURE 11-2

As an example of the use of such D/A switches, consider the absolute-value circuit of Figure 4-19c. The equivalent circuit using switches would appear as in Figure 11-3. In this case the switches are controlled by the outputs (when $x > 0$, then $U = 1$ and $\bar{U} = 0$) of the comparator.

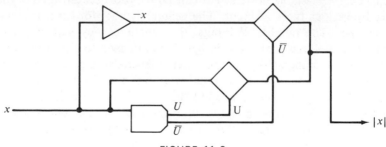

FIGURE 11-3

A *digital* (or logical) *inverter* is one that reverses the logic, changing the "on" state ($U = 1$) to an "off" state ($U = 0$) and viceversa. This is illustrated, along with the conventional symbolism, in Figure 11-4.

$U_2 = 1$ when $U_1 = 0$

$U_2 = 0$ when $U_1 = 1$

FIGURE 11-4

An AND gate will have two or more inputs. The output is on when, and only when, all the inputs are on. The conventional symbolism is shown in Figure 11-5 for the case where there are three inputs.

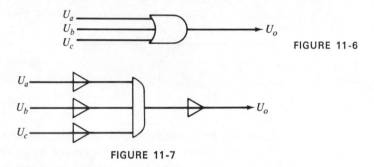

FIGURE 11-5

An OR gate is shown in programming-diagram form in Figure 11-6. Now the output U_o will be zero only when none of the inputs, U_1, U_2, or U_3 is 1; U_o will be 1 if any of the inputs are 1. Note that an OR gate may be made from an AND gate plus digital inverters, as shown in Figure 11-7.

FIGURE 11-6

FIGURE 11-7

Flip-flops represent another important form of logical element; these are, of course, bistable devices that can be tripped between the on and off states by various types of input. The general symbol for them is shown in Figure 11-8. The number of inputs, the functions they perform, and the significance of the alphabetical designations attached to the various inputs vary from one manufacturer to the other. Generally, S means that a signal applied to that type of input terminal will "set" the flip-flop (i.e., make its state 1). Similarly, a signal applied to the R input will reset it (i.e., make its state zero). A signal applied to the input marked P (other symbols also are used) will make it reverse its state, to 1 if originally zero, to zero if originally 1.

Probably the most important logical part of the hybrid computer is the *digital clock*. This establishes the timing of the logical operations and the duration of the various analog operating modes; it assures the synchronous operation of all logical elements. The need for precise timing

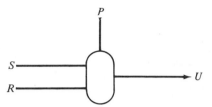

FIGURE 11-8

accuracy generally requires that the basic clock pulses be generated by a crystal-controlled oscillator. A typical crystal-oscillator frequency might be 1 MHz. Submultiples of this frequency, usually by factors of 10, can be generated as needed by means of ring-shift registers, to be discussed later. Together with counting registers, it is this clock that determines the precise timing of the operate and reset modes of the analog computer and the operation of other logical elements. For example, a continuous signal applied to the P input of a flip-flop might cause one state reversal for every clock pulse.

A series of flip-flops can be made into a *counting register* if some way of "carrying" from one binary place to the next can be devised. The logical device for accomplishing this and other similar tasks is the *differentiator*. This device simply produces a pulse of one clock-pulse duration every time the input signal to it changes from zero to 1. Figure 11-9 is a diagram of the simple square frequently used to represent this device in a program diagram.

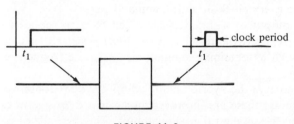

FIGURE 11-9

Flip-flops, inverters, and differentiators can be combined to make up a *binary counting register*, as shown in Figure 11-10. The rightmost flip-flop represents the least significant binary bit (i.e., the flip-flops appear in the same way as the binary numbers would be written). When any flip-flop changes from 1 to zero, the differentiator sends a pulse to the flip-flop to the left of it, causing a carry to take place. As many flip-flops are used as there are binary bits needed to represent the number.

BCD counting registers (binary coded decimal) are used when it is desirable to handle the logic in decimal form, as for display purposes. Four bits (i.e., four flip-flops) are used for each decimal place. A logic circuit effects a carry (i.e., sets the least significant bit of the next higher decimal

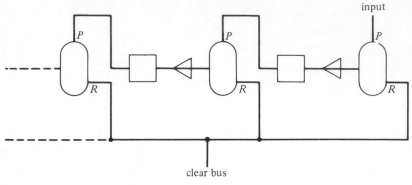

clear bus

FIGURE 11-10

place) and resets (i.e., "clears") all the bits in the present decimal place when a pulse arrives that would otherwise have raised the digit from 9 to 10 (binary 1001 to binary 1010).

Shift registers are designed to shift their contents to the next higher bit either at every clock pulse or else at every shift-command pulse. The contents of the highest bit is shifted out of the register completely and appears as an output pulse. This output pulse could, if desired, be the input to another, cascaded, shift register if more binary digits were needed in the chain. Such registers can be loaded in parallel (i.e., each individual bit can be loaded simultaneously). This pattern of 0's and 1's would then be shifted along the register once every clock or shift-command pulse.

If the output of a shift register is fed back to the least significant bit of the *same* register, the result is a *ring-shift register*. This can serve many functions, such as obtaining submultiples of pulse frequencies, as was discussed above.

In summary, the hybrid analog computer does contain a collection of logical elements; these are, however, much less extensive in capability than those of even the smallest digital computer. The methods of communication and control that exist between the analog and logical sections are shown in Figure 11-11. With such a computer, the dynamic-storage operations discussed in Chapter 4, the search for iterative solutions discussed in Chapter

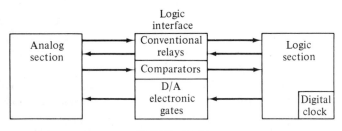

FIGURE 11-11

5, the search for boundary conditions described in Chapter 7, and the search for optimum parameters described in Chapter 9 will all be greatly facilitated. For full hybridization of analog and digital capabilities, it is necessary to proceed further, as is discussed next.

11-5 Analog/Digital and Digital/Analog Converters

Figure 11-11 shows that, up to now, there are very limited methods of communication between the analog and the logical (essentially digital) portion of the computer. To tie the system to a larger and more versatile digital computer requires a considerable extension of the interface equipment, especially including the addition of digital/analog (D/A) and analog/digital (A/D) coverters.

Various schemes are used for D/A and A/D conversion; only the simplest will be described here. A very rudimentary D/A technique will be described first.

Suppose that the analog-voltage range from $-V_r$ to $+V_r$ is to be covered by nine binary bits plus a tenth bit to represent the algebraic sign. Negative voltages are to be represented by the one's-complement form. Then $-V_r$ would be represented by binary 0000000000 and $+V_r$ by binary 1111111111. There would be a resolution of $2^{11} = 2048$ levels, providing an accuracy of about 0.1 per cent of full scale.

Figure 11-12 shows the analog and logic connections that would be used to convert this binary representation, stored in a register, into a corresponding analog voltage. The binary register, attached to the D/A converter, would ordinarily be loaded in parallel when the logic called for a D/A conversion. This would result in the immediate appearance of the corresponding analog voltage at the output terminal, e_o.

Note that the first gate in Figure 11-12, actuated by the sign bit, receives an analog-input signal V_r. Hence, if the binary quantity stored were 0000000000, only this gate would be open[1] (because of the digital inverter at its input) and the output voltage e_o would be $-V_r$, as it should be.

As other bits are added, indicating a less negative quantity, the gates connected to the $-V_r$ supply become open as the output voltage increases algebraically and comes closer and closer to zero. When the algebraic sign does change and the sign bit becomes 1, the first gate closes. However, the one's complement then is no longer used and the lowest "positive" number, 1000000000, meaning simply zero, would result; all gates are closed and e_o would be zero, as it should be. Then, as the binary register attains increasing positive values, various of the gates connected to the V_r supply are

---

[1]"Open" will mean here that the analog signal *is* transmitted; "closed," that it is not.

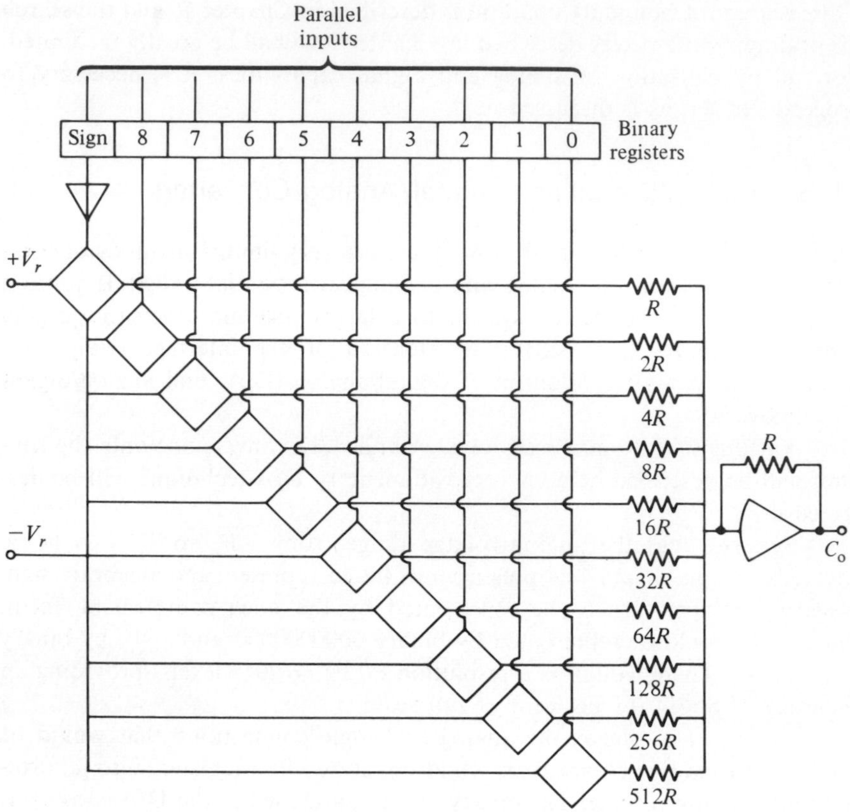

FIGURE 11-12

opened and an increasing positive V_r results. Finally, when the register contains 1111111111, all gates connected to $-V_r$ are open and the voltage e_o now finally attains its highest possible value, $0.999V_r$ V. (Modified versions of the scheme described are used when the digital indication of V is in binary-coded decimal form.)

The inverse type of device, the A/D converter, has been important for years, not only for interface equipment in hybrid-computer systems but also as the basic part of a digital voltmeter. One simple form of such a device performs this conversion by implicit methods employing a D/A converter, possibly one of the type just described. Figure 11-13 shows one method, based on the converter of Figure 11-12. Here the voltage produced by the D/A converter e_o is compared with the voltage V that is to be converted to digital form. When $e_o > V$, the U output of the comparator results in the clock pulse being transmitted to the subtract bus; when $e_o < V$, the $\bar{U}$ output results in the pulse being transmitted to the add bus.

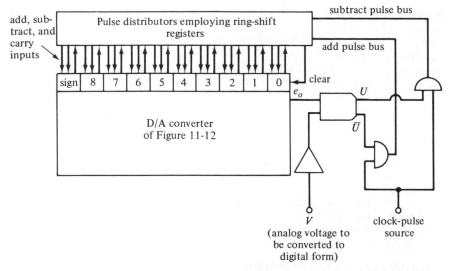

FIGURE 11-13

When the computer logic calls for A/D conversion, the register of the D/A converter is first cleared. The ring-shift registers of the pulse distributor then select the sign bit of the D/A converter's register and the first add or subtract pulse is sent to it. During the next clock-pulse interval, the pulse produced (add or subtract depending upon whether e_o is greater or less than V) is transmitted as either the add or subtract input to bit 8 of the register, then to 7, and successively until bit 0 is reached. By this time the correct binary value of V (within the accuracy limits) will be stored in the register. One point is important to note to understand this operation. When an add pulse is received and is applied to the add input of the bit being addressed, if that bit already holds a 1, nothing is changed. But, when a subtract pulse is received and is applied to a bit that already holds a zero, the value of that bit is changed to a 1, but a negative carry is effected [i.e., a subtract pulse is sent to the next higher bit (to the left in the diagram)].

All of this is best illustrated by example. Table 11-1 shows the sequence of operations when the voltage V is -2.55 V with V_r equal to 10 V (the usual value when dealing with a hybrid analog computer). The final result of the conversion would be a binary indication of the voltage corresponding to V being -2.558 V; this is within the 0.1 per cent (of full scale) accuracy described.

If this were a one-shot measurement of the voltage and conversion to digital form, the value now stored in the register would be transmitted for the next step of the computer operation. If this were a continuing operation, where repeated measurements of V were to be made as it varies with time (as would be the case with a digital voltmeter), then the contents of the D/A

TABLE 11-1

Register Content	e_o	Type of Pulse Applied	Pulse Applied to
0 000 000 000	−10.000	Add	Sign digit
1 000 000 000	0	Subtract	Digit 8
0 100 000 000	−5.000	Add	Digit 7
0 110 000 000	−2.500	Subtract	Digit 6
0 101 000 000	−3.750	Add	Digit 5
0 101 100 000	−3.125	Add	Digit 4
0 101 110 000	−2.812	Add	Digit 3
0 101 111 000	−2.656	Add	Digit 2
0 101 111 100	−2.578	Add	Digit 1
0 101 111 110	−2.559	Subtract	Digit 0
0 101 111 101	−2.558	None	None

converter's register would be transferred to a storage register. (If this were being done in a digital voltmeter, the results would be converted to decimal form for display purposes.) Under such circumstances, the register in the D/A converter would then be cleared with the next clock pulse. The clock pulse following this would result in the add or subtract pulse (depending upon the comparator's decision) being applied again to the sign bit of the register as the operation was repeated. The complete sequence of operations previously described would then be repeated and the values in the D/A converter's register would be corrected in the event the V had changed its value since the last cycle.

There are a number of other methods of A/D conversion. One consists of the simple arrangement shown in Figure 11-14. When this circuit is placed in operation, the comparator will become actuated and will remain actuated until the negative output of the integrator $-k_1k_2V_r t$ attains the same magnitude as the analog voltage being converted, V, i.e., until

$$k_1k_2V_r t = V$$

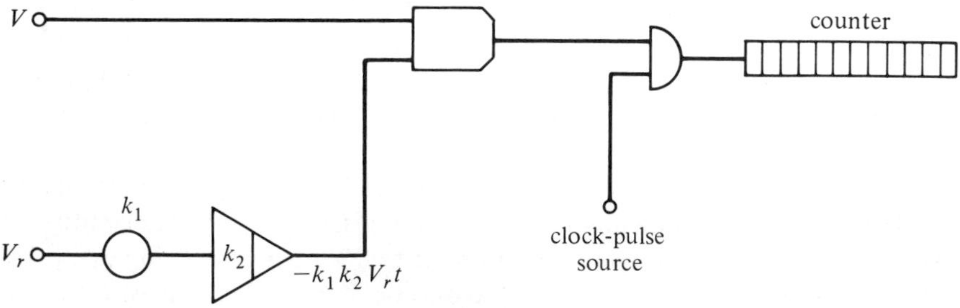

FIGURE 11-14

or

$$t = \frac{1}{k_1 k_2 V_r} V$$

The counter counts the clock pulses only as long as the comparator remains actuated and, hence, the final reading of the counter will be a measure of V. The method just described handles only positive values of V but relatively simple modifications of it will permit the handling of negative V's as well. The method of Figure 11-14 is considerably simpler than that of Figure 11-13; however, it is generally inclined to be less accurate and involves a longer execution time.

11-6 Attainment of Complete Hybridization

The tying together of the hybrid analog computer and the digital computer is finally accomplished by an *interface* which involves the digital clock, logic, registers, and the D/A and A/D converters just discussed. Normally, all control of the analog-computer operation comes from commands that arise at the digital end and are transmitted to the analog portion through the *control portion* of the interface. Among the control actions effected by the digital computer can be the setting of the servo-controlled analog potentiometers in accordance with the digital instructions. (It is also possible to set these potentiometers from a manually operated keyboard.)

In addition to the control portion, the interface will include a *data-handling portion* through which digital data can appear as an analog voltage, and vice versa. Obviously, this is where the roles of the D/A and A/D converters become essential.

It is difficult to describe in general the actual operation of the hybrid system unless the handling of some particular problem is discussed. For that purpose, let us consider the optimization of a control system's parameters. The cost function might be

$$C = \int_0^{t_{max}} e^2 \, dt$$

where e is the system error.

A digital program following the general form shown in Figure 8-15 and employing the relaxation technique might be used for this purpose. However, the first iterative operation, described in that diagram in the block as "Determine the cost function. . . ," would be performed in an analog fashion. For the first iteration, all the initial trial values of the parameters would have been specified during the initialization part of the program and would be used to set the servo-driven analog potentiometers that establish them in the analog program. A single, high-speed analog run would then be made and the integration operation described above performed to obtain the value of the cost function C. At the end of this run, this value of C would be converted to digital form and the subsequent digital steps, starting with the instruction, CALL RELAX, would continue. At the next iteration a new value of α_1 would have been proposed by the RELAX subroutine; hence, the corresponding potentiometer would have to be reset to this new value before the second analog run was initiated. The program would proceed iteratively in this fashion with α_2 next being adjusted after the (temporarily) best α_1 had been found. Finally, after a number of iterations and assuming that the program did not fail because of excessive trials or rounds (more of these, however, can be afforded than before with purely digital operation because of the great reduction in execution time for each run), the values of the optimum parameters and resultant cost function may be read out in digital form. While the optimization trials were taking place, the resulting responses could have been displayed on a cathode-ray oscilloscope.

The most time-consuming portion of the above-described procedure would be the repeated settings of the servo-driven potentiometer. (If the steepest-descent technique had been used this problem would have been intensified because then, for each trial, *all* the parameters would have had to be reset.) However, all-electrical potentiometers, involving no mechanical motion, are being introduced to overcome such a disadvantage.

In most hybrid applications the high-speed mode of the analog computer will be employed. However, when not many repeated runs need be made, normal time operation may be preferred instead. The digital-computer portion of the system might then be used to perform certain operations, such as division or finding a function of more than one variable, that the analog portion would have found difficult. With this type of operation the analog computer could be thrown into a hold mode during each of a series of intervals while the necessary digital computation was being carried out, being returned to the operate mode only after the digital computation had been completed and the results had been transmitted back to the analog portion. Analog extrapolating circuits could be used for updating the values of the digitally computed results in between these intervals.

The hybrid system is the ideal answer to the problem of simulating finite time delays with analog computation because here it is possible to use basically the same digital time-delay subroutine described in Chapter 10; the returned values of the delayed variable would be continuously fed back to the analog program. In this instance, unlike the previous one, the technique of placing the analog computer in the hold mode during the digital computation would no longer be necessary.

There is now only one more step that need be made to reach the ultimate of hybridization and that step is expected with the next generation of hybrid systems. It consists of digitally directed patching of the analog-computer configuration. When this time arrives, it will be possible to describe the analog-program configuration in terms of a block diagram expressed as a set of digital instructions and then let the system do the remainder of the programming, scaling, and patching.

11-7   The Final Decision: Analog or Digital or Both (or Neither?)

Before deciding on the method of simulation to be employed, a question should first be asked: Do we want computer simulation at all? Many examples have been given here where the need for such simulation was definitely indicated. But there have been many other instances when simulation has been misapplied. The computer-simulation model will never be as perfect a representation as is the system being simulated itself. When the latter is available and tests on it are feasible, economical, and safe, why not use it? The author is thinking of instances when he has seen either students or engineers in industry developing sophisticated control schemes based on tests of simulation models of the systems to be controlled when tests performed directly on the real systems would have been practical and the results much more meaningful. Although it is true that this latter approach may introduce the usual hardware difficulties, when it does happen to be practical, it is the most rational.

Now if we suppose that the need for a computer simulation model is definitely indicated, we are faced with the previously stated question.

Many engineers concerned with system simulation have spent entertaining hours engaged in dialogue about simulation methods. Those who have had their major experience with digital simulation can often see little to recommend the analog computer, while those whose major experience has been with the analog feel the same way about the digital computer, at least as far as simulation is concerned. At the risk of making such dialogue less entertaining by making it more rational, it is hoped that this book will have contributed some insight into the relative advantages each method possesses and the roles each finds the most appropriate. The only thing that can be added here is that the proper decision can be made only by one who is well acquainted with all approaches: analog, digital, and hybrid.

Additional Reading

1. T. D. Truitt, Hybrid Computation—What Is It?—Who Needs It?, *AFIPS Conference Proceedings*, Vol. 25 (1964), 249–269.

2. D. F. Hoeschle, Jr., *Analog-to-Digital and Digital-to-Analog Conversion Techniques* (New York: John Wiley & Sons, Inc., 1968).

3. G. A. Korn and T. M. Korn, *Electronic Analog and Hybrid Computers* (New York: McGraw-Hill, Inc., 1964).

4. Z. Nenadal and B. Mirtes, *Analogue and Hybrid Computers*, rev. ed. (New York: American Elsevier Publishing Co., 1968).

Index